155-SIR-13

ORGANIZATION DEVELOPMENT
PRINCIPLES AND PRACTICES

ORGANIZATION DEVELOPMENT

PRINCIPLES AND PRACTICES

W. Warner Burke

Teachers College,
Columbia University

Little, Brown and Company

Boston   Toronto

Library of Congress Catalog Card No. 81-83134

ISBN 0-316-11686-6

9 8 7 6 5 4 3 2

ALP

Published simultaneously in Canada
by Little, Brown & Company (Canada) Limited

Printed in the United States of America

TO THE MEMORY OF MY FATHER,
A. V. BURKE

PREFACE

This book is both a text for organization development and a personal statement about how I view the field, how I have practiced organization development as a consultant, and how I think the field should be defined and practiced. I have attempted to explain organization development objectively, however—that is, as it is typically defined, practiced, and perceived by many in the field. At the same time, I have allowed my own bias regarding style, approach, and conceptual preferences to be apparent. I believe the reader will be able to detect the difference between my describing, reporting, or explaining and my advocating a particular viewpoint or perspective.

This book, then, is a departure from much that has been written about organization development (OD). Much of what has been written either conveys abstract notions about OD or describes what a practitioner did, without reference to general concepts that may extend beyond the description at hand. Organization development is a consultative practice that is based on theory, research, and guiding principles. For a book to claim it is concerned with the *field* of OD, which I claim for this one, it must encompass both principle and practice. Moreover, I have attempted to describe some of my experience in relation to principles of consultation and organizational change. These descriptions are an attempt not only to link principle and practice but to enliven the text with actual case examples. We are dealing with a dynamic field, not a set of abstractions that have no relation to reality.

A few words of explanation: First, I use the terms *organization development practitioner* and *organization development consultant* interchangeably. The OD person is a practicing consultant and consultant practitioner—the terms are the same and mean that the person's consulting approach is active, not passive. Second, I believe strongly in diagnosis; I consider it the most important phase of OD practice. Since concepts and techniques for diagnosis are both critical to effective OD practice, approximately one-third of the book

vii

concerns diagnosis. Finally, the book is written with *practice* as the point of departure. To be sure, I have incorporated concepts, principles, and theory, but only as they relate to and undergird the practice of OD. Organization development is, after all, an applied field, a type of practice in consulting with organizations. I have also emphasized practice because it is not easy to convey exactly what OD is. Organization development is not a science, nor has it reached the stage of development where it can be described in a programmed, step-by-step manner. We are still learning about how to do it, and therefore we must continue to explain OD in terms of "This is what I did" or "This is what I think it means" and "This is how what I did and what happened links to research and theory."

We have learned much since the early 1960s, when OD had its beginnings; otherwise, this book could not have been written. Yet there is much more to learn, and the field is still young and evolving. Those entering OD today will influence the field's future to some extent. The fact that organization development is still malleable and dynamic is what makes it an exciting field. After almost two decades, I remain involved, enthusiastic, and challenged.

This book consists of eighteen chapters, organized in five parts. Part I concerns the definition of OD. It has been said that there are as many definitions of OD as there are those who practice and write about it. Thus, I have gone to some lengths—three chapters—to define the field. The defining process starts with a case example, continues with a coverage of OD's beginning and conceptual underpinnings, and ends with a presentation of how change is conceptualized for OD purposes. Part II is devoted to the primary concepts, mostly from social psychology, on which OD is based. Covered in four chapters, these concepts are (1) organizations as open systems; (2) norms, roles, and values in organizations; (3) reward systems; and (4) power, leadership, and management. Part III sets the stage for the practice of OD (Chapter 8) and includes two additional chapters dealing with diagnosis, perhaps the most important phase of OD work. Part IV, consisting of five chapters, covers the variety of interventions that may be used in OD practice. These interventions range from those focusing on the individual, on groups, and on relations between groups to those focusing on large system change. The concluding three chapters, comprising Part V, again address the *field* of OD by considering the evaluation of OD change efforts, the OD consultant as a person, and, finally, some perspectives on OD, both current and for the future.

Acknowledgments

I owe the greatest debt of gratitude to Len Goodstein and Craig Lundberg. They served as the best type of reviewer in reading earlier versions of the manuscript; that is, they were always critical, generous with suggestions, and consistently supportive and encouraging. I also received very helpful feedback from David Nadler, Tom Cummings, Kim Cameron, and Mark Plovnick.

I also owe a great deal of thanks and appreciation to my editor, Milton Johnson. He has displayed far more patience with my missed deadlines than anyone could ever expect. His editorship and support have been all that any author could ask.

Regina O'Rourke has also been all that an author could ask in helping me with the enormous workload of typing, duplicating, organizing materials, and the like. She did all this while maintaining a full-time job and completing her graduate degree in organizational psychology.

Without the support of my family, especially Bobbi, my wife, I suspect that I never would have undertaken this project. She and my daughter, Courtney, and son, Brian, were always patient and understanding on those many occasions that I trudged upstairs to my study.

W. Warner Burke

CONTENTS

Contents

PART I

DEFINING ORGANIZATION
DEVELOPMENT

Many people have said that organization development (OD) is difficult to define. A few have said that there are as many definitions as there are people who classify themselves as organization development practitioners—that definitions are legion. It is not surprising, then, that some people still raise the question that was asked when the field of organization development was established around 1960: "What is OD anyway?"

It is easy to define organization development theoretically: A process of change in an organization's culture via the application of behavioral science knowledge. Determining a definition based on what people in the field actually do, however, is not easy. Many activities are subsumed under the label of OD; some fit my brief definition, and some do not.

Perhaps the primary difficulty with definition is that OD is relatively young as a field of knowledge and practice. In the 1960s and early 1970s the field expanded, with people going in similar yet different directions. Organization development became not much more than a handy category for a disparate assemblage of activities and concepts.

Organization development has now begun to settle, to mature, and to become a more clearly recognized entity of knowledge and practice. It is now more generally recognized that OD is a process of organizational change that takes a system perspective (Chapter 1); that the field has an identifiable history, with links to appropriate and well-defined concepts and theories (Chapter 2); and that OD practice follows known and valid pathways and steps for planning and implementing change in an organization (Chapter 3). The first three chapters of this book thus set the context for defining and clarifying the nature and characteristics of organization development.

CHAPTER 1

Introduction

Organization development is a relatively young field. I refer to OD as a field, a body of knowledge and practice, but I would not call it a discipline. It is still too young to be a discipline, since that term implies that a subject or field of study is theoretically advanced and broadly researched, and OD is neither of these. Moreover, the term *organization development* did not even become part of our vocabulary until about 1960. Organization development is still in its infancy compared with such disciplines as psychology. Because of its youth, its growth and formation are still in process. Its practitioners continue to shape the field with their modifications of some older methods and their attempts at something new.

Also because of its youth, OD is not easy to define, at least not to everyone's liking, and definitions abound. Most people in the field agree, however, that OD involves consultants who try to help clients improve their organizations by applying knowledge from the behavioral sciences—psychology, sociology, cultural anthropology, and certain related disciplines. Most would also agree that OD implies change and, if we accept that improvement in organizational functioning means that change has occurred, then, broadly defined, OD means organizational change.

Not everyone agrees with this last statement, and I do not. Improvement in an organization's way of operating may mean changing from one procedure to a better one—such as putting an organization's payroll procedure onto a computer rather than processing checks by hand—but the fundamentals of *how* problems are solved, *how* decisions are made, and *how* people are treated may not have changed at all. This more fundamental aspect of change in the organization is the domain of organization development. The distinction between improvement and organization change may not be clear, however, and it is this distinction that compounds the problem of defining OD. A case example should help.

3

A Case Example

Several years ago I was asked to consult with a division of a large United States manufacturing corporation. The division consisted of two plants, both of which manufactured heavy electrical equipment. The division was in trouble at the time. There were quality control problems and customers were complaining. The complaints concerned not only poor quality but late delivery of these products—inevitably weeks if not months later than promised. Several weeks prior to my arrival at the divisional offices, a senior vice-president from the corporation's headquarters had visited with the division's top management team, a group of six men. The corporate vice-president was very much aware of the problems, and he was anything but pleased about the state of affairs. At the end of his visit, he made a pronouncement. In essence, he stated that, unless this division was "turned around" within six months, he would make the necessary arrangements to close it down. If he carried through with this threat, it would mean loss of jobs for more than 1,000 people, including, of course, the division's top management team. Although the two plants in this division were unionized, the vice-president had the power and the support from his superiors to close the division if he deemed it necessary.

Over a period of several months prior to my arrival as a consultant the division general manager had taken a variety of steps to try to correct the problems. He had held problem-solving meetings with his top management team; he had fired the head of manufacturing and brought in a more experienced man; he spent time on the shop floor talking with first-line supervisors and workers; he authorized experiments to be conducted by the production engineers to discover better methods; and he even conducted a mass rally of all employees at which he attempted to persuade them to do better. After the rally signs were placed throughout the division stating that the goal was to become number one among all the corporation's divisions. None of these steps seemed to make any difference.

The general manager also sought help from the corporate staff of employee relations and training specialists. One of these specialists made several visits to the division and eventually decided that an outside consultant with expertise in organization development could probably help. I was contacted by this corporate staff person, and an initial visit was arranged. Only a few weeks before my arrival, the corporate vice-president had made his visit and his pronouncement.

My initial visit consisted largely of (1) talking at length with the general manager; (2) briefly observing most of the production operations; (3) visiting with the top management team in an informal meeting at which questions were raised and issues explored; and (4) finally discussing the action steps I proposed. I suggested that we start at the top. I would interview each member

4

of the top management team at some length and report back to them as a group what I had diagnosed from these interviews; then we would jointly determine the appropriate next steps. They agreed to my proposal, and a couple of weeks later we began to take the steps I had suggested.

I began by interviewing the six members of the top management team (see Exhibit 1.1) for about an hour each. Many reasons were given for the division's problems, and some of the presumed causes ironically contradicted one another. What did surface fairly clearly was the fact that, although divisional goals were generally understandable, they were not specific enough for there to be clarity about priorities. Moreover, there were interpersonal problems, as, for example, the head of marketing and the head of employee relations not getting along. (The marketing manager believed that the employee relations manager was never forceful enough, and the employee relations manager perceived the marketing manager as a ''blowhard.'') We decided to have a two-and-a-half-day meeting at a hotel some ninety miles away to work on achieving clearer priorities and ironing out some of the interpersonal problems.

The meeting was considered successful because much of what we set out to accomplish was achieved—a clearer understanding of the problems and concerns and a priority for action. The key problem needing attention did indeed surface. It was as if a layer or two of an ''organizational onion'' had been peeled away, and we were finally getting at not only some causes but some specifics that we could tackle with confidence that we were moving in the right

EXHIBIT 1.1

Organization Chart: Top Management Team of Manufacturing Division

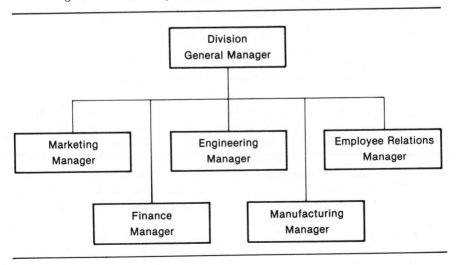

direction. The specific that surfaced from this off-site meeting of the top team was the lack of cooperation between two major divisional functions—engineering and manufacturing.

As the organization chart in Exhibit 1.1 shows, the division was organized according to functions. The primary advantages of a functional organization are the clarity of organizational responsibilities resulting from the divisions of labor and the opportunities for continuing development of functional expertise within a single unit. There are disadvantages, however, primarily stemming from the distinct divisions of responsibility. In other words, marketing does marketing and manufacturing manufactures, and the twain rarely meet. In this case, the problem was between engineering and manufacturing. The design engineers claimed that the manufacturing people did not follow their specifications closely enough, whereas the manufacturing people claimed that the design engineers did not consider that the machinery for manufacturing was old and used. Because of the condition of the machinery, the manufacturing people were not able to follow the design engineers' specifications to the desired tolerance level. Each group blamed the other for the drop in overall product quality and for the delays in delivery of the product to their customers.

This kind of conflict is common in organizations that are organized functionally. The advantages of such organization are clear, of course, but a premium is placed on the need for cooperation and communication across functional lines. Moreover, when managers are in the midst of such conflict, the pressures of daily production schedules make it difficult for them to pull away and clearly diagnose the situation, especially in terms of what is cause and what is symptom. Managers in high-productivity-oriented organizations thus spend a great deal of time "fighting fires," or treating symptoms. An outside consultant who is not caught up in this day-to-day routine can be more objective in helping to diagnose problem situations. This was my primary role as a consultant to this manufacturing division.

The next step in my consultative process was to deal with this problem of intergroup conflict. Another off-site meeting was held about a month later, with twelve attendees—the top six people from engineering and the equivalent group from manufacturing. These men were predominantly engineers—either design engineers assigned to the engineering function or production engineers working in the manufacturing operation. These two functions had interacted closely, or they were supposed to. The design engineers sent plans (similar to blueprints) to manufacturing to have the specified electrical equipment produced. As noted earlier, the design engineers complained that the manufacturing people did not follow specifications to the desirable degree ("No wonder quality was poor," they lamented), and the production engineers complained that the design people established specifications calling for tolerances that were significantly more stringent than their machinery could handle. The production people stated further that their machinery was too old. In order to meet the design specifications, new machinery would have to be purchased, and the cost would be prohibitive. "And besides," they added, "those design guys never set foot on the shop floor anyway, so how would they know?"

These comments and the attitudes they reflect are illustrative and common. Communication is rarely what it should be between groups in such organizations. It is also common, if not natural, for functional groups to maintain a distance from one another and to protect their turfs.

Using a standard intergroup problem-solving format from organization development technology, I worked with the two groups (1) to understand and clarify their differences; (2) to reorganize temporarily into three four-person cross-functional groups to solve problems; and (3) to plan specific action steps they could take to correct their intergroup problems. The purpose of this kind of activity is to provide a procedure for bringing the conflict to the surface so that it can be understood and managed more productively. The procedure begins with an exchange of perceptions between the two groups—how each group sees itself and the other group. This initial activity is followed by an identification of the problems that exist between the two groups. Finally, mixed groups (members from both functions) work together to plan action steps that will alleviate the conflict and solve many of the problems. See Burke (1974) for a detailed description of this activity.

The outcome of this intergroup meeting clearly suggested yet another step. A major problem needing immediate attention was that the manufacturing group was not working well as a team. The design engineers produced evidence that they often got different answers to the same design production problem from different manufacturing people. Thus, the next consulting step was to help conduct a team-building session for the top group of the manufacturing function. Approximately two months after the intergroup session, I met off-site for two days with the production engineers and general foremen of manufacturing. In this session, we set specific manufacturing targets, established production priorities, clarified roles and responsibilities, and even settled a few interpersonal conflicts.

By this time I had been working with the division off and on, from my initial contact, for close to nine months. After my team-building session with the manufacturing group, I was convinced that I had begun to see some of the real causes of the divisional problems; until then I had been dealing primarily with symptoms, not causes. I noticed, for example, that the first-line supervisors had no tangible way of rewarding their hourly workers; they could use verbal strokes—"Nice job, Alice" or "Keep up the good work, Joe"—but that was about it. They could use negative reinforcement, however, if they so

7

chose—for example, threatening a one- or two-week layoff without pay if performance didn't meet standards. This type of action was within the bounds of the union contract.

The hourly employees were paid according to what is called a measured day-work system. Their pay was based on what an industrial engineer had specified as an average rate of productivity for a given job during an eight-hour day. Incentive to produce more for extra pay was not part of the system.

I suggested to the division general manager that a change in the reward system might be in order. At that suggestion, the blood seemed to drain from his face. What I then came to understand was that the present president of the corporation was the person who, years before, had invented the measured day-work system. He did not believe in incentive systems. The division general manager made it clear that he was not about to suggest to the corporate president that the measured day-work system should perhaps be scrapped. I discussed the matter with my original corporate contact, the staff specialist. He confirmed the situation and stated that change in the reward system was not in the offing. I was extremely frustrated at this point. I thought that I had finally hit upon a basic cause of divisional if not corporate production problems, but it became apparent that this root of the problem tree was not going to be dug up. My consulting work with the division ended shortly thereafter. What I urged as a next step in the overall problem-solving process—to change some elements of the reward system for hourly employees, if not the entire system—was not a step the division general manager was willing to take. The corporate staff person was also unwilling to push for change in this aspect of the system.

The point to this consultation case is as follows: What I used as a consultant was the standard methodology of organization development, but the project was *not*, in the final analysis, organization development. Having described the case, I will now use it as a vehicle for clarifying what OD is and what it is not.

Definitions

In the consultation, I used OD methodology and approached the situation from an OD perspective. The methodological model for OD is *action research;* data on the nature of certain problems are systematically collected (the research aspect) and then action is taken as a function of what the analyzed data indicate. The specific techniques used within this overall methodological model (few of which are unique to OD) were (1) diagnosis—interviews with both individuals and groups and observation, followed by analysis and organization of the data collected; (2) feedback—reporting back to those from whom the data were obtained on the collective sense of the organizational problems; (3) discussion of what these data mean and planning the steps that

8

should be taken as a consequence; and (4) taking those steps. In OD language taking a step is making an *intervention* into the routine way in which the organization operates. In the consultation case there were three primary interventions: team building with the division general manager and the five functional heads who reported directly to him, intergroup conflict resolution between the engineering and manufacturing groups, and team building with the top team of the manufacturing group. These interventions, team building and intergroup conflict resolution, are described and explained more fully in Chapters 13 and 14, respectively.

The case example does not qualify as an effort in organization development because it meets only two of the three criteria for OD, at least as I have defined them (Burke and Hornstein 1972). For change in an organization to be OD it must (1) respond to an actual and perceived need for change on the part of the client, (2) involve the client in the planning and implementation of the change, and (3) lead to change in the organization's culture.

As a consultant I was able to meet the first two criteria but not the third. For cultural change to have taken place, the reward system would have to have been modified. In another organization perhaps it would have been not the reward system but some other aspect of the culture. Thus, the bias presented in this book is that organization development is a process of change in an organization's *culture*. By fundamental change, as opposed to fixing a problem or improving a procedure, I mean that some significant aspect of an organization's culture will never be the same. In the case example, it was the reward system. In another case, it might be a change in the organization's structure, requiring new forms of authority and probably leading to different conformity patterns, since new norms would be established, especially in the area of decision making.

Now that we have jumped from a specific case to more general concepts, perhaps we should slow down and define some terms. Any organization, like any society, has its own unique culture. A given culture consists of many elements, but the primary element is the unique pattern of norms—standards or rules of conduct—to which members conform. Other significant elements of an organization's culture are its authority structure and how power is exercised, values that are unique to the organization, rewards (what they are and how they are dispensed), and communication patterns. These and other cultural dimensions will be covered in more depth in later chapters.

For an organization to develop, change must occur, but this does not mean that *any* change will do. We are concerned with change in the organization's culture—change that will more fully integrate individual needs with organizational goals; change that will lead to greater organizational effectiveness through better utilization of resources, especially human resources; and change that will provide more involvement of organization members in the decisions that directly affect them and their working conditions.

9

At least by implication and occasionally directly, I shall define OD several times throughout this book. The following definition is somewhat general and perhaps vague, but it provides a starting point: Organization development is a planned process of change in an organization's culture through the utilization of behavioral science technology, research, and theory.

Before I proceed further, two pertinent questions should be addressed. First, what if an organization's culture does not need any change? Then OD is neither relevant nor appropriate. Organization development is not all things to all organizations. It is useful only when fundamental change is needed. Second, how does one recognize when fundamental change is needed? Perhaps the clearest sign is when the same kinds of problems keep occurring. No sooner does one problem get solved than another just like it surfaces. Another sign is when a variety of techniques is used to increase productivity, for example, and none seems to work. Yet another is when morale among employees is low and the cause can be attributed to no single factor. There are undoubtedly further questions and more elaboration could be provided, but let us continue.

A Total System Approach

The target for change is the organization—the total system, not necessarily individual members (Burke and Schmidt 1971). Individual change is typically a consequence of system change. When a norm, a dimension of the organization's culture, is changed, individual behavior is modified by the new conforming pattern. Organization development is a total system approach to change. (This quality of OD is the focus of Chapter 4.)

Most people who work in OD agree that it is an approach to a total system and that an organization is a sociotechnical system (Trist 1960). Every organization has a technology, whether it is producing something tangible or rendering a service, and this technology is a subsystem of the total organization and represents an integral part of the culture. Every organization also is composed of people who interact around a task or series of tasks, and this human dimension constitutes the social subsystem. The emphasis of this book is on the social subsystem, but it should be clear that both subsystems and their interaction must be considered in any effort toward organizational change.

The case example at the beginning of this chapter illustrates the sociotechnical qualities or dimensions of an organization. The problem between the engineering and manufacturing groups was both a technical one (out-of-date machinery) and a social one (lack of cooperative behavior). The case also illustrates another important point. A cardinal principle or guideline of OD is to begin any consultation with what the client considers to

10

be the problem, with what he or she deems critical, not necessarily with what the consultant considers important. Later in the consultative effort specific directions for change can be advocated. The consultant begins as a facilitator and then gradually moves on to make specific recommendations.

This process of facilitation followed by advocacy is a disputed issue within the field of organization development. As I shall discuss more thoroughly in Chapter 4, practitioners and academicians in the field of OD are divided according to their views of organization development as a contingent or a normative approach. The contingent camp argues that OD practitioners should only facilitate change, not focus it; the client determines the direction of change, and the OD practitioner helps the client get there. The normative camp, significantly smaller, argues that, although the approach to OD should be facilitative at the beginning, before long the practitioner should begin to recommend, if not argue for, specific directions for change. As the reader will no doubt discern from my presentation of the case in this chapter and from the particular slant I give to certain statements in the text, I place myself in the normative camp—the minority group. I am taking a position, and I shall explain my reasons in Chapter 4; but I shall make every attempt to be comprehensive and as objective as possible in my coverage of OD.

In the consultation case example, I dealt almost exclusively for more than nine months with what the client considered the central problems and issues. As I became more confident about what I considered to be causal factors rather than symptoms, I began to argue for broader and more directed change. Until then, it was my opinion that we had been putting out fires for the most part, not determining the systemic arsonists.

When one takes a position, regardless of how authoritative, the risk is one of encountering resistance. As is obvious from my description of the case, I didn't consult much longer than the first nine months. The total time was about a year. As it turned out, I did help; the division did turn around in time to keep the corporate vice-president from acting on his threat. As a consultant, I take satisfaction in this outcome. From an OD perspective, however, I consider that my work was a failure. That assessment stems from two perspectives, one concerning research and the other concerning values.

Research evidence regarding organizational change is now very clear. Change rarely if ever can be effected by treating symptoms, and organizational change will not occur if effort is directed at trying to change individual members. The direction of change should be toward the personality of the organization not the personality of the individual. My knowledge of the research evidence, my realization in the consultation case that a modification in the organization's reward system was not likely, and my acceptance that OD, by definition, means change led me to conclude that, in the final analysis, I had not conducted an organization development effort.

The values that underly organization development include humanistic

11

and collaborative approaches to changing organizational life. Although all OD practitioners do not agree, an effort at decentralizing power is also included in OD for most organizations. In the consultation case, it seemed that providing first-line supervisors with more alternatives for rewarding their workers positively not only was more humanistic but would allow them more discretionary and appropriate power and authority for accomplishing their supervisory responsibilities. Changing the reward system was the appropriate avenue as far as I was concerned, but this change was not to be and, for my part, neither was OD.

What I have just stated is likely to raise many more questions than answers. Let us move on now to more clarity and, I hope, answers.

CHAPTER 2

The Growth of
Organization Development

The primary purpose of this chapter is to explain the origins of OD. First, we shall trace its history, primarily from the perspective of certain precursors or roots, next from the standpoint of significant events, and finally through certain individual's contributions to the major theoretical underpinnings. We shall then use this background material to establish our understanding of the field of OD as we know it today and to set the stage for definition in Chapter 3.

Precursors and Roots

As is true for most fields and disciplines, determining the birth of organization development is difficult. In all likelihood, it had multiple births. If we consider OD from the standpoint of its primary mode, consultation, we can then trace its beginning all the way back to Old Testament times, with Moses as one of our first recorded clients (Exodus 18:13–27). Moses had what might be called a very decentralized system; thousands of people had direct access to him. Moses was leader, counselor, judge, and minister to all. His father-in-law, Jethro, no doubt because he was concerned for his son-in-law's mental health, suggested what amounted to a reorganization. He proposed that Moses select a few good men to be rulers of thousands. They would have direct access to him and would bring to him only the problems they could not solve. Each of these rulers, in turn, would have lieutenants who would be rulers of hundreds and would have direct access to the rulers of thousands and would bring to them only the problems they could not handle; and so on, down to the lowest, the rulers of ten persons. This was the birth of one of the first pyramidal organizations. It is possible, of course, that this idea of organization was not original with Jethro, since, before Moses's deliverance, the Hebrews had been enslaved by the Egyptians, who had a highly organized society. In any case, OD consultants today are faced with much the same

13

problems—the mental and emotional well-being of their clients and the occasional need for reorganization.

History records many examples of consultants, from Jethro to Machiavelli to Henry Kissinger. More direct roots to OD as a field, however, were planted well within this century. The major historical event that helped to set the stage for the later evolvement of organization development was the Hawthorne studies. These well-known studies at the Hawthorne Works of Western Electric dramatically contrasted with the mechanistic treatment of people in organizations established by Frederick Taylor (1911). The work of Mayo (1933), Roethlisberger and Dickson (1939), and Homans (1950) established in no uncertain terms that psychological and sociological factors made significant differences in worker performance. Moreover, the findings from the research at the Hawthorne Works ushered in an era in which employees began to be considered human beings, not merely cogs in the organizational machinery. This era was delayed or extended because of two significant societal events, the Great Depression and World War II. In the late 1940s and early 1950s, however, what was begun at Hawthorne a quarter of a century before began to take hold.[1]

I do not mean to imply that the Hawthorne studies were a direct precursor to OD. They were, rather, a major piece of the groundwork necessary for the field to develop eventually. Another related precursor was industrial psychology, especially as it began to flourish during and immediately following World War II. These early days of industrial psychology were characterized by paper and pencil tests for recruiting and management development purposes, but knowledge was also being accumulated in the areas of leadership and personnel research, that is, the impact of organizational life on employees, and the reverse, and job design. It is interesting to note, regarding job design, that in the late 1940s work simplification was the goal, whereas today it is the opposite, job enlargement and enrichment.

Also in the late 1940s and the 1950s two other precursors to OD were developing—the survey method of research, which was later coupled with direct feedback of the research data to those from whom the survey was collected, and sensitivity, T-group, or laboratory training (all three labels for essentially the same activity).

Although OD has multiple precursors, four seem to be the most significant historically, at least for the United States: the Hawthorne studies, industrial psychology, survey feedback, and sensitivity training. These precursors not only helped to set the stage for organization development, but they also provided a necessary base of knowledge.

---

[1] For an update on the impact of the early Hawthorne studies and their meaning for the 1970s, see Cass and Zimmer (1975), which is a report on the symposium held on the occasion of the fiftieth anniversary of the original work.

The Hawthorne Studies

Beginning in 1924 and continuing into 1933, the Western Electric Company sponsored a series of experiments for studying worker productivity and morale at its Hawthorne Works in Chicago. The researchers, from the Harvard Business School, were led by Fritz Roethlisberger, T. N. Whitehead, Elton Mayo, and George Homans and by W. J. Dickson of Western Electric. A full discussion of these studies is in Roethlisberger and Dickson (1939).

The studies can be categorized according to types of experiments, types of workers studied, and time period. The four categories of experiments, listed chronologically, were:

1. The illumination experiments
2. The relay assembly group experiments
3. The interviewing program
4. The bank wiring group studies

The intent of these studies was to determine the effect of working conditions on productivity and morale. In the illumination experiments, lighting was changed in a variety of ways for a test group consisting of women. A control group was also studied. As lighting was increased, productivity increased, but, to the surprise of the investigators, productivity continued to increase even when lighting was subsequently decreased to significantly less than it had been originally. Other variations were tried. In some cases, even when the researchers pretended to change the illumination, the women responded positively. Throughout these experiments, regardless of whether the workers were in the test group or the control group, production either increased or did not change significantly. The researchers concluded that, if light was a factor with respect to employee output, it was only one among many. They further hypothesized that worker attitude was a significant factor.

The next series of studies was with a small group of six women who assembled part of the standard telephone. The variables studied were shorter working periods, incentive pay, personal health, and supervision. The conditions of the study were (1) that the women worked in a special, separate area; (2) that they were continuously observed by a researcher; (3) that they were consulted by the researcher-observer prior to any change; and (4) that, although the observer served as a supervisor of sorts, it was clear to the women workers that he was not a formal part of managment. Over a period of two and a half years, in spite of many changes, productivity steadily increased to a level 30 percent higher than it had been before the experiments, and morale among the six women had improved steadily. Their absenteeism record was superior to that of the other regular workers, and there was no turnover. Also, regardless of the direction of the change the researcher made, overtime output continued to increase. The conclusion was that there is no cause-and-effect relationship between working conditions and productivity. The women themselves told the researchers what the primary factors were:

1. More freedom on the job
2. No boss
3. Setting their own work pace
4. Smaller group (Their pay was based on their performance as a small group, not as the usually larger one of thirty or more; thus, they had more control over the relationship between their performance and pay.)
5. The way they were treated

This series of experiments had clearly shown the researchers the importance of worker attitude. Managers at Western Electric were impressed with these studies, particularly with what they perceived to be a considerable amount of latent energy and willing cooperation, which could be tapped under the right conditions.

In an attempt to investigate attitudes more thoroughly, a third set of studies was launched in 1928. This program began as a vast data-collection process using individual interviews. Some 21,000 interviews were conducted by 1930. The interviews tended to become counseling sessions, and the researchers learned a great deal about employee attitudes, particularly those relating to supervision, worker relationships, and the importance of perceived status. A major outcome of these interview studies was learning how to teach supervisors about handling employee complaints, teaching them that an employee's complaint frequently is a symptom of some underlying problem, one that exists either on the job, at home, or in the person's past.

The researchers' desire, however, was to investigate social relations on the job more extensively. Thus, the final set of studies was conducted with a bank wiring group of fourteen men. This group's job was to wire and solder banks of equipment for central connecting services. Again the group was separated for study, and data were collected by observers. The findings of this study concerned the importance of group norms and standards and the informal organization.

The Hawthorne studies are significant as a precursor to organization development because:

1. They demonstrated the important influence of psychological or human factors on worker productivity and morale.

2. They signaled the criticality of certain variables for worker satisfaction: autonomy on the job (workers being able to set their own work pace),

the relative lack of a need for close supervision of people who know their jobs, the importance of receiving feedback on the direct relationship between performance and reward, and having choice and some influence regarding change.

3. They ushered in more humanistic treatment of workers on the job.

4. They provided evidence for later theory, such as Herzberg's motivation-hygiene notion. (The hygiene portion of Herzberg's theory is that there is no cause-effect relationship between working conditions and productivity. This is explained in more detail later in this chapter.)

5. They provided the stimulus and data for much of what we now know about group dynamics, especially in a work context. The bank wiring group was analyzed thoroughly by Homans, and this study plus others in the series resulted in his theory about work groups, his leading-edge thinking about group norms, and his now classic book, *The Human Group*.

There are undoubtedly other reasons, but these stand out and demonstrate the significance of this early research and theory in setting the stage for organization development.

Industrial Psychology

Industrial psychology is now called industrial and organizational psychology, at least by the American Psychological Association, and the expanded label reflects the field. In earlier days, however, prior to but especially during and immediately following World War II, industrial psychology was largely limited to business-industrial and military organizations. Its primary thrust was testing. Questionnaires for selection and screening were created by the hundreds and then tested for reliability and validity. As a result of the war effort, psychological testing came into its own. Industrial psychologists were also involved in training and development, especially supervisory and management training, during and after the war.

A research project conducted at the International Harvester Company by Edwin Fleishman (1953) during the late 1940s and early 1950s is typical of this era of industrial psychology, as it combined supervisory training and the development of a psychological test. This series of studies, conducted over a period of more than three years, is highly significant for another reason, however; it was another precursor for organization development.

Fleishman was interested in the study of leadership and in the consequences of supervisory training; that is, whether supervisors' attitudes and behavior would change as a result of a two-week training program on leadership principles and techniques. Using several questionnaires, Fleishman took measures before the training and immediately following

17

the program. Measures were also taken from a control group of supervisors and from the bosses and subordinates of both groups, the trained and untrained supervisors. In addition to measures taken right after the training, the same tests were administered at various intervals, ranging from 2 to 39 months later.

These tests reflected two primary functions of leadership: *initiation of structure*—provision of task direction and conditions for effective performance; and *consideration*—the leader's sensitivity to and consideration of subordinates' needs and feelings. Prior testing had shown that first-line supervisors in International Harvester were strong in initiation of structure but were rarely considerate of their subordinates as people. The training program then focused on increasing the consideration function.

Measures taken immediately following the training showed that the supervisors who had received the training scored significantly higher in consideration in comparison with both their own previous scores and the control group's scores. Further measures taken over time with the trained group revealed a startling outcome. These supervisors not only gradually reverted to their original behavior—not being very considerate—but in a number of cases they ended up being *less* considerate than the control group.

On further investigation, Fleishman found that the bosses of the trained supervisors also scored high on initiation of structure and low on consideration. The few supervisors who had considerate bosses continued to score high over time on consideration. There was a direct relationship between the attitudes and behavior of the supervisors and those of their bosses. Moreover, this relationship was stronger than the effects of training.

Schein (1972) explains the outcome of Fleishman's research directly and succinctly:

> . . . *the effects of training were intimately related to the culture, or climate, of the departments from which the men came.* These climates had as much of an effect on the trainee as did the training. Consequently, the training was effective, in terms of its own goals, only in those departments in which the climate from the outset supported the training goals. (p. 44)

As early as 1953, therefore, we knew (or at least the knowledge was available) that organizational change was not likely to occur as a result of an individual change strategy unless, of course, the objective of the training was in the same direction as a prior decision for overall organizational change. Practitioners of OD did not seem to learn this for a long time, as we shall see with further tracings of OD beginnings.

I want to make it clear that industrial psychology has made many other contributions to OD. I have singled out the Fleishman study because it seems to have pointed the way to what organization development was to become.

18

Survey Feedback

As noted in the previous section, psychologists rely rather extensively on questionnaires for data collection and for diagnosis and assessment. Leadership questionnaires typically have been associated with the group of psychologists at Ohio State University in the 1950s. Questionnaires for organizational diagnosis, however, are more likely to be associated with the psychologists of the 1950s and 1960s at the Institute for Social Research of the University of Michigan. Rensis Likert, the first director of the institute, started by founding the Survey Research Center in 1946. Kurt Lewin had founded the Research Center for Group Dynamics at the Massachusetts Institute of Technology (M.I.T.). With his untimely death in 1947, the Center was moved to the University of Michigan later that year. These two centers initially constituted Likert's institute. The two primary thrusts of these centers, questionnaire surveys for organizational diagnosis and group dynamics, combined to give birth to the survey feedback method. As early as 1947 questionnaires were being used systematically to assess employee morale and attitudes in organizations.

One of the first of these studies, initiated and guided by Likert and conducted by Floyd Mann, was done with the Detroit Edison Company. From working on the problem of how best to use the survey data for organization improvement, the method we now know as survey feedback evolved. Mann was key to the development of this method. He noted that, when a manager was given the survey results, any resulting improvement depended on what the manager did with the information. If the manager discussed the survey results with his subordinates, particularly through group discussion, positive change typically occurred. If the manager did not share the survey results with his subordinates, however, and failed to plan certain changes for improvement jointly with them, nothing happened—except, perhaps, an increase in employee frustration with the ambiguity of having answered a questionnaire and never hearing anything further.

Briefly, the survey feedback method involves, first, the *survey*—data collection by questionnaire to determine employees' perceptions of a variety of factors, most focusing on the management of the organization; and second, the *feedback*—results of the survey reported back systematically in summary form to all people who answered the questionnaire. *Systematically,* in this case, means that the feedback occurs in phases, starting with the top team of the organization and flowing downward according to the formal hierarchy and within functional units or teams. Mann (1957) referred to this flowing-downward process as the "interlocking chain of conferences." The chief executive officer, the division general manager, or the bureau chief, depending on the organization or subunit surveyed, and his or her immediate group of subordinates receive and discuss feedback from the survey first. Next, the

19

subordinates and their respective groups of immediate subordinates do the same, and so forth downward until all members of the organization who had been surveyed (1) hear a summary of the survey and then (2) participate in a discussion of the meaning of the data and the implications. Each functional unit of the organization receives general feedback concerning the overall organization and specific feedback regarding its particular group. Following a discussion of the meaning of the survey results for their particular group, the boss and his or her subordinates then jointly plan action steps for improvement. Usually, a consultant meets with each of the groups to help with data analysis, group discussion, and plans for improvement.

Thus, this rather orderly and systematic way of understanding an organization from the standpoint of employee perceptions and processing this understanding back into the organization so that change can occur, with the help of an outside resource person, not only was a direct precursor to and root of organization development, it is an integral part of many current OD efforts.

Sensitivity Training

From a historical viewpoint, it would be interesting to know how many events, inventions, or innovations that occurred in 1946 had lasting impact through the subsequent decades. Apparently, once the war was over, people were somehow freed to pursue a variety of creative endeavors. One such innovative event occurred in the summer of 1946 in New Britain, Connecticut. Kurt Lewin, at the time on the faculty of M.I.T. and director of the Research Center for Group Dynamics, was asked by the director of the Connecticut State Inter-Racial Commission to conduct a training workshop that would help to improve community leadership in general and interracial relationships in particular. Lewin brought together a group of colleagues and students to serve as trainers (Leland Bradford, Ronald Lippitt, and Kenneth Benne) and researchers (Morton Deutsch, Murray Horwitz, Arnold Meier, and Melvin Seeman) for the workshop. The training consisted of lectures, role playing, and general group discussion. In the evenings, most researchers and trainers met to evaluate the training to that point by discussing participant behavior as they had observed it during the day. A few of the participants who were far enough from their homes to stay in the dormitory rooms at the college in New Britain asked if they could observe the evening staff discussions. The trainers and researchers were reluctant, but Lewin saw no reason to keep them away and thought that, as participants, they might learn even more.

The results were impactive and far-reaching, to say the least. In the course of the staff's discussion of the behavior of one participant, who happened to be present and observing, the participant intervened and said that she disagreed with their interpretations of her behavior. She then described the event from her point of view. Lewin immediately recognized that this intrusion provided a richness to the data collection and analysis that was otherwise unavailable. The next evening many more participants stayed to observe the staff discussions. Observations alone didn't last, of course, and three-way discussions occurred among the researchers, trainers, and participants. Gradually, the staff and participants discovered that the feedback the participants were receiving about their daytime behavior was teaching them as much or more than the daytime activities were. The participants were becoming more sensitive to their own behavior in terms of how they were being perceived by others and the impact their behavior was having on others. This serendipitous and innovative mode of learning, which had its beginning that summer in Connecticut, has become what Carl Rogers (1968) labeled "perhaps the most significant social invention of the century" (p. 265).

Sensitivity training, T-group, and laboratory training are all labels for the same process, consisting of small group discussions in which the primary, almost exclusive source of information for learning is the behavior of the group members themselves. Participants receive feedback from one another regarding their behavior in the group, and this feedback becomes the learning source for personal insight and development. Participants also have an opportunity to learn more about group behavior and intergroup relationships.

T-groups (T is for training) are educational vehicles for change, in this case individual change. When this form of education began to be applied in industrial settings during the late 1950s for organizational change, the T-group became one of the earliest so-called interventions of organization development.

Early Events

As the T-group method of learning and change began to proliferate in the 1950s, it naturally gravitated to organizational life. Sensitivity training began to be used as an intervention for organizational change; in this application the training was conducted inside a single organization, and members of the small T-groups were either organizational "cousins"—from the same overall organization but not within the same vertical chain of the organization's hierarchy—or members of the same organizational team, so-called family groups. As French and Bell (1978) reported, one of the first events to improve organizational effectiveness by sensitivity training took place with managers at some of the major refineries of Exxon (then known as Esso) in Louisiana and southeast Texas. Herbert Shepard of the corporate employee relations department and Harry Kolb of the refineries division used interviews followed by three-day training laboratories for all managers in an attempt to move management in a more participative direction. Outside trainers were used, many of them the major names of the National Training

Laboratories at the time, such as Lee Bradford and Robert R. Blake. Paul Buchanan conducted similar activities when he was with the Naval Ordnance Test Station at China Lake, California. He later joined Shepard at Esso.

At about the same time, Douglas McGregor of the Sloan School of Management at M.I.T. was conducting similar training sessions at Union Carbide. These events at Esso and Union Carbide represented the early forms of organization development, which usually took the form of what we now call team building (Burck 1965; McGregor 1967).

Also during that period—the late 1950s—McGregor and Richard Beckhard were consulting with General Mills. They were working on what we now call a sociotechnical systems change effort. They helped to change some of the work structures at the various plants so that more teamwork and increased decision making took place at the shop-floor level; more ''bottoms-up management began to occur. They didn't want to call what they were doing ''bottoms-up,'' nor were they satisfied with ''organization improvement,'' so they eventually labeled their effort ''organization development.'' This label also became, apparently independently, the name for the work Shepard, Kolb, Blake, and others were doing at the Humble refineries of Esso.

The first sustained, long-term organization development efforts were conducted with TRW Systems, the aerospace division of TRW, Inc. (Davis 1967), and with the Harwood-Weldon Manufacturing Corporation (Marrow, Bowers, and Seashore, 1967). During the early 1960s, Herb Shepard, who had left Esso for the academic world at Case Western Reserve, consulted with TRW Systems and worked particularly with the internal employee relations managers, Jim Dunlap and Shel Davis. Team building was the primary intervention used in those early days. Later, as OD became more sophisticated and diversified, TRW Systems began to use a variety of methods. In fact, the external and internal consultants at TRW during the 1960s helped to invent much of the OD technology we use today, such as the organization mirror and quick techniques for team diagnosis (Fordyce and Weil 1971).

The primary method at Harwood-Weldon started with an action research approach (Coch and French 1948) and gradually incorporated the method of survey feedback developed at the University of Michigan.

These events and their precursors and roots created the climate and methodology for organization development to grow and flourish.

Conceptual and Theoretical Underpinnings

Organization development has other roots in the area of concepts, models, and theories. Some people in or related to the burgeoning field of OD in the 1960s not only were doing but were thinking and writing as well. Some took

22

an individual viewpoint, others a group perspective, and still others more of a macro or total organizational frame of reference.

What follows is a synopsis of some of the thinking of a fairly select group of people, who have helped to provide most of the theoretical and conceptual underpinnings of organization development. Ten theorists or conceptualizers were selected to represent the theory that is associated with organization development, because no single theory or conceptual model is representative or by itself encompasses the conceptual field or the practice of OD. What we have instead is a group of mini theories that have influenced the thinking and consultative practice of OD practitioners. I refer to them as mini theories because each helps to explain only a portion of organizational behavior and effectiveness.

The ten theories or theory categories were selected because they best represent the theory we do have within the field of OD. Some prominent names in the field of OD were not included because their contributions have been more descriptive than theoretical, such as Blake and Mouton's (1978) Managerial Grid, a model of managerial styles (see Chapter 8); more practice-oriented, such as Beckhard (1969); Schein (1969); and Walton (1969); or more broadly explanatory and provocative, such as Bennis (1966, 1967, 1969, 1970). The selection is a matter of judgment and could be debated. The ten theories are presented in three major categories: the *individual* approach to change—Maslow and Herzberg, expectancy theorists Vroom and Lawler, job satisfaction theorists Hackman and Oldham, and Skinner; the *group* approach to change—Lewin, Argyris, and Bion; and the *total system* approach to change—Likert, Lawrence and Lorsch, and Levinson.

The Individual Perspective

Psychologists have taken two major approaches to the understanding of human motivation: need theory and expectancy theory. One of the early proponents of need theory was Murray; later representatives were Maslow and Herzberg. Expectancy theory, a more recent approach to understanding human motivation, is usually associated with Lawler and Vroom. Applications of need theory in organizations have centered around job design, career development, and certain aspects of human relations training, whereas expectancy theory has been applied with respect to both needs and reward systems. I shall focus first on need theory and some of its applications, since Maslow and Herzberg have probably been the most influential historically.

NEED THEORY—MASLOW AND HERZBERG   According to Maslow (1954) human motivation can be explained in terms of needs that people experience to varying degrees all the time. An unsatisfied need creates a state of tension,

23

which releases energy in the human system and, at the same time, provides direction. This purposeful energy guides the individual toward some goal that will respond to the unsatisfied need. This process—a unsatisfied need providing energy and direction toward some goal—is how Maslow defined motivation. Thus, only unsatisfied needs provide the sources of motivation; a satisfied need creates no tension and therefore no motivation.

Briefly, the foundation of Maslow's theory is his arrangement of human needs into a hierarchical system. The hierarchy consists of five levels, beginning with the basic or physiological needs, such as the needs for oxygen, food, and water. Next in the hierarchy are the safety or security needs—the needs for a secure environment, order, predictability, and the like. Third in the hierarchy is the need for belonging—a person's desire to be accepted by significant others. The fourth level is an individual's ego-status need. At this level a person wants to be recognized by others as unique, as having special talents, as having achieved important objectives, and so forth. For this need and the need for belonging to be met, the individual is dependent on others. For the fifth and final level of need, the need for self-actualization, the person is not dependent on others. At this level one has a need to realize one's potential, to prove oneself *to* oneself. Realizing this need is acquiring a sense of personal growth and development, stretching to one's full potential. The fifth need level completes the hierarchy. One final key point, however, is that Maslow used the term *hierarchy* because he believed that a person would not experience a next-higher level of need until the previous level or levels had been satisfied.

To discuss motivation more fully in regard to Maslow, we must also consider the particular goals associated with each level of need. The following chart depicts the kinds of goals or goal objects that are associated with each need level in an organizational context:

Need Level	*Goal Objects*
Self-actualization	Autonomy on the job, opportunity to determine criteria for job and for effectiveness
Ego-status	Title, carpet on the private office floor, promotions, salary
Belonging	Being part of work team, playing on company's softball team
Safety and security	Seniority, salary, fringe benefits
Basic (physiological)	Clean, safe air to breathe, proper ventilation, hazard-free environment

24

In summary, Maslow contended that we progress through this five-level need system in a hierarchial fashion and that we do so one level at a time. The hierarchy represents one continuum from basic needs to self-actualization.

It is on this last point, a single continuum, that Herzberg parts company with Maslow. Herzberg (1966; Herzberg, Mausner, and Snyderman 1959) maintains that there are two continua, one concerning dissatisfaction and the other concerning satisfaction. It may be that the two theorists are even more fundamentally different in that Herzberg's approach has more to do with job satisfaction than with human motivation. The implications and applications of the two are much more similar than they are divergent, however.

Specifically, Herzberg argues that only the goal objects associated with Maslow's ego-status and self-actualization needs provide motivation or satisfaction on the job. Meeting the lower-order needs simply reduces dissatisfaction; it does not provide satisfaction. Herzberg calls the goal objects associated with these lower-order needs (belonging, safety, and basic) hygiene or maintenance factors. Providing fringe benefits, for example, prevents dissatisfaction and thus is hygienic, but this provision does not insure job satisfaction. Only motivator factors, such as recognition, opportunity for achievement, and autonomy on the job insure satisfaction.

Herzberg's two categories, motivator factors and maintenance or hygiene factors, do not overlap. They represent qualitatively different aspects of human motivation. We can depict Herzberg's theory graphically as follows:

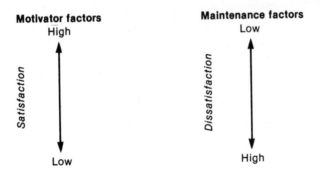

It is important to note one other point of Herzberg's. He states that not only does the dimension of job dissatisfaction differ psychologically from job satisfaction, but it is also associated with an escalation phenomenon, or what some have called the principle of rising expectations—that the more people receive, the more they want. This principle applies only to job dissatisfaction. Herzberg uses the example of a person who received a salary increase of $1,000 one year and then receives only a $500 increase the following year.

Psychologically, the second increase is a cut in pay. Herzberg maintains that this escalation principle is a fact of life and that we must live with it. Management must continue to provide, upgrade, and increase maintenance factors—good working conditions, adequate salaries, and competitive fringe benefits—but should not operate under the false assumption that these factors will lead to greater job satisfaction.

Job enrichment, a significant intervention within OD and a critical element of quality-of-work-life projects, is a direct application of Herzberg's theory and at least an indirect one of Maslow's.

EXPECTANCY THEORY—LAWLER AND VROOM   Expectancy theory (Lawler 1973; Vroom 1964) has yet to have the impact on organization development that need theory has had, but it is gaining in acceptance and popularity. This approach to understanding human motivation focuses more on outward behavior than on internal needs. The theory is based on three assumptions:

1. People believe that their behavior is associated with certain outcomes—the performance-outcome expectancy. People may expect that, if they accomplish certain tasks, they will receive certain rewards.
2. Outcomes or rewards have different values (valence) for different people. Some people, for example, are more attracted to money as a reward than others are.
3. People associate their behavior with certain probabilities of success—the effort-performance expectancy. People on an assembly line, for example, may have high expectancies that, if they try, they can produce 100 units per hour, but their expectancies may be very low that they can produce 150 units, regardless of how hard they may try.

Thus, people will be highly motivated when they believe (1) that their behavior will lead to certain rewards, (2) that these rewards are worthwhile and valuable, and (3) that they are able to perform at a level that will result in the attainment of the rewards.

The theory further states that, given that people believe their behavior will lead to certain outcomes or rewards, the extent to which they will be motivated is a function of the multiplicative relationship between the value the reward holds for them and the perceived probability that their effort will result in the reward. The multiplicative relationship means that one without the other results in zero—no motivation. People may value the potential reward, but if they do not expect that their efforts will lead to the obtainment of the reward, they will not be motivated. If people believe that their efforts will lead to the reward but do not care for the reward, they will not be motivated. There are degrees of mixture of these two factors, of course, and the mixture will determine the amount of motivation. The amount of motiva-

26

tion a person will have is equal to $E \times V$, the expectancy times the valence of the reward.

Research has shown that high-performing employees believe that their behavior, or performance, leads to rewards that they desire. Thus, there is evidence for the validity of the theory. Moreover, the theory and the research outcomes associated with it have implications for how reward systems and work might be designed and structured (see chapter 6).

JOB SATISFACTION—HACKMAN AND OLDHAM   Hackman and Oldham's (1980) work design model is grounded in both need theory and expectancy theory. Their model is more restrictive in that it focuses on the relationship between job or work design and worker satisfaction. Although their model frequently leads to what is called job enrichment, as does the application of Herzberg's motivator-hygiene theory, the Hackman and Oldham model has broader implications. Briefly, Hackman and Oldham (1975) contend that there are three primary psychological states that significantly affect worker satisfaction: (1) experienced meaningfulness of the work itself, (2) experienced responsibility for the work and its outcomes, and (3) knowledge of results, or performance feedback. The more that work is designed to enhance these states, the more satisfying the work will be. A more thorough explanation of the Hackman and Oldham model is provided in Chapter 6.

POSITIVE REINFORCEMENT—SKINNER   The best way to understand the full implications of the applications of B. F. Skinner's (1971, 1953) thinking and his research results is to read his novel, *Walden Two* (1948). The book is about a utopian community designed and maintained according to Skinnerian principles of operant behavior and schedules of reinforcement. A similar application was made in an industrial situation in the Emery Air Freight case ("At Emery" 1973). By applying Skinnerian principles, which are based on numerous research findings, Emery quickly realized an annual savings of $650,000. (The Emery case is discussed more fully later in this section.)

Skinner is neither an OD practitioner nor a management consultant, but his theory and research are indeed applicable to management practices and to organizational change. For Skinner, control is key. If one can control the environment, one can then control behavior. In Skinner's approach, the more the environment is controlled, the better, but the necessary element of control is the rewards, both positive and negative. This necessity is based on a fundamental of behavior that Skinner derived from his many years of research—a concept so basic that it may be a law of behavior—that people (and animals) do what they are rewarded for doing. Let us consider the principles that underly this fundamental of behavior.

In the famous case of Pavlov's dog, after continuously pairing food with the sound of a bell, Pavlov eventually elicited a salivation response from the

27

dog with the bell sound only. The key word here is *elicited.* Skinner believes most behavior is *emitted.* He agrees that Pavlovian, or classical, conditioning is real but believes that it proves only that reflexes can be conditioned to various stimuli. Most behavior is more a result of an active process by a person than of a passive, reflexive response to certain stimuli in the environment. For Skinner, then, the primary subject matter of psychology is the study of emitted responses and their consequences. When we emit a response—that is, do something, such as writing a book—we tend to increase this response when it is followed by reinforcement. When the consequence of a certain behavior is reinforcement or reward, the behavior tends to be repeated. Absolutely identical behavior will not necessarily be repeated, but similar acts having essentially the same effect will certainly occur. Moreover, the act does not have to be continuously reinforced for it to be repeated. One of the most dramatic findings of psychological research has been the principle of partial reinforcement. In a comparison of behavior that has been reinforced all the time with the same behavior of a similar organism that has been reinforced only occasionally, after all reinforcement for both has stopped, the behavior of the partially reinforced respondent will last significantly longer than that of the continuously reinforced respondent. (This explains, of course, why many people continue to go to the golf course on weekends even though they may hit only one beautiful shot out of about every twenty attempts.)

The first phase of learned behavior is called shaping, the process of successive approximations to reinforcement. When children are learning to walk, they are reinforced by their parents' encouraging comments or physical stroking, but this reinforcement typically follows only the behaviors that lead to effective walking. Programmed learning, invented by Skinner, is based on this principle. To maintain the behavior, a schedule of reinforcement is applied, and, generally, the more variable the schedule is, the longer the behavior will last.

Skinner therefore advocates positive reinforcement for shaping and controlling behavior. Often, however, when we consider controlling behavior, we think of punishment—"If you don't do this, you're gonna get it!" According to Skinner, punishment is no good. His stance is not based entirely on his values or whims, however. Research clearly shows that, although punishment may temporarily stop a certain behavior, negative reinforcement must be administered continuously for this process to be maintained. The principle is the opposite of that for positively reinforced behavior. There are two very practical concerns here. First, having to reinforce a certain behavior continuously is obviously not very efficient. Second, although the punished behavior may be curtailed, it is unlikely that the subject will learn what to do; all that is learned is what *not* to do.

Thus, the way to control behavior according to Skinnerian theory and research is to reinforce the desirable behavior positively and, after the shaping process, to reinforce the behavior only occasionally. An attempt should be made to ignore undesirable behavior and not to punish (unless, perhaps, society must be protected) but, rather, to spend time positively shaping the desired behavior. The implications of Skinner's work for organizations is that a premium is placed on such activities as establishing incentive systems, reducing or eliminating many of the control systems that contain inherent threats and punishments, providing feedback to all levels of employees regarding their performance, and developing programmed-learning techniques for training employees.

The application of Skinner's work to OD did not occur systematically until the 1970s. Thus, his influence is not as pervasive as Maslow's is, for example. Skinner's behavior-motivation techniques as applied to people also raise significant questions regarding ethics and values: Who exercises the control, and is the recipient aware? Thus, it is not a question of whether Skinner's methodology works, but rather how and under what circumstances it is used.

The Emery Air Freight example, mentioned at the beginning of this section, illustrates how and under what circumstances Skinner's methodology may be applied in an organizational setting. At Emery supervisors were taught to use positive reinforcement, but not punishment, as a motivational tool. In keeping with Skinnerian principles, two main supervisory practices were stressed: recognition coupled with rewards and feedback. In a workbook provided for supervisors, as many as 150 types of recognition and rewards were suggested, ranging from a smile with an encouraging nod to detailed praise for excellent work. Praise and recognition were applied to specific behavior as soon as possible after the act had occurred. For the behavior to be shaped at Emery, supervisors used praise and recognition at least twice a week during the early weeks and months and then tapered off, providing praise only occasionally and never at a predictable time. Supervisors were also instructed to provide concrete and specific feedback to workers regarding their performance. Supervisors let the worker know specifically what was being rewarded; for example, a supervisor would say, "Mac, I liked the initiative you showed in getting those crates into the large containers. You're performing consistently now at 98 percent of standard." As workers were able to see more clearly, by this specific feedback, which behavior was being rewarded, they began to associate the feedback with reward—what Skinner refers to as "noncontrived reinforcers." The more workers associated the specific feedback they received with the recognition and praise, the more the feedback itself became a reward. Even when the workers' performance feedback came to them in the form of written reports, such as computer printouts listing workers' rates of production compared with the standard, the form itself became a reward.

At Emery the behavior to be shaped was first identified—for example, putting more crates into each container. As workers packaged more crates per container, this behavior was recognized and rewarded by the supervisor, frequently at first and less frequently and intermittently later. In the process, the supervisor also indicated, by feedback to workers, the specific behavior that was associated with the desired direction or standard. Gradually, the feedback became a positive reinforcer.

The Group Perspective

THE GROUP AS THE FOCUS OF CHANGE—LEWIN The theorist among theorists, at least within the scope of the behavioral sciences, is Kurt Lewin. His thinking has had a more pervasive impact on organization development, both direct and indirect, than any other person's. It was Lewin who laid the groundwork for much of what we know about social change, particularly in a group and by some extrapolation in an organization. Lewin's interest and, easily determined by implication, his values have also influenced OD. As a Jew who escaped Hitler's Germany in the 1930s, it was not coincidental that Lewin was intensely interested in the study of autocratic versus democratic behavior and matters of influence and change (Marrow 1969). Thus, his own and his students' research findings regarding the consequences of such variables as participative leadership and decision making have had considerable impact on the typical objectives of most if not all OD efforts.

According to Lewin (1951, 1948), behavior is a function of a person's personality, discussed primarily in terms of motivation or needs, and the situation or environment in which the person is acting. The environment is represented as a field of forces that affect the person. Thus, a person's behavior at any given moment can be predicted if we know that person's needs and if we can determine the intensity and valence (whether the force is positive or negative for the person) of the forces impinging on the person from the environment. Although Lewin borrowed the term *force* from physics, he defined the construct psychologically. Thus, one's perception of the environment is key, not necessarily reality. An example of a force, therefore, could be the perceived power of another person. Whether or not I will accomplish a task you want me to do is a function of the degree to which such accomplishment will respond to a need I have and how I perceive your capacity to influence me—whether you are a force in my environment (field).

Lewin made a distinction between imposed or *induced* forces, those acting on a person from the outside, and *own* forces, those directly reflecting the person's needs. The implications of this distinction are clear. Participation in determining a goal is more likely to create own forces toward accomplishing it than is a situation in which goal determination is imposed by others. When a goal is imposed on a person, his or her motives may match accomplishment of the goal, but the chances are considerably more variable or random than if the

30

goal is determined by the person in the first place. Typically, then, for imposed or induced goals to be accomplished by a person, the one who induced them must exert continuous influence or else the person's other motives, not associated with goal accomplishment, will likely determine his or her behavior. This aspect of Lewin's theory helps to explain the generally positive consequences of participative management and consensual decision making.

Another distinction Lewin made regarding various forces in a person's environment is the one between *driving* and *restraining* forces. Borrowing yet another concept from physics, quasi-stationary equilibria, he noted that the perceived status quo in life is just that—a perception. In reality, albeit psychological reality, a given situation is a result of a dynamic rather than a static process. The process flows from one moment to the next, with ups and downs, and over time gives the impression of a static situation, but there actually are some forces pushing in one direction and other, counterbalancing forces that restrain movement. The level of productivity in an organization may appear static, but sometimes it is being pushed higher—by the force of supervisory pressure, for example—and sometimes it is being restrained or even decreased by a counterforce, such as a norm of the work group. There are many different counterbalancing forces in any situation, and what is called a force-field analysis is used to identify the two sets of forces.

Change from the status quo is therefore a two-step process. First, a force-field analysis is conducted, and then the intensity of a force or set of forces is either increased or decreased. Change can occur by adding to or increasing the intensity of the forces Lewin labeled driving forces—that is, forces that push in the desired direction for change—or by diminishing the opposing or restraining forces. Lewin's theory predicts that the better of these two choices is to reduce the intensity of the restraining forces. By adding forces or increasing the intensity on the driving side, a simultaneous increase would occur on the restraining side, and the overall tension level for the system—whether it is a person, a group, or an organization—would intensify. The better choice, then, is to reduce the restraining forces.

This facet of Lewin's field theory helps us to determine not only the nature of change but how to accomplish it more effectively. Lewinian theory argues that it is more efficacious to direct change at the group level than at the individual level.

If one attempts to change an attitude or the behavior of an individual without attempting to change the same behavior or attitude in the group to which the individual belongs, then the individual will be a deviate and either will come under pressure from the group to get back into line or will be rejected entirely. Thus, the major leverage point for change is at the group level—for example, by modifying a group norm or standard. According to Lewin (1958):

31

> As long as group standards are unchanged, the individual will resist change more strongly the farther he is to depart from group standards. If the group standard itself is changed, the resistance which is due to the relation between individual and group standard is eliminated. (p. 210)

Adherence to Lewinian theory involves viewing the organization as a social system, with many and varied subsystems, primarily groups. We look at the behavior of people in the organization in terms of (1) whether their needs jibe with the organization's directions, usually determined by their degree of commitment; (2) the norms to which people conform and the degree of that conformity; (3) how power is exercised (induced versus own forces); and (4) the decision-making process (involvement leading to commitment).

Chapter 5 provides an elaboration of Lewin's thinking as it applies to organizational behavior and OD.

CHANGING VALUES THROUGH THE GROUP—ARGYRIS   It is not possible to place the work of Chris Argyris in one category, one theory, or one conceptual framework. He has developed a number of mini theories, whose relationship and possible overlap are not always apparent. He has always focused largely on interpersonal and group behavior, however, and he has emphasized behavioral change within a group context, along the same value lines as McGregor's (1960) Theory Y. The work described in *Management and Organizational Development: The Path from XA to YB* (Argyris 1971) best illustrates this emphasis. Since Argyris has made many theoretical contributions, we shall briefly cover his work chronologically, discussing it as early, middle, and recent Argyris work.

Argyris's early work (1962) may be characterized as emphasizing the relationship of individual personality and organizational dynamics. His objective was to look for ways in which this relationship could be satisficed; that is, that the person and the organization both might compromise so that each could profit from the other—*satisficed* meaning that there is an improvement but that it is less than optimal for each party. Although the relationship may never be optimal for both parties, it could still be better for both. For this relationship between the individual and the organization to be achieved, the organization must adjust its value system toward helping its members to be more psychologically healthy—less dependent on and controlled by the organization—and the individuals must become more open with their feelings, more willing to trust one another, and more internally committed to the organization's goals.

Argyris has always believed that organizations, especially pyramidally structured ones, tend to stifle people, to overcontrol them, and to treat them as children, thus making them something less than their projected potential. It is not surprising, therefore, that Argyris was captured by the early thrust of

32

sensitivity or T-group training in the 1950s. He published the article "T Groups for Organizational Effectiveness" (Argyris 1964). It was also during this period and within the same behavioral framework that Argyris developed his three-facet theory of interpersonal competence. He postulated that an interpersonally competent individual is one who *owns up,* openly expressing what he or she thinks and feels; *expresses feelings* to others when experiencing an emotion; and *experiments,* trying new behaviors and seeking to learn from these attempts. Thus, one who is interpersonally competent relates with others openly and seeks greater self-awareness and growth through risk taking.

In his thinking, research, and writing during the late 1960s and early 1970s, Argyris became more closely associated with organization development. His thrust of this middle period was in (1) theorizing about competent consultation, and especially about the nature of an effective intervention, and (2) operationalizing organizational change in behavioral terms by McGregor's Theory Y. Regarding the first aspect, Argyris (1970) contends that, for any intervention into an organization-social system to be effective, it must generate valid information, lead to free, informed choice on the part of the client, and provide internal commitment by the client to the choices taken. More on this aspect of Argyris's work is provided in Chapter 10. For the second aspect, Argyris connects behaviors (he calls them Pattern A) with McGregor's Theory X and Theory Y (Pattern B). Argyris specifies the behavioral manifestations of someone who holds either of the sets of assumptions about human beings in organizations that were postulated earlier by McGregor (1960). Pattern A behaviors are characterized as predominantly intellectual rather than emotional, conforming rather than experimenting, individually oriented rather than group-oriented, involving closed rather than open communications, and generally mistrusting rather than trusting. This pattern is the opposite of interpersonally competent behavior. Thus, Pattern B is an extention of Argyris's earlier facets of interpersonal competence.

More recently, Argyris has turned his attention to the gaps in people's behavior between what they say (he calls it espoused theory) and what they do (theory in action). People may say that they believe that McGregor's Theory Y assumptions about human beings are valid, for example, but they may act according to Pattern A. Argyris goes on to argue that as people become more aware of these gaps between their stated beliefs and their behavior, they will be more motivated to reduce the differences, to be more consistent. In one project, Argyris tape-recorded managerial staff meetings, analyzed the recorded behaviors, and then showed the managers where their actions were not consistent with their words (Argyris 1973). More recently, in collaboration with Don Schön, Argyris studied and elaborated the learning process involved in obtaining greater self-awareness and organizational awareness

33

about human effectiveness (Argyris and Schön 1978). Argyris and Schön argue that most organizations accomplish no more than "single loop learning," that problems are solved or fixed and a single loop of learning is accomplished. For significant organizational improvement and for insuring long-term survival and renewal, however, change must occur in more fundamental ways. Although problems must be solved in a single loop, new ways of learning *how* to solve problems must be learned as well. Another loop is thus added to the learning cycle—what Argyris and Schön refer to as "double loop learning." This process of learning is analogous to if not the same as the way OD is defined in this text, as a planned process of change in the organization's culture—how we do things and how we relate to one another.

THE GROUP UNCONSCIOUS—BION   Most people believe that everyone has an unconscious; Freud has clearly had an effect. Wilfred Bion believes, as others do, that there is also a group unconscious—a collective unconscious that is more than the sum of the individual unconsciouses—and he gives compelling but complex arguments (Bion 1961; Rioch 1970).

Bion believes that every group is actually composed of two groups, the work group and the basic-assumption group; that is, every group *behaves* as if it were two groups, one concerned with group accomplishment and rational actions, the other concerned with activity that stems from the unconscious and is irrational. Bion does not mean simply that a group is both rational and irrational. He goes far beyond this commonly accepted dichotomy.

The work group is the aspect of group functioning that is concerned with accomplishing what the group is composed to do, the task at hand. The work group is aware of its purpose, or at the outset knows that its initial task is to establish clarity of purpose. The work group is sure about, or quickly becomes sure about, roles and responsibilities in the group. The work group is also clearly conscious of the passage of time and the procedures and processes needed to accomplish the task.

How many times have you been a member or leader of a group that fit such a description? I suspect that it has not been very often, if ever. Bion states that groups do not behave in this clearly rational and sensible way because there is always another group operating simultaneously—the basic-assumption group.

Bion theorizes that all groups function according to basic assumptions, that groups operate as if certain things are inevitable. Perhaps an analogy will help to explain. In the early days of automobiles, many people made the basic assumption that no motorized vehicle could go faster than a horse, and these people acted accordingly. In fact, some of them eventually lost money because they bet heavily on their assumption. The point is that they acted as if their belief were true and inevitable.

There are three types of basic-assumption groups: the dependency group,

34

the fight-flight group, and the pairing group. The dependency group assumes that the reason the group exists is to be protected and to be assured of providence by its leader. The group members act immaturely, childishly, and as if they know little or nothing as compared with the leader. The leader is all-powerful and wise. In the dependency group, the leader is typically idolized. We mortals are neither omnipotent nor omniscient, however, and the group members soon realize that they must seek a "new messiah." The cycle then repeats itself with a new leader.

The fight-flight group assumes that it must preserve itself, that its survival is at stake, so group members act accordingly. Taking action is the key to survival, as in the proverbial Army command: "Do something even if it's wrong!" It is the *group* that must be preserved, so individuals may be sacrificed through fight or abandonment (flight). The leader's role in this basic-assumption group is clear: to lead the group into battle or retreat. The best leader is one who acts in a paranoid manner, assuming that "They're out to get us, gang!" Eventually and inevitably the leader will not meet all the group's demands, at which point the group panics and searches for a new leader.

In the pairing group the assumption is that the group's purpose is to give birth to a new messiah. The leader in this case is purely incidental, and the group must quickly get on with the business of bringing forth the new savior. Two members therefore pair off to procreate. The two may be both male, both female, or male and female, but the basic assumption is that, when two people pair, the pairing is sexual in nature, even though it takes the innocent form of establishing a subcommittee. Although new life and hope may be provided, the new messiah, as the Christian Messiah, will soon be done away with. All the basic-assumption groups behave as if the leader must be replaced or, to use Bion's more dramatic and graphic terminology, as if the leader must be crucified.

Although the work group and the basic-assumption group are functioning simultaneously, their degree of activity varies. At times the work group is predominant and at other times the basic-assumption group holds sway.

Another Bion concept is his idea of valency. With this construct, he accounts for individual differences in groups. He contends that some people have a greater tendency to enter into (collude with) a basic-assumption group than others do. The comparison is in the work group; some people are more cooperative than others. The difference is that cooperative behavior in the work group is a conscious, deliberate effort, whereas valency for the basic-assumption group is exclusively an unconscious process.

Bion has never been an OD practitioner; he is a psychotherapist. His theory, however, is applicable to interventions with teams, consultation with leaders, and diagnosis of possible processes of collusion. For a direct application and extension of the latter group or organizational dynamic, see

Harvey's "Abilene Paradox" (1974a), an extension of Bion's theory that explains collusive behavior on the part of members of a group. More general application of Bion's theory is also provided in Chapter 12.

For the OD practitioner serving as a consultant to an organizational team, Bion's theory is particularly useful for diagnosing internal problems, especially those concerning team members' relationships with the leader.

The Total System Perspective

PARTICIPATIVE MANAGEMENT, THE ONE BEST WAY—LIKERT Likert is best known for two concepts: the linking pin notion of management and the four-system model of organizations. He is also known for his unequivocal advocacy of participative management as *the* approach to be taken by managers, regardless of organizational type. Likert's method for organization development is survey feedback. I shall cover each of these concepts in turn.

Likert's (1961) idea of the linking pin originated from his desire to design organizations in a more decentralized form without eliminating the hierarchical structure. He also wanted to incorporate more opportunity for group activity, especially group decision making, in the managerial process. Thus, each manager is simultaneously a member of two groups, one in which he or she manages and is the leader and one in which he or she is a subordinate and follows the leadership of a boss. By being a member of both these hierarchical groups, the person becomes a key *link* within the vertical chain of command. This linkage manifests itself primarily in activities involving communication and resolution of conflict. The manager-subordinate, therefore, is the primary conduit for information and facilitates the resolution of conflict, by virtue of the linking position, when there are differences between the two vertically connected organizational groups. An organization chart is drawn so that groups overlap vertically rather than in the more traditional way, as separate boxes connected only by lines. Exhibit 2.1 shows this concept of organizational structure.

Likert (1967) has described four major models or systems of organization design: the autocratic, the benevolent autocratic, the consultative, and the participative. He uses seven organizational functions to describe the four models differentially: leadership, motivation, communication, interaction and influence, decision making, goal setting, and control. His "Profile of Organizational Characteristics," a diagnostic questionnaire, is organized according to these seven functions and four models. Organizational members' answers to the questionnaire provide a perceptual profile of the organization. The profile is derived from the respondents' views of how the seven functions are managed and depicts which of the four systems seems to be predominant, at least in the eyes of the respondents.

36

EXHIBIT 2.1

Likert's Linking Pin Design of Organizational Structure and Managerial Role

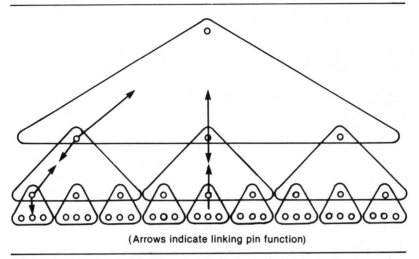

(Arrows indicate linking pin function)

Source: R. Likert, *New Patterns of Management* (New York: McGraw-Hill, 1961). Reprinted by permission.

The autocratic model—System 1 in Likert's terminology—is character-ized by strictly top-down management, with little or no leeway for subor-dinates to affect decisions. Communication is one-way, starting from the top, motivation is by use of the stick, and control is tight and concentrated at the top. System 2, benevolent autocracy, is less punitive and uses the carrot more than the stick; people are treated more humanely, and top management will listen to subordinates, but it is always clear who ultimately controls the organization. In consultative management, System 3, managers not only listen to subordinates but genuinely want their ideas. Managers *consult* with their subordinates in the decision-making process but reserve the right to make the final decisions themselves. Communication is more two-way, motivation is mostly by carrot rather than stick, subordinates have influence on their own organizational goals, and control is more decentralized. Par-ticipative management, System 4, is at the opposite end of the spectrum from the autocratic model. In a System 4 organization, leadership is participative, motivation is developed according to Maslow's higher-order needs, com-munication is always two-way and open, influence and interpersonal rela-tions are cooperative and trusting, decisions are frequently made in groups and by consensus, goals are mutually established, and control is highly decen-

37

tralized and widespread. As indicated earlier, Likert advocates System 4. Thus, he is a normative theorist, declaring one best way, rather than a contingency theorist. In his book *The Human Organization* (1967), he provides research evidence to support his position.

Likert not only argues that there is one best way to manage, he also espouses one best way to conduct an organization development effort. His method is survey feedback, the survey instrument being his "Profile of Organizational Characteristics" and the feedback being organized and analyzed according to the four-system model of organizational management. In an organization development effort, then, Likert's approach is highly data-based, but the diagnosis is largely limited to the functions he deems important. Once the survey data are collected, they are given back in profile form to organizational family units—to a boss and his or her team. This group then considers the data in light of their particular situation and organizational mandate, then decides on a plan for changes they want to make, and finally takes the necessary action for implementing the plan. Approximately a year later, the organization should take another survey to check progress and to plan and implement further changes.

Although organizational change agents may be uncomfortable with Likert's one best way and may prefer an approach that is more contingent and perhaps more flexible, they can be very sure of the direction and the objectives of the change effort.

IT ALL DEPENDS—LAWRENCE AND LORSCH   For an organization to operate efficiently and effectively, one person cannot do everything, and every organizational member cannot do the same thing. In any organization, therefore, there is a division of labor. Lawrence and Lorsch (1969, 1967) call this *differentiation*. In an organization with many divisions, some people must provide coordination, so that what the organization does is organized in some fashion. Lawrence and Lorsch label this process *integration*. Their approach is sometimes referred to as a theory of differentiation-integration. A more appropriate label, however, and the one they prefer, is *contingency* theory. They believe that how an organization should be structured and how it should be managed depend on several factors, primarily the organization's environment, or its marketplace. The central elements of the Lawrence and Lorsch contingency theory are differentiation, integration, the organization-environment interface, and the implicit contract between the employees and management.

Differentiation means dividing up tasks so that everything that needs to be done is accomplished. To determine the degree of differentiation in an organization, Lawrence and Lorsch consider four variables: (1) goal certainty—whether goals are clear and easily measured or ambiguous and

38

largely qualitative; (2) structure—whether the structure is formal, with precise policy and procedures, or loose and flexible, with policy largely a function of current demands; (3) interaction—whether there is considerable interpersonal and intergroup communication and cooperation or very little; and (4) timespan of feedback—whether people in the organization see the results of their work quickly or it takes a long time. The more that units within an organization differ from one another along these four dimensions, the more differentially structured the organization is. Some units may be very sure of their goals while others are not so sure, and some units may follow strict and precise work procedures while other units are still trying to formulate working procedures. It should be clear, therefore, that highly differentiated organizations are more difficult to coordinate. In a pyramidal organization, the coordination and the resolution of conflict are handled by the next higher level of management. When organizations are simultaneously highly differentiated and decentralized with respect to management, Lawrence and Lorsch argue that integrator roles are needed, that certain people must be given specific assignments for coordinating and integrating diverse functions. These people may or may not be in key decision-making positions but they ensure that decisions are made by someone or by the appropriate group.

How should an organization be structured, differentiated, and centralized (pyramidal) or decentralized? We already know the answer—that it depends—but on what does it depend? Lawrence and Lorsch argue that it depends primarily on the organization's environment, on whether the environment is complex and rapidly changing, as in the electronics industry, or relatively simple (one or two major markets) and stable (raw materials forthcoming and predictable and market likely to remain essentially the same in the foreseeable future). The more complex the environment, the more decentralized and flexible management should be. Lawrence and Lorsch's reasoning is that, the more rapidly changing the environment, the more necessary it is that the organization have people monitoring these changes, and the more they should be in a position to make decisions on the spot. When the organization's environment is not particularly complex and when conditions are relatively stable, management should be more centralized, since this way of structuring is more efficient.

Lawrence and Lorsch consider matters of conflict resolution because conflicts arise quickly and naturally in a highly differentiated organization, and the management of these conflicts is critical for efficient and effective organizational functioning. Moreover, if the organization is highly differentiated *and* decentralized, conflict is even more likely.

Finally, how well an organization operates is also a function of the nature of the interface between management and employees. Lawrence and Lorsch recognize the importance of individual motivation and effective supervision. They tend to view motivation in terms of expectancy, believing that employees' motivation (and morale) is based on the degree to which their expectations about how they should be treated are actually met by management in the work environment.

In summary, Lawrence and Lorsch are known as contingency theorists. They advocate no single form of organizational structure or single style of management. The structure and the style depend on the business of the organization and its environment—how variable or how stable it is.

Currently, Lawrence and Lorsch are among the most influential theorists for OD practitioners. There is something appealing about the idea of considering contingencies before acting.

THE ORGANIZATION AS A FAMILY—LEVINSON   Harry Levinson believes that an organization can be psychoanalyzed and that an organization operates like a family, with the chief executive officer as the father. According to Levinson, all organizations "recapitulate the basic family structure in a culture." Thus, the type of organization Levinson understands best, of course, is the family-owned business, and his theory about organizations and how they operate and change has its roots in Freudian psychoanalytic theory (Levinson 1972a, 1972b).

Levinson does not look at organizations exclusively through psychoanalytic glasses, however. He is well aware that structure, the type of business, the kinds of people who are attracted to the organization as employees, and the outside environment affect the internal behavioral dynamics of organizations. More important for Levinson's diagnosis of an organization, however, is the nature of the organization's personality (we might call it culture). He believes that an organization has a personality, just as an individual does, and that the health of an organization, like that of a person, can be determined in terms of how effectively the various parts of the personality are integrated. He refers to this process as maintaining equilibrium. Levinson also believes that implicit psychological contracts exist between management and employees, based on earlier experiences from family life. If the employees behave themselves (are good boys and girls), the parents (management) will reward them appropriately. Thus, the psychological contract is characterized by dependency. Note that this aspect of Levinson's theory is similar to Argyris's theory.

Continuing the psychoanalytic paradigm, Levinson theorizes that the chief executive officer represents the ego ideal for the organizational family and that this ideal, for better or for worse, motivates the kinds of people who are attracted to the organization in the first place, the interaction patterns among people in the organization, especially in matters of authority, and the kinds of people who are promoted. If a chief executive officer stays in office for a long time, the personality of the organization slowly crystallizes over the years; those who aspire to the ego ideal stay in the organization, and those who do not leave. Accordingly, Levinson believes that history is a critical factor in diagnosing an organization.

Levinson is a clinical psychologist who became more interested in organizational health than in individual psychodynamics as a result of his work at the Menninger Clinic. He has applied the principles of individual clinical therapy to his consulting practice with organizations. His approach as a consultant is (1) to immerse himself as deeply as possible in the psychodynamics of the organization; (2) to take a thorough history of the organization, just as a clinician would in the initial session with a patient; (3) to work predominantly with top management, since they tend to shape the personality of the organization and are therefore in the best position to change it; and (4) to pay particular attention to the stress factors in the organization and to how organizational members cope. In regard to this last point, Levinson is considered the "great worrier" among OD theorists. He worries about executive stress (Levinson 1975) and about the incidence in an organization of such variables as psychosomatic illnesses, absenteeism, and business pressures, such as the all-out emphasis many organizations place on meeting the so-called bottom line. Levinson is very interested in what people do with their energy, in whether human energy in the organization is directed toward goal accomplishment or toward coping with stress.

In summary, as a consultant, Levinson uses the clinical case method in diagnosis, intervenes primarily at the top of an organization, and bases his theory on psychoanalysis. In his own words:

> You've got to take into account all the factors in an organization, just as you gather all the main facts of a person's life in taking a case history. But you need a comprehensive theory like psychoanalysis to make sense of all the facts, to make it hang together in a useful way. (1972a; p. 126)

Summary

At the risk of oversimplification, I have summarized ten theorists by categorizing them according to their perspectives and emphases and according to potential applications of their theoretical approaches. A summary of these factors is given in Exhibit 2.2. Keep in mind that there is no single, all-encompassing theory for organization development. What we have are several mini theories that help us understand certain aspects of organizational behavior and OD. Taken together and comparatively, they become more

41

EXHIBIT 2.2

Summary of Primary OD Theorists According to Their Perspectives, Emphases, and Applications

Perspective	Theorist	Emphasis	Application
Individual	Maslow and Herzberg	Individual needs	Career development, job enrichment
	Vroom and Lawler	Individual expectancies and values	Reward system design, performance appraisal
	Hackman and Oldham	Job satisfaction	Job and work design, job enrichment
	Skinner	Individual performance	Incentive systems, reward system design
Group	Lewin	Norms and values	Changing conformity patterns
	Argyris	Interpersonal competence and values	Training and education
	Bion	Group unconscious, psychoanalytic basis	Group behavior diagnosis
System	Likert	Management style and approach	Change to participative management
	Lawrence and Lorsch	Organizational structure	Change contingent on organizational environment
	Levinson	Organization as a family, psychoanalytic basis	Diagnosis of organization according to familial patterns

useful to the practitioner who must cope with an ever-changing, complex, total organization.

Thus, organization development comes from many sources and has its roots in more than one methodology and in a variety of theories and concepts. The background provided in this chapter, though varied, nevertheless has commonality. The trunk from these roots might be expressed as the attempt to improve an organization with methods that involve people and to create conditions whereby the talents of these people are used more effectively.

CHAPTER 3

Organization Development and the Process of Change

Now that we have some background on the origins of organization development, we can proceed toward a more definitive definition and a more thorough understanding. As stated in Chapter 1, OD is a planned process of change in an organization's culture through the utilization of behavioral science technology and theory. The focus of this chapter is on the "process of change" and "utilization of . . . theory" portions of that definition. The organization's culture will be the focus of Chapter 4, and coverage of the technology comes in Parts III and IV.

Although the practice of organization development may be based on portions of several theories from the behavioral sciences, as stated in the previous chapter, there is no single, all-encompassing theory of OD. This no doubt constitutes a weakness of the field, but it is not surprising, since OD is very young as a field, having its origins around 1960, and is based on several disciplines. Nevertheless, most practitioners agree that three models are the underlying and guiding frames of reference for any OD effort: (1) the action research model; (2) Lewin's three-step model of system change—unfreezing, moving, and refreezing; and (3) phases of planned change as delineated by Lippitt, Watson, and Westley (1958). The three models are not mutually exclusive, and all stem from the original thinking of Kurt Lewin.

Action Research

In practice, the words *action research* are reversed (L. D. Brown 1972), for initially research is first conducted and then action is taken as a direct result of what the research data are interpreted to indicate. As W. L. French and Bell (1978) have pointed out, action research came from two independent sources, one a person of action, John Collier, who was commissioner of Indian Affairs from 1933 to 1945, the other a person of research, Kurt Lewin.

Collier worked to bring about change in ethnic relations and was a strong advocate of conducting research to determine the "central areas of needed action" (Collier 1945). He labeled this kind of research *action research*.

Although Lewin was an academic—a scholar, theoretician, and researcher—he was just as eminent a man of action (Marrow 1969). Moreover, he pulled it all together when he stated that there is "no action without research, and no research without action" (Lewin 1946). Lewin and his colleagues and students conducted many action research projects in several different domains: community and racial relations, leadership, eating habits, and intergroup conflict. The action research project that is perhaps most relevant to OD was conducted by John R. P. French (a student of Lewin's and now a professor at the University of Michigan) and his client, Lester Coch. Their famous study of workers' resistance to change in a pajama factory not only illustrated action research at its best but provided the theoretical basis for what we now call participative management (Coch and French 1948). A summary of this study should help to explain the process involved in action research.

The Coch and French Study

The study took place in the late 1940s in one of the plants of the Harwood Manufacturing Company. This plant, located in the western part of Virginia, manufactured pajamas. In their attempts to stay competitive with other manufacturers of sleep wear, Harwood management occasionally made changes in the way work was conducted. Serious production problems usually occurred when changes were made—efficiency decreased, absenteeism and job turnover increased, and workers complained. Like most sewing plants, this one employed mostly women, some 500. They were recruited and hired from the rural areas surrounding the small town in Virginia. Although it was relatively easy to recruit new workers, the time required to train them was costly. When a worker was transferred to a new job, the average relearning time was eight weeks, and the relearning period for highly experienced workers was even longer. Although the changes typically made were minor ones, workers resisted. Some refused to change and quit instead. Some of the changes were as follows: (1) hand pressers who formerly stacked their work in half-dozen lots on a flat piece of cardboard would start stacking their work inside a box; (2) pajama folders who formerly folded tops with prefolded pants would be required to fold the pants as well; and (3) pajama examiners who formerly clipped threads and examined every seam would change to clipping only certain threads. For the first two changes, more time would be allowed by the time-and-motion-study person (less time in the third instance), since workers' incentive pay was on a piece-rate basis.

The usual procedure that management used for making changes was to hold a group meeting with the employees involved in the change, to explain the reason and need for the change, and to have the time-study person explain thoroughly the basis of the new piece rate. The change would then be implemented. This usual way of bringing about changes in the Harwood plant created strong resistance on the part of the workers, however, as manifested in the long relearning time, absenteeism, grievances, and turnover.

Management had not been successful in overcoming this resistance, so they hired an outside consultant, John R. P. French, to work with Lester Coch, the industrial relations and personnel manager at the plant. With Coch's help, French studied the problem thoroughly. They conducted interviews, observed the work itself, and perused previous production records. Coch and French then devised a study that they wished to conduct—the research phase of the action research approach. After obtaining management's approval, they arranged for the next change to be conducted in three different ways:

1. For eighteen employees, they used the same method as before. In research terminology, these employees were referred to as the control group.
2. At the same time, for another group of thirteen employees in another part of the plant, they held a group meeting, explained the need for a change, presented a tentative plan, sought the group's approval—allowing for modifications where warranted—and then had the group select from among themselves three "special" operators to try the new arrangement, fine-tune the new procedure, and then later serve as trainers for the other workers. This research group was referred to as the representative group.
3. The third procedure was like the second, except that, rather than selecting representatives, the group was divided into two groups of seven and eight employees, respectively, and all employees in these two subgroups served as special operators. These employees were referred to as the total-participation groups.

The results of the study were dramatic. The control or no-participation group improved very little in efficiency. Resistance occurred as before: 17 percent quit their jobs in the first forty days of the study, grievances and absenteeism increased, and so on. The representative group improved significantly. At the end of fourteen days they had reached their former levels of production, no one had quit, and there was only one grievance and no absenteeism. The two total-participation groups relearned the fastest. Not only did they reach their previous level of production more rapidly, but they surpassed it by 14 percent within thirty days. By the end of the forty-day study period, this new, higher rate of production had been stabilized. There were no quits among the total-participation groups, no grievances, and no absenteeism.

Coch and French later repeated the study in other parts of the plant and achieved the same results. Management was so impressed that they began to implement participative modes of management throughout the plant and in other Harwood plants. This decision by management represents the *action* phase of action research. Later, in the 1950s, the Harwood Company acquired one of its major competitors, the Weldon Company, and gradually changed its management approach to one of greater employee participation. The story of these changes and the accompanying results is told in Marrow, Bowers, and Seashore's *Management by Participation* (1967).

Wendell French (1969) and Frohman, Sashkin, and Kavanagh (1976) have taken the action research model and made it directly applicable and relevant to the organization development process. Exhibit 3.1 shows French's

EXHIBIT 3.1

Action-Research Model for Organization Development

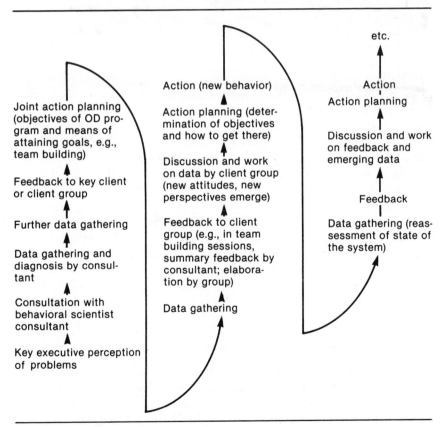

Source: W.L. French, "Organization Development: Objectives, Assumptions, and Strategies," © 1969 by the Regents of the University of California. Reprinted from *California Management Review,* Volume XII, No. 2, p. 26 by permission of the Regents.

adaptation. The OD steps included in this action research model will be covered in detail in later chapters.

Lewin's Three-Step Procedure of Change

According to Lewin (1958), the first step in the process of change is *unfreezing* the present level of behavior. To reduce prejudice, for example, the unfreezing step might be catharsis (G. W. Allport 1945) or participation in a series of sensitivity training sessions (Rubin 1967). For organizational change, the unfreezing step might be a series of management training sessions in which the objective for change was a more participative approach (Blake, Mouton, Barnes, and Greiner 1964; Shepard 1960) or data feedback from a survey that showed serious problems in the managerial process of the organization (Bowers 1973; Nadler 1977).

The second step, *movement*, is to take action that will change the social system from its original level of behavior or operation to a new level. This action could be organization restructuring (Foltz, Harvey, and McLaughlin 1974), team development (Beckhard and Lake 1971), or any number of what OD practitioners call interventions.

The *refreezing* step involves the establishment of a process that will make the new level of behavior "relatively secure against change" (Lewin 1958). This refreezing process may include different conforming patterns, or new norms, such as collaboration rather than competition (Davis 1967; R. Tannenbaum and Davis 1969), a new approach to managing people (Marrow, Bowers, and Seashore 1967; Seashore and Bowers 1970), or a new reward system that will positively reinforce the desired behavior change (Lawler 1977).

Thus, according to Lewin, bringing about lasting change means initially unlocking or unfreezing the present social system. This might require some kind of confrontation (Beckhard 1967) or a process of reeducation. Next, behavioral movement must occur in the direction of desired change, such as a reorganization. Finally, deliberate steps must be taken to ensure that the new state of behavior remains relatively permanent. These three steps are simple to state but not simple to implement. Lippitt, Watson, and Westley (1958) have helped to clarify these steps by elaborating on them.

Phases of Planned Change

The Lippitt, Watson, and Westley (1958) model of planned change expands Lewin's three steps to five phases. They use the word *phase* deliberately, since *step* connotes a discrete action or event rather than the more likely reality, that step 1 has probably not been completed when step 2 is being taken, and so forth. Their five phases are:

1. Development of a need for change (Lewin's unfreezing)
2. Establishment of a change relationship
3. Working toward change (moving)
4. Generalization and stabilization of change (refreezing)
5. Achieving a terminal relationship

Lippitt, Watson, and Westley viewed the change process from the perspective of the change agent. Their concept of a change agent is a professional, typically a behavioral scientist, who is external or internal to the organization involved in the change process. In OD terms, this person is the OD practitioner or consultant. Lippitt and his colleagues go on to state:

> The decision to make a change may be made by the system itself, after experiencing pain (malfunctioning) or discovering the possibility of improvement, or by an outside change agent who observes the need for change in a particular system and takes the initiative in establishing a helping relationship with that system. (Lippitt, Watson, and Westley 1958, p. 10)

With respect to phase 1—the development of a need for change—Lippitt, Watson, and Westley suggest that the unfreezing occurs in one of three ways: (1) a change agent demonstrates the need by, for example, presenting data from interviews that indicate that a serious problem exists; (2) a third party sees a need and brings the change agent and the potential client system together; or (3) the client system becomes aware of its own need and seeks consultative help.

By establishment of a change relationship, phase 2, these authors mean the development of a collaborative working effort between the change agent and the client system. Lippitt and his colleagues make an important point when they note that "often the client system seems to be seeking assurance that the potential change agent is different enough from the client system to be a real expert and yet enough like it to be thoroughly understandable and approachable" (p. 134). Striking this balance is critical to effective consultation in organization development.

Most of their elaboration on Lewin's three steps is in the moving phase, or, as Lippitt and his colleagues call it, working toward change. There are three subphases to this third major phase:

1. Clarification or diagnosis of the client system's problem, which consists primarily of the change agent's collecting information and attempting to understand the system, particularly the problem areas
2. Examination of alternative routes and goals, which involves establishing goals and intentions of action and also includes determining the degree of motivation for change and the beginning of a process of focusing energy

49

3. Transformation of intentions into actual change efforts, which is the doing part—implementing a new organization structure, conducting a specific training program, installing a new reward system, and the like

Refreezing, or the generalization and stabilization of change, is the fourth major phase. The key activity in this phase is spreading the change to other parts of the total system. This phase also includes the establishment of mechanisms or activities that will maintain the momentum that was gathered during the previous phases. Lippitt and his colleagues call this a process of institutionalization. Hornstein et al. (1971) view this institutionalization process in two ways: (1) as normative support for the change and (2) as structural support for the change. By normative support they mean that, in the refreezing phase, organization members are conforming to new norms (see Chapter 5). To ensure this form of institutionalization, organization members must be involved in the planning and implementing of the action steps for change. Involvement leads to commitment—in this case, commitment to new norms. Structural support may take the form of new organizational arrangements—that is, new reporting and accountability relationships, as reflected in a new organization chart—or the placement of guardians of the new culture, the new conforming patterns. These guardians, or facilitators, of the new culture are people whose job it is (1) to monitor the state of the organization's effectiveness; (2) to see that the information that is monitored is reported to the appropriate people in the organization; (3) to provide help in understanding the information, especially in the diagnosis of problems; (4) to assist in the planning and implementation of action steps for further changes; and (5) to provide additional expertise in helping the organization to continue to change and renew where appropriate. Their primary responsibility, therefore, is to help regulate change as an organizational way of life. Hornstein and his colleagues go on to state:

> Initially, this role is typically fulfilled by an outside consultant to the organization. Frequently, he attempts to work in conjunction with some person (or persons) inside the organization. If the internal person is not trained in OD, the external consultant will usually encourage the internal person(s) and other key individuals in the organization to develop their own resources in this area. (Hornstein et al. 1971, p. 352)

In other words, the more the consultant can arrange for OD-trained people to be permanent organization members, the more likely it is that the initiated change will last and become institutionalized as a way of life.

For the final phase, Lippitt and his colleagues argue for the achievement of a terminal relationship. What they mean is that the relationship between the change agent and the client must end. They contend that it is common for clients to become dependent on change agents and that change agents' ultimate goal is to work themselves out of a job. The underlying value of this model for change is that it creates within the client system the expertise to solve its own problems in the future, at least those problems that fall within the same universe as the original change problem.

The Generic Model for Organizational Change

The three models covered so far in this chapter—action research; Lewin's three steps of unfreezing, moving, and refreezing; and Lippitt, Watson, and Westley's five phases of planned change—are all part of a generic model for bringing about organizational change. This is not accidental, of course, since all three models are based on the original thinking of Kurt Lewin.

The generic model might be described as a process by which a consultant collects information about the nature of an organization (the research) and then helps the organization to change by way of a sequence of phases that involve those who are directly affected—the organization members themselves. This more general model consists of the following elements:

1. An outside consultant or change agent
2. The gathering of information (data) from the client system by the consultant for purposes of understanding more about the inherent nature of the system, determining major domains in need of change (problems), and reporting this information back to the client system so that appropriate action can be taken
3. Collaborative planning between the consultant and the client system for purposes of change (action)
4. Implementation of the planned change, which is based on valid information (data) and is conducted by the client system, with the continuing help of the consultant
5. Institutionalization of the change

Behavioral Attributes of Change

We now turn to an explanation of some of the primary behavioral attributes of change. This exposition will help us to understand more thoroughly the behavioral bases that underlie the model of change for organization development.

People resist change—or do they? Does an employee resist an upward change in pay rate or vacation allowance? Does a homemaker resist the replacement of a cranky old dishwasher for a new one? Does a manager resist an imposed schedule change that requires him to represent his division at an important reception for the new company president rather than finishing his quarterly budget? All these changes are likely to be welcomed warmly and to

51

be implemented with great cooperation from the people concerned. What distinguishes these changes from the changes that people resist strongly is the fact that their nature and effects are relatively well known and are enthusiastically desired. The degree of people's resistance to change depends on the kind of change involved and how well it is understood. What people resist is not change but loss, or the possibility of loss (Marris 1975). This loss is generally one of two kinds.

Loss of the Known and Tried

Change often involves a shift away from a known situation, with all its familiarity and possible advantages. The people concerned are exchanging the known for the unknown; certainty for uncertainty; stable, existing patterns of behavior and adaptation for the need to evolve new patterns; tried rewards for untested ones. In addition to the uncertainty of the satisfactions to be gained from the new situation, the people being asked to make the change are required to spend a great deal of effort and psychological energy in getting to know the new situation and in tolerating and coping with frustration until they can evolve new work or living patterns. In psychological terms, newness and the need to cope with it constitute *stress*. If the long-term rewards to be gained from the change are no greater than those enjoyed formerly, the stress cost outweighs the future advantage. If the new advantages outweigh the old but are not well understood by those making the change, again the effort involved will not seem worthwhile. Only if the advantages are greater and are desired sufficiently to outweigh the efforts required to make the transition are people likely to change willingly.

Loss of Personal Choice

People are not simply and naturally resistant to change. What comes closer to a universal truth about human behavior is that people resist the *imposition* of change. Brehm's (1966) research and his theory of *psychological reactance* help to explain this human phenomenon. When one's feeling of freedom is in jeopardy, the immediate reaction is likely to be an attempt to regain this sense of freedom. This reaction is so strong, in fact, that people frequently will not bother to defend their beliefs and may even change them in order to maintain opposition to others' attempts at changing them. In some cases the issues of advantage and change are in conflict, leading to a situation in which people may prefer to continue on a path that is not in their best interests rather than to give up the feeling of free choice. Research shows, for example, that, when a smoker is *told* to stop smoking, his or her typical reaction is either to continue as usual, or to increase the rate. Brehm's theory is that, when people believe themselves free to behave in a certain way, they will experience psychological reactance (that is, they will resist) if that freedom is threatened or eliminated. The degree of ease and success with which an organizational change is introduced is therefore directly proportional to the amount of choice that people feel they have in determining and implementing the change.

Involvement and Commitment

A common-sense principle of human behavior that is corroborated by considerable research is that, the more people are involved in decisions that directly affect them, the more they will be committed to implementing those decisions (Lewin 1958). This principle helps to explain why some elegantly and appropriately designed plans never get implemented. When a single person or a small group of people plans a change that will involve a much larger group of other people, without involving the others in the planning, the likelihood of successful implementation is diminished. The larger group is likely to perceive the plan as something being imposed on them, and their reactance is aroused. Although they may agree that the plan is intrinsically logical and appropriate, there will be no *psychological commitment* to it if they have not been involved in the planning itself and have had no influence on its content or choice in whether to contribute to it. This lack of psychological commitment does not necessarily cause complete resistance to implementation, but the best that can be expected (unless organizational loyalty is extraordinarily high) is passive compliance.

Methods of Implementing Change

Now that we have covered some of the primary behavioral attributes of change and a basic principle of behavior related to change—that involvement leads to commitment—we shall consider the implications of these attributes and this basic principle by comparing two very different methods for implementing change. In some circumstances a top-down method, one extreme, may be appropriate; in others, a more participative approach, the other extreme, will help to guarantee implementation.

Top-down Unilateral Decree

The most dramatic, traditional, and perhaps still most frequently used method for making a change in an organization is the top-down unilateral decree. This is a form best suited to crises, such as war or accident, or in situations in which time is precious or argument or discussion would be disastrous, such as in the middle of a religious ceremony). This method requires a source whose authority is accepted and whose directives are clear.

The most commonly cited case of this form of introducing change is the military, but situations calling for top-down decree abound in daily life. The father who sees his four-year-old daughter standing up in the back of his open sports car while he is driving at 60 mph does not wait to ask if the child feels like sitting down. He yells an order. There is no doubt that, in crisis situations, when everyone understands and accepts the authority, the top-down autocratic order is the fastest and most effective way to institute change. What is not so well understood, however, is that this technique is dysfunctional in other circumstances, creating the reactance that Brehm described.

The autocratic introduction of change has been a traditional hallmark of the tough American manager. In organizations where the quality of managerial toughness is valued for itself, this method will probably be called for more often than it would be elsewhere. The second circumstance in which top-down autocratic change management is appropriate is in organizational cultures where it is an intrinsically valued and expected mode. It would be more appropriate, for example, in the German Army than in the Israeli Army or in some sectors of the Norwegian Merchant Marine. Even now the German Army is structured relatively rigidly around top-down unilateral methods, even in situations where there is sufficient time and opportunity for other ways of operating. In contrast, the Israeli Army uses a more participative style in most situations short of actual combat, and some Norwegian merchant ships have adopted participative methods at sea, reverting to traditional autocratic methods only when they come into port, in order to interface effectively with the more traditional harbor organizations.

Participative Change

To exact greater commitment, the method for introducing change should be a participative process. The overall form may still be from the top down, but the more the process follows Likert's linking pin format (Likert 1961), which involves overlapping teams in the hierarchy, or the more it is managed through a series of ad hoc committees composed of the people who will eventually have to make the change work and therefore need to be involved, the more successful it is likely to be.

It is important to make a clear distinction between *participative decision making* and *participative communication*. Participative decision making is a sharing in the diagnosis, analysis, development, and choice of solution for a particular problem or situation—in determining ways to implement the solution and manage the change process. Participative communication is the opportunity to contribute information to a decision-making process, either about the problem itself or about how recommended solutions are likely to work or can best be implemented. It is also important to distinguish between levels of participative decision making. In a large organization, it is clearly more effective to assign a small group of people or one individual to develop an initial plan and then to invite the larger community to review it and become involved in elaborating, planning, and managing implementation for the parts of the plan with which they are most closely involved.

When the term *participative management* is used, many managers hear *participative decision making* and immediately fear a change that would mean a loss for them, at least in terms of how they perceive their control of a situation. Their anxiety about loss of control leads them to resist with great vigor what they imagine will happen. Consequently, they are not able to benefit from their subordinates' participative communication or from appropriate levels of participative decision making, which would enable them to collect much better data about problems, possible solutions, and implementation. Unfortunately, too few managers have confidence in their subordinate's mature, common-sense understanding that decisions are best made by a small number of people, so long as others who are affected have a chance to express their opinions and to become involved with the direction and implementation of changes that affect their own work situations. Participative communication and choice of an appropriate level of participative decision making and implementation are the key issues in successful implementation of change.

A Case Example

A case example of a change effort that used a participative approach will help to illustrate the foregoing point.

Several years ago I consulted with a medical school that was considering an overall change in the curriculum. Prior to my arrival, a curriculum change had been in the planning process for two years. The planning was being done by a small committee of approximately ten people, from both the faculty and the administration. The committee was planning on behalf of a total faculty group of approximately two hundred people.

In the early stages of my work it became clear that the committee had a sound plan and was very enthusiastic about it but that the faculty as a whole was suspicious. The committee had been working on and off for two years, but no one on the outside knew anything about the new plan, and rumors were rampant.

In my meetings with the committee, members expressed their concern about faculty suspicion and rumors and their fears that their new plan would not receive the necessary faculty vote for ratification. The committee chairman wanted it to pass with a two-to-one vote but was realistic enough to know that, at that moment, a vote would probably produce the opposite ratio. I began by confronting the committee with the probability that, if they wanted ratification, they would have to risk possible modifications to their plan. For overall faculty commitment to occur, something more than information sharing would be required. Simply explaining the new plan to the faculty would not overcome suspicion and guarantee ratification, regardless of the logic and elegance of the new curriculum design.

Resistance could be expected because of the degree of change involved in the plan. The plan called for greater coordination across courses and a shift away from the solo-instructor model toward more team teaching, with consequent loss of some freedom for the instructors. It thus involved some degree of loss of choice.

I explained that, although the committee could remain in control of the planning, its responsibility and roles would need to shift to managing the change process rather than remaining as planner of curriculum content. The committee began to plan the organization of the further planning process. It formed itself into a steering committee and assigned major managerial roles to each member. Four individuals were chosen to head the more detailed curriculum planning for each of the four medical schools years, and four primary subcommittees were formed. These subcommittees were composed of faculty members other than those on the original committee. At that point, thirty to forty additional faculty members were involved.

Other special committees were then formed as extensions of the four primary subcommittees. These "sub-subcommittees" became involved in planning specifics, such as how cell biology would be taught within an overall organic systemic approach. Eventually, some one hundred faculty members were involved in planning at least one piece of the new curriculum. With so many people involved and with such a complex new plan, it took most of a year to get the job done. When the faculty vote finally came, however, the new curriculum was ratified by a four-to-one margin.

Next came implementation. The committees had informally selected people to head the major elements of the new curriculum. These people became the prime movers of the new plan, which was implemented one year at a time. For the initial academic year of the new plan, only the first-year curriculum was changed. The following year the second-year curriculum was changed, and so on, taking four years to complete implementation.

A new organizational structure was also created. Each medical school year was managed by a course master. The four course masters had several instructors under their jurisdiction for teaching each year's curriculum. The course masters were accountable to the associate dean of education, who had been chairman of the steering committee. The new organizational structure of the school was a matrix, with each faculty member having a departmental boss and a course master boss. The departmental functions were limited to clinical services, research, and graduate training rather than classroom instruction, so that the traditional academic departments formed a matrix with the course structure (see Exhibit 3.2).

Although some of the details of the original committee's plan were modified, the grand design was not changed fundamentally. Because half the

EXHIBIT 3.2

Matrix Structure for a Medical School

	Associate dean of education			
Academic departments	First-year courses	Second-year courses	Third-year courses	Fourth-year courses
Clinical services				
Research				
Graduate training				

faculty eventually was involved in the planning, ratification became a formality rather than a heated contest. The conflicts and anxiety that people experienced over what they stood to lose, the disagreements about what should be done, and the time needed to understand and become involved in the new plan all could be worked through in the committee and subcommittee stages of implementation. Although other changes have been made since, this way of teaching and this organizational structure still remain in effect.

Summary

In an attempt to summarize and integrate the three models of change considered in this chapter, Exhibit 3.3 shows a comparison of Lewin's (1958) three steps, the action research model for OD provided by Wendell French (1969), and Lippitt, Watson, and Westley's (1958) phases of planned change. As shown in the exhibit, the action research model for OD is the main reference point for comparison.

The remainder of the chapter was concerned with the psychological nature of change and its implications for change implementation. It should be clear that, for organizational change to be implemented effectively, careful planning of the implementation process must occur. Except in crisis situations, a more participative mode is likely to have greater success than autocratic decree will. The key elements for success are *inclusion of affected people* and *adequate time*. The time issue is directly related to the maturity of management. A

EXHIBIT 3.3

Summary Comparison of the Three Models of Change

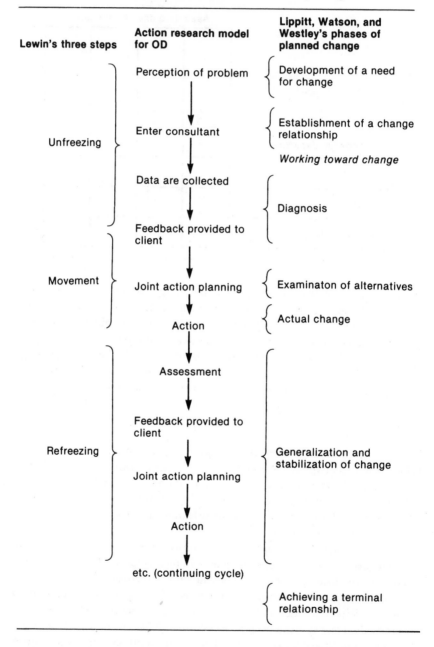

Lewin's three steps	Action research model for OD	Lippitt, Watson, and Westley's phases of planned change
	Perception of problem	Development of a need for change
Unfreezing	Enter consultant	Establishment of a change relationship
		Working toward change
	Data are collected	Diagnosis
	Feedback provided to client	
Movement	Joint action planning	Examinaton of alternatives
	Action	Actual change
	Assessment	
Refreezing	Feedback provided to client	Generalization and stabilization of change
	Joint action planning	
	Action	
	etc. (continuing cycle)	
		Achieving a terminal relationship

manager must have a mature attitude to refrain from enjoying the sense of omnipotence that goes with the successful exercise of top-down autocratic change and instead to defer the immediate gratification of seeing something happen for the much longer-term satisfaction that comes from involving others, working slowly and patiently, and ultimately seeing the changes take deep root.

Successful management of change by a process similar to that used in the case example has a major advantage. The organization's leadership will be able to use this process as an opportunity to model more modern participative forms of management, which can then become an ongoing part of the organization's culture.

Finally, the change process that has been described is an application of the principles of human behavior discussed briefly in this chapter. We are concerned with (1) *providing people with choices,* so that their feelings of freedom will not be unduly curtailed and thus their resistance will be minimized, and (2) *involving people* at some level of participative decision making and communication regarding the direction of organizational change, so that *commitment* to change implementation will be enhanced.

59

PART II

CONCEPTS FOR ORGANIZATION DIAGNOSIS

Diagnosing an organization—that is, collecting information from and about it, analyzing this information, and then casting the information within a systemic and systematic framework—is the most important aspect of organization development practice. A good diagnosis will point the way toward, if not determine, the steps that must be taken to change and improve an organization. To diagnose well, one must know where to look and what to look for, which is the focus of Part II.

In discussing where to look, the emphasis is on the notion of system. An organization is a system—an open system, with information and material coming in and with internal use and transformation of this information and material into something going out. Where to look, then, is toward the organization as a system. Dimensions for diagnosis are systemic ones, including the organization's structure, its process of rewards and punishments, the way its members monitor the organization's environment, and characteristics of the organization's culture (Chapter 4).

Regarding what to look for, the bias of this book becomes clear. Social-psychological concepts are chosen for guiding this aspect of the looking process—norms, roles, and values, (Chapter 5), rewards (Chapter 6), and power (Chapter 7). Since organization development is defined as a process of change in an organization's culture, *it follows that what must be considered in diagnosis are the elements or dimensions that comprise that culture. The concepts of Part II are the primary elements or dimensions. Thus, the theoretical heritage and perspective for the diagnostic phase of organization development practice is social psychology. Diagnosis is by no means limited to these primary dimensions; they simply represent the major guides.*

CHAPTER 4

The Organization
as a System

Organizations as Open Systems

When you think of an organization, what goes through your mind is probably a name or something tangible, such as a building or a product. When I think of the U.S. Senate, for example, what frequently runs through my mind is an image of the U.S. Capitol building. That building, however, besides providing shelter and bounded space, is more a symbol than an organization. The U.S. Senate as an organization is more appropriately described as the *interaction* of 100 people and their staffs and the *events* surrounding their endeavors.

When you think of an organization, you also may think in terms of purpose, as an organization consists of people working together toward the accomplishment of some objective. When you think of Coca-Cola, for example, you may not only think of the name but may also conjure in your mind's eye a bottling plant. You are likely to think of their purpose as making soft drinks. After some more thought you probably would state more specifically and accurately, however, that the organization's purpose is making money. Saying that the purpose of a business is to make money, however, is at once an accurate but limited statement. The Coca-Cola Company has more than money making as a corporate purpose. Additional purposes probably include providing attractive jobs for people and not polluting the environment.

The point is that any organization is more complicated than its purpose, location, and name—although even name can be very important (Mancuso 1978). According to Katz and Kahn (1978) the model for really understanding the nature of any organization is:

> . . . that of an energic input-output system in which the energic return from the output reactivates the system. Social organizations are flagrantly open systems in that the input of energies and the conversion of output into further

63

energic input consist of transactions between the organization and its environment. (p. 20)

Their model for understanding organizations is not as complex as this quotation makes it sound.

Any human organization is an open system. An organization is open
because of its absolute dependency on the environment in which it resides.
Closed systems exist only in the world of nonliving matter. Even a biological
cell is an open system, since it depends on its environment for survival—for
taking in oxygen, for example.

For survival, then, an organization takes in energy from its environment.
Energy is broadly defined and may include money, raw materials, or the
work of people. This energy is then transformed into a product or service and
thrust back into the environment. The output may encompass the same
segments of the environment that were used as energic inputs or others. One
critical element of input is money, which may take the form of a bank loan.
After transformation into a product and sale in the marketplace (another
aspect of the organization's environment), the income from sales provides
additional input. For a product-making organization to survive in the long
term, sales income must become the primary input. The sales income then
reactivates the system. Diagramatically, the cyclical model is

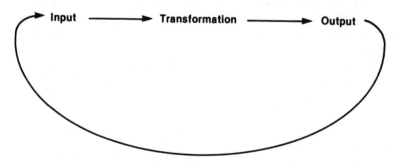

Thus, for example, a bank loan (input) provides money to purchase raw
materials (more input) so that a product can be made (transformation) and
then sold (output) to consumers, and their payments provide money for further input, reactivating the cycle.

To identify the boundaries of an organization, therefore, is not to consider
its name, location, or purpose (these may add to the definition) but rather to
follow

the energic and informational transactions as they relate to the cycle of activities of input, throughput, and output. Behavior not tied to these functions
lies outside the system. . . . Open systems [therefore] maintain themselves

through constant commerce with their environment, that is, a continuous inflow and outflow of energy through permeable boundaries. (Katz and Kahn 1978, pp. 21, 22)

Although they are permeable and open, organizations are also entities, with internal elements or parts that are easy to identify: physical and technological parts, such as buildings, machines, desks, and paper; task or work-related elements, such as specific jobs, roles (boss, subordinate), functions (accounting, manufacturing), and suborganizations or subsystems, such as departments, divisions, or profit centers; and, most important, people—male or female, black or white, skilled or semiskilled, old or young. All these parts compose a whole, a total organization that represents an entity different from the simple sum of its elements and dimensions. General Motors is more than the sum of Chevrolet, Fisher Body, Oldsmobile, and the other subsystems, and, similarly, a hospital is something more than the operating room and its staff, the various wards, beds, nurses, doctors, patients, and so on, put together.

Calling our entity of study an organization is therefore calling it a system—more specifically and accurately, an open system. The implication of this labeling and understanding for organization development is as follows.

As an effort toward change, OD takes a total system approach. Thus, it is imperative that we understand the nature of an organization as a social and technical system and the process of change within such a system. In this chapter we shall attempt to gain these prerequisite understandings.

Although we rarely tackle the entire system at once, we attempt to keep the total in mind as we go about changing parts, since the change of one part will affect other parts, perhaps all other parts eventually. An OD technique that illustrates this attempt is open-systems planning. The technique is an approach to planning that not only emphasizes the total system but also stresses the organization's relationship with its environment. Open-systems planning is actually an *intervention* among the OD phases of planned change. As a phase of OD it is a technique for facilitating change. I am getting ahead of myself here, since OD interventions are not covered until Part IV, but attempting to explain organizations as open systems can be too abstract. Examples can help, and, in this case, considering open-systems planning as a technique for helping an actual organization to change should help to illustrate (1) that organizations are open, permeable systems and (2) how this conceptual frame of reference is applied in OD practice.

Open-Systems Planning

Open-systems planning is an approach to organizational planning based on the premise that an organization is an open system and therefore is continually affected by its external environment and simultaneously has an effect on that external environment. A fundamental part of the planning process is to examine and analyze this relationship of the organization with its environment.

Open-systems planning is also based on the important assumption that it is beneficial to plan for the future by (1) understanding and building on current resources and strengths and (2) attempting to shape that future according to what organizational members desire. It is also necessary to try to predict what the future will be and thereby make plans to cope with it. These predictions are based largely, if not exclusively, on estimate, guesswork, extrapolation, hunch, and the like, regardless of how educated or scientific they may be.

The planning is done by a core organizational group—typically, the top team of the entire organization or of one of the subsystems of the organization. Open-systems planning may be conducted by any unit of an organization; the process and principles are the same. The OD practitioner serves in two capacities. First, he or she guides the planning process by asking relevant questions to be addressed by the group. Second, the practitioner serves as a group facilitator by providing observations and suggestions regarding the group's process—how well the members are working together as a group. (For more information on this second role of the OD practitioner, see Chapter 13.)

We can understand the process better by considering an actual organizational example. Several years ago I observed a consultant's work with an institutional food-management group as they went through the steps of open-systems planning. Let us consider the steps first, and then the case.

STEPS IN OPEN-SYSTEMS PLANNING   Although there are some variations, the usual steps in open-systems planning are as follows (Jayaram 1976):

1. Create or map present expectations and domains coming from the external environment.
2. Create or map present expectations, domains, and responses to the external environment from inside the system. A final part of this step is to identify the core process of what the organization actually does, to determine the organization's identity and core mission more systematically.
3. Identify the transactions that occur across the boundaries of the system, from external to internal and the reverse.
4. Identify the inherent value systems represented by the transactions.
5. Given no change in the present organization and its *modus operandi,* make a projection into the future.
6. Create an ideal future, the desired state.
7. Compare the present with the ideal future.

8. Identify the areas of agreement and consensus about the desired future state, uncertainty and only partial agreement, and disagreement.

9. Decide what to do (action steps) about each piece of the plan in three time dimensions: tomorrow, six months from now, and two years from now.

10. Determine the follow-up schedule for action steps and for updating the plan.

A CASE EXAMPLE Most large institutions that provide meals, such as colleges and universities, hospitals, and corporations, do so by a contractual arrangement with an outside food-management company. These companies do not own any of the buildings or equipment but simply provide the management of the dining facilities, including procurement and disbursement of food, recruitment and management of personnel, and maintenance. As they were dissatisfied with the quality of their food service and with the organization's performance in general, the management team of a university's food service decided, with the assistance of an outside consultant, to use open-systems planning as a way of determining what needed to be changed. This management team of six individuals and their organization of one university's dining service for students, faculty, and administration comprised the system for planning purposes. The system was a unit of a larger corporation, of course, which had similar units in many other institutions across the United States.

The team began by identifying the domains in their system's environment that created expectations for certain responses on the part of their organization. The procedure was to sketch, on a chart pad or chalkboard, a circle that represents the system and then to identify environmental domains by drawing arrows from around and outside toward the circle. Exhibit 4.1 shows a partial picture of the team's work on step one.

Having mapped the environmental domains that represent expectations and demands, the team members then identified their responses to these domains. Exhibit 4.2 shows some of these internal responses. They are depicted by the arrows inside the circle. The small circle inside the larger one is a pictorial representation of the system's core process. After this mapping of external demands and internal responses, what do we know of what the organization really does? What would fundamentally describe the system's identity?

After identifying the nature of the transactions that occur across the system's boundaries (where the arrows meet in Exhibit 4.2) in step 3 of the open-systems planning process, the members discussed the values that seemed to underlie these transactions (step 4) and the way the team managed the food service at the university. They gradually began to agree that they were actually in the business of "the efficient production of garbage"! These were the words that belonged in the inner circle. By mapping out all the domains and studying the implications of what the picture showed, they

EXHIBIT 4.1

*Partial Outcome of an Institutional Food-Management Team's Identification
of Environmental Domains that Create Expectations and Demands
for Response by Their Organization*

realized that, in the desire to be cost-effective and profit-making, they had
created an efficient operation for garbage production. The cafeteria line was
extremely well organized so that students could be processed as rapidly as
possible, and food waste containers and locations for placing dirty dishes and
trays were strategically placed at exits so that few lines were formed to
lengthen the dining period unnecessarily. Dining tables and chairs were ar-

EXHIBIT 4.2

*Partial Outcome of an Institutional Food-Management Team's
Identification of Their Internal System's Responses
to Environmental Expectations and Demands*

ranged in neat rows, resulting in appropriately placed aisles so that movement in and out of the dining room would be unimpeded and quick. There were no major student complaints, only grumbles that did not seem to form a pattern. The Wednesday night meal of steak or something equally special was appreciated by the students but was not thought of as "a big deal."

The team came to the conclusion that two or three years down the road (step 5) they would be even more efficient at rapidly processing students in and out of the dining room, with perhaps an increased incidence of indigestion but a well-run and sanitized garbage-production operation nevertheless. They decided in step 6 that they did not want to be identified so strongly with that image and that, instead of the efficient production of garbage, the core process should be "providing a pleasant dining experience." During the process of responding to the remaining four steps, they planned a different picture for the future. Part of the plan included rearranging the physical structure of the dining room, including new decorations, so that tables were situated to facilitate small-group conversation rather than rapid eating and departure. In addition, one night each week was planned as an international evening, with the meal consisting of some sort of ethnic food. On those evenings the dining room would also be decorated to symbolize the particular international meal—red-checkered tablecloths for Italian, music from "Zorba" for Greek, and so on. Their plan was to add certain qualities to the management of their food service without necessarily sacrificing cost-effectiveness and efficiency. The details of their follow-up action steps were planned so that these additions could be made and yet they could continue to meet their profit goals.

General Systems Theory Applied to Organizations

Having considered an actual organization and the applicability of one type of OD technology, open-systems planning, we shall now examine the theory on which organization development and open-systems planning are based—general systems theory. Katz and Kahn (1978), my primary source for this chapter, place their view of organizations within the context of general systems theory. This view is based further on the earlier work of von Bertalanffy (1956).

According to Katz and Kahn, ten characteristics distinguish open systems. We shall briefly define each of these and draw on our previous institutional food-management organization case for examples.

1. *Importation of energy:* No human organization is self-contained or self-sufficient; thus, it must draw energy from outside to insure survival. The energy the food-management group drew from its environment was primarily university money as a function of the contract for services; (b) raw materials—foodstuffs and related materials; and local labor for cooks, servers, and so on, who were hired from the local community.

2. *Throughput:* The food-management group took the raw materials and, with the work of their labor force, transformed these materials into meals for their consumers, who were mostly university students.

3. *Output:* The meals and the accompanying service served as the output for the food-management organization.

70

4. *Systems as cycles of events*: Providing quality food and attractive service helps to ensure that the food-management organization's contract with university will be renewed and perhaps even increased, so that the input-throughput-output cycle will continue. Katz and Kahn use the term *events* (after F. H. Allport 1962) to explain the nature of an organization's structure and the boundaries. An organization does not have a physical boundary, as a human being does (skin that encloses bones, muscles, organs, and so on) to identify it as a system. As noted earlier, an organization's building does not suffice as the identifying feature of structure and boundary. Events rather than things provide identity; and social structures, the chain of events between and among people, establish boundaries. For the food-management organization, the identifying and boundary-setting events were contracting, purchasing, hiring a work force, preparing and serving food, disposing of waste, collecting monies from the university to purchase more raw materials, and eventually contracting again. Such a cycle of events is what establishes and identifies an open system—for our purposes, an organization.

5. *Negative entropy*: According to general systems theory, the "entropic process is a universal law of nature in which all forms of organization move toward disorganization or death . . . [but] by importing more energy from its environment than it expends, the open system can store energy and acquire negative entropy" (Katz and Kahn 1978, p. 25). When an organization is losing money, the managers do not typically ask "How can we stop this terrible entropic process?" but they do understand that, unless positive action is taken, they and all their employee colleagues can be out of jobs, for the organization will cease to exist under such a condition. For a profit-making organization, storing energy consists of having capital and lines of credit. For a university, it is having a healthy endowment. For the food-management company, it is having and maintaining the goodwill of students, good relations with the university's administration, and reputable, high-quality food brokers.

The point is that organizations are not self-sufficient; they are unstable and will not function or grow unless active and deliberate effort is made. The process of interpersonal trust serves as an analogy. Trust between people is a very unstable process, which must be maintained constantly. When one party to the relationship behaves at all strangely or suspiciously, the trust in the relationship is automatically in jeopardy, and deliberate action must be taken for the trusting quality to be maintained. Similarly, constant effort must be expended not only for the maintenance of an organization but for its very survival.

6. *Information input, negative feedback, and the coding process*: If an organization obtains feedback on how well its output is being received, it can respond to its consumers more effectively in the future. This is especially true if the feedback is negative; then corrective action can be planned and taken. When

71

students complain about the food, the food-management team can take action to change some elements within the input-throughput-output events. It is rare for all information in an organization's environment that could be utilized as feedback to be tapped. Some kind of coding occurs, as organizational members are selective and try to simplify all the possibilities into fundamental categories that seem to be most relevant for a given system. The institutional food-service managers would probably pay much more attention to negative feedback from students than to that from faculty, because there is a significant quantitative difference, depending, of course, on the faculty-student ratio. More important for the selective or coding process, however, is that student board fees provide the primary source of funds used by the university to pay for the food-management company's services.

7. *Steady-state and dynamic homeostasis*: Organizations that survive are typically considered steady, but this does not mean that little activity is occurring. As Katz and Kahn (1978) depict it: "A steady state is not a motionless or true equilibrium. There is a continuous inflow of energy from the external environment and a continuous export of the products of the system, but the character of the system, the ratio of the energy exchanges and the relations between parts, remains the same" (p. 26). Lewin's (1947) concept of quasi-stationary equilibrium is relevant here. An organization's *apparent* equilibrium actually is up at one moment (during one event in the cycle) and down at another, but the overall averaging of these ups and downs gives the appearance of a stationary or steady-state situation.

To counteract entropy, organizations attempt to grow and to control more and more of their environment—that is, to expand the original system. This counteracting process implies change. In terms of Lewin's concept of equilibrium, the average of an organization's ups and downs does not always remain at the same level. Even so, the basic character of an organization tends to remain the same. To say that Citicorp or Bank of America is now a financial intermediary institution, for example, is to reflect the organization's movement into a broader field of services, not necessarily to state that it is getting out of the banking business.

The institutional food-management group decided to make some changes so that their effort would be directed more toward providing pleasant dining than toward efficient garbage production, but their modifications did not mean that they were changing the nature of their corporation's business fundamentally.

8. *Differentiation*: As an organization continues to offset the entropic process and therefore grows (not always meaning expansion, but sometimes creating new businesses and eliminating old ones), differentiation and elaboration occur; that is, specialization and division of labor evolve. The food-management group, when they decided to have a special ethnic dinner

each week, had to determine who within their organization had the expertise to make this change work.

9. *Integration and coordination*: To maintain stability, there cannot be too much differentiation. A certain degree of unification and coordination is necessary. According to Katz and Kahn (1978), integration is accomplished through shared norms and values. Organization structure, roles, and authority are the social system vehicles managers use to achieve integration and coordination.

10. *Equifinality*: According to von Bertalanffy's principle, an organization can attain the same goal from several different starting points and by a variety of paths. The food-management group might have decided on the changes they made without going through the open-systems planning process, and they could have achieved their mission of providing a pleasant dining experience in ways other than having an ethnic dinner each week.

An organization's success and effectiveness in a systems sense is contingent on two processes—openness and selectivity. The organization's managers must operate according to the foregoing ten open-system characteristics, but they should be selective in their inputs and outputs, especially with respect to the feedback they obtain from the environment.

As a way of summarizing at this point, let me state again my purpose in starting with an OD technique as a way of entering the theoretical world of organizations as systems. It should be clear that managers of organizations need to be constantly aware that they are managing a system that has permeable boundaries, is dependent on its environment for survival, and will go out of existence unless it is actively managed. In their role as a consultant to managers, OD practitioners can provide considerable assistance when they facilitate planning in general, particularly when they use open-systems planning, since the technique keeps managers cognizant of their organization as an open system and of their dependence on the organization's environment, however it is defined, for survival. There are other advantages to using open-systems planning as a part of any organization development effort— such as the typical by-product, a management team that is stronger in terms of interpersonal relationships—but the most important benefits are that the process insures thinking and planning in open-system terms and greater clarity regarding organizational mission and purpose.

A Total and Open-System Approach

In Chapter 1, I defined OD as a total system approach. Now the word *open* is added, because ignoring an organization's dependence on its environment risks planting the seeds for bankruptcy or extinction.

The OD consultant therefore considers the total organization and its envi-

73

ronmental relations in conducting a diagnosis—that is, in attempting to understand the organization as an entity. The ultimate purpose of this understanding is to put the consultant in a position to help the client organization (1) to understand itself better, (2) to know what is effective or ineffective about its functioning, and (3) to plan appropriate steps for increasing its effectiveness. This purpose could be claimed for any organizational consultant; what distinguishes the OD consultant is the emphasis on the total system, the facilitative and collaborative nature of the consultation, and the change objective.

The objective for change is systemic; that is, some aspect of the system such as the organization's managerial structure or the reward system is selected for change (see Chapter 1). This selection is made as a result of a previous diagnosis and in collaboration with the relevant people from the client organization.

The change objective is systemic for at least three reasons. First, when some aspect of the system is changed, other aspects eventually will be affected, thus making for a total system approach. If the consultant works in one part of the organization and does not consider and plan for the consequences of his or her actions for other parts of the system, the consultative effort will probably be aborted (Burke 1980c).

Recall the case example in Chapter 1—the manufacturing division that was experiencing performance problems, especially in the areas of quality control and timely delivery of products. Standard OD interventions were used—team building with the top management group, intergroup conflict resolution between engineering and manufacturing, and team building with the top group of the manufacturing department. Eventually, I suggested that change in the division's reward system would result in the kind of outcome desired by the general manager. The general manager resisted this suggestion, stating that the reward system was corporatewide and that the current president had designed it. That change effort was thus aborted.

The point here is that, even if the reward system had been modified, other aspects of the total organization would have been affected. The way in which authority was exercised would have had to change to a more positive approach, and worker relationships would have differed. The workers might have become more competitive, but the consequent outcome more likely would have been the formation of new norms regarding productivity. This outcome is predictable when we consider the evidence from the Hawthorne studies (Chapter 2). Other effects would also occur, because an organization is an open system, each subpart of the system relating to every other part and the system consisting of cycles of events. Had the general manager of the manufacturing division agreed to changing the reward system, we would have begun to move toward total system change, and I would have needed to establish a longer-term contract.

74

The second reason for the OD consultative effort to be systemic is based on our knowledge of how to bring about change in an organization. One of the precursors of OD is sensitivity training (see Chapter 2), which is educational and individually focused regarding the objective for change, improvement, and learning. Sensitivity training was a primary intervention for organizational change in the early days of OD. As we discovered through experience and research, however, although training may lead to individual change (Bunker and Knowles 1967; Crawford 1962; Dunnette 1969; Rubin 1967; E. H. Schein and Bennis 1965) and in some cases to small group change (Hall and Williams 1966, 1970), there is scant evidence that attempting to change individuals will in turn change the organization (J. P. Campbell and Dunnette 1968). The Fleishman research of the 1950s at International Harvester, mentioned in Chapter 2, is further evidence that individual training alone does not affect the total organization for purposes of change.

The target for change, then, is the system, not the individual (Burke and Schmidt 1971). This systemic target is primarily the organization's culture, especially the group and organizational norms to which members conform. This stance is based, in part, on the original work of Kurt Lewin. His theories and research led him to conclude:

> As long as group standards are unchanged, the individual will resist change more strongly the further he is expected to depart from group standards. If the group standard itself is changed, the resistance which is due to the relation between individual and group standard is eliminated. (Lewin 1958, p. 210)

Others since Lewin also have shown in their research that work performance and satisfaction are greater when workers perceive that they influence the formulation of work-group norms (Bowers 1964; Likert 1961; A. S. Tannenbaum and Kahn 1957, 1958; Bachman, Smith, and Slesinger 1966; Hornstein, Callahan, Fisch, and Benedict 1968). The classic study by Coch and French (1948), based on Lewinian theory, clearly demonstrated this relationship of commitment, norms, and change (see Chapter 3). Since individual and group behavior in an organization is largely determined by group norms (part of the organization's culture), the changing of certain of these norms and their accompanying values should be a major focus of an OD effort.

The third reason an OD effort should be systemic relates to the open system characteristics of importation of energy and negative entropy. For an organization to survive, energy must be taken into the organization in a variety of forms and transformed into products or services that add value to the consumer, and the entropic process must be reversed. According to Katz and Kahn (1978), "by importing more energy from its environment than it expends, the open system can store energy and acquire negative entropy"

(p. 25). The OD consultant's job in this case is to pay particular attention to how human energy is used in the organization. Are employees' efforts thwarted because of excessive bureaucracy? Is energy bottled up because of an overly centralized control and authority structure? Or are people's efforts dissipated because power and authority are so diffused in the organization?

The OD consultant's job is to pay considerable attention to the use of human energy and to help the client organization change things (norms, rewards, or authority structure) so that this energy can be focused more appropriately toward accomplishment of the organization's goals. Thus, negative entropy is more effectively established. The consultant can do this job optimally only by taking a systemic viewpoint and approach.

Summary and Conclusions

Some people consider that OD means organizational development, but for most people it is organization development. According to Vaill (1971), organizational development means

> development that occurs in organizations. The phrase says nothing about *what* is being developed: persons, groups, departments, technologies, ideas, problems, and relationships are all fair game. Nor does the phrase imply by itself, that any of these developments are at all "organized." The phrase does imply, however, that the organization itself, as a totality, is *not* the object of development. [The] focus [of organization development] is clear; it means "development of organizations. " The phrase does not deny that subunits of the organization may occupy attention, but implies that concern for such subunits occurs *because* the total organization is the major object of interest. (p. 264)

Vaill clearly notes grammatically the approach I am taking to OD in this book. This is a system bias, not an individual one. Herman (1972, 1977), for example, has argued otherwise, but I believe the weight of evidence on how organizations, not just pieces of them, are changed is heavily on the side of a total system viewpoint.

The purpose of this chapter has been to delineate the nature of an organization as a system and to define OD within this frame of reference. I have defined OD as a process of cultural change, and I like the earlier definition of organizational culture by Katz and Kahn (1966)—that the culture of the system reflects:

> The norms and values of the formal system and their reinterpretation in the informal system,
>
> the history of internal and external struggles,
>
> the types of people the organization attracts,

its work processes and physical layout,

the modes of communication, and

the exercise of authority within the system. (p. 66)

These six dimensions are useful for OD practice, especially in organization diagnosis. They help the practitioner to work more comprehensively.

Although, as a consultant, I consider these dimensions, my primary diagnostic bias is more social-psychological. The five primary variables for me are norms, roles, values, rewards, and power. The remainder of Part II will be devoted to coverage of these variables, developing an understanding of each of them and clarifying their role or function in diagnosing organizations.

CHAPTER 5

Norms, Roles, and Values

Occasionally I have served as advisor or coach to people who were training to become organization development consultants. On one such occasion I coached two young men who were consulting to an organization involved in youth crisis work. The organization, mostly volunteers, provided help to young people in trouble. The typical case was a drug problem. Members of the organization, mostly college students and high school seniors, maintained a telephone hot line twenty-four hours a day and counseled troubled youths or referred them to more professional help. A psychologist on the faculty of the local college served as advisor to the young people who operated the organization. The operation was not going well. Responsibilities for some roles and activities were not clearly defined, and many members were frustrated about not being able to get things done. When the members learned that they could receive some free consultation, the organization readily agreed to become a client.

After their initial data collection and diagnostic effort, my two consultants-in-training were baffled. Their client's frustration apparently had affected them as consultants, for they complained that they didn't have a real organization to work with. Other than a so-called executive committee, which rarely met, and one half-time, paid employee, who seemed to be little more than a caretaker for the building, there were none of the expected or normal characteristics of an organization and definitely none of the formal ones, such as an organization chart or a control or auditing system, even though they received some financial aid from government sources. The consultants-in-training proclaimed that their client was simply "not an organization!" I agreed with them that their client was not an organization in the usual and formal sense but pointed out that these young people, who at least occasionally worked toward a common effort, did constitute a social and technical system. Their technology, using the term loosely, was rendering a

78

particular kind of service, and their interpersonal and working relationships composed the social aspect of the system, which should become the consultant's primary focus of attention. I explained that, even though their client did not look like an organization, a sociotechnical system did indeed exist. I suggested further that they concentrate their diagnostic efforts on the social aspects, with particular emphasis on the norms that governed the members' behavior. Rather than trying to determine their client's effectiveness in certain formal organizational characteristics, which didn't exist, I urged them to look for conforming patterns among the membership, to discover what norms they did conform to, especially implicit ones. With that suggestion and some further encouragement on my part, the two consultants agreed to tackle their "nonorganization" client once again.

Several weeks later the aspiring consultants returned. This time they proclaimed that they had found the "don't hassle" norm, an implicit norm that governed much of the behavior of the students who worked in the youth organization. Although no individual among the client group seemed to be consciously aware of this norm, when it was brought to the surface by the two consultants, the students readily admitted that there was an implicit agreement among the students not to hassle one another. The behavioral expression of the norm seemed to be "You do what you want and I do what I want, and we don't bug one another about the consequences." As a result of this conforming pattern, when things did go wrong—for example, when the phone was not answered by the person who was supposed to be on duty or when people had differences with one another—these problems were rarely if ever addressed. As an outgrowth of the consultants' help in identifying the "don't hassle" norm and agreeing that it did indeed exist and was not functional—preventing them from accomplishing much of what they genuinely wanted to do in their voluntary effort—the students agreed to change the norm. The replacement norm (actually two norms) became that it was legitimate, especially for the good of the organization, (1) to disagree with one another and (2) to hold one another accountable for jobs that need to be done.

At the conclusion of their project, the two now-experienced consultants were pleased that they had actually helped their client and that they had learned experientially something about a system and about how to consult in the face of initial ambiguity.

Norms

As noted in Chapter 4, two main dimensions of an organization's culture are "the norms and values of the formal system and their reinterpretation in the informal system" (Katz and Kahn 1966, p. 66). Although it may not be realistic behaviorally to separate norms from values, for purposes of achieving greater understanding I shall cover each one separately. Remember that

79

the purpose of Part II is to consider an organization as an open system that has a unique culture consisting of a number of dimensions to be examined diagnostically, so that an organization development effort will be based on sound concepts as well as on appropriate theory and research.

Definition

Norms are standards or rules of conduct to which people conform. Behavior, therefore, reflects the extent to which people conform to or deviate from the standards. When people say that a particular group is highly resistant to change, they usually mean that conformity to a certain norm or set of norms is strong. Social psychologists have reported often that, even though group norms ''can be changed, the more striking characteristic about them is their enduring quality and the fact that they may be the sources of resistance to change in organizational structure or practices'' (Cartwright and Zander 1960, p. 181). We have all felt the pressure to conform at times. There is value in conformity; for civilized society to exist, conformity to certain rules must occur. This is also true for organizations. We also know two other qualities of conformity, however: that creative change rarely if ever springs from such behavior, and that we sometimes conform to rules or standards that do not make sense from the perspective of either productive individual behavior or effective organizational performance. Conforming to the ''don't hassle'' norm discussed earlier is a good example of these two other qualities.

People are usually aware of their conformity, but, especially in organizations, they are often not aware of many of the norms to which they are conforming. Norms can be classified as either explicit or implicit. Explicit norms are the standards to which we consciously conform. Examples of explicit norms in organizations are dress codes, working hours, communication restrictions, and the like. Implicit norms are those rules we follow without being aware that we are conforming to anything. These conforming patterns can be recognized but usually not by the actors. Implicit norms are identified, if at all, after the fact or by some outside party. In OD the outside party is the consultant.

In organizational terms, explicit norms reflect the formal organization and implicit norms the informal side. Herman (1970) has depicted an organization in these terms, using an iceberg as a metaphor to illustrate the relative difference between the formal and informal organization. By depicting the formal organization above the waterline and the informal one below, he argued that most of behavior in an organization is manifested by the informal organization (Exhibit 5.1). The iceberg also represents the balance between behavior shaped by explicit norms—the tip above the waterline—and behavior influenced by implicit norms—the greater amount below the waterline.

80

EXHIBIT 5.1

The Organization Depicted as an Iceberg: Relativity of the Formal Organization to the Informal Organization and of Explicit Norms to Implicit Norms

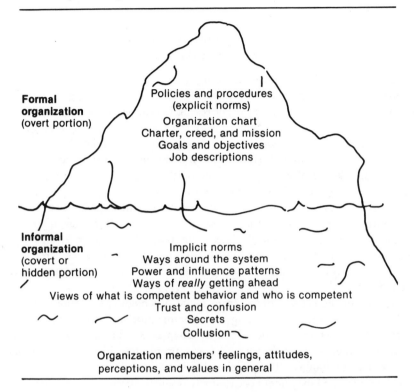

Formal organization
(overt portion)

Policies and procedures
(explicit norms)
Organization chart
Charter, creed, and mission
Goals and objectives
Job descriptions

Informal organization
(covert or hidden portion)

Implicit norms
Ways around the system
Power and influence patterns
Ways of *really* getting ahead
Views of what is competent behavior and who is competent
Trust and confusion
Secrets
Collusion

Organization members' feelings, attitudes,
perceptions, and values in general

Much of the diagnostic work in organization development involves determining the nature of organizational behavior that occurs below the surface—how these behaviors affect people and the organization positively or negatively. During the diagnostic phase of OD especially, the consultant is concerned with:

1. determining the norms, particularly the implicit ones, that influence organizational members' behavior;
2. bringing these norms to the surface, by a feedback process, for organizational members to consider;
3. considering these norms in terms of those that seem to be helpful and those that hinder effective working relationships; and
4. changing the norms that are considered to be dysfunctional (the intervention phase in OD).

81

Although these four steps do not explain the process fully, they summarize a primary thrust of organization development. Referring again to the iceberg, we can describe this primary thrust of OD as "lowering the waterline."

The Relevance and Importance of Norms
for Organization Development

In Chapter 2 we discussed the first recognition of the importance of norms in understanding organizational behavior—the Hawthorne studies, particularly the work of Homans (1950). The researchers at the Hawthorne Works of Western Electric found that norms were the key factors in determining the rate and amount of work group productivity. In related studies at Hawthorne, researchers also found that, if they wanted to change any of those norms, the degree of success was based on the extent to which the workers themselves determined what the new norms would be.

Lewin was one of the first to call our attention to the importance of norms for purposes of change within a group or an organization. Lewin's thesis regarding change in a social system, discussed in Chapter 2, was that resistance to change would be strong if individual group members were asked to deviate from a group norm but would not exist if the norm itself were changed.

In one of the classic studies from social psychology, Coch and French (1948) applied Lewinian thinking to an organizational problem in a pajama factory. (This study was described in Chapter 3.) The published article describing their action research work was appropriately titled "Over-coming Resistance to Change." The problem they investigated concerned changes in work patterns. Management occasionally required these changes so that the company could become more efficient and could remain competitive in the marketplace. Workers' resistance to these job changes was reflected in the length of time it took for them to learn a revised job—for example, stitching or folding pajamas differently—and then build up again to the standard of 60 units of work per hour. Resistance also took the form of increased absence from work and, in many cases, of workers' simply quitting their jobs. Thus, with each change management introduced, a considerable price was paid in worker turnover. Coch and French analyzed the problem according to Lewin's force field analysis (see Chapter 2). They were interested in the forces that acted on a worker to produce up to a standard and more and in the forces that restrained higher production. Their diagnosis focused on the forces toward and away from the workers' producing the standard of 60 units of work per hour—that is, the degree of conformity to the norm of 60 units, an explicit norm. It should be noted that management, not the workers, had established the quota of 60 units per hour. Although few workers produced much more than 60 units, most did achieve the standard or slightly more. The problems occurred when management changed the dimensions of a job and then expected the workers to reach the standard again quickly. Even though transfer bonuses were provided with a change of job, so that the workers who were paid on a piece-rate basis would not suffer a pay cut, the relearning to standard took well over a month.

To understand more about how to overcome this resistance to change, Coch and French devised an experiment that investigated the different outcomes among three conditions of change: (1) a control condition, in which management carefully explained the need for the change and how the new work process would be done, patiently answered questions, and then installed the new method; (2) participation through representation, by which workers were elected from among the ranks of colleagues to meet with management to help plan the change and then trained their fellow workers in the new work process; and (3) total participation, whereby all members of a work group designed and implemented the change. The results of the experiment were dramatic. Thirty-two days after the change the control group still had not achieved the standard. By the end of fourteen days the representative group averaged 61 units per hour. The total-participation group, however, not only relearned their jobs more rapidly but two weeks after the change achieved a standard of production that averaged 14 percent higher than the earlier one.

After reporting the results of the experiment, Coch and French addressed the obvious questions:

1. Why did the nonparticipative control group take so long to recover as compared with the other two? They cite a number of reasons and conclude:

   > Probably the most important force affecting the recovery under the no-participation procedure was a group standard, set by the group, restricting the level of production to 50 units per hour. Evidently this explicit agreement to restrict production is related to the group's rejection of the change and the new job as arbitrary and unreasonable . . . . there was a definite group phenomenon which affected all the members of the group. (Coch and French 1948, p. 529)

2. Why did the two other groups produce significantly more and do it faster? Their interpretation related to Lewin's theory regarding own and "induced" forces. The representative and total-participation groups owned or were more in control of the forces promoting the change, whereas the forces affecting the control group were primarily induced by management.

This summary of the Coch and French study does not tell the whole story. The reader is encouraged to go to the original source, which has also been reprinted in several books of readings.

My purpose in relating the study here has been to demonstrate (1) the importance of diagnosing an organization by the norms to which members conform, (2) the fact that people will be more committed to the implementation of decisions that directly affect them if they are involved in making those decisions, (3) a significant corroboration of some aspects of the Hawthorne studies, and (4) the role of action research in organization development. Coverage of the Coch and French study also sets the stage and provides the background for a later consideration of participative management in Chapter 7.

Roles

According to Katz and Kahn (1978), "organizational integration is a fusion of role, norm, and value components" (p. 44). A role is a set of behaviors that a person is expected to perform. These expectations are the norms that help to establish the role. How people behave in organizational roles is determined by (1) their personal characteristics, (2) their understanding of what is expected by others, and (3) their desire to conform to the norms that establish the expectations.

The concept of role is important to organization development because it represents a primary link between the individual and the organization. From an OD standpoint, the more we understand roles, the more we are in a position to determine the adequacy of fit or integration of individual needs and goals with the organization's mission and objectives.

In organizational language, roles are defined by job descriptions, which typically are written documents outlining the requirements and responsibilities of specific jobs. In the language of social psychology, job descriptions provide the sets of expectations that define organizational roles. It was not surprising that no one in the youth crisis organization described earlier in this chapter had a job description. This lack of definition for the members' responsibilities in their organization created what social psychologists call role conflict and role ambiguity. In the youth crisis organization, there was more role ambiguity, because roles had never been clarified.

The concepts of role conflict and ambiguity are highly germane to organization development, because research has demonstrated that, when either is high, organizational effectiveness suffers (Beehr 1976; House and Rizzo 1972; Kahn et al. 1964). Role conflict is experienced by an individual when expectations regarding his or her role contradict one another. Role ambiguity occurs when the person does not know or understand what is expected. In either case the individual experiences stress. This increase of stress was demonstrated particularly in the research work of Kahn and his colleagues (1964). Organizational change and complexity are significant contributing factors to organizational members' role conflict or ambiguity and

84

therefore stress. It should be emphasized that change and complexity in organizations are even more prevalent now than they were when Kahn and his colleagues conducted their research in the early 1960s.

When OD practitioners are working on role problems, they are in a position not only to help the organization by reducing role conflict and ambiguity, thus clarifying organizational members' responsibilities, but to help the individual by reducing factors that contribute to human stress.

OD Interventions Relating to Role Problems

OD practitioners have responded to role problems in several different ways. In OD language, these ways are referred to as interventions (see Part IV). Dayal and Thomas (1968) have developed what they call the role-analysis technique. The technique is particularly useful as an activity for a newly formed team or work unit but also can be very practical for an established group.

Dayal and Thomas believe that an effective role analysis consists of three parts:

1. a discussion of the purpose of the role;
2. a determination of its prescribed and discretionary components; and
3. an examination of the role's linkages with other roles.

The setting for the role-analysis technique is usually within an organizational unit where considerable interdependence among members of the unit is necessary for effective work to be accomplished. Typically, therefore, this technique and two others covered later occur within the broader framework of the OD interventions referred to as team building. The techniques are not limited to a team but they are certainly more appropriate in an organizational family unit.

Dayal and Thomas begin with the most focal role in the group. This role is often but not always the leader or unit head. The technique involves an extended meeting of the unit members, beginning with a group discussion initiated by the person who occupies the most focal role. This person lists for the others the activities he or she feels constitute his or her role, especially distinguishing between activities that the person believes to be prescribed—necessary components of the role, typically found in a job description—and those that are discretionary—areas in which the person has leeway and must exercise judgment. A general discussion of the list by all group members follows. Greater clarification is usually achieved as a result of this discussion, and activities may be added to or deleted from the original list.

The second step in the role-analysis technique is also led by the person in the focal role. For this step, the focal person lists what he or she expects from each of the other roles within the unit. Again discussion follows, resulting in greater clarification and perhaps some changes.

For the third step, the other members list what they consider to be the focal-role individual's obligations to them. Discussion follows in much the same way as before.

The final step is for the focal-role incumbent to document the major points that evolved from the group discussions. This written report consists of (1) the prescribed and discretionary aspects of the role, (2) the obligations of the focal role to each of the other roles, and (3) the expectations of this focal role from the other members.

At the next meeting, before the next focal role is considered, the first focal role's written document is discussed and clarified further, as necessary. The same procedure is then followed for each of the remaining roles within the group.

As noted earlier, Dayal and Thomas find this technique particularly useful as a start-up activity for a new team or work unit. They also point out that the technique can facilitate and expedite the integration of a new member into an established team. The final written documents for all roles, according to Dayal and Thomas (1968), "provide a composite picture of the linkages among positions—the interdependence—in a management group. These have value if assessed periodically by individuals who can obtain some notion of (a) how expectations and obligations are being met and (b) to what extent role elements are out of date, unworkable, and in need of replacing or change" (p. 497). It should be noted that the theoretical grounding for the role-analysis technique comes from the work of W. Brown (1960), Jaques and Brown (1965) and Kahn et al. (1964).

Huse (1975) has developed a technique that is similar to Dayal and Thomas's role analysis. His technique, known as the job-expectation technique, follows essentially the same format except that Huse argues that the first focal role dealt with in the meetings should be the easiest one, so that momentum can be gained, and that the leader's role should be considered last. Huse presumably believes that the leader's role will usually be the toughest to analyze and that, when all others have preceded it, a clearer picture of the leader's team will be in place, which should then facilitate the analysis.

Roger Harrison (1972) has also developed an approach for dealing with role problems, but his technique, role negotiation, deals more with behavior than with components of a given role. This technique is more behaviorally corrective (through negotiation) than Dayal and Thomas's or Huse's techniques. Harrison's role negotiation has four steps:

1. *Contract setting:* Agreements are reached to be open and honest, to

86

write down expectations and demands explicitly, and to be willing to bargain and negotiate regarding behavioral change.

2. *Diagnosis.* Members think about the way working relationships are conducted between themselves and the other members of the group and what they would change if possible. They then list for all other group members what they would like the other people (1) to do more or do better, (2) to do less or stop doing, and (3) to keep on doing. The lists are then exchanged and a discussion ensues for clarification only; no negotiating or debating takes place at this point.

3. *Negotiation:* The group selects the issues for negotiation. The negotiating process, usually done in pairs, is based on a *quid pro quo*; that is, unless an exchange can occur, there is little use in discussion. Harrison argues that "unless behavior changes on both sides the most likely prediction is that the status quo will continue" (Harrison 1972, p. 90). The process therefore consists of the two individuals making "contingent offers to one another of the form, 'if you do X, I will do Y'. The negotiation ends when all parties are satisfied that they will receive a reasonable return for whatever they are agreeing to give" (p. 91).

4. *Follow-up:* The group is asked to live with their agreements for a specified period and to get back together later to review and possibly to renegotiate.

Harrison contends that his role-negotiation process generally focuses on work relationships and particularly deals directly with problems of power and influence. Since the latter problems frequently are acute, Harrison believes that his straightforward and highly structured approach helps to deal with the issues realistically.

Although there is no so-called hard evidence to support Harrison's argument or the contentions that Dayal and Thomas and Huse make for their techniques, their case reports the experience of other independent practitioners lends credence to the usefulness of these interventions in dealing with problems of role conflict and ambiguity.

In a study of hospital managers and administrators, Adams (1978) has also shown that role ambiguity contributes to individual stress. For Adams, however, the most important sources of stress on the job are dysfunctional norms. He describes these norms as implicit and embedded within an individual's daily working conditions. Examples of these norms include (1) the pressure to take on more work than time allows for adequate response to deadlines (it being apparently better to be viewed as overworked than to meet deadlines), (2) the tendency to receive feedback on one's performance *only* when it was considered unsatisfactory, and (3) avoiding obvious conflict rather than dealing with it openly and straightforwardly.

Although Adams would undoubtedly support the use of the role-analysis and negotiation techniques we have considered, he would argue that, in the prior step of diagnosis, when individual stress is found to be high for a significant number of people, the consultant should take a broader perspective than one's role. As Adams points out, French and Caplan (1972) found that role ambiguity and conflict were not the only sources of chronic organizational stress; heavy work load, lack of participation in decision making, poor relationships, and territoriality problems also contributed to it.

The significance of these factors is twofold: (1) in the diagnostic phase of OD work it is imperative that the consultant view the organization as a total system with a culture and members' conforming patterns as a primary carrier of that culture; and (2) with the systems perspective, it is clear that norms and roles are highly intertwined—as the Adams study demonstrates—and that to consider one without the other is like assuming that water consists of only one element, oxygen or hydrogen, not both.

Values

The attempt to understand human organizations is even more complicated than just described, however, because values are intertwined with norms and roles. To illustrate, let us assume that a manager in an organization makes two statements: "The way we do things around here is to follow the chain of command" and "This way of doing things is preferable to other ways because we are able to accomplish our objectives in an orderly and therefore more effective fashion." The first statement reflects a norm; the second reflects a value. Peoples' values evolve from their beliefs about what is good and what is bad.

Social psychologist Milton Rokeach has spent most of his professional life studying peoples' beliefs and values. Although his definition is somewhat pedantic, it is perhaps preferable and certainly more explanatory than a mere reference to "good and bad" or "should and ought." He has defined both a value and a value system:

> A *value* is an enduring belief that a specific mode of conduct or end-state of existence is personally or socially preferable to an opposite or converse mode of conduct or end-state of existence. A *value system* is an enduring organization of beliefs concerning preferable modes of conduct or end-states of existence along a continuum of relative importance. (Rokeach 1973, p. 5)

An organization, like an individual, has a value system. This "enduring organization of beliefs" is reflected in what members consider to be preferable and appropriate or inappropriate organizational behavior. Conformity to appropriate behavior and avoidance of the inappropriate is a behavioral carrier of the organization's culture. In terms of organizational behavior, therefore, it is difficult to separate a norm from a value, since both involve conformity or nonconformity. The point to remember, however, is that a norm is neither good nor bad, valuable nor invaluable, and conformity can be viewed objectively. What people *believe* about the appropriateness of their and other's conformity and their concomitant preferences regarding a given norm constitute a value.

These beliefs of organizational members sometimes take the form of myths or rituals. Organizational stories and ritualized behavior serve both as sources of data for diagnosis and understanding and as indicators of key norms and values in the system.

Organization Development Values

At the risk of redundancy, but in order to keep focused and to maintain perspective, it should be noted that we consider values because they are an integral element of an organization's culture. Following the line of thought and belief that organization development constitutes cultural change, it is obviously important that we understand the nature of organizational values as thoroughly as possible. We also need to understand the value system of the field of organization development itself and the carriers of this professional culture—OD practitioners and consultants. Thus, in this section we shall first examine the values represented by the field of organization development. Next we shall summarize what appear to be the primary values reflected in the workplace today. We shall then look at the degree of match between current trends and OD values. Finally, we shall consider what may be the greatest value dilemma for OD as it is currently practiced.

We can gain some understanding of the values represented by organization development by referring to the field's roots, especially sensitivity training. This method of education and change has a humanistic value orientation, the belief that it is worthwhile for people to have the opportunity throughout their lives to learn and develop personally toward a full realization and actualization of their individual potentials. Some people now believe that this preference (Rokeach's term) not only is worthwhile but should be a right.

Another OD value that came even more directly from sensitivity training is that peoples' feelings are just as important a source of data for diagnosis and have as much implication for change as do facts or so-called hard data and peoples' thoughts and opinions, and that these feelings should be considered as legitimate for expression in the organization as any thought, fact, or opinion.

Yet another OD value stemming from sensitivity training is that conflict, whether interpersonal or intergroup, should be brought to the surface and dealt with directly, rather than ignored, avoided, or manipulated.

89

Before I go further (my list could continue), let us return to one of the original sources. When sensitivity training was at the height of its popularity in the United States, E. H. Schein and Bennis (1965) stated what they considered its two main value systems: a spirit of inquiry and democracy.

The spirit of inquiry comes from the values of science. Two parts of it are relevant: the hypothetical spirit—being tentative, checking on the validity or assumptions, and allowing for error; and experimentalism—putting ideas or assumptions to the test. In sensitivity training, "all experienced behavior is subject to questioning and examination, limited only by the threshold of tolerance to truth and new ideas" (E. H. Schein and Bennis 1965, p. 32). A corollary value mentioned by Schein and Bennis is being authentic in interpersonal relations.

The second main value system, the democratic value, has two elements: collaboration and conflict resolution through rational means. The learning process in sensitivity training is a collaborative one between participant and trainer, not a traditional authoritarian student-teacher relationship. By conflict resolution through rational means, Schein and Bennis did not mean that irrational behavior or emotion was off limits, but "that there is a problem-solving orientation to conflict rather than the more traditional approaches based on bargains, power plays, suppression, or compromise" (p. 34).

Most important—what Schein and Bennis called "the overarching and fundamental value" (p. 35)—is the matter of choice. Freedom from coercion and from the arbitrary exercise of authority is the most preferred end state of existence.

Schein and Bennis wrote about and espoused those values in the 1960s, when individualism, rebellion toward authority, and questioning the rights of certain traditional institutions were in vogue. What about OD today? Does the field still maintain the values that evolved from sensitivity training? Without definitive evidence one way or the other, this is a difficult question to answer. For some indications, however, let us examine two sources of information: some informal data I have collected and Tichy's (1978) findings.

For a number of years I have served as a faculty member in the Columbia Graduate School of Business program, "Advanced Organization Development and Human Resource Management." The program is designed for experienced practitioners. One of the sessions I conduct in this program deals with values. The session involves an exercise in the identification of one's values, primarily those that relate to organization development. Since it is difficult to respond to a direct question of what ones values are, and since most of us would tend to respond in a socially desirable manner anyway, I begin the exercise with three other questions:

1. When you are about to contract with a client for possible OD work (an entry situation), what has caused you *not* to want to be involved, to pull away, not to do it?

2. Give an example of a situation in which you were already involved in an OD effort and then wanted to get out of it.
3. Under what conditions or in what kinds of situations have you felt good or satisfied as a consultant?

After the participants have had time to write their individual responses, I ask them to examine what they have written and to extract or determine from their responses the values they reveal. I then ask them to state these values in writing, following these guidelines: (1) the statement is a belief I hold, not a "should" for others; (2) the statement communicates right or wrong, good or bad; and (3) the statement cannot be proved quantitatively or scientifically.

In the words of the participants in several of these sessions, involving approximately seventy-five people, mostly male, the following values predominate:

1. Everyone has the right to learn, grow, and value themselves.
2. It is essential that I, as an OD consultant, respect the right of people to be themselves.
3. It is right to be insecure about what is right.
4. I value improving the quality of work life.
5. It is good to move in life toward an ideal self—that is, a congruent self.
6. An OD consultant's behavior must be congruent with his or her own values.
7. Value-free OD is a myth and therefore the consultant must clarify and declare his or her assumptions, beliefs, and biases as part of the client's data base for making choices.
8. OD consultants should help to create environments in which people have the opportunity *to make choices,* to realize their potential, and to contribute to the organization's well-being.
9. We must have a concern for human dignity.
10. My knowledge and discoveries are "mine"; I can only help others to discover their own.

There have been many more statements, and not all participants agreed with all ten of these statements, but most did. They represent at least part of the OD system of values for these practitioners.

From these statements we can easily draw two conclusions: (1) they are well within the mainstream of the earlier values from sensitivity training, even though most of these participants had not been heavily involved (few would classify themselves as T-group trainers); and (2) statements concerning organizations are noticeably absent. It is possible, of course, that this absence results from the nature of my three original questions, but the participants met in small groups after the individual work, and there was an opportunity to broaden their statements.

91

Also with a small group of OD practitioners, Tichy (1978) found that, although they were concerned with such organizational matters as productivity, they apparently felt somewhat impotent (to use Tichy's label) in bringing about change in these areas. Many admitted, also, that they intervened in areas or with techniques that were not directed at the primary needs or "hurts" of the organization, that they used techniques in which they were skillful and comfortable but that these interventions ultimately did not have much organizational influence.

To repeat a warning, my data and those of Tichy are based on small, select groups of OD practitioners, which may or may not represent the mainstream of consultants in OD work. Thus, we cannot generalize. My personal impression, however, is that these responses are certainly not far off the mark, but may vary in degree. The conclusion, albeit more impressionistic than rigorously scientific, is that most OD practitioners hold these kinds of humanistic values and act accordingly as consultants, believing that organizations should serve humans, not the reverse. Thus, OD consultants more frequently are attracted to and use interventions that help individuals (1) to be more involved in decisions that directly affect them; (2) to be assertive regarding their needs, if not their rights; (3) to plan their careers; (4) to become more a part of their work group; (5) to obtain more interesting jobs or to enrich the ones they have; (6) to have opportunities for additional training, education, and personal development; (7) to be more involved with their superiors in establishing the objectives and quotas they are expected to reach; and, in general, (8) to receive respect and fair treatment.

These values and their consequent interventions in OD are not inappropriate or unneeded. It is, painfully obvious that most organizations treat their most valued resources—employees—as if they were expendable. The all-too-frequent attitude among managers is, "If our employees don't like the jobs we provide, they can find employment elsewhere; we pay them a fair wage and they receive excellent fringe benefits." In the name of efficiency and economic or top management pressure, some people in organizations may be bored, some may be discriminated against, and many may be treated unfairly or inequitably regarding their talent and performance. If OD helps to correct these imbalances, it is long overdue, but what about the organization? If it doesn't survive, there will be no jobs, no imbalances to correct. Of the two words represented by OD, practitioners heretofore have spent more time on development than on organization. They are equally important, however; if either is out of balance, the OD consultant's goal is to redress the imbalance. Weisbord (1977) has stated it well:

> OD's right goal—its central purpose—grows from its proper setting. If the proper setting is organizations, then there is only one right goal for OD: to confront an issue which most certainly predates the Industrial Revolution. That is

92

the tension between *freedom* and *constraint*. OD's right purpose is to *redress the balance* between freedom and constraint. (p. 4)

He goes on to point out that there is always tension between the two—the autonomy of the individual and the requirements of the organization—and that either can be out of kilter. Furthermore, it is practically impossible to determine the proper balance, but, when either factor is obviously out of balance, the OD consultant's goal is to work toward reducing the heavier side.

With these points in mind, let us now turn to the larger picture of societal values and how they are shifting with respect to organizations. We should then be in a position to determine to some extent whether OD is appropriate and is equipped for future organizational needs.

Values in the Current Work Place and Future Trends

Two of the most respected social research organizations in the United States are the Institute for Social Research (ISR) of the University of Michigan and the firm of Yankelovich, Skelly and White, Inc., in New York City. Studies conducted by these two organizations will provide the basis for our understanding of current values held by most United States workers and our prediction of future trends.

Quinn and Staines (1978) of ISR, on behalf of the United States Department of Labor, conducted a national survey on the quality of work life and on such related factors as the relationships between work and family life and work and leisure. A major finding of this survey was that, compared with similar surveys conducted by ISR in 1969 and 1973 (Quinn and Shepard 1974), a pronounced decline in job satisfaction had occurred, particularly among college graduates. Some specific job-related problems concerned work schedules, difficulties in getting job requirements changed, worry about exposure to health and safety hazards, and shortage of time for leisure activities.

According to the ISR survey, the following value shifts have occurred since the 1960s.

1. *Less unquestioned acceptance of authority by young people:* In the 1969 survey, almost 70 percent accepted authority with few if any reservations. In the 1977 survey, a majority indicated that they felt free to disagree with a boss's commands. In reviewing this survey, Rosow (1979) explains that

> even as younger, more educated workers resent authoritarianism, they are
> not opposed to the *proper* exercise of authority. . . . They respect authority
> properly exercised with restraint and with rationality, but reject authority
> which is abusive or arbitrary. This poses a challenge for large bureaucratic

93

organizations—to rationalize their work procedures and learn the art of managing conflict with consent. (p. 4)

2. *Reduced confidence in institutions:* In all categories—government, business, religion, and labor—esteem has dropped and mistrust has increased. Rosow (1979) believes that people are looking more to their work place for support than to the family, church or synagogue, or the more traditional sources of social support.

3. *Less tolerance for work for the sake of work:* The Protestant ethic of working hard for delayed reward is not as acceptable as it had been before. When asked if hard work always pays off, almost 70 percent of the young people responding in the late 1960s said yes. Less than a decade later, 75 percent said no. Young people are not unwilling to work hard, but work is not necessarily their primary source of satisfaction. Leisure time and other aspects of life have become much more important than they used to be. More workers of all ages now want a better balance among work, leisure, family, and community.

4. *Less satisfaction with financial rewards:* Workers of all ages are concerned that their income and fringe benefits will not keep pace with rising taxes and inflation. Using Herzberg's terminology, this means that hygiene factors will continue to play a central role in overall job satisfaction.

5. *More demand for participation in decision making:* The 1977 ISR survey showed that 54 percent of all workers (62 percent of young people) believed they had a right to be involved in decisions that affected them directly. This percentage, too, was a significant increase over past years' surveys. People don't want to run the company, but they want to have more influence on their immediate work situations.

A significant part of the ISR survey by Quinn and Staines was conducted with young people. Yankelovich (1978) refers to this group as the "new breed." According to Yankelovich, this new breed of Americans, "born out of the social movements of the 60s and grown into a majority in the 70s, holds a set of values and beliefs so markedly different from the traditional outlook that they promise to transform the character of work in America in the 80s" (p. 46). His description of the new breed includes the following characteristics:

1. They refuse "to subordinate their personalities to the work role" (p. 49).
2. They desire self-fulfillment.
3. They want to work with pleasant and likable people.
4. They definitely want a paid job and are willing to work hard and produce, but if the job's rewards do not meet their expectations, they will no longer be motivated. Loyalty to the organization for its having provided a job, pure and simple, is a thing of the past.

94

It is readily apparent that Yankelovich's descriptions, based on his organization's survey results, corroborate the findings of the ISR survey.

OD and the New Values

Exhibit 5.2 is a summary of some of the shifts from the older, more traditional values regarding work and organizational life to the newer ones, as manifested by the new breed. For each value dimension, I have also included a phrase that depicts OD's stance. I have taken some liberties in portraying the OD value system. I have incorporated many of the value statements from the OD practitioners we considered earlier, but I also have gone beyond those statements and have made some interpretations and generalizations of my own regarding the field of organization development.

If my summaries are reasonably accurate, two things are clear. First, as Yankelovich stated, some major shifts are indeed occurring with respect to

EXHIBIT 5.2

A Comparison of Value Shifts with the Values of OD

Value dimension	Shift from	Shift to	OD values
Motivation	Security	Security and fulfillment	All of Maslow's needs hierarchy is important
Authority	Acceptance	Challenge if perceived as arbitrary	Confrontation of authority may be appropriate
Participation in decision making	Not appropriate	May be a right	Very appropriate
Work itself	Primary mode of self-identity and activity	One of several modes and activities	Work is only one component of life
Job	Provides security	Should be rewarding and interesting	Job enrichment is a major OD intervention
Career	Most important to to have a job	Most important to have a career path	Career development is a major OD intervention
Organizational loyalty	Strong	Weak	Should depend on management approach (a situational value)
Organizational demands	Acceptance of restraint	Preference for autonomy	Balance is the desirable end state
Family	Secondary to work	At least equal in importance to work	Equal importance to work
Leisure	A luxury	A right	Balance with work is the desirable end state

95

values in the work place. Second, organization development seems, overall, to be in a good position to respond to these value shifts.

One other perspective regarding value shifts should be mentioned. Although current OD values may stem largely from sensitivity training, other sources or roots of organization development have also contributed, especially sociotechnical systems. A prominent person in the area and one of its most articulate spokesmen is Eric Trist. In a recent paper (Trist 1978), he has examined the quality of working life (QWL) movement as a response to value shifts that are occurring in the work place. Trist believes that a new work ethic is emerging, which is beginning to influence the nature of jobs and broader organizational life. The behavioral sciences have made it clear that workers have needs beyond the *extrinsic* requirements of a job—wages, hours, seniority, and the like. For a worker to have ultimate satisfaction with a job, *intrinsic* requirements must be met, such as the needs for a job (1) to be reasonably demanding of a person's talents, (2) to provide an opportunity for learning, and (3) to provide some degree of autonomy. The job must contribute to a person's desire for a higher quality of life, not be a detriment to it. Exhibit 5.3 gives Trist's summary of this shift. It does not represent a shift *from* extrinsic *to* intrinsic, a substitution of one for the other, as was depicted in Exhibit 5.2, but rather shows an addition of necessary properties that are required of jobs currently and will be in the future. One other qualification is that some of Trist's intrinsic properties, such as recognition and support, desirable future, and psychosocial, are not strictly *intrinsic*. Trist's point is that the properties of jobs should acquire more of these qualities, regardless of their category.

Trist states that job changes toward an improved quality of working life will not endure unless they are made in a supportive organizational context.

EXHIBIT 5.3
Properties of Jobs

Extrinsic properties	Intrinsic properties
Fair and adequate pay	Variety and challenge
Job security	Continuous learning
Benefits	Discretion, autonomy
Safety	Recognition and support
Health	Meaningful social contribution
Due process	Desirable future
Conditions of employment	The job itself
Socioeconomic	Psychosocial

Source: E. Trist, "Adapting to a Changing World," in *A New Role for Labour: Industrial Democracy Today,* ed. G. Sanderson (Toronto: McGraw-Hill Ryerson, 1978). Originally published in the *Labour Gazette,* 1978. Reprinted with permission from the *Labour Gazette,* Government of Canada.

He claims that a new organizational paradigm that is needed and is being established will reinforce the intrinsic qualities of a job. Trist characterizes the old, more traditional organizational paradigm as having a technological imperative that regards the person as no more than an extension of the machine and consequently as an expendable spare part. The new paradigm is based on the principle of joint optimization: the person and the machine are complementary, and the person is valued for his or her judgment rather than technical skill alone.

As an example, it is interesting that, in the 1960s, the United States astronauts were trained to ride in a space capsule and to monitor the instruments—not to fly the craft. The first flights had monkeys aboard, and NASA originally planned for the astronauts to perform little more than the monkeys had. The astronauts rebelled and demanded that the spacecraft be designed for person-piloting as well as autopiloting. More than one mission was saved because the astronauts were able to maintain a significant portion of flight control (Wolfe 1979).

Exhibit 5.4 is Trist's summary of the paradigmatic shifts that he believes are under way. He believes these shifts are occurring for two reasons. First, the QWL movement has been substantial, despite recessional setbacks during the early 1970s. Second, because we are becoming a conserver society, recognizing that there are limits to certain physical resources, there is a greater need than ever before to develop human resources as much as possible—to learn to do more with less.

As is seen readily in Trist's two summaries, his perception, based on a

EXHIBIT 5.4
Shifts in Organizational Paradigms

Old paradigm	New paradigm
The technological imperative	Joint optimization
Employee an extension of the machine	Employee complementary to the machine
Employee an expendable spare part	Employee a resource to be developed
Maximum task breakdown and single, narrow skills	Optimum task grouping and multiple, broad skills
External controls (supervisors, specialist staffs, procedures)	Internal controls (self-regulating subsystems)
Tall organization chart, autocratic style	Flat organization chart, participative style
Competition, gamesmanship	Collaboration, collegiality
Organization's purposes only	Members' and society's purposes also
Alienation	Commitment
Low risk-taking	Innovation

Source: E. Trist, "Adapting to a Changing World," in *A New Role for Labour: Industrial Democracy Today,* ed. G. Sanderson (Toronto: McGraw-Hill Ryerson, 1978). Originally published in the *Labour Gazette,* 1978. Reprinted with permission from the *Labour Gazette,* Government of Canada.

sizable number of QWL projects launched in the United States and in Norway, Sweden, and Canada, parallels the value shifts identified earlier.

The Value Dilemma for OD

I have stated that organization development is a process of cultural change and that the value system of an organization is a significant component of its culture. For the organization to change significantly, then, its values must change. From what values to what other values should it change, and what would the new culture look like? Who determines the direction and desired end state for the change? Is organization development a body of knowledge and practice that helps managers and administrators to bring about change regardless of direction? Are OD practitioners facilitators only? Or does the field of organization development represent a certain direction of change, an implied if not clear-cut desired end state? Are OD practitioners more than facilitators, and should they be? Practitioners and academics in organization development are divided on these questions. Most believe in a contingent approach to OD, but some argue for a normative approach. The contingent camp argues that OD practitioners should only facilitate change, not focus it. They believe that the client should determine the direction of change, and the consultant should help the client to get there. Moreover, they argue, there is no one best way to organize—to structure an organization—no one best way to manage people, and no one best way to design, for example, an organization's reward system. The course of these directional decisions depends on many factors: the organization's environment, the nature of the work force, the organization's type of business or service, and so forth.

Those who argue for a normative approach—a much smaller group—believe that, although the consultative approach should be facilitative at the outset, the consultant-practitioner eventually should begin to recommend and encourage specific directions for change.

This value dilemma in OD—contingent versus normative—is manifested in different ways. I described the dilemma earlier as two camps. This portrayal may not be accurate, for many experience the dilemma internally, not clearly on one side or the other. Tichy (1974), for example, found that, compared with three other types of consultants or change agents, OD consultants were highest in value-action incongruence. The OD consultants believed that they should encourage if not push for humanistic and participative management practices, but, in practice, they admitted that they were primarily concerned with the more traditional and typical problems of how to increase efficiency and productivity. In concluding their excellent review of the status of organizational development, Friedlander and Brown (1974) stated that "the future of OD rests in part on its values and the degree to which its practice, theory, and research are congruent with those values" (p. 355). According to

98

Bowen (1977), "value conflicts, perhaps even more than a dearth of research or techniques (although research difficulties are oft-cited constraints to development of the profession), currently limit further development of the theory and practice of OD" (p. 544). Argyris (1970) believes that value conflicts within the consultant diminish his or her effectiveness.

Bowen (1977) has proposed a way out of the dilemma. He argues that, if consultants perform the three tasks delineated by Argyris (1970) when intervening in an organization, the conflicts can be resolved. These tasks actually constitute criteria for an effective intervention. The first task—the most important according to Bowen—is the generation of *valid information,* so that the consultant's diagnosis is based on needs for change that organizational members genuinely experience. Second is recognition that the client has *choice* regarding what the intervention will be; and third is that, in exercising this choice, the client will have *internal commitment* to the decision that has been made. Bowen (1977) clarifies further:

> This position for the consultant is *not* value-free. It merely substitutes one set of values—criteria for the proper conduct of the consultation—for another set—preconceptions about the "good" organization and the necessity of change . . . . Allegiance to valid information rather than to change on a particular normative concept of the organization encourages the consultant to approach the client system with fewer preconceptions of the type that are likely to make debilitating value dilemmas inevitable. (p. 552)

Bowen clearly puts himself in the contingency camp.

It is ironic that Bowen uses Argyris (1970) as the authoritative base for his argument. On the basis of a number of other writings by Argyris, I would place him on the normative side. First, Argyris has been a proponent of a more humanistic treatment of people in organizations for many years (Argyris 1973, 1964, 1957). Second, he has argued that the consultant sometimes should intervene authoritatively. Occasionally the consultant (Argyris uses the term *interventionist*) may see the relevance of some theory or research to the organizational problem at hand. On such occasions, the consultant may be "asked to be authoritative, without being authoritarian; to be confronting, without being punitive; to be clear, without becoming didactic. In short, it may be legitimate for the interventionist to be authoritative and to create the conditions where others can question and confront his views and behavior" (Argyris 1971, pp. 157–58). Finally, more recently, Argyris and Schön (1978) have argued for "double-loop learning" in organizations, as opposed to "single-loop learning." By single-loop learning they mean simple problem solving, closing a single loop by merely fixing something that was wrong. No learning occurs regarding how to avoid or prevent the problem in the future. By double-loop learning they mean not only problem solving but also organizational change, the second loop. Organizational members learn new patterns of behavior and change accordingly. If Argyris's other writings are indicative (Argyris 1973, 1971), the direction for these changes would be toward an organizational culture that would look like McGregor's Theory Y behaviorally.

I agree that the consultant should be facilitative, especially at the beginning of an OD effort. For me the cardinal principle of entry-level consultation is to take the client where he or she is. The consultant must deal first with the client's problems or hurts. As more is learned about the organization's culture, especially its norms and values, and if the consultant is knowledgeable about behavioral science theory and research, he or she gradually moves closer to being able to make authoritative interventions. The consultant does not make the directional decisions for change but suggests certain directions to the client and then, if the client agrees, works closely with him or her to help implement the changes. As authoritative consultants we must be selective, of course, first determining the client's readiness for change (which was clearly not the situation in the case described in Chapter 1) and then deciding which areas of behavioral science knowledge are applicable in a given situation. We must be selective for another reason also: our applicable knowledge is meager, but, compared with what most managers and administrators know about applied behavioral science, we are or should be in a more authoritative position.

A Normative View of Organization Development

The final question to be addressed regarding the issue of contingent versus normative organization development is what normative is. What is the norm that we should advocate when we are implementing change in an organization's culture?

The normative shift concerns values more than any other aspect of the organization's culture. Changes in certain norms would support value shifts that had already been determined. The shift is generally toward a humanistic treatment of members at all levels in the organization. More specifically, the direction of change would be toward an organizational culture with the following characteristics:

1. The growth and development of organization members is just as important as making a profit or meeting the budget.
2. Equal opportunity and fairness for people in the organization is commonplace; it is the rule rather than the exception.
3. Managers exercise their authority more participatively than unilaterally and arbitrarily, and authority is associated more with knowledge and competence than with role or status.

100

4. Cooperative behavior is rewarded more frequently than competitive behavior.
5. Organization members are kept informed or at least have access to information, especially concerning matters that directly affect their jobs or them personally.
6. Members feel a sense of ownership of the organization's mission and objectives.
7. Conflict is dealt with openly and systematically, rather than ignored, avoided, or handled in a typical win-lose fashion.
8. Rewards are based on a system of both equality-fairness and equity-merit.
9. Organization members are given as much autonomy and freedom to do their respective jobs as possible, to insure both a high degree of individual motivation and accomplishment of organizational objectives.

Although this list is more value-laden, it is not unlike Beckhard's (1969) characteristics of an effective organization:

1. The total organization, the significant subparts, and individuals manage their work against *goals* and *plans* for achievement of these goals.
2. Form follows function; that is, the program or task or project determines how the human resources are organized.
3. Decisions are made by and near the sources of information, regardless of where these sources are located on the organizational chart.
4. The reward system is such that managers and supervisors are rewarded or punished comparably for short-term profit or production performance, growth and development of the subordinates, and creating a viable working group.
5. Lateral and vertical communication is relatively undistorted. People are generally open and confronting. They share all the relevant facts, including feelings.
6. There is a minimum of inappropriate win-lose activities between individuals and groups. Constant effort is made at all levels to treat conflict and conflict-situations as *problems,* subject to problem-solving methods.
7. There is high conflict (clash of ideas) about tasks and projects and relatively little energy spent in clashing over *interpersonal* difficulties, because they generally have been worked through.
8. The organization and its parts see themselves as interacting with each other and with a larger environment. The organization is an open system.
9. There is a shared view, and management strategy to support it, of trying to help each person or unit in the organization to maintain integrity and uniqueness in an interdependent environment.

101

10. The organization and its members operate in an action-research way. General practice is to build in *feedback mechanisms* so that individuals and groups can learn from their own experience.[1]

A different but compatible perspective on the nature of an effective organization—what a new culture that operationalized many of the values I've covered would look like—is provided by Peter Vaill's (1978) description of "high-performing systems." His theory base and perspective is steeped in the sociotechnical systems context, especially the notion of joint optimization. (See the summary of Trist's thinking earlier in this chapter and some of the basic readings on sociotechnical systems, such as Pasmore and Sherwood 1978.)

My coverage of the nature or end state of the cultural change is still very general and perhaps even vague, but organization development is relatively young as a field, and additional experience, theory, and research will provide greater specificity and clarity. It is best, therefore, to consider these characteristics of a new organizational culture as preliminary. It should be clear that normative change primarily concerns values; other aspects of change, such as organizational structure, the substance of a fringe benefit package, the design of a management information system, or a decision to install a new reward system, are all contingent matters. If puzzling questions remain about the specific direction of some of these latter examples of change, however—if "what it depends on" is unclear or doesn't appear to matter much—a guide should be sought from within the value system to which the organization aspires.

A most appropriate question about my coverage and viewpoint regarding organizational values and change is: "What right do I have to say what an organization's values should be, to impose my values on anyone else?" Fundamentally, I have no such right. For me to assume that I can act as a value-free consultant, however, is pure nonsense. It is most important for me to work toward as much clarity of my values as possible and to declare these values relatively early in the consultant-client relationship. Most are clear anyway if the client has paid any attention to my behavior and to my recommendations. I believe this fear of imposition is a false obstacle. As a perceived expert, I have a certain amount of power, but I have never had a client who was unable to say no to me.

Regarding value change, then, OD values are in line with societal shifts that are already under way. In some respects OD practitioners are simply trying to catch up with and respond to these shifts. Recent research evidence and certain theories in the behavioral sciences are also compatible with many of these value changes—as I will attempt to show in the next two chapters.

[1] *Source:* R. Beckhard, *Organization Development: Strategies, and Models,* © 1969. Addison-Wesley Publishing Company, Reading, Mass., pp. 10–11. Reprinted with permission.

Summary

Norms, roles, and values are social-psychological concepts that are essential for understanding an organization's culture. Norms are concepts that represent standards or rules of conduct to which people conform, and conformity is the behavior. An important classification of norms is whether they are explicit or implicit. Explicit norms are standards, rules, and policies that are public and usually formal. Implicit norms are informal and are usually not within the conscious awareness of organization members. Implicit norms govern organziation members' behavior far more than explicit ones do. Since norms are significant in governing organizational member's behavior, understanding them and particularly revealing those that are implicit are key activities in organization development practice.

Roles are sets of expectations about individuals' behavior in a particular context. The organizational term for a role is a job description. When there is role conflict—contradictory expectations regarding a given role—or role ambiguity—unclear or nonexistent expectations—organization members experience personal stress. Organization development practitioners can help by using certain interventions that reduce role conflict and ambiguity, thereby alleviating stress for individuals in the organization.

Values are enduring beliefs that certain modes of behavior or end states of existence are preferable to others. "It is better to tell the truth than to lie" and "Happiness consists of maximizing one's potential" are examples of value statements. Values among organization development practitioners are largely individualistic rather than systemic. The central value is that organizations should serve humans, but in practice the reverse is typical. Values in our society seem to be shifting toward the person, and OD practitioners are positioned well to facilitate this shift within organizations. Not everyone agrees, however, that this trend toward the person over the organization is actually occurring. Scott and Hart (1979) believe that the opposite is taking place. See Chapter 18 for an exposition of their observations and hypotheses.

A value dilemma for OD practitioners is whether to advocate a certain direction for change in the client organization—the normative stance—or only to facilitate change, regardless of direction. Some combination may be best, beginning the consultation with facilitation and then gradually moving toward taking a position about directions for change.

CHAPTER 6

Reward Systems
in Organizations

I recently consulted with a company vice-president and his subordinate managers about reward problems in their organization. Results from an earlier attitude survey had indicated that a significant number of employees in all levels of the managerial hierarchy felt that their work performance was not given adequate recognition. In my one-day meeting with the vice-president and his managers, we spent almost a quarter of the time dealing with this recognition problem—how to provide recognition for good work performance. The following five action steps are a sampling of the ideas we generated:

1. Set aside ten minutes every week to ask each of my subordinates about his or her work; simply ask something like "How's it going?"—and stay for the answer. This activity should be rewarding in itself, and it would provide an opportunity to determine more adequately who is performing well.
2. Ask my boss to write an occasional brief memo of recognition to one of my subordinates who is performing well. The higher-level recognition may have greater impact.
3. Have reports of completed projects signed by the person or persons who actually did the work, rather than by the next superior person in the hierarchy (which was typical in this organization).
4. Provide occasional opportunities for subordinates to make presentations to the next higher level of management, rather than to their immediate boss. This activity would give people who are doing high-quality work a chance not only to gain wider recognition but to demonstrate their competencies to higher levels of management—"Where it counts more!"
5. Give special assignments to people who are performing their routine work particularly well. In such areas as accounting, for example, a special-

assignment project to study the feasibility of some new method could be rewarding because it would remove the person temporarily from a job that might have become boring. Special assignments that involve travel might be particularly rewarding for some people.

These ideas are not profound and they may not be out of the ordinary for many organizations. As these managers worked on their recognition problems, I was nevertheless impressed with two things. First, they held considerable respect for the complexity of the problem with which they were dealing. They knew that an occasional pat on the back was not only insufficient but also oversimplified. Second, since they worked in a division of a much larger company, they had little control over the more tangible or extrinsic rewards, such as salary and fringe benefits. Even a promotion for one of their subordinates was not solely their decision. Thus, their recognition list had to go beyond the obvious, and their action steps would require more conscious and deliberate effort from them than would such a step as making certain that all their deserving subordinates received an equitable annual increase in salary.

Recognizing good work performance and providing an organizational reward system that simultaneously (1) meets human needs, (2) increases the quality of work life, and (3) leads to greater organizational effectiveness is no small matter. Yankelovich (1978) has stated: ''Perhaps no question will dominate the workplace in the 1980's more than how to revamp incentives to make them a better match for the work motivations of the New Breed'' (p. 50). He was referring to the different values of the young people who were born in the 1960s and entered the work force in the middle and late 1970s.

In this chapter we shall consider some of the fundamentals about rewards in organizations, regardless of whether members are new or old breed. Certain principles of behavior and rewards are well known, reliable, and valid in terms of prediction, and are readily applicable to all members of an organization. People differ, of course, in terms of both needs and what is viewed as rewarding. As we shall see, a major strength of any organization's reward system is its flexibility, its capacity to respond to a variety of individual needs and values.

The Nature of Rewards

There are no *laws* of behavior, or we simply have not yet discovered them. One type of behavior that comes close to being a law, in that it is highly predictable, is that people will continue to do what they have been rewarded for doing. This simple statement, which we learn in our first psychology course if not before, is actually more complex than may be apparent. One person's

105

reward may be another person's punishment, for example, or something may be rewarding for a person under some conditions but not under other conditions.

Rewards can be broadly classified in two categories: extrinsic rewards and intrinsic rewards. A synonym for *intrinsic* is *inherent,* and thus an intrinsic reward is one that is difficult if not impossible to distinguish from the act that produces the reward. Behaving in a definite way, working on or accomplishing a particular task, or performing a certain act may be rewarding in and of itself. Painting a picture, writing a book, or making a presentation before an audience can be intrinsically rewarding in that the artist, writer, or speaker can receive satisfaction from experiencing the consequences of his or her work as it unfolds or materializes. Regardless of what the viewer, reader, or listener may experience or think, the creator's experience of what he or she does may be fun, satisfying, pleasantly surprising, fulfilling, emotionally pleasing— that is, *rewarding.*

An extrinsic reward is like a prize for one's performance. The prize is something outside or extraneous to the person and is typically something tangible, material, and easily identifiable or articulated. This contrasts with the frequent difficulty in expressing precisely what might be intrinsically rewarding. The most obvious examples of extrinsic rewards in an organization that employs people are salary, fringe benefits, promotions, and seniority or tenure.

An organization's reward system involves *what* constitutes rewards, both extrinsic and intrinsic, and *how* these rewards are administered by management.

Reward Systems and Organization Development

Most people with any experience working in or consulting with an organization are undoubtedly familiar with what has been discussed so far in this chapter. Other books about organization development have barely mentioned anything about reward systems in organizations (W. L. French and Bell 1978; Huse 1980; Margulies and Raia 1978). Why, then, do I devote an entire chapter to them?

Perhaps because the concept of rewards is so basic to human behavior, it is taken for granted and thus overlooked. Learning, for example, does not occur without reward of some kind. For this very reason, which is basic to human behavior, rewards should be stressed, not taken for granted or overlooked. Arguing that any organization development effort should *start* with rewards, Lawler (1977) states that "the reward system implications of an organization change project should always be considered *before* the project is begun" (p. 221). By "before," Lawler means, in OD language, prior to intervention, during the diagnostic phase. I not only agree with Lawler but rely fairly heavily on his work for the basis of this chapter.

People active in the field of organization development have brought to the organizational arena some critical dimensions of organizational behavior that had previously been ignored, such as the impact of group behavior on individuals or on the system as a whole. Ironically, these same practitioners have been naive about other organizational dimensions that are just as critical to understanding and to change, such as power and politics. Having been criticized in recent years for this naiveté, especially with respect to power (Beer 1976b; Burke 1972) and politics (V. E. Schein 1977; Tichy 1978), most practitioners have begun to be more cognizant of these dimensions. With an occasional exception, however (Levinson 1972a; Weisbord 1976), the reward dimension continues to be neglected. Part of the reason for this neglect is that many OD practitioners are uneasy about the close association of reward and manipulation. The values of organization development include a strong belief that processes of behavior modification, when applied to the organizational setting, can be used manipulatively. They can be applied nonmanipulatively as well, but the potential for manipulation concerns many practitioners.

Thus, understanding the nature of reward systems and the consequences for human performance in organizations and for change is necessary for an effective OD effort. It is possible that the consequences of some aspects of an organization's reward system might have the opposite effect of what was intended. Kerr (1975), for example, cites some unintended consequences from areas that are meaningful for OD. He points out that management rarely evaluates new projects that are meant to bring about change—such as management by objective (MBO), job enrichment, or a training program. The people who are expected to conduct such evaluations frequently are the same people who are responsible for the change project. Kerr (1975) states the dilemma this way:

> Having convinced top management to spend the money, they usually are quite animated afterwards in collecting rigorous vignettes and anecdotes about how successful the program was. The last thing many desire is a formal, systematic, and revealing evaluation. Although members of top management may actually *hope* for such systematic evaluation, their reward systems continue to *reward* ignorance in this area. And if the personnel department abdicates its responsibility, who is to step into the breach? The change agent himself? Hardly! He is likely to be too busy collecting anecdotal ''evidence'' of his own, for use with his next client. (p. 774)

Reward and Motivation

Reward and motivation are interrelated, because the former is often a result of the latter. Although OD practitioners may not have paid much attention to the reward part of this relationship, they certainly have kept motivation in the forefront. This emphasis is undoubtedly a function of the popularity of

107

Maslow's and Herzberg's theories, as noted in the section on values in Chapter 5. It is interesting that these theories have represented a primary thrust in OD but yet have created a limited arena for OD work. Consulting from these theoretical bases means focusing on the individual—emphasizing such activities as job enrichment, career development, and training—rather than on the organization as a system. I do not mean to imply that motivation is unimportant, but rather that it is important to know where to focus for purposes of organizational change. My argument, therefore, is that OD practitioners should focus their efforts more on rewards than on motivation. There are three reasons for this argument:

1. Focusing on motivation for purposes of organizational change lacks leverage; one is apt to miss the more important elements for bringing about change. Managers occasionally ask, "How can I motivate my people more?" My reply is, "You cannot motivate anyone but yourself." Managers and leaders have no control over anyone else's needs or motives. The domain of their control is within the reward system—what they can provide that *may* respond to their subordinates' needs and desires. If what managers provide does indeed respond to subordinates' needs, they will be motivated. Thus, managers can reward; they may or may not increase motivation.

2. An attempt to increase motivation focuses on the individual, not on the system. As I have defined it, organization development is a process of organizational change from a systems perspective. This is not to say that such activities as job enrichment, career development, and training are useless interventions for organization development, but that interventions of this type should be a consequence of a larger focus on the total organization, in support of the overall system change effort.

3. Dealing with motivation from a needs perspective, as Maslow does, necessitates an inward look with respect to others. From this perspective we attempt to learn what peoples' needs are. The problem is that frequently it is difficult for people to be clear about their own needs or motives, much less someone else's.

Another perspective on motivation and rewards, discussed in Chapter 2, is expectancy theory (Lawler 1973; Vroom 1964). The underlying assumption of this theory is that human beings rationally evaluate situations they encounter. This evaluation is based on individuals' perceptions of how much effort will be required to achieve some outcome and how valuable that outcome is to them. Expectancy theory thus consists of a probabilistic estimate and the notion of valence or value—that is, the extent to which the reward is considered worthwhile. If people want a particular reward, such as a promotion, and if they believe that exerting a certain amount of effort will lead to that reward, they will be motivated. There are two ifs here, and, according to the theory, they are interactive. If one of the ifs is zero, then motivation will be zero, regardless of the quantity of the other. If people want and value a reward but believe that, regardless of their efforts, they are not likely to obtain it, their motivation will be nil. If they believe that their efforts will produce a given reward but that the reward holds no value for them (for example, a promotion means a geographical move and the dislocation is a greater negative outcome for them), they will not be motivated.

As Hamner, Ross, and Staw (1978) point out:

> The implications of such a theory to a practitioner is substantial. By training and illustration, employees can be shown that effort will lead to performance. Managers should take steps to strengthen the perceived relationship between performance and outcomes. (p. 230)

As we shall see, Lawler (1977) takes this relationship into account when he describes and considers the implications of the dimensions of an organization's reward system.

Diagnosing an Organization's Reward System

There are three primary sources of rewards within an organization (Nadler, Tushman, and Hatvany, forthcoming). For diagnostic purposes and in general, these sources are:

1. The formal organizational arrangements—pay, fringe benefits, bonus procedures, incentive systems, and the like.
2. The nature of the work to be done—is it interesting and meaningful? Does the work require my unique talents or could anybody do it? Is the total work of the organization worthwhile and meaningful?
3. The social environment—do I like to work with the people around me? Is the nature of the supervision pleasant or unpleasant?

When considering an organization's reward system, it also is important to pay equal attention to intrinsic and extrinsic rewards. As Lawler (1977) has noted, "No study has yet been done that definitely establishes one as more important than the other" (p. 165). Both types of rewards are important, but they are not interchangeable; what satisfies intrinsically is not likely to satisfy extrinsically, and the reverse.

More specifically, Lawler's four necessary properties of an organization's reward system for producing a high quality of work life are as follows:

1. The system must have enough available rewards for employee's basic needs.
2. The system must compare favorably with other organizations; that is, the organization must be competitive in the labor marketplace.
3. The distribution of rewards in the organization must be perceived by employees as equitable.
4. The system must treat employees as individuals.

In addition to providing a high quality of work life, managers naturally want their organization to be effective. According to Lawler, a reward system contributes to an organization's effectiveness in four major ways: (1) by the attractiveness of the reward system for recruiting and holding people as members; (2) by the degree of attendance at work—whether people like coming to work or there is a great deal of tardiness and absenteeism; (3) by the relationship of rewards to performance and whether people perceive such a relationship; and (4) by the match of reward system to organizational structure—whether people at higher levels receive more rewards than those at lower levels. The first two points concern the degree of attractiveness and the impact of the reward system on organizational effectiveness, and the latter two address degree of fit—between rewards provided and members' performance and between the reward system and the organization's authority structure.

Lawler points out that, for a reward system to be effective, it must have five identifiable characteristics. The first is *importance*; the rewards must be important to the employees, both managers and the rank and file. This characteristic stems from the valence notion in expectancy theory. Second, the reward system should have as much *flexibility* as possible. Because individuals differ, their needs are never exactly the same. The more choice the individual has with respect to rewards, the greater is the likelihood of high motivation and performance. The choice may be as elaborate as accepting a raise in salary versus taking more vacation time or as simple as going home early when the production quota for the day is met versus working more for extra pay. TRW Systems' successful experiment with a "cafeteria-style" choice of fringe benefits is an example of arranging a reward system to respond to individual needs. This cafeteria-style system has not been easy to implement, but the gains made in employee morale and satisfaction have been well worth the effort.

A third characteristic of rewards that contributes to organizational effectiveness is *frequency*. Generally, the more frequently rewards can be given, the better the results are. Whether the rewards can be provided frequently without losing their value to the recipient, however, must be considered. Fourth, *visibility* of rewards is important. This visibility is highly related to peoples' needs for ego status and recognition.

Finally the *cost* of rewards is important, because there obviously are limits. Significant bonuses cannot be given weekly, and not everyone can be promoted. High costs can reduce organizational effectiveness, and so the price of rewards is a significant consideration in the process of administration.

Lawler (1977) has evaluated the most common extrinsic rewards in organizations according to these five characteristics. Exhibit 6.1 is a summary of his evaluation. According to Lawler, none of the types of extrinsic rewards rates high on all five criteria. Pay comes the closest, but the problem is its high cost. Lawler (1977) points out that:

organizations have little control over how important different outcomes are to individuals. However, organizations do control which outcomes they use. It is important that each organization carefully diagnose its situation and use the one or ones that are right for its particular situation. (p. 175)

Thus far, we have considered mostly extrinsic rewards. Intrinsic rewards cannot be as easily categorized because they are more individualistic, especially in terms of what people value. Intrinsic rewards are more closely associated, however, with a person's job itself.

In considering the three primary sources of rewards noted earlier, the one source that has the greatest potential for contributing to intrinsic reward is the nature of the work itself. Intrinsic rewards are more psychological and therefore relate signficantly to people's feelings, perceptions, and needs. According to Hackman and Oldham (1975), three key psychological states affect individuals' satisfaction with their work:

1. Experienced meaningfulness—the extent to which people experience their work as worthwhile and important
2. Experienced responsibility—the extent to which people feel responsible and accountable for the outcomes of their work
3. Knowledge of results—the extent to which people are informed regularly about the effectiveness of their work performance

Hackman and Oldham are noted for their research in job design (1975) and work redesign (1980) and for their application of this research knowledge (Hackman 1977). Based on this knowledge they have concluded that, for a job to contribute to the three key psychological states, five criteria must be met. The first three criteria all contribute to meaningfulness of the work: (1)

EXHIBIT 6.1

Evaluation of Extrinsic Rewards

Reward category	Average importance	Flexibility in amount	Visibility	Frequency	Dollar cost
Pay	Moderate to high	High	Potentially high	High	High
Promotion	High	Low	High	Low	High
Dismissal	High	Low	High	Low	High
Status symbols	Moderate	High	High	Low	Moderate
Special awards, certificates, and medals	Low	High	High	Low	Low
Fringe benefits	High	Moderate	Moderate	Low	High

Source: E. E. Lawler III, "Reward Systems," in *Improving Life at Work,* ed. J. R. Hackman and J. L. Suttle (Santa Monica: Goodyear, 1977). Reprinted by permission.

skill variety—the degree to which the job demands a variety of activities; (2) task identity—the degree to which the job is characterized by a clearly identifiable piece of work, which has a beginning and an end; and (3) task significance—the degree to which the job has an impact on others. Meaningful work thus occurs when people are able to do a variety of activities that result in a whole piece of work that has a visible outcome and that significantly affects the lives or work of others. The other two criteria are autonomy—the degree to which the job provides independence and freedom of choice in carrying out the various aspects of work—and feedback—the degree to which the job occupant receives information about the effectiveness of his or her work performance.

A nationwide survey by Quinn and Shepard (1974) corroborates the work of Hackman and Oldham. From their factor-analytic study, they found six primary factors that contributed to job satisfaction: comfort (working conditions), challenge, financial rewards, relations with co-workers, resource adequacy, and promotion. In line with Hackman and Oldham, Quinn and Shepard also found that the survey items that contributed most to challenge—that is, to intrinsic job satisfaction—were

1. Interesting work (the heaviest factor-loading)
2. The opportunity to develop one's own special abilities
3. The opportunity to see the results of one's work
4. The opportunity to do the things one does best
5. The freedom to decide how to do one's own work
6. Problems one is expected to solve being hard enough

Of the three general reward sources in an organization (Nadler, Tushman, and Hatvany, forthcoming), extrinsic rewards come from the formal arrangements—pay, incentive systems, and the like—and intrinsic rewards from the second source—the work itself, especially its degree of meaningfulness. The third source of rewards, which may be either extrinsic or intrinsic, is the social environment—the people with whom one works and associates in the organization. Herzberg (1966) classifies supervisory relationships as a hygiene factor and therefore as more extrinsic than intrinsic. Supervisory style, approach, or method perhaps could be considered extrinsic, but for supervisory relations in general, especially at the peer level, feelings about others in the organization may be considered intrinsic. As Katz and Kahn (1978) point out, affiliative expression is an expansion of one's ego; therefore, identification with others is part of one's self-identity.

Whether it is intrinsic or extrinsic, it is clear that social environment makes a difference. Van Zelst (1952) showed that construction workers who were given a choice of work mates, rather than having them assigned by the foreman, significantly outperformed the work groups who had no choice. In general, then, how people feel about others in their organization, especially those with whom they work closely, affects their motivation. How and how much managers shape the social environment constitutes another aspect of the organization's overall reward system.

To conclude this section on diagnosing an organization's reward system, we should consider one final, critical element: the degree of congruence between the organization's reward system and other management systems, such as control and decision making. The more congruent the reward system is with other systems within the organization, the less conflict employees will experience, especially regarding their roles. Thus, congruence is desirable for optimal organizational functioning.

Lawler (1977) has summarized what he considers the reward system practices that are most congruent with a more traditional, or Theory X (McGregor 1960), approach to management, and the practices that are most congruent with a more participative, or Theory Y, approach (see Exhibit 6.2).

Lawler emphasizes that congruence is more important than type of

EXHIBIT 6.2

Appropriate Reward System Practices

Reward system	Traditional, or Theory X	Participative, or Theory Y
Fringe benefits	Vary according to organization level	Cafeteria-style—same for all levels
Promotion	All decisions made by top management	Open posting for all jobs; peer group involvement in decision process
Status symbols	Many—carefully allocated on the basis of job position	Few—low emphasis on organization level
Pay:		
Type of system	Hourly and salary	All salary
Base rate	Based on job performed; high enough to attract job applicants	Based on skills; high enough to provide security and attract applicants
Incentive plan	Piece rate	Groupwide and organizationwide bonus, lump sum increase
Communication policy	Very restricted distribution of information	Individual rates, salary survey data, all other information made public
Decision-making locus	Top management	Close to location of person whose pay is being set

Source: E. E. Lawler III, "Reward Systems," in *Improving Life at Work*, ed. J. R. Hackman and J. L. Suttle (Santa Monica: Goodyear, 1977). Reprinted by permission.

EXHIBIT 6.3

Reward System Diagnostic Checklist

Where to look

1. Formal arrangements—administration of compensation, promotions, and the like (primarily extrinsic rewards)
2. Work itself—job satisfaction, working conditions, design of jobs, and so forth (primarily intrinsic rewards)
3. Social environment—supervisor-subordinate relationships, peer relationships, and so forth (both extrinsic and intrinsic rewards)

What to look for

A. Concerning the quality of work life, how effectively does the organization maintain the four necessary reward system properties:
    1. To what extent does the system have enough available rewards for employees' basic needs?
    2. How favorably does the system compare with other comparable organizations' reward systems?
    3. To what extent do the employees perceive the reward system to be administered equitably?
    4. To what extent does the system treat employees as individuals?

B. Concerning the impact of the reward system on overall organizational effectiveness:
    1. To what extent does the organization attract and hold people; that is, what is the *rate* of turnover and who turns over?
    2. Do employees enjoy and want to come to work; that is, what is the degree of absenteeism and tardiness?
    3. Do employees perceive that the rewards they receive are directly related to their work performance?
    4. To what extent does the reward system reinforce the organization's authority structure; for example, do employees at higher levels in the managerial hierarchy receive more rewards than those at lower levels?

C. Concerning the work itself, to what extent do jobs provide meaningfulness of work:
    1. Skill variety
    2. Task identity
    3. Task significance

    To what extent do jobs provide

    4. Autonomy for employees, especially in terms of *how* the work is to be done
    5. Feedback for the employees regarding the effectiveness of their work performance?

D. Concerning the social environment, how do employees feel about their relationships with their
    1. Supervisors
    2. Fellow employees

E. How congruent is the reward system with
    1. The authority and decision-making structure
    2. Management's public statements, if any, about how it treats its employees

Note: For more specificity regarding the diagnosis of jobs, see the *Job Diagnostic Survey* developed by Hackman and Oldham (1975) and Hackman (1977, pp. 133–36.)

management approach. He thus takes a contingency position. A normative stance in OD would advocate a reward system congruent with Theory Y assumptions and a participative management approach.

To summarize this section on reward system diagnosis, I have prepared a checklist for the consultant in organization development to consider, if not actually use (see Exhibit 6.3).

Reward System Interventions

Extrinsic Interventions

Part IV will give more extensive coverage of interventions in OD, but coverage of some interventions that relate directly to rewards is appropriate in this chapter.

Some of the examples in the summary shown in Exhibit 6.3 represent potential interventions in an organization's reward system. An intervention may be installment of a new element within the reward system, such as open job posting, or a change in a previous one, such as from an incentive plan based on individual piece rate to one based on group output. Although several alternatives for modification in an organization's reward system are available, as we shall see later in this chapter, change is not easy. Reward systems often are of long standing and represent precedence that is sometimes considered to be sacred. In the case example in Chapter 1, my efforts as a consultant to effect change in such a system were futile. In that situation, the basis of wages for the hourly paid employees—the measured-day-work system— was congruent with the organization's managerial approach—traditional, top-down, and centralized—and perhaps that is why there was such strong resistance to the different system I advocated, which was based more on linking pay to performance. In retrospect, it appears that centralizing decision-making control was a more important value in that organization than increasing performance through incentives.

The case example from Chapter 1 provides us with an opportunity to relate rewards to the concepts of norms, roles, and values in Chapter 5. Not only was centralized decision making a more important value than an incentive system, but expectations regarding workers' roles seem to have been firmly grounded. Job enrichment would have been out of the question, and worker norms for rate of productivity were strongly conformed to. Much like the employees at the Hawthorne Works of Western Electric, the workers in the electrical equipment plant described in Chapter 1 conformed to a rate of production closely aligned to the amount of pay established by the measurements of industrial engineers for an average rate of worker productivity per day. The workers probably agreed, either explicitly or implicitly, to a rate of production that was neither more nor less than the measured-day-

115

work rate. Understanding such norms, roles, and values in an organization helps to determine the potential for change in the reward system.

We shall now consider some of the major potential interventions that can be made in an organization's reward system. We shall begin with the most important element of any organization's reward system—pay.

PAY   In a recent off-site meeting with a company vice-president and his managerial staff, we began the all-day session by providing an opportunity for people to discuss their feelings about the overall organizational change effort we were involved in. We had allocated about ninety minutes for such a discussion. To my surprise, they spent almost twice that time discussing, if not complaining about, the company's system for administering their pay.

Some years before, the company had adopted the Hay plan (Belcher 1974; Berg 1976), a job-evaluation system that analyzes jobs according to the (1) knowledge required, (2) problem-solving requirements, and (3) account-abilities. In the Hay plan, points are assigned to each job according to how much knowledge and problem-solving ability are required and where the job is located in the managerial hierarchy—how much accountability is required. Certain jobs in an organization are selected as anchor positions, and all others are compared with these anchor jobs for point assignments. The Hay plan is very popular in the United States, especially in the East, and is a highly rational system. This system, and any other system, of course, are administered by people, however, who are never completely rational. Different people see jobs differently, and managers frequently argue over points because the more points assigned to a job, the higher the pay. Equity is obviously the key to any system of pay administration, but what may seem equitable to one person may not appear so to another. In the long discussion of pay and the Hay system at the off-site meeting, arguments arose over what was considered to be equitable and fair. We finally were able to move on to broader issues and to the larger purpose of the meeting, but the length and heat of the discussion indicated the degree of importance people attach to the *way* they are compensated.

The Hay plan, like most systems of pay administration, is based on job evaluation—the requirements of a given job. There are alternatives, however. One alternative that has gained some recent popularity is the skill-evaluation plan. With this plan, a person is paid for what he or she is capable of doing rather than what is actually done. Thus, the person is paid for ability rather than for performance and earns more by knowing more jobs rather than by necessarily performing well in one. This type of pay plan encourages people to learn new skills. Companies in the United States that have implemented this type of system—pay based on amount of knowledge and skill—include General Foods and Procter and Gamble. The system has been installed on a plant basis in these companies, not across the whole organization.

116

There are problems with this type of pay arrangement, as Lawler (1977) has noted: people may "top out" fairly quickly if the organization doesn't continue to expand or somehow provide learning opportunities; the plan requires a considerable amount of training; and, finally, the system may be limited to certain types of organizations, such as process production plants, the only places where it has worked successfully so far.

Since there is a limited amount of experience with this type of pay system, it is difficult to generalize about its applicability. Where it has been implemented, however, the advantages that accrue seem to outweigh the disadvantages significantly.

There are at least two other ways of administering pay, both involving a choice. The first choice is whether the company will have an hourly paid work force *and* a salaried one or an all-salaried system, regardless of type of employee. The second choice is whether, when raises in pay are administered, the raises are distributed one pay period at a time over a 6- or 12-month period—the typical procedure—or employees receive the full amount of their annual increase, in a lump sum, at the time of the announced raise.

With respect to the first choice, there is some evidence, albeit scant, that an all-salaried pay system increases quality of work life and organizational effectiveness, but tradition regarding pay dies hard. Not many organizations have experimented with an all-salaried pay system. Most important, the all-salaried scheme "is likely to be effective only if it is part of an overall management strategy and organization design that emphasizes employee participation, meaningful work, and mature treatment of employees" (Lawler 1977, p. 188).

Regarding the second choice—when a raise is administered—with a lump-sum arrangement, organization members typically can choose when to receive their increase. If an employee elects to receive the full amount of the increase as soon as it is effective, a small amount (percentage) is deducted to offset the organization's cost. The money that is advanced is thus treated as a loan. In these days of rapidly increasing inflation, this mode of receiving a raise can be an attractive choice for employees. As mentioned, there is no evidence regarding the effectiveness of this pay arrangement for morale or organizational performance. Employees are generally enthusiastic about this alternative, however. It is also safe to assume that, when employees are provided a choice in decisions that directly affect them, their commitment to the organization is likely to increase.

INCENTIVE SYSTEMS For incentive to work—to increase the quality of work life and organizational effectiveness—pay must be directly related to employees' performance. This may seem to be an obvious conclusion, but such incentive systems as stock options and profit-sharing plans, for example,

117

do not make much difference in organizational effectiveness because they are so broadly administered. It is difficult for employees to see how their individual performances contribute directly to company profits. An important criterion for effective incentive systems, therefore, is that employees are able to see a relationship between the pay they receive and their work performance.

Three other criteria are also key to the effectiveness of any incentive system. First, the more objective the measure of performance is, the better the results will be. When the quality of performance is determined subjectively, there is opportunity for arbitrariness on the part of the decision makers, and mistrust and suspicion can become pervasive, if not destructive. Second, it is best for performance to be group or organizationally based, since individual incentive plans can breed competitiveness, which may be detrimental overall. Finally, the effectiveness of incentive systems is contingent on individual personalities. Lawler (1966) has found that people who have a high need to achieve prefer incentive plans, whereas people who have a high need for security do not.

One form of incentive system is reward schedules based on Skinnerian principles of behavior modification. When this system has been applied in an organizational setting, the results have not been uniform, especially with respect to variable-ratio schedules of reward. Variable-ratio schedules, as opposed to a fixed-ratio or continuous mode of reinforcement, have been shown in the laboratory to produce responses that are the most resistant to extinction. Experiments with variable-ratio schedules have been performed in industry (Yukl and Latham, 1975), but the results have not matched laboratory outcomes. The problem is that studies in industrial settings have not followed Skinnerian principles to the letter. According to those principles, continuous reinforcement is applied at the outset in order to establish the desired response. Once the response has stabilized, the schedule is then gradually shifted from continuous to a variable ratio. One case study that did follow Skinnerian principles closely was the Emery Air Freight experiment (''At Emery'' 1973). Although control groups and other conditions appropriate to a reliable scientific study were not applied, the case report was impressive. For organization development purposes, however, this case presented problems, as mentioned in the last chapter. Employees were placed on specific reward schedules without their knowledge. What is needed for a definitive study is an approach in which (1) Skinnerian principles are closely followed and (2) employees are made aware of and have a choice about participating in a reward system based on these principles. Some might argue that these two conditions are incompatible for any kind of effective outcome, but until such an approach is attempted, the question remains unanswered.

Another incentive system is the Scanlon plan. This system was first attempted in the 1930s, worked successfully then, but for some reason was not

118

used very widely for a number of decades. In recent years, however, the plan has become more popular than ever before (Driscoll 1979).

Three primary elements compose a Scanlon plan. The first element is financial incentive tied to unit or total organizational productivity—typically, a monthly bonus paid to everyone regardless of level in the organization. Second is a committee system of workers and management; elected representatives from among the workers meet with management, usually monthly, to diagnose production problems and to suggest corrective action. Although the committee composition is representative of workers rather than involving participation by most or all workers, this second element is not unlike the quality control circles (see Chapter 13) developed in Japan in the 1950s (Gregerman 1979). The third element of the Scanlon plan is participative management; the belief or philosophy is (1) that workers are capable of self-directed efforts toward organizational goals and (2) that they should be given more opportunity for taking responsibility and utilizing their competencies. It should be apparent that this philosophy relates directly to McGregor's Theory Y assumptions about human behavior in organizations.

Strengths of the plan include but are not limited to the following:

A bonus system is based on group or overall organizational performance; thus, teamwork and coordination are reinforced.

If the involved organization is unionized, the union is typically strengthened rather than threatened.

The organization becomes more adaptable to change, since employees are rewarded for helping the organization to remain or become more competitive in the marketplace.

Employees gain a better sense of and commitment to the organization's objectives.

Problems with the Scanlon plan seem to relate to how the plan is implemented rather than to its substance. For more information on the details of the plan and its results in a variety of settings, see Lesieur (1958), Lesieur and Puckett (1969), and Moore and Goodman (1973).

PROMOTION   Although not everyone in an organization desires to move up in the ranks, most employees do. Consequently, the offer of a promotion can be a powerful reward for many. Succession planning, as it is sometimes called, is usually performed by the people responsible for the management development function in an organization, but the *decisions* regarding promotion are often made in secret and by only a few top managers. An alternative to this typical procedure is open job posting, which is utilized for lower and middle-level positions in an organization but not usually for top management positions. When a position is available, a description is posted on a prominent bulletin board or announced in an internal organizational publication or memo, and people who believe that they can meet the requirements of the job are eligible to apply. Although there are some problems with open job posting—extra administrative work, more time required, and telling those who do not get the job why they did not—the advantages seem to carry more weight. These advantages include a potential for better promotion decisions, a potential for increased employee motivation, and the creation of a more open system of communication.

FRINGE BENEFITS   The usual format for fringe benefits is either an identical package for all employees or one for hourly workers, another for salaried employees, and a third for top managers. A recent alternative to these typical formats is the so-called cafeteria-style fringe benefit compensation plan. The plan is based on the simple fact that different employees have different needs, which is especially true for different age groups. Older employees desire more retirement benefits, while younger workers may want more vacation time. With the cafeteria-style plan, employees are told what is available within the total fringe benefit package of, for example, ten elements, and they can choose any six. Another alternative is to give employees a total pay package for fringe benefits; they can then choose to spend the money in any way they may desire. No research studies have yet determined the effectiveness of cafeteria-style plans, but two United States organizations have implemented such plans—TRW, Inc., and the Educational Testing Service. TRW's plan has been in effect since 1974, and it is considered very workable and satisfactory.

SUMMARY   The interventions considered thus far have been primarily extrinsic rewards. The *type* of change in an organization's reward system may not be as important as the *way* the change is implemented—the process—and, of course, organization development is "working the process." According to Lawler (1977), three factors are critical in the process of administering a reward system. First, *openness* seems to be more effective than secrecy (Lawler 1972). Open job posting, for example, avoids secrecy regarding job placement and promotion. Second, *participation* of employees in decisions regarding their rewards, especially the design and administration of pay and other reward systems, can lead to greater productivity (Cammann and Lawler 1973). Third, when employees are provided with *choice*, motivation appears to be affected positively.

Managers hope that the rewards they provide will lead to high performance, and they tend to rely more heavily on extrinsic rewards, or perhaps they understand them more easily. According to Nadler, Hackman, and

120

Lawler (1979), there are six necessary conditions in which extrinsic rewards motivate performance:

1. Important rewards can be given.
2. Rewards can be varied depending on performance.
3. Performance can be validly and objectively measured.
4. Information can be made public about how rewards are given.
5. Trust within the organization is high.
6. Superiors are willing to explain and support the reward system in discussions with their subordinates.

Intrinsic Interventions

Interventions that concern one's career in general are likely to be intrinsic. Career development itself, to be discussed in Chapter 12, may be a major intervention in organization development. We shall now consider work redesign, a primary type of intervention that may provide intrinsic reward. The fundamental objective of a work redesign intervention is to change the basic relationship between people and their jobs so that (1) the dysfunctional effects of repetitive work may be minimized; (2) individual differences may be taken into account; (3) a proper fit may occur between job requirements and individual talent; (4) individual needs for growth and development may be met; and (5) individual needs for meaningful social relationships may be met.

Hackman and Oldham's (1975) job characteristics model is designed for planning and redesigning jobs so that these five objectives may be achieved. It is based on the three psychological states mentioned earlier and the job dimensions that provide meaningfulness, autonomy, and feedback. In summary, "internal rewards are obtained by an individual when he *learns* (knowledge of results) that he *personally* (experienced responsibility) has performed well on a task that he *cares* about (experienced meaningfulness)" (Hackman 1977, p. 129).

Hackman (1977) has shown how his and Oldham's job characteristics model ties directly to an earlier but still prevalent form of work redesign—job enrichment. According to several sources (Hackman et al. 1975; Walters and Associates 1975), there are five primary principles for enriching jobs:

1. *Forming natural work units:* Without unduly sacrificing efficiency, workers are assigned tasks that are clearly identifiable and represent a whole element of work rather than having one person work on one piece of the whole, a second on another piece, and so forth.
2. *Combining tasks:* The more tasks that can be combined into one worker's

121

job, the more skill is required and, at least potentially, the more meaningful the work becomes.

3. *Vertical loading:* One of the most common complaints of workers, including managers, is that they do not have sufficient authority to exercise the responsibilities of their job effectively. Vertical loading means giving employees more control over the way they conduct their work, thereby contributing to increased autonomy on the job.

4. *Establishing client relationships:* Workers are provided greater opportunities for contact with the ultimate users of their product or service. As Hackman (1977) points out, these increased contacts provide more feedback for the workers, greater variety of skill and greater significance of tasks, and autonomy.

5. *Opening feedback channels:* More sources are provided for workers to learn about the consequences of their work performance.

It is obvious that these five principles are not mutually exclusive—for example, following principle 4 will help in accomplishing principle 5—nor are they exhaustive, but they are highly representative of others' concepts of job enrichment (Herzberg 1974) and fundamental to the redesign of jobs in order to increase meaningfulness of work and to provide more feedback and autonomy. Job enrichment should be distinguished from job enlargement, which involves horizontal loading only; that is, responsibility is increased, thus giving workers more jobs to do, but authority is not.

Intrinsic rewards are encompassed mostly within the work itself. The social environment—whether people like and respect their fellow workers, their supervisors, and higher level managers—also contributes to intrinsic satisfaction, but the more we attempt to identify intrinsic rewards, the more individualized the list becomes. We can summarize by listing some further principles. Work is likely to be intrinsically rewarding for people when (1) they have opportunities to achieve and to utilize their talents significantly; (2) they have opportunities to develop themselves personally, technically, or professionally; (3) they are recognized for effective work in general and high performance in particular; (4) they have autonomy on their jobs and a reasonable amount of freedom to fail; and (5) they are provided with work that is meaningful and worthwhile.

Finally, whether the social environment of the work place represents potential for more intrinsic rewards than extrinsic ones, or the reverse, is really not important. What is important is to recognize the potential for at least two kinds of interventions. One intervention is obvious—providing employees with as much choice as possible regarding who their fellow workers will be. Such action is not usually feasible on a widespread basis but, within certain naturally existing work units (Van Zelst 1952), some degree of previously ignored choice may indeed be possible.

EXHIBIT 6.4

Interventions in Organizational Reward Systems

Reward category	Traditional form	Potential intervention
Pay:		
Base rate	Based on job evaluation	Based on skill and knowledge attained
Type of system	Hourly and salaried; increases spread over time	All salaried; lump sum payment
Incentive systems	Piece rate individualized	Piece rate based on group or organization performance; reward schedules; Scanlon plan
Promotion	Secretive and centrally controlled	Open job posting
Fringe benefits	Same for all, or three different forms—hourly, salaried, and top management	Cafeteria-style
Work itself	Close supervision; repetitive; divided tasks	Work redesign; job enrichment; career development
Social environment	Work mates determined by management; feedback to managers from subordinates not allowed or practiced	Employees have choice regarding fellow workers; feedback from subordinates to managers routinely provided

Another potential intervention in the social environment, directly concerning supervisor-subordinate relationships, is systematic feedback to supervisors and managers from their subordinates, rather than relying on the standard approach—worker performance appraisal. Very few organizations use a feedback process, usually through a periodic survey or a management training program. The potential benefit of such a process, however, is that, as supervisors and managers receive feedback, they can take steps to improve their relations with their subordinates and consequently to improve the quality of work life and the overall social environment.

As a summary of our discussion of reward system interventions, Exhibit 6.4 compares the traditional forms of reward systems with potential changes in these forms.

Other Reward Processes

Two additional processes of reward in an organization are both worthy of attention and relevant to organization development: performance appraisal and self-fulfilling prophecy.

123

Performance Appraisal

Most large organizations have some system of performance appraisal. These systems are often criticized by employees, for none are perfect. According to a recent study conducted in almost 300 companies by The Conference Board (Lazer and Wikstrom 1977) there are four major characteristics of an effective performance appraisal system:

1. *Reliability and validity:* For reliability to exist, two or more evaluations should rate a single employee's work performance essentially the same. Reliability therefore is a function of *objectivity* of performance measurement, already mentioned as a critical factor for an effective reward system. A system may be reliable but not valid, however. For validity to exist, the appraisals must be useful for making judgments about employees' potential in the jobs currently held, not other jobs.

2. *Job-relatedness:* The appraisal must measure criteria that are relevant and important to a given job.

3. *Standardization:* The form and administration of the appraisal system should be the same across a variety of jobs. Appraisal information is often used to make comparisons among employees across several units. If the form and administration are not standard, these comparisons will possess no validity.

4. *Practicality:* The system should not be difficult to administer, and it should serve the organization's objectives of establishment and maintenance of a fair and equitable reward system, effective human resource planning, and career development.

More specifically, the Conference Board study noted eight general categories of objectives for most organizations' performance appraisal systems:

1. Management development
2. Performance measurement
3. Performance improvement
4. Compensation
5. Identification of potential
6. Feedback
7. Manpower planning
8. Communications

The problem with most performance appraisal systems is usually the process of administration. Most managers find the process very difficult and discomforting, as for example, when too many of the objectives are attempted in a once-a-year one-hour session. Under such circumstances, employees are

124

usually more interested in the compensation objective and significantly less interested in the others—if at all. A list of problems could extend for several pages, as anyone familiar with large organizations can confirm, but, for purposes of organization development, the following are pertinent.

OD practitioners have considerable opportunity for effective consultation in trying to improve performance appraisal systems. The performance appraisal system is critical to OD, because a considerable portion of an organization's reward system is implemented within this single process. OD practitioners can help (1) by training managers in the effective conduct of sessions with subordinates—how to listen, ask questions, and provide feedback; (2) by working with management to design or redesign the system; and (3) by providing information, based on research and sound theory, that will suggest possible alternatives to present systems, such as using multiple raters for appraising an employee's work performance, which is likely to be more valid than a single rater, even if the rater is the employee's boss.

Self-fulfilling Prophecy

It is difficult to state just how the self-fulfilling prophecy works, but there is little question that the phenomenon exists (Rosenthal 1976). Rosenthal has defined the concept, originally developed by Robert Merton (1948), as follows: "One prophesies an event, and the expectation of the event then changes the behavior of the prophet in such a way as to make the prophesied event more likely" (Rosenthal 1976, p. 129). From a reward standpoint, if a manager believes positively about a person, he or she is likely to behave in such a way as to elicit confirming behavior from that person. A manager thus may be able to motivate a subordinate merely by believing that he or she is capable of high performance and then recognizing (rewarding) any performance in that direction. Consequently, higher performance by the subordinate is even more likely in the future. The so-called halo effect is a related concept, but the self-fulfilling prophecy is based as much on the prophet's behavior as on the belief.

Although the self-fulfilling prophecy obviously is not part of an organization's formal reward system, it is potentially the most powerful aspect of the system, whether it is a formal or an informal one. Since it is difficult to determine precisely how the concept works, it is not possible to teach managers a step-by-step process for fulfilling their prophesies for motivational and reward purposes. It is a function for the OD consultant, however, to help managers become more aware of the behavioral phenomenon and of how their behavior may influence and reward subordinates. Performance appraisals are affected by the rater's prophecy, and managers must be aware that the process is usually unconscious. The OD consultant can thus help to bring this behavioral process to the manager's attention.

Summary

I contended early in this chapter that most consultant-practitioners in organization development have neglected reward systems. This neglect has occurred, perhaps, because rewards are so basic and fundamental, or because motivation has received most of the attention. Since rewards *are* so fundamental and since it is far more productive to concentrate on the reward side of the motivational equation—rewards responding to needs—than to attempt to diagnose individual needs, it is important to emphasize reward systems in OD diagnosis and intervention.

For organizational diagnosis of reward systems, it is useful to look at (1) formal arrangements, such as pay and fringe benefits; (2) the work itself; and (3) the social environment. Within these sources of rewards in organizations, the consultant should also conduct a diagnosis of both extrinsic and intrinsic rewards. Both types of rewards contribute to motivation, but extrinsic rewards must be carefully administered for a linkage to exist. For pay to lead or contribute to higher performance, for example, employees must perceive a direct relationship between their work performance and the pay they receive.

The work itself is the domain in which most intrinsic rewards potentially operate. Meaningful work, feedback regarding performance, and autonomy on the job contribute most to high levels of satisfaction.

Within the social environment, how employees feel about their fellow workers affects motivation in general and job satisfaction in particular. How employees feel about the kind of supervision they receive also contributes to motivation and job satisfaction.

Finally, an organization's performance appraisal system may be the most critical vehicle for reward system administration. It is therefore important for OD consultants to become involved in this area of administration and management.

126

CHAPTER 7

Power, Leadership, and Management

We have already considered three of the four primary social-psychological concepts for diagnosing an organization: norms, values, and rewards. The fourth concept is power. The reason for including power is both significant and straightforward. Organization development signifies change, and, *for change to occur in an organization, power must be exercised.* For purposes of OD, therefore, the consultant must understand the nature of power, from both a personal and an organizational perspective, and be able to determine, within an organization, who has power, how power is exercised, and where the leverages for change (exercising power) are likely to be.

Our initial concern in this chapter will be with power itself—individual need for power and the consequences of this need on leadership and management, sources of power for an individual in a social context, and organizational sources of power. We shall then consider leadership and management, which are defined as the exercise of power, and finally we shall address the implications of what we know about power, leadership, and management for organization development.

This chapter ultimately makes three major points:

1. Since organizational change involves the exercise of power, it is imperative that the OD consultant recognize the importance of this concept and learn how power is manifested in individual and organizational behavior. In the early days of OD practice, issues of power were generally considered a necessary evil, to be avoided if possible. More recently, however, OD consultants have begun to deal more realistically with power in organizations. In this chapter, therefore, my desire is to expedite this more recent trend by attempting to add to and clarify our base of knowledge and its applicability.

2. From the standpoint of what may be applicable for the effective management of organizations, consideration of the research literature on leadership, especially some recent findings, and of evidence and observations

127

from related areas has significant implications for authoritative interventions within organization development.

3. Based on further and more recent knowledge and understanding of power, leadership, and management I shall bolster the argument given in Chapter 5—that organization development should be normative rather than contingent in terms of certain change objectives.

I have emphasized the point that power must be exercised for organizational change to occur. An actual case will help to illustrate this point.

Case Example

Ron had been the new regional manager for only a month when he asked me to help him with an off-site meeting he planned to have with his staff. Ron was head of one of five regions of a nationwide financial institution. His region had been losing money for the past four years, and his mandate was "to turn the region around" and make it profitable again. As a vice-president of the corporation, Ron was responsible for a regional business with millions of dollars in revenues and a total employee population of 1,000. The managers who reported to Ron had responsibilities typical of such a business—marketing, operations, finance and accounting, credit, consumer sales, human resources, and planning.

Ron wanted to have a two-day off-site meeting to get his staff to agree to profit goals for the next two years and to establish a more clear-cut strategy for his region. He wanted to accomplish this, by involving his staff in the decision-making process. This approach was a change for his staff. The former regional manager was not autocratic, but neither did he believe in participative management. He managed one-on-one with his staff, rather than in a group setting. Ron was more charismatic, however, was more oriented toward a participative approach, and was less tolerant of the status quo.

Although some of the staff believed that the off-site meeting was somewhat premature, they all thought that the idea of the meeting was a good one. At the meeting, everyone participated actively, short- and longer-range profit goals were determined, and the beginnings of a regional strategy were initiated. Ron was pleased with the meeting and its outcomes. Later, some organizational changes were made in the managerial structure, the new strategy began to be implemented, and the region gradually turned around.

Ron had exercised power to change his region's profits from a loss to a gain. He achieved the change by presenting a model of leadership that demonstrated high commitment and energy and that involved his staff in policy making. Ron's leadership was strong but not authoritarian; he exerted influence but could also be influenced. He exercised his power for change in four primary ways: (1) by holding the off-site meeting early and establishing a clear thrust to his managerial tenure; (2) by insisting on establishment of short- and long-range profit goals; (3) by insisting that the region have a clear-cut business strategy; and (4) by involving his staff in the key decisions so that they were highly committed to implementation. Ron's power was thus exercised through the position he held and by his particular approach to leadership, which was charismatic, energetic, and participative.

Although this case is brief and only touches on some of our concerns, let us keep it in mind as a context for reality and concreteness as we proceed to an examination of the concepts that are the focus for this chapter.

Power

Most people who have thought about it tend to agree that power means the ability or capacity to influence others (Votaw 1966). This definition of power allows an easy comparison and integration with the concept of leadership. Power is the *capacity* to influence, and leadership is the *process* or act of influencing.

Until recently, Machiavelli seemed to be the authority on power. To paraphrase one of his truly brilliant insights, for example: The more one acts on one's power the more one is apt to lose it. Recent work by others has added significantly to our understanding of power, however, and this newer understanding has been predominantly, though not exclusively, in the personal rather than the political domain.

Power and Motivation

David McClelland, the Harvard psychologist noted for his work on need for achievement, has devoted much of his research in the last decade to a better understanding of a person's need for power (McClelland 1975). Relating his work theoretically to Freud and Erikson's theories of ego development, McClelland has postulated, with supportive research data, that there are four distinct stages in the development of a person's orientation to power.

STAGE I: INCORPORATION OF POWER FROM OTHERS Stage I, which is experienced even in infancy, involves incorporating power from another person—from a source of power outside oneself. Early in life this feeling of strength comes from parents; later in life it may come from friends, from a spouse, or from an admired leader or mentor. Thus, by experiencing or sharing the power of a stronger person, the individual self feels powerful.

STAGE II: INDEPENDENT POWERFULNESS Stage II is independence of the self. As McClelland (1975) puts it, "I can strengthen myself" (p. 15). As the person learns self-control, a degree of powerful feeling usually occurs. McClelland's research shows that a major expression of this stage later in life is

129

possession of objects that one experiences as part of the self. These possessions are usually power-related, such as a powerful or high-status automobile, guns, and even credit cards. The possession of powerful things, as an extension of self, facilitates the feeling of power.

STAGE III: POWER AS AN IMPACT ON OTHERS   The primary form of behavior in this stage is competitive behavior that is intended to win. Another less readily apparent form is helping behavior, for "in accepting . . . help, the receiver can be perceived as acknowledging that he is weaker, at least in this respect, than the person who is giving him help" (McClelland 1975, p. 18). Research by McClelland and by Winter (1973) shows that a significant number of teachers behave predominantly according to this Stage III helping orientation. It is likely, also, that many therapists and consultants operate extensively at this stage of power-orientation development.

STAGE IV: DERIVING POWER FROM A HIGHER AUTHORITY   The final stage is deriving power from a higher authority and doing one's duty accordingly. McClelland has found that many people satisfy their power motivation by "joining organizations in which they subordinate personal goals to a higher authority" (McClelland 1975, p. 20). At this stage the need for power, though not exclusively altruistic, is largely socialized and institutionalized, rather than personal. At Stages II and III, the motivation for power is primarily for purposes of self-aggrandizement. In Stage IV, power is sought more for the good of the organized effort.

Each stage has an implied relationship to maturity, and pathological behavior may be manifested at any of the stages: in Stage I, if the person feels totally controlled by outside forces; in Stage II, if the person is compulsive about trying to control everything; in Stage III, if the person tries to control others regardless of values or ethics; and in Stage IV, if the person has a martyrdom or messianic delusion.

Characteristics of Successful Managers

In other work, McClelland relates his theory and research more directly to management (McClelland and Burnham 1976). He documents empirically what most of us have suspected all along, that more successful managers have a stronger need for power than less successful managers do.

A popular misconception is that a good manager has a high need to achieve. Having a high need to achieve means that one wants to do things oneself. Self-accomplishment is paramount, and the ability to do something better than others can or better than one did it before is the most gratifying. In contrast, effective management means that a person's needs are satisfied by seeing *others* achieve. The greatest satisfaction comes from influencing others to achieve, not from achieving the tasks oneself.

Entrepreneurs typically have a high need to accomplish, but when this high need for achievement is coupled with a low need for power, delegation comes slowly, if at all—a situation that causes many of the problems in a growing family business. Conversely, managers with a high need for power and a low need for accomplishment may spend their time politicking and plotting rather than achieving.

Using subordinates' ratings of their organizations' degree of clarity and amount of team spirit as indices of successful management, McClelland and Burnham found that, if a manager was high in power motivation, low in need for affiliation, and high in inhibition (that is, the power need was socialized, mature, and not expressed for self-aggrandizement), the organization's degree of clarity was greater (subordinates knew the goals and what was expected of them) and the team spirit was higher.

There are good reasons for this outcome. Managers who have a high need for affiliation usually want to be liked and to be popular. As a result, their decision making tends to be impulsive, being done to please someone at the moment rather than in rational support of the overall good of the organization. Managers with a high need for power that is *personally* oriented (typically Stage III of power orientation and Stage II of career development) are not builders of the institution, according to McClelland and Burnham. They tend to demand personal loyalty from their subordinates—loyalty to them as individuals rather than to the organization. The institutional managers (high need for power at Stage IV) are the most successful because they encourage loyalty to the institution rather than to themselves. As a result, the successful Stage IV manager creates a climate with clarity, team spirit, and opportunities for accomplishment.

The profile of the desirable institutional manager thus has three major elements: high need for power, low need for affiliation; and high inhibition. In addition, successful institutional managers like and are oriented toward organizations. They typically join more organizations and feel greater responsibility for developing them. They enjoy work, like the discipline of work, and have a preference for getting things done in an orderly fashion. They place the good of the organization above self-interest. They are judicious; that is, they have a strong sense of fairness. They are generally more mature—less ego-centered and less defensive. They are also more willing to seek advice from experts, and they have longer and broader vision regarding the future.

Finally, McClelland and Burnham (1976) point out that successful managers tend to have a style of management characterized by participative and coaching behavior; that is, they are concerned with the needs and development of their subordinates. This corroborates the research of J. Hall

(1976) and others, which will be covered later in this chapter. In summary, according to McClelland and Burnham (1976):

> The general conclusion of these studies is that the top manager of a company must possess a high need for power, that is, a concern for influencing people. However, this need must be disciplined and controlled so that it is directed toward the benefit of the institution as a whole and not toward the manager's personal aggrandizement. Moreover, the top manager's need for power ought to be greater than his need for being liked by people. (p. 101)

Power in Interpersonal Relationships

Social psychologists who theorize and conduct research tend to define power in fairly restrictive terms. J. R. P. French and Raven (1959), the most influential theorists in this group, define power in terms of behavioral acts. When person A causes person B to do something B would not have done ordinarily, power has been exercised by A. Although their definition of power may be restrictive, French and Raven have been remarkably instructive in their identification of the primary *sources* of power, at least within the context of interpersonal and person-to-group relationships. According to them, a person with power is one who holds resources that others desire. The relationship is therefore a matter of reciprocity. French and Raven cite five primary sources or bases of power:

1. *Reward power*—having rewards others want and will *do* something to obtain;
2. *Coercive power*—having resources that can be used to punish and that others will *do* something to avoid;
3. *Expert power*—having information or knowledge that others wish for themselves or wish to benefit from and that they will *do* something to acquire or benefit from;
4. *Legitimate power*—having authority associated with a position or role that others accept as the person's right by the very (legitimate) act of holding such a position or role; because of values they deem important, others will *do* something in obedience to this acknowledged power; and
5. *Referent power*—having power because of personal attraction, commonly termed *charisma*. The person has power because others not only admire him or her but wish to be like and to be identified with that person. Power is exercised as a result of the others' wish to please the powerholder, to use Kipnis's (1976) term.

To be the chief executive officer of an organization and simultaneously to be viewed as an expert *and* as charismatic is to be *very* powerful indeed. This combination, though very attractive to those with high power motivation, is rare. People may have two, three, or perhaps even four of these power bases but rarely all five. Moreover, the fifth power base, referent power, has a wider range than the other bases; that is, it typically draws more compliance from others than if the powerholder were operating predominantly from a legitimate base, for example. As a further explanation of these five sources of power, each of them can be considered in terms of whether the powerholder is liked by the recipients of his or her power and whether private compliance is likely to occur. With respect to compliance, we can easily see that any base of power can induce public compliance; if a person desires the reward the powerholder can provide, the person will comply with what the powerholder wants. It is not so obvious, however, whether the person will comply privately—whether he or she will internalize the desire to do what the powerholder wants without constant monitoring and rewarding. Exhibit 7.1 summarizes the relationship of these dimensions to the five bases. As can be seen from this summary, referent power has the strongest base of the five, because it is more psychological and emotional.

In concluding this section, I should stress that the exercise of power involves a reciprocal relationship. One holds power when he or she controls resources that others desire, and a powerholder can exercise power only to the degree that the receiving person allows it. It is difficult to provide examples of absolute power—perhaps a judge who can decree the death penalty for someone who does not wish to die—but so long as the recipient has *choice,* power is reciprocal and limited.

Power and Organizational Change

We shall now consider briefly the relationship between the reciprocal notions of power implementation, or leadership, and changing an organization, particularly that organization's culture.

EXHIBIT 7.1

Personal Attractiveness of Powerholder and Private Compliance of Power Recipient as a Function of Power Base

Base of Power	Personal Attractiveness of Powerholder for Others	Private Compliance
Reward	May be liked by others, but not necessarily	No (perhaps yes in the long run)
Coercive	Will be disliked by others	No
Legitimate	Will typically be treated with indifference by others	Tends to be yes
Expert	Will typically be treated with indifference by others	Tends to be yes
Referent	Will be liked very much by others	Definite yes

Among the elements of an organization's culture are the roles and positions people occupy, the norms to which organization members conform, and the values held by these members as well as by the organization as a whole. In most organizations the primary source or base of power for managers is a legitimate one. Their position and role is legitimized by organizational rules (norms), policy, custom, and the authority vested therein. Thus, managers' power is only as extensive as the degree to which organization members conform to the norms and values associated with the positions and roles held by the managers.

Changing an organization is thus a reciprocal process, and change does not occur without the exercise of power. An organization's culture can be described in terms of a unique pattern of norms and values that have evolved and developed over time. Research shows that leaders conform more to group and organizational norms than other members do and that, ironically, they are in the best position to change them. The more limited managers' power base is, the more they must rely on participative methods for bringing about change, despite the principle that the more people are involved in making decisions that directly affect them, the more they will be committed to implementing the decisions.

How does this bear on organizational change efforts? First, most managers' bases of power are limited in both number and scope. Second, most managers' primary source of power is their position and role and is thus dependent on organization members' internalized values concerning legitimacy and their degree of conformity to what is deemed proper. Third, if D. T. Hall's (1976) appraisal of value shifts among the work force—from "what's good for the organization" to "what's good for me"—is correct, management approaches will have to change accordingly. Fourth, the changing nature of the work force, including management, to incorporate more women and minorities will require different management styles from those in the past. Finally, if Lodge's (1974) data-based prediction is accurate—that we are moving toward a communitarian society and gradually leaving behind the so-called rugged-individual values—then organizational behavior will change as employees demand a more sharing and less autocratic attitude from managers. This leads to two important points:

1. More than one model of leadership and management should be represented among top management. With diversity among the work force, multiple models, especially within the mentoring process, will help to provide the critical integration needed for any organized effort.

2. A participative approach to management, coupled with a decentralized structure, will facilitate a broader sharing of power, with more people feeling empowered by the organization.

These points help set the stage for a discussion of power that is inherent within the structure and culture of an organization.

Returning to the case described earlier in this chapter; we see that Ron, the regional manager, had a fairly strong base of power. In French and Raven's terms, he had reward power in that he could raise salaries, could determine the amount of bonus for his staff, and could promote individuals into higher positions. He also had coercive power by having the authority to decrease salaries, to eliminate bonuses, and to demote or fire individuals. Although his expertise was limited, he did have some expert power, since he had been promoted to his position from within the marketing ranks of the division. He was seen as very knowledgeable regarding marketing, sales, and consumer services. His legitimate power was based on the position he held as regional manager. This power stemmed from the organizational authority associated with the position and therefore overlapped with two other sources, reward and coercive power, but his position also afforded him another source—information. By virtue of his position, he was privy to certain inside information, which came from his peers in other regions and from his boss, who in turn had access to information from higher up in the organization. With respect to referent power, the situation for Ron was mixed. He was attractive in that he exuded considerable energy, was far more enthusiastic and optimistic than pessimistic, and demonstrated a strong American value—the "can-do" philosophy. He frequently made such statements as, "It's really very simple; we can easily do it." This high energy and can-do approach were mistrusted by some of his staff, however. They were afraid of being overwhelmed and of making mistakes because of hasty decision making. For some, then, Ron had referent power; for others he did not.

Ron's position as a source of information who was well connected within the overall corporation added to his base of power. As we shall see in the next section, being connected in the right places is a source of power that French and Raven merely allude to.

Organizational Sources of Power

Rosabeth Kanter (1977) has argued that the French and Raven typology, though important and explanatory, does not fully exemplify all sources of power in an organization. She takes a broader sociological view and delineates sources of power that are specifically organizational, not interpersonal. According to Kanter, "The accumulation of power in a corporation is closely tied to the overall state of the system" (p. 174). She identifies two main social system routes to power in an organization: *activities* and *alliances*.

ACTIVITIES Three types of activities are key: *extraordinary* activities—being the first in a new position or endeavor, making certain organizational changes, or taking significant risks and succeeding; *visible* activities—the importance of being visible, attracting attention to what you are doing or are about to do; and *relevant*—activities relating if not specifically addressing activities to pressing organizational problems.'

These activities may empower an individual in an organization in that the first two types provide opportunities for one to have impact, and the third type assures access to key information and to important connections, which Kanter calls alliances.

ALLIANCES Alliances provide power through or from others. The most important alliance is with sponsors. The sponsor role is very close to if not the same as that of mentor. Kantor's point is that having an important sponsor higher in the organization provides power in the form of someone (1) to fight for you, (2) to help you bypass the hierarchy at critical times, and (3) to show that you are important—what Kanter labels "reflected power." A second type of alliance is with peers, as peer acceptance is necessary to any organizational base of power; and a third type of alliance is with subordinates. Unless a manager develops subordinates, he or she will not have a solid base from which to operate and from which to move on, leaving people who are clearly able to take over when an opportunity comes for the manager to assume a higher position.

Kanter's coverage of the concept of powerlessness is instructive for two reasons. She helps to further our understanding of power itself, and she explains clearly and objectively the problems of integrating women and minorities into the ranks of management. To be powerless in an organization is to have responsibility without system power. According to Kanter (1977):

> People held accountable for the results produced by others, whose formal role gives them the right to command but who lack informal political influence, access to resources, outside status, sponsorship, or mobility prospects, are rendered powerless in the organization. . . . they lack control over their own fate and are dependent on others above them. (p. 186)

Examples include first-line supervisors, holders of certain staff positions, and frequently women and minorities. The emphasis here must be on behavioral responses to powerlessness and their consequences for the organization. When people feel powerless, the natural response is an attempt to rid themselves of the emotion, because powerlessness doesn't feel good. To protect and defend themselves, powerless people often will attempt, ironically, to control others. This response often manifests itself in bossy and critical behavior. In citing a study by Hetzler (1955), Kanter points out that organization members who are low in status and advancement potential preferred leadership that was highly directive, rigid, and authoritarian. Moreover, she states:

136

> If managers or supervisors who encounter resistance from those they are try-
> ing to direct tend to become more coercive in their power tactics, it is a vicious
> cycle: Powerless authority figures who use coercive tactics provoke resistance
> and aggression, which prompts them to become even more coercive, control-
> ling, and behaviorally restrictive. (Kanter 1977, p. 190)

Further manifestations of powerlessness include (1) rule-mindedness—
as controlling rules may represent one of the few avenues for exercising
power; and (2) territoriality, sometimes referred to as "turfmanship"—as
protecting one's domain can provide a sense of exercising power.

The consequences of powerlessness obviously do not afford the kind of efficiency and effective management that is desirable for an organization. Rollo
May (1972) takes the consequences of powerlessness even further. He contends that powerlessness corrupts, that extreme powerlessness frequently
leads to madness and violence.

The solution to problems involving powerlessness is to create conditions
whereby people can be empowered. This means providing people with more
opportunity for exercising authority on their own or in groups, especially
those people who are held accountable for results produced by others and who
have little or no access to resources.

Power and Organization Diagnosis

Now that we have a better understanding of power and its place in the life of
an organization, we turn to a discussion of how an OD practitioner may use
this knowledge. As noted earlier, in diagnosing an organization, certain
social-psychological concepts guide my understanding as a consultant:
norms, roles, values, rewards, and power. To understand power in an
organization, I must learn *who* the primary decision makers are, *where* they
are located in the managerial hierarchy, and *how* their decisions typically are
made. It is also helpful for me to understand the sources of power a client
manager appears to have. Are his or her sources limited to the usual
three—legitimate (position and role), reward, and coercive—or does the
manager also possess a high degree of relevant expertise? What about referent
power? Do the manager's subordinates seem to be loyal, to admire and
respect their boss, and to feel pleased to be associated with him or her?

Considering the organization in systemic terms, what proportion of the
work force, including management, appears to be out of the mainstream, to
feel alienated, or to have authority by virtue of their position but not be informally or politically linked to the power centers of the organization? The
greater the proportion of the work force that falls into these categories, the
more likely it is that feelings of powerlessness will pervade the organization.
As a consequence, organizational morale will be lower than normal or

137

necessary, and the efficiency and overall productivity of the work force is likely to fall short of potential.

Can a particular leadership or management style be identified within the organization? Useful frames of reference for such identification can be found in the work of Blake and Mouton (1978) and Likert (1967). If a predominant style can be identified, what are the consequences of that style? Is there a connection between style and the extent to which organization members may feel powerless?

The point is that power is the paramount energy source for running the human side of the organization. How this energy source is used behaviorally will determine not only the nature of a prime facet of the organization's culture but how effectively the organization is likely to be managed.

As a manager exercises power to achieve change in an organization, so must the OD consultant exercise power if the client is to be influenced. The primary source of power for the consultant is expertise. How the consultant uses this source may lead to either a positive or a negative influence. The nature of this use is partly a function of the OD consultant's personal need for power. In Chapter 17, I give examples of how my own above-average need for power created problems for me as a consultant. For now we shall proceed with a relatively impersonal coverage of how such consultant need relates to a client.

Power and the OD Consultant

It is reasonable to assume that most managers, especially those in the middle to upper ranks, have an above-average need for power. Schutz (1967) has found that Harvard Business School students tend to score higher than average on a measure of "desire to influence or control others." McClelland and Burnham's (1976) findings also support this assumption. Consultants undoubtedly have a stronger than average need to influence as well; even the desire to help can be considered a desire to influence. In a longitudinal career study, McClelland (1965) found that teachers and business managers scored significantly higher than average in need for power, and that psychologists and clergymen, though not scoring as high, nevertheless scored higher than average. Managers and those who like to help others are therefore likely to be above average in their need for power.

In the consulting relationship, therefore, we have the potential for competitive needs to influence on the part of the consultant and the client manager. The *sources* of power are different, however. For the consultant, the primary source is expertise. The client has at least three sources: reward, coercive, and legitimate. Thus, their modes of reciprocal influence are likely to differ. It is possible, of course, for the client or the consultant to have referent power, but the consultant must rely primarily on his or her expertise.

This expertise is based on (1) knowledge from the behavioral sciences and organizational theory, (2) the ability to know how and when to apply such knowledge, and (3) interpersonal competence. With such expertise, the OD consultant must be sensitive to the power needs of the client manager and, accordingly, must look for ways to help that client share power and delegate authority where appropriate, while convincing him or her that power in an organization is not a zero-sum game—that sharing power is not necessarily losing it. The form of power may change, but an overall loss will not necessarily occur. It is possible, for example, to manage a team of subordinates participatively (sharing power at that level) and at the same time enhance one's power base as a manager in the overall organization. Having a cohesive team with team spirit, which often results from a participative approach to leadership, provides a stronger base of power for the team leaders in the larger organization than having splintered and disgruntled subordinate team members.

In addition to being sensitive to the client's need for power and to one's own need to influence, the consultant must also be prepared to take a position regarding how power is exercised in the organization. McClelland and Burnham's (1976) results and Kanter's (1977) findings imply that the consultant should lean in the direction of participation, delegation, and involvement of subordinates in decision making. More specifically, the OD consultant should look for ways to help the client manager involve his or her subordinates in the decision-making process for their unit within the organization. The consultant should help the client *empower* his or her subordinates so that their energy can be channeled toward team and organizational achievement rather than toward passive hostility, inappropriate competitiveness, and an overdependence on rules—the behavior that typically occurs as a consequence of feelings of powerlessness. Thus, the consultant's position regarding the exercise of power should be more normative than contingent. Note that I say "more than," not "rather than." In some organizations a greater decentralization of power would not be wise. Power in a university, for example, is often sufficiently and sometimes overly decentralized, if not diffuse. As a consultant to a university, I might advocate a greater *centralization* of power. In most organizations, however, power is concentrated in limited domains, usually according to a strict hierarchy, and OD consultants are more likely to be in a position to argue authoritatively that power should be exercised more participatively and decentrally.

The next major section of this chapter is devoted to leadership. As power is the *potential* to influence, leadership is the *act* of influencing, the exercise of power. My intent is to provide a summary of what we know about leadership. A more important reason for discussing leadership, however, is to provide the OD consultant with support for taking a normative position regarding the use of power. I have advocated that, in most situations, a participative approach

139

to the use of power and the practice of leadership and management is more effective than a unilateral one. The discussion of leadership should strengthen that argument.

Leadership

In this section we shall briefly consider some earlier literature on leadership. We shall then discuss some major differences of opinion and theory about leadership, consider some more recent evidence, and, finally, relate all this information to management and organization development.[1]

Early Research

Although the "great-man theory" of leadership is out of vogue and lacks empirical support, this kind of thinking undoubtedly stimulated early research approaches to the study of leadership. It is also likely that the average person still believes that becoming a great leader is largely preordained—you either have it or you don't. The *trait* approach to the study of leadership, which dominated the literature in the decades between the two world wars and to some extent following World War II, was based, at least implicitly, on the great-man theory. The initial studies were correlational, searching for personality traits that related systematically with leadership effectiveness. Research might show that, under some conditions, a certain trait would correlate significantly, but a later study under different conditions would demonstrate the opposite effect. This kind of research continued for a number of decades, but researchers apparently began to despair of this approach shortly after World War II, and they began to take another approach. This was particularly true for the psychologists at Ohio State University during the 1950s. Using observational and questionnaire techniques, they began to focus on behavior, not on personality traits. The center of attention was how leaders acted, not whether they were courageous or brave, for example. Independent studies began to show similar patterns. What emerged from research in the 1950s was the stability of two primary dimensions of leadership, called by various names: group task roles and group-building and maintenance roles (Benne and Sheats 1948); initiation of structure and consideration (Stogdill 1974); task and socioemotional leadership (Bales 1950); and, building on this early research later in the 1960s, task-motivated and relationship-motivated leadership (Fiedler 1967), concern for production and concern for people (Blake and Mouton 1964), and task and relationship leadership (Hersey and Blanchard 1969). When Blake and Mouton (1978) graphed these two dimensions along nine-point scales and described leader behavior in terms of the eighty-one various combinations, the "style" era of

[1] This section is based largely on a previously published article (Burke 1979).

leadership study was born (See Exhibit 7.2). Blake and Mouton contend that some styles are more effective than others—the 9,9 style being the best, of course. Hersey and Blanchard argue, however, that there is no one best way, that situational differences require different styles. Fiedler asserts that leadership is interactive and contingent. He claims that the leader's personality or style is a factor, but the situation is also; and these two variables interact in such a way that task-motivated leaders are more effective than relationship-motivated leaders in some situations but the opposite is true for other conditions (Fiedler 1974). I agree with Fiedler in many respects, since my own research tends to support his theory (Burke 1965).

EXHIBIT 7.2

The Managerial Grid

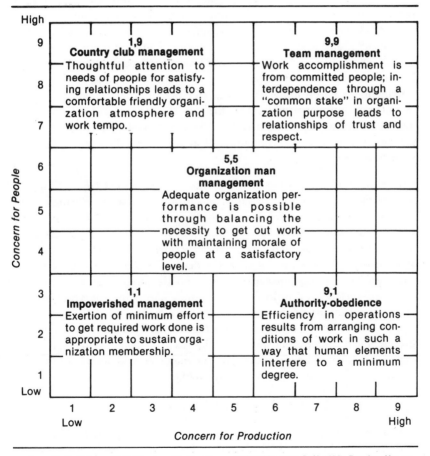

Source: R. R. Blake and J. S. Mouton, *The New Managerial Grid* (Houston: Gulf, 1978). Reprinted by permission.

Recent Research

The recent literature is characterized by a debate between those who argue for a normative approach to the development of leaders, claiming one best way, and the situationalists or contigency theorists, claiming that it all depends. The former theory is best represented by Blake and Mouton (1978) and the latter by Hersey and Blanchard (1977). There is also debate or at least strong criticism regarding leadership research. Some critics have argued that the multitude of empirical studies on leadership has yielded very little (McCall and Lombardo 1978).

It is unfortunately true that many, perhaps most, of the more than 3,000 books and articles reviewed in Stogdill's *Handbook of Leadership* (1974) are trivial—and some are even worthless. If we consider the cumulative effect of many of these studies and look for patterns across independent research reports, however, there is some substance that is worthy of note.

The normative versus situationalist difference has been argued for almost two decades, and it appears that the situational advocates are ahead in the debate. What does the evidence show? I have kept reasonably current with leadership research over the past fifteen to twenty years, and I believe some statements based on more recent research are in order. Having classified myself as a contingency advocate in the past, this more recent set of evidence has caused me to take a second look. This second look resulted from a consideration of evidence from four different areas. What follows is a summary of these four areas.

HALL'S MANAGERIAL ACHIEVEMENT QUOTIENT   Jay Hall's (1976) findings are impressive because they are based on data from more than 11,000 male managers and because of the clear pattern that emerges from his data analysis. To study leadership effectiveness or success, one must define or establish reasonable criteria for what is effective or successful. Hall chose the criterion of achievement within the organization, determining a managerial achievement quotient (MAQ) for each manager.[2] This quotient is determined by one's age and level or rank in the organization. The higher one's rank or level in the organization and the younger one is, the higher the MAQ is. Thus, a vice-president who is 38 years old has a higher MAQ than a 48-year-old vice-president in the same organization. At the risk of oversimplifying Hall's findings, a summary of the research shows that managers with high MAQs, compared with those with moderate or low MAQs:

1. Will have higher need for self-actualization

---

[2] I use the terms *leader* and *manager* interchangeably, but perhaps I shouldn't. In an award-winning article, Zaleznik (1977) makes an interesting and compelling case for fundamental differences between the two.

2. Will emphasize the higher-order need (self-actualization and ego status)
3. Will have subordinates who also rate themselves highest on self-actualization and ego status
4. Will be more competent interpersonally
5. Will involve their subordinates more in decision making and problem solving
6. Will use a participative style of management, as rated by themselves and by their subordinates

By comparison, people with low MAQs tend to be (1) hygiene or maintenance seekers, regarding their own motives as well as the management of others, (2) interpersonally incompetent, and (c) "impoverished" in their managerial approach, as Blake and Mouton label a 1,1 style of management.

A later study, which replicated Hall's 1976 research, compared approximately 1,000 women managers with a comparable group of men (Donnell and Hall 1980). The results were essentially the same; high-achieving women apparently behave the same as male managers who have high MAQs.

CITICORP'S MANAGEMENT DEVELOPMENT PROGRAM   Since 1977, Citicorp has been conducting a "managing people" program for their middle to top-level managers. The program is held off-site for one week and is specially designed for Citicorp management. The design is based on a set of managerial practices that have been empirically determined to be representative of the corporation's best managers. Top management selected thirty-nine managers whom they considered to be "corporate property"—the people who would manage and lead the corporation some day. An additional thirty-nine managers were selected who were considered to be good managers but not as good as the first group. These two sets of managers were then rated by their subordinates on fifty-nine managerial practices. The practices were stated in behavioral terms, such as, "Your manager emphasizes cooperation as opposed to competitiveness among members of his (her) work group." Subordinates rated their managers on a five-point scale in terms of how much they perceived that their managers behaved as described in the statement. From the original group of fifty-nine practices, twenty-two were found to distinguish between the two sets of managers significantly, regardless of the manager's position and job responsibilities. Other practices that also discriminated were a function of situational differences, typically highly structured responsibilities rather than those with low structure.

The training program was therefore designed around the management practices that discriminated between the high-performing managers and those who were considered average. Each training day is devoted to a particular category of practices, such as coaching, and on that day the participants receive feedback in the form of subordinate ratings on that practice.

What is striking about the twenty-two practices which set the high-performing managers apart is that most of them could be used to script a role for a participative manager.

THE JAPANESE MANAGEMENT APPROACH   Assuming that we agree that, on the whole, Japanese management is very successful, what accounts for that success? There are many reasons, of course, most of them embedded deep within Japanese culture—their beliefs, attitudes, and values. One characteristic that stands out, however, is the consistently participative manner in which they manage.

More information on this Japanese approach can be found in an early article by Drucker (1971), in the later work of William Ouchi (Ouchi and Price 1978; Ouchi and Jaegar 1978), and, within the context of organization development, in some of my articles (Burke 1977; Kobayashi and Burke 1976). Although there are significant cultural differences, the consequences of involvement and participative management may be universal (Hatvany and Pucik 1981).

MASCULINITY AND FEMININITY RESEARCH   The fourth category, which does not relate to management directly, is the research of Janet Spence and Robert Helmreich (1978) on masculinity and femininity. The major hypothesis guiding their series of studies with males and females is that masculinity and femininity represent dual characteristics of personality and behavior, rather than a single continuum, that each of us may be characterized as having some degree of *both* masculinity and femininity rather than being in a ''psychological location'' between bipolar opposites. Their research evidence provides strong support for this contention.

Spence and Helmreich developed several questionnaires for their research, one of which results in scores on masculinity and femininity. Based on these scores, they classified people according to the following matrix, depending on whether a person's scores are above or below the median score:

Masculinity

	Below median	Above median
Femininity — Above median	Feminine	Androgynous
Femininity — Below median	Undifferentiated	Masculine

Source: Adapted from J. T. Spence and R. L. Helmreich, *Masculinity and Femininity: Their Psychological Dimensions, Correlates, and Antecedents,* University of Texas Press, 1978. Reprinted with permission.

Among the many studies Spence and Helmreich have conducted, three are noteworthy for our purposes here. Each of these studies was correlational, relating some index of success or accomplishment with degree of androgyny—high scores on both masculinity and femininity. One study compared grade point average of MBA students with degree of androgyny. Another study compared scientists' impact, as measured by the number of times they were mentioned in the *Science Citation Index*—an indication of scientific success—with degree of androgyny. A third study compared MBA graduates' annual income with degree of androgyny. In all three studies, they found a significant positive correlation between the index of achievement and the degree of androgyny. Summarizing and combining these findings, we can conclude that there is a relationship between achievement and androgyny.

COMPARING THE THEORIES   Consider, first, Hersey and Blanchard's (1977) model of situational leadership:

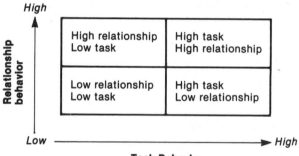

Task Behavior

Source: P. Hersey and K. H. Blanchard, *Management of Organizational Behavior* 3rd ed. p. 103, (Englewood Cliffs, N.J.: Prentice-Hall, 1977). Reprinted by permission of the author.

We can easily superimpose Blake and Mouton's (1978) managerial grid over this model, with the upper right quadrant being similar to their 9,9 style, the lower left quadrant like the 1,1 style, and so forth. The 5,5 grid style would fall in the middle of the situational leadership model. Hersey and Blanchard claim that, for a leader, being in one quadrant is just as effective as being in any other, depending on the situation. Blake and Mouton, with Likert's support, I suspect, would argue that being in the upper right quadrant is best; in the middle, where the lines intersect, is second best; the lower right quadrant is third best; and so on, with the lower left quadrant being the least effective for management and leadership.

The argument goes on. In addition to Blake and Mouton's (1978) theory and findings, we have Likert's (1967) earlier but similar findings, as well as the Japanese management approach and Jay Hall's (1976) highly persuasive results. Although the research of Spence and Helmreich is outside the area of our main topic, it may indeed relate to it. As another imagery exercise, superimpose Spence and Helmreich's 2×2 classification table over the

Hersey and Blanchard situational leadership model. Isn't task behavior similar to masculinity and relationship similar to femininity, at least as our culture has defined them? Based on Spence and Helmreich's findings, and assuming that this superimposing is not merely a mental exercise, which quadrant would you prefer if you were a leader?

I have been selective with the four categories, and I may have stretched some things to show relationships and similar patterns. Until I see accumulated evidence and contrary patterns for a more effective approach to the development of leaders, however, I would advise managers and leaders to set a developmental goal for themselves—learning more about how to acquire participative management skills.

I should note that Blake and Mouton (1981) do not think that superimposing their grid over Hersey and Blanchard's (1977) model is appropriate. They contend that the situational leadership model is additive, while theirs is an *interactive* theory. The Hersey and Blanchard dimensions—task and relationship—are independent of one another and therefore combine arithmetically. The basic assumption of Hersey and Blanchard's (1977) model

> is revealed in the high task/high relationship of 9 + 9. This entails a 9 of control by the boss, which means that he or she completely structures the way the work is done. When the 9 of relationship is added through complimenting, rewarding, or "stroking" the subordinate for executing work as instructed, the result is paternalism/materialism; compliance by a subordinate is reinforced with socio-emotional support. (Blake and Mouton 1981, p. 13)

Assumptions underlying the two grid dimensions, however, hold that they are interactive, not independent of one another. Thus, a 9,9 leader is team-oriented and manages participatively, not paternalistically. He assumes, for example, that subordinates naturally desire to be productive and, when they are given a chance to accomplish tasks in concert with the boss, they will experience a high degree of relationship behavior from him. By leading in a 9,9 rather than a 9 + 9 manner, the leader combines production (task) and relationship behavior in a single behavioral act, rather than emphasizing task one moment and then stressing relationship behavior later.

Implications for OD Consultation

When a planned change or intervention is proposed by an OD consultant, the proposal is most vulnerable if it constitutes a change in the power structure of the organization. Most consultants prefer a contingency approach in these circumstances and therefore take no position regarding the change (V. E. Schein and Greiner 1977; Tichy 1978). Their stance is facilitative—helping the client to implement whatever change he or she chooses to make. I suggest that a normative position is frequently the more authoritative and therefore more appropriate stance to take.

In the case example of Ron, the regional manager, my advocacy of a more participative approach was not necessary. He was already so inclined. My consultative task was to help him design and conduct a variety of techniques for involving his subordinates in key decision-making areas. In my work with the medical school curriculum committee (see Chapter 3), however, I did argue for more decentralization of power.

Organization development consultants often should take a normative approach regarding certain kinds of changes (interventions), such as decentralization of power and participative management, but at other times they should allow their recommendations to be more contingent. My rule of thumb involves research and values. I prefer to be normative regarding change when the direction of change can be supported by sound research results, even though the evidence may not be conclusive, and by values that enhance human dignity and use human resources more fully. Actions involving a wider sharing of power and a participative approach to management usually respond to these change directions.

With respect to organization design and structure, however, there appears to be no one best way. Burns and Stalker (1961) and Lawrence and Lorsch (1967) have underscored this position with ample evidence. Under certain environmental conditions in an organization, a high division of labor and centralized control may be more appropriate than a highly decentralized structure and less differentiated labor. Perhaps there is an incongruence of values here, but not necessarily. It is possible to share power and manage participatively in a steep, hierarchical organization in which control is very centralized. Delegation is key, of course, as is team management. It is also possible to combine a participative, if not democratic, form of management within the structure and control system of a hierarchical organization. Russ Ackoff not only has designed such a structure but has helped to implement it successfully in several organizations. In response to such questions as how employees throughout the organization can be given opportunities in decisions that directly affect them and how involvement and participation can be practiced so that any necessary hierarchy and central control can be maintained, Ackoff (1974) designed what he calls the *circular* organization. In the circular organization, all managers report to boards that are superior to them in the hierarchy. Each board is composed of (1) the manager of the unit to be considered, (2) subordinate managers or workers, and (3) the manager's boss, who serves as the board chair. Thus, each board consists of three levels of management, and consequently each manager is a member of three different boards: the board to which he or she reports, the board to which his or her superior reports, and, as chairperson, the boards to which each of his or

147

EXHIBIT 7.3

Ackoff's Circular Organization

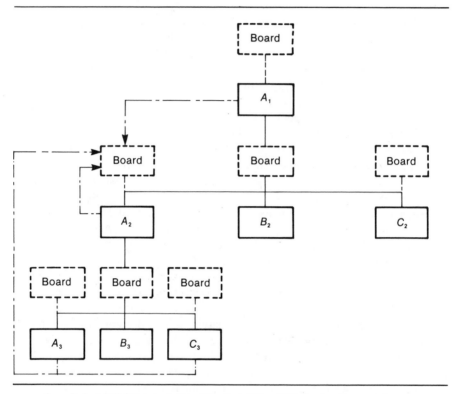

Source: R. L. Ackoff, *Redesigning the Future* (New York: Wiley, 1974). Reprinted by permission.

her immediate subordinates reports. Exhibit 7.3 is Ackoff's representation of this circular organization.

These boards do not manage as such, but they establish policy and evaluate each manager's performance, removing him or her if necessary. As Ackoff (1974) states:

> The immediate subordinates of any manager, acting collectively, can re- move him from his position. But the board cannot fire him, it only controls the occupancy of the position, not the occupant. On the other hand, no manager can remove a subordinate without agreement of the board to which that subordinate reports. This means that each manager's performance would be evaluated by those immediately below him as well as by his im- mediate superior. (p. 52)

Ackoff also points out that, in addition to increasing humanization in the organization, the circular board design has the advantages of (1) more adequately preparing managers for higher positions, because they can be exposed to as many as five levels of management by virtue of their multiple board memberships, and (2) greater integration of activities at different levels and greater coordination of different activities at the same level. Although the circular organization may seem cumbersome, Ackoff contends that it has worked very successfully, particularly in certain segments of government and industry in Mexico.[3]

The argument that hierarchy and organizational control are incompatible with a participative or democratic approach to management and with decentralized power is obviously out of date.

Summary

Power is defined as the *potential* for influence. The study and understanding of power is an important topic in a book on organization development because, if change is to occur in an organization, power must be exercised by some person or group. The potential must be acted upon.

Just as one has a need for achievement or a need for affiliation, McClelland has hypothesized a human need for power. There are individual differences regarding the amount of need, of course, but McClelland states that we all pass through four developmental stages of power, at least potentially. Each succeeding stage represents a higher level of maturity regarding one's need for power, and some people, perhaps most, never reach the fourth stage. McClelland's stages are (1) being dependent on others for power, (2) becoming independent, (3) influencing others, and (4) deriving power from higher authority. McClelland has presented evidence to show that successful managers are likely to have an above-average need for power and that this need is manifested in a mature, socialized manner. There is also evidence that people in the helping professions, including organization development practitioners, are likely to have higher needs for power than the general population has. Since both consultants and successful client managers have these high needs, conflict may not be inevitable, but it is certainly possible.

French and Raven have postulated five primary sources or bases of power: reward, coercive, expert, legitimate, and referent. A client's bases are generally legitimate (by virtue of position), reward, coercive, and perhaps expert, at least within the organization. A consultant's primary base is expert. So long as the client perceives expertise on the part of the consultant that is different from the client's expertise, power conflicts are less probable.

Kanter has extended the earlier work of French and Raven by tracing certain sources of power to the organization itself. She argues that organization

---

[3] Reported in a presentation November 8, 1979, at Columbia University's Graduate School of Business executive program, "Advanced Organization Development and Human Resource Management."

149

members' participation in certain activities and formation of key alliances will empower them within the organization. Kanter argues, further, that feelings of powerlessness on the part of organizational members cause individual stress or depression and potentially can cause disruptions in the work. These feelings are particularly evident in women and minorities.

From the perspective of organization development, power is a central concept for diagnosis. Power means energy and, for change to be planned and channeled, this energy must be focused. Consultants should therefore look not only for the key leverages of power in the organization but also for evidence of powerlessness, for where powerlessness exists, we will find unused and inappropriately focused energy.

Leadership is the exercise of power. Recent evidence supports a normative position on this use of power—a participative approach. Although OD consultants should maintain a contingency position regarding some kinds of changes in an organization, such as structural changes, they often can authoritatively espouse a participative style of leadership.

PART III

THE SOCIAL TECHNOLOGY
OF ORGANIZATION DEVELOPMENT

Parts III and IV concern organization development activities. The question being addressed in these chapters is, simply, "What do you do when you do OD?" The answer to this question can be given as seven steps: (1) locate a client or respond to a potential client's request for assistance, (2) make an agreement with the client regarding what the two of you are going to do, (3) gather information from and about the client organization, (4) report your summary and understanding of this information to the people from whom you collected the information, (5) collaborate with the client in planning activities that will respond to problems and issues that were identified from the summary and understanding of the information collected, (6) help the client to conduct and implement the planned activities, and (7) work with the client to determine the degree of success of these activities. Organization development practitioners have developed labels for these seven steps, as follows:

1. *Scouting and entry*
2. *Contracting*
3. *Diagnosis*
4. *Feedback*
5. *Planning change*
6. *Intervention*
7. *Evaluation*

Part III will consider the first four steps, Part IV will deal with the remaining three. More specifically, in Part III we shall explain the steps, present some models of organizations that help significantly with the diagnostic phase, cover some of the primary techniques for diagnosing an organization, and, finally, deal with the process of feedback—that is, holding up a mirror so that the organization's members can determine the state of their system's health.

CHAPTER 8

The Practice of
Organization Development

In this chapter and the remainder of the book, we shall concern ourselves with
the *practice* of organization development. Some practitioners rely heavily on
standard packages—grid organizational development, such instruments or
questionnaires as Likert's "Profile of Organizational Characteristics," and
the like—while others prefer to keep their practices more organic, deriving
interventions that are especially tailored to the client organization.
Regardless of style or bias, however, most OD practitioners conform to the
action research approach—collecting information about the organization
and using this information for making changes—and most follow the seven
basic phases of an OD effort. The action research approach, explained in
Chapter 3, provides the umbrella for the specific phases of an OD effort.
These phases will be discussed in greater detail here, but first we shall consider again an actual case of organization development consultation, which
should help our understanding of the seven phases.

A Case Example

At the beginning of Chapter 7, we briefly considered the case of Ron, a
regional manager for a large financial institution. The case example was
presented in the context of power—what power Ron had as a regional
manager and how he exercised it. I reintroduce the case example now from
the perspective of consultation according to the phases of organization
development.

CONTACT   I was called initially by Carol, the manager of human resources,
who reported directly to Ron, the regional manager. Carol explained that she
was calling me because she knew that I had consulted for the corporation
before (in other divisions) and was familiar with their business, and because I

153

came highly recommended. She further explained that Ron was new in his position as regional manager and was anxious to make some changes. He was considering an off-site meeting with his senior management group and believed that an outside consultant might be helpful. Carol then asked if I would be interested and, if so, if we could have lunch together soon to explore the matter.

EXPLORATION   At the lunch meeting a few days later, Carol and I asked one another many questions. She was interested in what I had done before, how I liked to work, what I might do or suggest if such-and-such were to happen, what I knew about her company's business, and whether I would be interested in continuing to consult with them if the initial effort went well. I asked her such questions as why the business had been losing money for four years in a row; what Ron's predecessor was like; what Ron was like—his managerial style, his previous job history; how people in the region, especially the senior management group, felt about him, and whether any of the others thought they should have become the new regional manager instead of Ron; how the senior management group worked together—whether off-site meetings were common occurrences; and so forth. Toward the end of our exploratory discussion, Carol explained that she needed to talk further with Ron and that she would be in touch with me again soon.

MEETING WITH RON   The following week Carol called and scheduled a meeting for me with Ron. In my meeting with Ron, it was soon clear to me that he trusted Carol a great deal. He was essentially sold on me, and all we needed to do was discuss details. He explained that, although he had been in the region for more than three years—as head of consumer services—he had only been regional manager for a month. He felt pressure from higher management to make the region profitable, and he reasoned that he must have his senior management group solidly with him in order to "turn the region around." He further stated that he wanted to have an off-site meeting with his senior management group (1) to establish two-year profit goals, (2) to develop an overall regional business strategy, and (3) to begin the process of building a senior management *team*.

For my part, I explained that I would like to conduct individual interviews with the members of his senior management group, including himself, determine if they thought an off-site meeting was appropriate (we would not have the meeting if enough of them said no), summarize and analyze the information from the interviews, meet with him again to go over the data, plan the meeting (if warranted), and clarify our respective roles—that he would lead the meeting and I would help. In OD language, my role would be a *facilitating* one.

154

AGREEMENT   We reached agreement concerning what Ron wanted and how I wanted to proceed. This verbal agreement was followed a few days later with an exchange of letters to confirm our agreement in writing.

INTERVIEWS   Over a one-week period, I conducted one-hour interviews with each member of the senior management group. Exhibit 8.1 is an organizational chart of the group. I explained to each manager that the interview would be confidential and that only a summary of the interviews in aggregate form would become public.

Although I asked many questions in each interview, I asked four general questions of everyone:

1. What are the strengths of the region?
2. What are the weaknesses of the region?
3. Are you in favor of the off-site meeting?
4. What should be the objectives of the off-site meeting?

The interviews went well. All the managers were cooperative and expressed themselves openly and candidly, and I took many notes.

SUMMARY AND ANALYSIS OF INTERVIEWS   Although some of the managers thought the off-site meeting was somewhat premature, because Ron had only been in his position one month, others believed that the timing was right.

EXHIBIT 8.1

Organization Chart: Regional Business Unit of a Larger Financial Institution

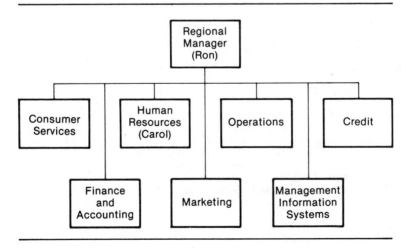

Regardless of the timing, however, all thought that an off-site meeting was a good idea. Thus, the summary of my interviews was categorized according to the three other questions—strengths and weaknesses of the region and objectives of the off-site meeting. Exhibit 8.2 provides a partial listing of some of the major points made in the interviews. As is typical for such an activity, the weaknesses listed outnumber the strengths. People, especially managers, tend to focus more on problems than on what is going well or is positive for the organization.

Some general problems in the region became clear to me as a result of the

EXHIBIT 8.2

*Partial Summary of Eight Interviews Conducted with a
Regional Senior Management Group*

Strengths of the Region

1. Senior management group is highly experienced in the business (7)
2. Commitment of work force; community spirit (5)
3. Considerable opportunity; natural market area (3)
4. Good people throughout (3)
5. Last four years we have experienced success in many areas (3)
6. Have become more of a marketing organization (3)
7. We are technologically superior and a market leader as compared with our competitors (3)
8. Creativity (2)
9. Managers think entrepreneurially (2)

Weaknesses

1. Our marketing and services system (6)
2. Try to do too many things at once; do not establish priorities (3)
3. Region priorities are always secondary to individual manager's (3)
4. Lack of management depth (3)
5. Little planning (3)
6. Structure (2)
7. High costs (2)
8. Overly change-oriented (2)
9. Poor reward system (2)
10. Low morale (2)
11. Internal competition (2)
12. High degree of mistrust (2)

Objectives of Off-Site Meeting

1. Agree on the regional structure (7)
2. Set financial objectives for next two years (6)
3. List of things we need to do and stop doing (4)
4. Must hear from Ron about his team notions, ideas, expectations (4)
5. Some ventilation of feelings needed (3)
6. Must come together more as a top management team (3)
7. Establish standards for performance (3)
8. Increase mutual respect (2)

Note: The number in parentheses after each item indicates the number of respondents who specifically mentioned that point. The total number of interviewees was eight.

interviews. Although the group believed that they were highly knowledgeable and experienced in their business, they recognized that continuing to make no profits was not going to get them where they wanted to go, especially in their individual careers. There was also a conflict over whether theirs was a marketing and sales organization or a consumer services organization. Actually, it had to be both, but, from the standpoint of strategy and with respect to individuals' roles and responsibilities in lower levels of management, there was considerable ambiguity. This ambiguity contributed to problems of priorities, numbers 2 and 3 in the list of weaknesses. The emphasis on structure and financial objectives was therefore appropriate in the major objectives for the off-site meeting.

PLAN FOR THE OFF-SITE MEETING   Ron and I met before the off-site meeting to go over my summary and analysis of the interview information and to plan the meeting. I gave Ron the summary and analysis of the interviews just as I would later give it to the entire group. Thus, Ron received the same information but received it earlier. The purposes of this advance notice were (1) to use the information as a basis for planning an agenda for the meeting and (2) to allow Ron to have time to understand and react to the information before the meeting. Ron would then have an opportunity to discuss his reactions to the information, particularly his feelings, so that, if he felt defensive, for example, he could talk about it with me and not be as defensive during the meeting. In such situations, especially if it is the first time, bosses frequently receive more criticism for problems than any other members of the group. Even if interview comments are not specifically directed at the bosses, they may feel responsible and accountable for the problems because of their positions, regardless of where the actual causes may lie. In Ron's case, he was not angry and he was not particularly defensive. He didn't think he had contributed to the weaknesses and problems any more than anyone else had. If he had been regional manager longer than a month, of course, his feelings might have been different. Ron was pleased with his group's openness and accuracy regarding the issues, and he was enthusiastic about the upcoming meeting.

Our plan for the meeting was simple and straightforward. We wanted as little interference and distraction as possible, so we would hold the meeting at a hotel-resort location that was fairly remote yet comfortable. The site was less than two hours away from the region's headquarters by automobile, and it met our criteria. Regarding the agenda, we planned to begin at 4 P.M. on Wednesday. Ron would open the meeting with a statement of his goals and expectations regarding the meeting, and I would follow with a summary of the interviews. The group would then have a chance to react to and discuss the interview summary. Before dinner Ron would present some financial data that would show clearly how the region compared with the other regions (they were close to the bottom), and after some discussion we would eat dinner together as a group. Thursday morning would be devoted to setting a two-year profit goal and to establishing priorities among the many objectives. Thursday afternoon we would discuss potential obstacles to reaching the profit goal and to realizing some of the more specific objectives of the region, such as clarifying their objectives regarding the balance of marketing versus service. Friday morning we would discuss an overall strategy that would incorporate the profit goal and these objectives, and Friday afternoon would be devoted to a summary of the meeting, to members' reactions to and critique of the meeting, and to a discussion of the specific plans for follow-up.

THE OFF-SITE MEETING   The meeting proceeded essentially as planned. We took a two-hour break for lunch and some physical recreation in the middle of the day on Thursday and then worked from 2 P.M. to about 7 P.M. On Friday we had a quick lunch and continued to work until about 3 P.M., when we adjourned. This was somewhat short for such a meeting, but adequate. During the summary and critique of the meeting, I also participated, giving my reactions to the meeting, providing the group with some of my observations of them as a group, and making suggestions about how they could improve their work together as a team. Everyone considered the meeting to have been worthwhile and useful, and Ron was particularly pleased. He believed that the formation of a team, as opposed to an administrative aggregate of senior managers, had begun, and I agreed.

AFTER THE OFF-SITE MEETING   A few weeks after the meeting, Ron and I met again and agreed on a plan for my continued consultation. Some of the changes I helped to make were (1) installation of a planning function reporting directly to Ron; (2) a reorganization of the consumer services area, particularly regarding the functions of marketing and sales as they related to service (an off-site meeting with the head of consumer services and his management group was part of the planning for these changes); (3) modifications in the reward and performance-appraisal processes of the region (I worked with Carol in this area); and (4) development of the senior management group into more of a team. Eventually, though certainly not overnight, the profit picture for the region began to change, and they did indeed move from the red to the black.

Now that we have the case as an illustration of organization development consultation, let us reconsider the steps I took so that we can translate the activities into OD language and understand more thoroughly the concepts and principles of this kind of consultation.

Phases of OD Practice

With some slight modifications, I shall follow the seven phases of OD consulting delineated by Kolb and Frohman (1970). Based on the Lewinian concepts of unfreezing, change, and refreezing and on Lippitt, Watson, and

Westley's (1958) phases of planned change, but oriented more specifically to current OD practice, Kolb and Frohman give seven phases to be followed in an OD consultation: scouting, entry, diagnosis, planning, action, evaluation, and termination. I have modified their list by putting scouting and entry together, separating contracting and feedback into distinct phases, using intervention instead of action, and eliminating termination. What Kolb and Frohman call *scouting*, I call *entry*, and I consider *contracting* a more appropriate term for what they label as *entry*. Our differences are simply in labels and emphasis; the overall process is the same, except for termination, which I will explain later. Thus, my seven phases are:

1. Entry
2. Contracting
3. Diagnosis
4. Feedback
5. Planning change
6. Intervention
7. Evaluation

We shall consider each of these phases in turn, using the case example to illustrate the particular characteristics of OD consultation.

Entry

Contact between the consultant and client is what initiates the entry phase. This contact may result either from the client's calling the consultant for an exploratory discussion about the possibility of an OD effort, as in the case example, or from the consultant's suggesting to the client that such an effort might be worthwhile. For an external consultant, the contact is likely to result from the client's initiative. For an internal consultant, either mode could occur. Internal consultants, being employees, typically feel some commitment to their organizations, or it may be part of their job descriptions to call on managers in the organization and suggest preliminary steps that might lead to an OD effort. Internal consultants also may have experienced success with organization development in one subsystem and may wish to spread this effect further within the organization. Initiating contacts with clients therefore comes naturally for internal OD practitioners, and there is certainly more opportunity for informal contacts to occur—at lunch, at committee meetings, and so forth—when questions can be asked and suggestions explored.

After the contact, the consultant and the client begin the process of *exploring* with one another the possibilities of a working relationship. The client is usually assessing (1) whether he or she can relate well with the consultant, (2) whether the consultant's previous experience is applicable to the present situation, and (3) whether the consultant is competent and can be trusted.

159

My lunch meeting with Carol served as the beginning of the exploration process. I repeated the process with Ron, the regional manager, but this second round was rapid, since it had already been facilitated by Carol's previous meeting with and assessment of me.

During the exploration process, the consultant is assessing (1) whether he or she can relate well with the client, (2) the motivation and values of the client, (3) the client's readiness for change, (4) the extent of resources for supporting a change effort, and (5) potential leverage points for change—whether the client has the power to make decisions that will lead to change or whether higher authority must be sought. In my conversation with Ron, I became satisfied that he was motivated and ready for change, that he had the resources, and that he had the leverage—enough autonomy to take considerable action without getting approval from higher management.

There are additional criteria and ways of determining a client's readiness for change. Pfeiffer and Jones (1978), for example, have developed a useful fifteen-item checklist for such a determination. They urge the consultant to check, among others, such things as flexibility of top management, possible labor contract limitations (which could be crucial if job enrichment, for example, were a potential intervention), any previous experience the organization may have had with OD (or what some may have called OD, regardless of what the activities were), structural flexibility with respect to the organization's design, and the interpersonal skills of those who would be involved at the outset.

Contracting

Assuming that the mutual explorations of the consultant and the client in the entry phase progress satisfactorily, the next phase in the process is negotiating a contract. If the entry process has gone smoothly, the contracting phase is likely to be brief. The contract is essentially a statement of agreement that succinctly clarifies what the consultant agrees to do. If it is done thoroughly, the contract will also state what the client intends to do. The contract may be nothing more than a verbal agreement, with a handshake, perhaps, or it may be a formal document, with notarized signatures. Most often, the contract is considerably more informal than the latter extreme, typically involving an exchange of letters between the two parties.

Unlike other types of contracts, the OD contract states more about process than about content. According to Weisbord (1973), it is

an explicit exchange of expectations . . . which clarifies for consultant and client three critical areas:

1. What each expects to get from the relationship;
2. How much time each will invest, when, and at what cost;
3. The ground rules under which the parties will operate. (p. 1)

My contract with Ron was fairly straightforward. The letters that we exchanged simply confirmed in writing what we had agreed to in our meeting. The letters summarized what I would do and some of what he planned to do. The case as I described it was indeed the implementation of our contract.

In our meeting following the off-site meeting, Ron and I agreed on a further contract, which was also confirmed in writing in an exchange of letters between us.

It is a good practice in OD consultation to renew or renegotiate the contract periodically. In my consultation with Ron, the second contract was essentially an extension of the first, occurring about three months after the earlier one. The timing of the renewal or renegotiation is not as important as seeing that this phase is periodically repeated. It is also a good practice to have the agreement in writing. Although an exchange of letters may not necessarily constitute a legal document, the written word usually helps to avoid misunderstandings.

Diagnosis

The next chapter will be devoted more thoroughly to this phase of organization development, but a brief description is in order at this point. There are two steps within the diagnostic phase: gathering information and analyzing it. Diagnosis has usually begun even at the entry phase—if the consultant is alert. How the client reacts to the possibility of change at the outset may tell a great deal not only about the client as an individual but also about the part of the organization's culture that he or she represents. Initially, therefore, information gathering is accomplished through the consultant's observations, intuitions, and feelings. Later, more systematic methods are used, such as structured interviews, questionnaires, and summaries of such organizational documents as performance records and task force reports. Once the data are collected, the consultant must then put all the varieties of information together, summarize the information without losing critical pieces, and finally organize the information so that the client can easily understand it and be able to work with it so that appropriate action can be taken.

As we shall see in Chapter 9, there are several models to help the consultant with both steps of the diagnostic phase: knowing *what* information to seek and knowing *how* to analyze and interpret the information.

In my initial work with Ron and his management group, I relied on three methods of data gathering: interviews, my observations, and my reading of two documents—one concerning Ron's thinking about long-range planning and another that summarized the issues regarding the problem of marketing versus service orientation.

My diagnosis consisted of (1) summarizing the data according to the categories of the interview questions (see Exhibit 8.2) and elaborating on

161

what the interviewees had said and (2) drawing certain conclusions from the combination of my observations and some relationships I perceived in the interview results.

Feedback

How effectively the consultant has summarized and analyzed the diagnostic information will determine the success of the feedback phase to a significant extent. This phase, which will be covered in detail in Chapter 10, consists of holding meetings with the client system—usually first with the boss alone and then with the entire group from whom the data were collected. The size of the group would determine the number of feedback sessions to be held. If the client system consisted of a manager and his or her immediate subordinates only, then two sessions would be required—one with the manager alone and the second with the entire group, including the manager. If more than these two levels of the overall managerial hierarchy were included—for example, four levels of management, involving thirty or more people—then as many as four of five feedback sessions may be necessary. A feedback session should allow for ample discussion and debate, and a small group that does not involve multiple levels of management is best for such purposes.

A feedback session generally has three steps. First, the consultant provides a summary of the data collected and some preliminary analysis. Next, there is a general discussion in which questions of clarification are raised and answered. Finally, some time is devoted to interpretation. At this stage some changes may be made in the consultant's analysis and interpretation. Thus, the consultant works collaboratively with the client group to arrive at a final diagnosis that accurately describes the current state of the system.

In my work with Ron and his management group, I followed essentially the steps I've just outlined. The feedback phase consisted, first, of our discussion of the interview results early in the off-site meeting. Toward the end of the meeting, I provided additional feedback, which was a combination of my observations of the group as they worked together for two days and my further analysis of the interview data. I told them, for example, that I had observed that their competition with one another, a weakness some of them had identified, conformed to a particular norm. The norm seemed to be: "Let's see who among us can best identify and analyze our problems and weaknesses as a region." Everyone tackled every issue and problem, and it appeared that winning the game of "best analysis" was critical to all. My diagnosis, with which they agreed, was based in a social-psychological frame of reference and was particularly related to the concept of norm (see Chapter 5).

Planning Change

The planning phase sometimes becomes the second half of the feedback session, as happened with Ron and his group. Once the diagnosis was understood and deemed correct, action steps were planned immediately. It has been noted that a good diagnosis determines the intervention. The only required planning may be the implementation steps—what to do. The more complex the diagnosis or the larger the client system, however, the more likely it is that the planning phase becomes a later event, following the feedback sessions. It may be best generally to allow some time to pass between feedback and planning—a few days, perhaps, but probably no more than a week. This passage of time might allow the feedback to sink in and would create an opportunity for more thought to be given to the planning process.

The purposes of the planning phase are (1) to generate alternative steps for responding correctively to the problems identified in the diagnosis, and (2) to decide on the step or order of steps to take. The OD practitioner again works collaboratively with the client system during this phase, primarily by helping to generate and explore the consequences of alternative action steps. The final decision of what steps to take is the client's, not the consultant's.

Intervention

The intervention phase consists of the action taken. Part IV of this book covers the range of intervention possibilities. The possibilities are numerous, and the selected interventions should be a direct reflection of and response to the diagnosis. Some examples of interventions at the individual level are job redesign and enrichment, training and management development, changes in the quality of working life, management by objectives, and career development. At the group level, interventions might include team building, process consultation, or the installation of autonomous work groups or quality control circles. Resolving intergroup conflict might be an intervention, as might changing such structural dimensions of the organization as reporting relationships, moving toward or away from decentralization of authority, modifying physical settings, or creating informal structures in the organization.

The interventions used in Ron's region were team building, process consultation, some minor structural changes, career development, and a change in the region's reward system—installation of a bonus plan for managers.

Whatever the intervention may be, the OD practitioner continues to work with the client system to help make the intervention successful. As Kolb and Frohman (1970) point out: "the failure of most plans lies in the *unanticipated consequences* of the change effort" (p. 60). The OD consultant's job is to help the client anticipate and plan for the unanticipated consequences.

Evaluation

It is usually best for someone other than the consultant to conduct an evaluation of any OD effort. The consultant cannot be totally objective, and it is difficult to concentrate on what needs changing and on evaluating its success at the same time (Lewicki and Alderfer 1973).

The mode of evaluation may range from clients' saying that they are pleased with the outcome to a systematic research effort employing controls and multiple data analyses. A more objective and systematic evaluation is obviously better, at least for determining cause and effect. It is difficult to do a highly scientific evaluation of OD efforts. The main problem, of course, is control; it is almost impossible to have a proper control group for comparison. Furthermore, the client is usually more interested in taking action that will pay off than in objectively determining whether the action results were attributable to the OD intervention. What is important to the client is whether the action taken was successful according to the organization's usual standards—profits, reduction of costs, or higher performance in general; what *caused* the success is less important. This was essentially the case with Ron and his region, and so no formal evaluation was conducted. Evaluation did occur, however, as I periodically checked and asked for feedback; and the profit results, although they did not necessarily prove a cause-effect relationship, were sufficient evaluation.

Regardless of its form or index, evaluation is very important because the process usually reinforces the change effort, and it is a primary way to learn about the consequences of our actions.

In a later chapter we shall consider evaluation in more depth. It should be clear that some form of evaluation is a critical part in the OD process. Although the evaluative effort does not have to meet all the standards of rigorous research and the scientific method, it must at least provide adequate data for making reasonable decisions regarding further changes.

Termination of the OD Effort

The foregoing seven phases constitute what I consider the primary, sequential actions a practitioner takes in an organization development effort. My list differs slightly in emphasis and labels from the earlier list of Kolb and Frohman (1970), but the phases are essentially the same, with one exception Kolb and Frohman's termination phase. They argue that "the consultant-client relationship is by definition temporary" (Kolb and Frohman 1970, p. 61), that the effort either succeeds or fails. If it fails, termination is abrupt; if it is successful and the goals are reached, the consultant may not leave so abruptly, but the relationship terminates because there is no further need for consultative help. It should be noted that Kolb and Frohman's seventh step is consistent with the phases of planned change delineated earlier by Lippitt, Watson, and Westley (1958).

I do not include termination in my list of phases for three reasons. First, termination is not an applicable phase for internal OD practitioners. Although they may conclude specific programs and projects with their clients, they should not terminate the relationships. A primary role of internal practitioners is to serve as guardians of the new culture. They help to regulate the social change that has become a new routine in organizational life (Hornstein et al. 1971). This regulation may take a variety of forms, ranging from periodic checks with client managers regarding the continuing effectiveness of changes to more systematic follow-up activities, such as conducting annual surveys, attending a manager's staff meetings as a process consultant, or helping to design and conduct off-site planning or diagnostic meetings for departments or divisions.

The second reason concerns external OD consultants. A termination phase is and should be more common for external consultants than for internal ones, but it is not necessarily a requirement for effective consultation. A major goal of an external OD consultant is to see that internal resources are established for the kind of help he or she is providing. As soon as possible, internal practitioners should begin to take over the work the external consultant initiates. Thus, although the external consultant's activities with the client organization may decrease, they do not necessarily have to be terminated. Kolb and Frohman's argument for termination is to prevent the client from becoming dependent on the consultant. As an external consultant I have had long-standing relationships with some clients, but I have never experienced these relationships as a great dependency on me. Although dependency may occur as a problem in personal therapy, it rarely becomes an issue in consultation with organizations. I know of consultant-client relationships that have continued for more than a decade, and I consider them healthy and useful for both parties. An organization has a constant need for periodic, objective diagnostic check-ups by external consultants—a need that exists, incidentally, whether or not the organization's managers see it.

Finally, I do not think a termination phase is appropriate because, when OD practitioners follow the action research model, they naturally generate new data for further diagnosis and action. The process is cyclical (W. L. French 1969), and since an organization both is dynamic and naturally follows the entropic process, there is always a great deal of consultative work to be done.

Phases, Not Steps

Phases is a more appropriate term than *steps* for describing the flow of events in OD work. *Steps* implies discrete actions, while *phases* better connotes the reality of OD practice—a cycle of changes. Although it is useful for our understanding of OD practice to conceive of distinct phases, in actual practice they blend, overlap, and do not always follow one from the other. Diagnosis, for example, comes early in the OD process and intervention later, but when one is collecting information from the organization for diagnostic purposes, an intervention is occurring simultaneously; when the OD practitioner begins to

165

ask questions about the organization and its members, he or she is intervening.

Phases is an appropriate term also because of the cyclical nature of the OD process. As the process continues, new or undisclosed data are discovered. These data affect organization members, and the members react, creating additional information for diagnosis. Further action is then planned as a consequence of the new, perhaps more refined diagnosis.

Another implication of the cyclical nature of OD relates to the characteristics of open social systems, as delineated by Katz and Kahn (1978) and discussed in Chapter 4. Two of these characteristics are relevant—the notion that organizations proceed through cycles of events over time and the notion that systems seek equilibrium. The first characteristic, that organizational life runs in cycles, is precisely the reason that OD is cyclical. Since organizations are cyclical, OD must also be in order to respond in an appropriate and timely manner. Major events in organizations—planning, budgeting, quarterly reports—are repeated over time; as these events are repeated, new data are likely to be generated each time. Two quarterly reports are rarely the same, and plans and budgets change continuously. Consequently, the diagnosis of an organization in December will be at least somewhat different, from the diagnosis conducted the previous June—significantly different if a significant intervention has occurred during the six-month interim. If things in the organization are significantly different six months later, and if these differences are disturbing to organization members, they will seek equilibrium—back to the former state. Organization development involves change. When change occurs in one of the organization's components or subsystems, other subsystems act to restore the balance. Pressure is brought to bear on organizational behavior that is different from the norm—from the organization's culture as it has evolved. Thus, in OD practice, for change to last, recurring diagnoses must be undertaken to determine the state of earlier interventions, and further actions (interventions) are usually needed to reinforce the new behaviors. The long-run objective is to institutionalize the change so that possibilities of changing the OD change will be resisted within the normal pattern of open-system life—equilibrium seeking.

Summary

In this chapter we have considered the seven primary phases of organization development consultation, using a case example to illustrate the phases. Although it is instructive to consider these phases—entry, contracting, diagnosis, feedback, planning change, intervention, and evaluation—as discrete steps, and although the consultative flow of events essentially follows the order of the seven phases, in practice the phases are not discrete; they

166

blend together and overlap. When the consultant enters the client organization to collect information—by interviews, questionnaires, or observations—the intervention phase, sixth among the ordered group of seven, has already begun; and although evaluation is listed as last, it begins at the entry stage as far as the client is concerned.

These phases are therefore guides for OD consultation. They are highly useful for planning and for ordering sequences of activities and events, but they should not be considered as discrete, rigid steps to follow nor as the only phases of consultation in organization development.

CHAPTER 9

Diagnostic Models
and Theories

Without a framework for understanding the information an OD practitioner collects about a client organization, the data may remain nothing more than a mass of confusion—merely an array of comments from a variety of people, representing nothing more than who said what about whom and never rising above the individual and interpersonal level. For information about the organization to become understandable and workable, it must be treated in organizational terms. As noted earlier, organization development represents a systemic approach to change, and the data for diagnosis are largely in system language; the categories for diagnosis are system labels.

In this chapter we shall cover selected models of and theories about organizations. These models and theories are useful in the diagnostic phase of OD consultation because they help to organize and systematize the mass of confusion. There are a number of models and theories from which the OD practitioner may choose, some that are merely descriptive and others that emphasize specific dimensions for diagnosis, therefore providing direction for change. The purpose of this chapter is not only to explain some of these models and theories but also to provide the practitioner with some criteria and bases for making choices.

I have been selective in my choice of models and theories to be considered in this chapter. First, I have chosen only those that are behavior-oriented. There are a number of other frameworks or models of organizations, some emphasizing technological aspects, others financial aspects, and still others in informational terms. Organization development practitioners must rely on behavior-oriented models, however, because the role of the OD practitioner is to understand what *people* do or do not do in organizations, not what machines do. The man-machine interface is of definite interest, but only in terms of its consequences for the people involved. Word processing in the office of the future, for example, is of interest to OD practitioners, but only in terms of the changes people will have to make, not for the electronic wizardry involved (Lodahl and Williams 1978).

We shall explore a number of models for OD purposes. Although they differ from one another, all are based on the open-system notion of input-throughput-output, and all recognize that an organization exists in an environmental context and is a sociotechnical system. Some models place more emphasis on environmental factors than others do, and some stress certain dimensions of organizations, such as structure, more than others do, but they all recognize the same fundamentals—an open system that exists in an environment and consists of people and technology.

We shall first examine three models that are largely descriptive: a model of simplicity with structure, a model of complexity with structure, and a develop-your-own model.

Weisbord's Six-Box Model

A model is useful when it helps us *visualize* reality, and Weisbord's (1978, 1976) model meets this criterion very well. Weisbord depicts his model as a radar screen, with "blips" that tell us about organizational highlights and issues—good and bad; but, as air traffic controllers use their radar, we too must focus primarily on the screen as a whole, not on individual blips (see Exhibit 9.1)

Every organization is situated within an environment and, as the arrows in Exhibit 9.1 indicate, is influenced by and in turn has an impact on various elements of that environment. In Weisbord's model, the organization is represented by six boxes: purposes, structure, rewards, helpful mechanisms, relationships, and leadership. Weisbord believes that, for each box, the client organization should be diagnosed in terms of both its formal and its informal systems. A key aspect of any organizational diagnosis is the gap between the formal dimensions of an organization, such as the organization chart (the structure box), and its informal properties, such as how authority is actually exercised. The larger this gap is, the more likely it is that the organization is functioning ineffectively.

Weisbord provides key diagnostic questions for each of the six boxes. For the *purposes* box, the two most important factors are goal clarity—the extent to which organization members are clear about the organization's mission and purpose—and goal agreement—whether people support the organization's purpose. For *structure*, the primary question is whether there is an adequate fit between the purpose and the internal structure that is supposed to serve that purpose. With respect to *relationships*, Weisbord contends that three types are most important: (1) between individuals, (2) between units or departments that perform different tasks, and (3) between people and the nature and requirements of their jobs. He also states that the OD consultant should

EXHIBIT 9.1
Weisbord's Six-Box Organizational Model

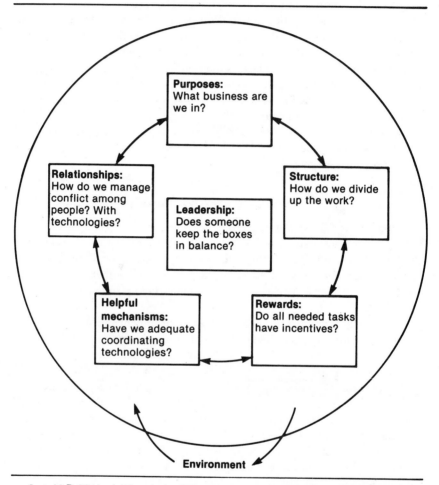

Purposes:
What business are we in?

Relationships:
How do we manage conflict among people? With technologies?

Leadership:
Does someone keep the boxes in balance?

Structure:
How do we divide up the work?

Helpful mechanisms:
Have we adequate coordinating technologies?

Rewards:
Do all needed tasks have incentives?

Environment

Source: M.R. Weisbord, "Organizational Diagnosis: Six Places to Look for Trouble With or Without a Theory," *Group and Organization Studies* 1(1976): 430–47. Reprinted by permission.

"diagnose first for required interdependence, then for *quality of relations*, and finally for modes of conflict management" (Weisbord 1976, p. 440).

In determining possible blips for the *rewards* box, the consultant should diagnose the similarities and differences between what the organization formally rewards—the compensation package, incentive systems, and the like—and what organization members *feel* they are rewarded or punished for doing.

170

Weisbord places the *leadership* box in the middle because he believes that a primary job of the leader is to watch for blips among the other boxes and to maintain balance among them. To help the OD consultant in diagnosing the leadership box, Weisbord refers to an important book published some years ago by Selznick (1957), citing the four most important leadership tasks. According to Selznick, the consultant should determine the extent to which organization leaders are (1) defining purposes, (2) embodying purposes in programs, (3) defending the organization's integrity, and (4) maintaining order with respect to internal conflict.

For the last box, *helpful mechanisms,* Weisbord refers analogously to "the cement that binds an organization together to make it more than a collection of individuals with separate needs" (Weisbord 1976, p. 443). Thus, helpful mechanisms are the processes that every organization must attend to in order to survive: planning, control, budgeting, and other information systems that help organization members accomplish their respective jobs and meet organizational objectives. The OD consultant's task is to determine which mechanisms (or which aspects of them) help members accomplish organizational purposes and which seem to hinder more than they help. When a helpful mechanism becomes red tape, it probably is no longer helpful.

Exhibit 9.2 gives a summary of the six-box model and the diagnostic questions to be asked.

We shall now move from the abstract, descriptive stage of the model to an illustration of how it may be used for diagnostic purposes. We refer again to the case example of Ron and his regional organization that is a unit within a larger financial corporation. Exhibit 9.3 is a reproduction of the summary of interview results (also Exhibit 8.2 in Chapter 8), and Exhibit 9.4 is a categorization of the interview data from Exhibit 9.3 within the six-box model. Note that some of the interview summary phrases are categorized within more than one box. I should also point out that some classifications are easier than others. It was difficult to classify S-8, creativity, for example. I chose "helpful mechanisms—informal" because it seemed that some informal mechanisms within Ron's organization must help foster creativity, but my classification was arbitrary. In practice, the client will have more to say about the appropriate boxes in such instances. It is also not absolutely necessary to classify everything.

Once the data are classified and the client has agreed or has rearranged some of the categories, we are in a position to formulate a diagnostic picture of the organization. What Exhibit 9.4 shows us, among other things, is that our primary problem areas—the blips on the radar screen—are in the "purposes" box, both formal and informal, the "structure—formal" box, the "relationships—informal" box, the "helpful mechanisms—formal" box, and the "rewards" box, both formal and informal. A clear strength is in

171

Add ENVIRON: Text

EXHIBIT 9.2
Weisbord's Matrix for Survey Design or Data Analysis

	Formal system (work to be done)	Informal system (process of working)
1. Purposes	Goal clarity	Goal agreement
2. Structure	Functional, program, or matrix?	How is work actually done or not done?
3. Relationships	Who should deal with whom on what?	How well do they do it?
		Quality of relations?
	Which technologies should be used?	Modes of conflict management?
4. Rewards (incentives)	Explicit system	Implicit, psychic rewards
	What is it?	What do people *feel* about payoffs?
5. Leadership	What do top people manage?	How?
	What systems are in use?	Normative "style" of administration?
6. Helpful mechanisms	Budget system	What are they actually used for?
	Management information (measures?)	How do they function in practice?
	Planning	How are systems subverted?
	Control	

Diagnostic questions may be asked on two levels:
1. How big a gap is there between formal and informal systems? (This speaks to the fit between individual and organization.)
2. How much discrepancy is there between "what is" and "what ought to be"? (This highlights the fit between organization and environment.)

Source: M. R. Weisbord, "Organizational Diagnosis: Six Places to Look for Trouble With or Without a Theory," *Group and Organizational Studies* 1(1976): 430–47. Reprinted by permission.

the "leadership—informal" box, and there are strengths in some of the same boxes that have problems.

We recall from the description of the off-site meeting with Ron and his senior management group and from the summary of what occurred following this meeting that the priorities of the meeting were to work on goals (purposes), strategy, and priorities (purposes), and on building a senior management team (relationships). Follow-up activities included some changes in the structure and reward system and installation of some improved helpful mechanisms, such as a more formal planning function. The strength of the leadership was instrumental in bringing about significant and rapid change. (See Chapter 7 for coverage of this aspect of Ron's approach and behavior.)

My diagnostic summary of the case example within the framework of the six-box model is obviously cursory. I have simply shown how the model may be used and how its use may help point to the parts of the client system that need the most immediate attention.

EXHIBIT 9.3

Partial Summary of Eight Interviews Conducted with a
Regional Senior Management Group

Strengths of the Region

1. Senior management group is highly experienced in the business (7)
2. Commitment of work force; community spirit (5)
3. Considerable opportunity; natural market area (3)
4. Good people throughout (3)
5. Last four years we have experienced success in many areas (3)
6. Have become more of a marketing organization (3)
7. We are technologically superior and a market leader as compared with our competitors (3)
8. Creativity (2)
9. Managers think entrepreneurially (2)

Weaknesses

1. Our marketing and services system (6)
2. Try to do too many things at once; do not establish priorities (3)
3. Region priorities are always secondary to individual manager's (3)
4. Lack of management depth (3)
5. Little planning (3)
6. Structure (2)
7. High costs (2)
8. Overly change-oriented (2)
9. Poor reward system (2)
10. Low morale (2)
11. Internal competition (2)
12. High degree of mistrust (2)

Objectives of Off-Site Meeting

1. Agree on the regional structure (7)
2. Set financial objectives for next two years (6)
3. List of things we need to do and stop doing (4)
4. Must hear from Ron about his team notions, ideas, expectations (4)
5. Some ventilation of feelings needed (3)
6. Must come together more as a top management team (3)
7. Establish standards for performance (3)
8. Increase mutual respect (2)

Note: The number in parentheses after each item indicates the number of respondents who specifically mentioned that point. The total number of interviewees was eight.

In summary, Weisbord's model is particularly useful (1) when the consultant does not have as much time as would be desirable for diagnosis, (2) when a relatively uncomplicated organizational map is needed for quick service, or (3) when the client is unaccustomed to thinking in system terms. In the latter case, the model helps the client to visualize his or her organization as a systemic whole without the use of strange terminology. I have also found Weisbord's model particularly useful in supervising and guiding students in their initial OD consultations.

EXHIBIT 9.4

A Classification of Interview Data in Exhibit 9.3 According to Weisbord's Six-Box Model

	Formal system			Informal system		
1. Purposes	S-3	W-2 W-8	M-2	S-9	W-2 W-3	M-3
2. Structure		W-1 W-6	M-1	S-6 S-8		
3. Relationships				S-2 S-4	W-11 W-12	M-5 M-8
4. Rewards		W-9		S-2 S-5	W-10	
5. Leadership		W-4	M-4	S-1 S-7 S-9		M-6
6. Helpful mechanisms		W-1 W-5 W-7		S-8		

Note: The symbols—S-1, S-2, W-1, W-2, M-1, M-2, and so forth—refer to the summary phrases in Exhibit 9.3: S-1 is the first *srength* listed, S-2 the second strength, W-1 the first *weakness,* M-1 the first objective for the off-site *meeting,* and so forth.

The Nadler-Tushman Congruence Model

For a more sophisticated client and when more time is available, a more complex model of organizations might be useful for OD diagnosis. In such instances the Nadler and Tushman (1977) congruence model should serve the purpose.

Nadler and Tushman make the same assumptions as Weisbord—that an organization is an open system and therefore is influenced by its environment (inputs) and also shapes its environment to some extent by outputs. An organization thus is the transformation entity between inputs and outputs. Exhibit 9.5 represents the Nadler-Tushman congruence model.

Inputs

Nadler and Tushman view inputs to the system as relatively fixed; the four they cite are the *environment,* the *resources* available to the organization, the organization's *history,* and *strategies* that are developed or evolve over time. These inputs help define how people in the organization behave, and they serve as constraints on behavior as well as opportunities for action.

As we know from the works of Burns and Stalker (1961), and Lawrence and Lorsch (1967), the extent to which an organization's environment is relatively stable or dynamic significantly affects internal operations, struc-

EXHIBIT 9.5
The Nadler-Tushman Congruence Model for Diagnosing Organizational Behavior

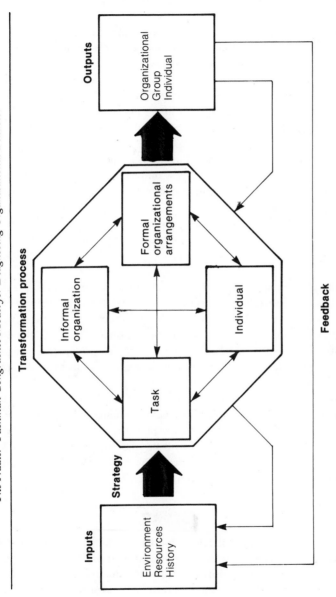

Source: D. A. Nadler and M. L. Tushman, "A Diagnostic Model for Organization Behavior," in *Perspectives on Behavior in Organizations*, ed. J. R. Hackman, E. E. Lawler, and L. W. Porter (New York: McGraw-Hill, 1977), pp. 85-100. Reprinted by permission.

175

ture, and policy. For many organizations a very important aspect of environment is the parent system and its directives. Many organizations are subsidiaries or divisional profit centers of larger corporations—such as Ron's unit in the case example—colleges within a university, or hospitals within a larger health care delivery system. These subordinate organizations may operate relatively autonomously with respect to the outside world—having their own purchasing operations, for example—but because of corporate policy may be fairly restricted in how much money they can spend. Thus, for many organizations we must think of their environments in at least two categories: the larger parent system and the rest of the outside world—government regulations, competitors, and the marketplace in general.

Resources within the Nadler-Tushman model include capital (money, property, equipment, and so on), raw materials, technologies, people, and various intangibles, such as company name, which may have a high value in the company's market.

An organization's history is also input to the system. The history determines, for example, patterns of employee behavior, policy, the types of people the organization attracts and recruits, and even how decisions get made in a crisis.

Although strategy is categorized as an input in the models, Nadler and Tushman set it apart. Strategy is the process of determining how the organization's resources are best used within the environment for optimal organizational functioning. It is the act of identifying opportunities in the environment and determining whether the organization's resources are adequate for capitalizing on these opportunities. History plays a subtle but influential role in this strategic process.

Some organizations are very strategic; that is, they plan. Other organizations simply react to changes in their environments or act opportunistically rather than according to a long-range plan that determines which opportunities will be seized and which will be allowed to pass. As Nadler and Tushman point out, however, organizations have strategies whether they are deliberate and formal or unintentional and informal.

Outputs

We shall move to the right side of the model to consider outputs before covering the transformation process. Thus we shall examine the organization's environment from the standpoint of both how it influences the system and how it becomes influenced by the system's outputs before we delve into how the organization operates internally.

For diagnostic purposes, Nadler and Tushman present four key categories of outputs: system functioning, group behavior, intergroup relations, and individual behavior and affect. With respect to the effectiveness of the system's functioning as a whole, the following three questions should elicit the necessary information:

1. How well is the organization attaining its desired goals of production, service, return on investment, and so on?
2. How well is the organization utilizing its resources?
3. How well is the organization coping with changes in its environment over time?

The remaining three outputs are more directly behavioral: how well groups or units within the organization are performing; how effectively these units communicate with one another, resolve differences, and collaborate when necessary; and how individuals behave. For this last output, individual behavior, we are interested in such matters as turnover, absenteeism, and, of course, individual job performance.

The Transformation Process

The components of the transformation process and their interactions are what we normally think of when we consider an organization—the people, the various tasks and jobs, the organization's managerial structure (the organization chart), and all relationships of individuals, groups, and sub-systems. As Exhibit 9.5 shows, four interactive major components compose the transformation process—changing inputs into outputs.

The *task component* consists of the jobs to be done and the inherent characteristics of the work itself. The primary task dimensions are the extent and nature of the required interdependence between and among task performers, the level of skill needed, and the kinds of information required to perform the tasks adequately.

The *individual component* consists of all the differences and similarities among employees, particularly demographic data, skill and professional levels, and personality-attitudinal variables.

Organizational arrangements include the managerial and operational structure of the organization, work flow and design, the reward system, management information systems, and the like. These arrangements are the formal mechanisms used by management to direct and control behavior and to organize and accomplish the work to be done.

The fourth component, *informal organization,* is the social structure within the organization, including the grapevine, the organization's internal politics, and the informal authority-information structure—whom you see for what.

177

Congruence: The Concept of Fit

As Nadler and Tushman point out, a mere listing and description of these system inputs, outputs, and components is insufficient for modeling an organization. An organization is dynamic, never static, and the model must represent this reality, as the arrows in Exhibit 9.5 do. Nadler and Tushman go beyond depicting relationships, however. Their term, *fit,* is a measure of the congruence between pairs of inputs and especially between the components of the transformation process. They contend that inconsistent fits between any pair will result in less than optimal organizational and individual performance. Nadler and Tushman's hypothesis, therefore, is that, the better the fit is, the more effective the organization will be.

Nadler and Tushman recommend three steps for diagnosis:

1. Identify the system: Is the system for diagnosis an autonomous organization, a subsidiary, a division, or a unit of some larger system? What are the boundaries of the system, its membership, its tasks, and—if it is part of a larger organization—its relationships with other units?
2. Determine the nature of the key variables: What are the dimensions of the inputs and components? What are the desired outputs?
3. Diagnose the state of fits. This is the most important step, involving two related activities: determining fits between components and diagnosing the link between the fits and the organizations outputs.

The OD consultant must concentrate on the degree to which the key components are congruent with one another. Questions such as the following should be asked:

> To what extent do the organizational arrangements fit with the requirements of the tasks?
>
> To what extent do individual skills and needs fit with task requirements, with organizational arrangements, and with the informal organization? Hackman and Oldham's (1975) job characteristics theory is a useful supplementary model for this part of the diagnosis, as is expectancy theory (Vroom 1964; Lawler 1973).
>
> To what extent do task requirements fit with both the formal and the informal organizations? Information-processing models are useful supplements for this aspect of the diagnosis (Galbraith 1977; Tushman and Nadler 1978).
>
> Exhibit 9.6 summarizes the fit questions to be raised.

For diagnosing the link between fits and outputs, the OD consultant must focus the outcome of the diagnoses of the various component fits and their

EXHIBIT 9.6

Definitions of Fits and Examples of Diagnostic Issues
from the Nadler-Tushman Congruence Model

Fit	The Issues
Individual-organization	To what extent individual needs are met by the organizational arrangements. To what extent individuals hold clear or distorted perceptions of organizational structures. The convergence of individual and organizational goals.
Individual-task	To what extent the needs of individuals are met by the tasks, to what extent individuals have skills and abilities to meet task demands.
Individual-informal organization	To what extent individual needs are met by the informal organization, to what extent does the informal organization make use of individual resources, consistent with informal goals.
Task-organization	Whether the organizational arrangements are adequate to meet the demands of the task, whether organizational arrangements tend to motivate behavior consistent with task demands.
Task-informal organization	Whether the informal organization structure facilitates task performance or not, whether it hinders or promotes meeting the demands of the task.
Organization-informal organization	Whether the goals, rewards, and structures of the informal organization are consistent with those of the formal organization.

Source: D. A. Nadler and M. L. Tushman, "A Diagnostic Model for Organization Behavior," in *Perspectives on Behavior in Organizations*, ed. J. R. Hackman, E. E. Lawler, and L. W. Porter (New York: McGraw-Hill, 1977), pp. 85–100. Reprinted by permission.

behavioral consequences on the set of behaviors associated with system outputs: goal attainment, resource utilization, and overall system performance. Considering the component fits, or lack thereof, in light of system outputs helps identify critical problems of the organization. As these problems are addressed and changes are made, the system is then monitored through the feedback loop for purposes of evaluation.

Hornstein and Tichy's Emergent Pragmatic Model

The emergent pragmatic model of organizational diagnosis (Hornstein and Tichy 1973; Tichy, Hornstein, and Nisberg 1977) is based on the premise that most managers and consultants "carry around in their heads" implicit theories or models about organizational behavior and about how human systems actually operate. These notions are usually intuitive, ill-formed, and difficult to articulate. Because they are largely intuitive, different observers and members of organizations have different theories, which gives rise to conflicts among consultants or between consultants and clients about what is really wrong with the organization and how to fix it.

179

To deal with these intuitive notions, Hornstein and Tichy have developed a procedure for helping managers and consultants articulate and eventually conceptualize their implicit models and therefore make them explicit. The procedure, known as an emergent pragmatic theory or model, consists of using a workbook and selecting items from among twenty-two sample labels or creating one's own labels from twenty-eight blank labels that are provided. These labels include such items as informal groupings, fiscal characteristics, turnover, goals, and satisfaction of members with their jobs. Individuals' selections represent the information they would seek in diagnosing an organization.

Hornstein and Tichy's approach to organizational diagnosis is one that is shared between consultant and client and among members of the client organization. The approach is identified as an emergent pragmatic theory because "the model *emerges* from an exploration of both the consultant's and client's assumptions about behavior and organizations . . . and draws on both the consultant's and client's organizational *experiences* as well as on empirical and theoretical work in the field" (Tichy, Hornstein, and Nisberg 1977, p. 367; emphasis added).

Another of Hornstein and Tichy's premises is that, consciously or not, organizational consultants tend to impose their theories and models of human systems on their clients. These impositions may or may not fit with the client organizations' realities, may or may not agree with client members' perceptions and beliefs, and may or may not jibe with the client organizations' underlying values. To assure better congruence, Hornstein and Tichy advocate a highly collaborative approach between consultants and clients, one that results in an emergent model that represents different perspectives and experiences.

There are five phases to the emergent-pragmatic approach. The consultant guides the client group through these phases.

1. *Exploring and developing a diagnostic model.* The first step of this phase is for members of the client group to work individually in the workbooks and select labels from the workbook for the organizational items that represent the most important dimensions of organization for the purpose of diagnosis—at least from each individual's point of view. The second step of this initial phase is for all members of the client group to agree on a common list. This agreement process consists largely of eliminating overlapping labels and arriving at a final list that represents all individual's selections.

The third step is to develop categories of organizational components from the common list of labels. This step is a group activity. Categories of labels representing organizational components might include such elements as formal structure, hard data (for example, a profit and loss statement), environmental interface, and organization member characteristics. A secondary but important consequence of this step is that the group begins to develop a common language, a shared organizational vocabulary. The terms and categories are therefore concrete, pragmatic, and more meaningful for the client members.

The final step of this initial phase is to make the model dynamic. For this activity, the group members first imagine that change may occur in one component of their model and then trace the effects of this change on all other components. They do this for each component of their model. The resulting matrix shows which components the group members believe are the most and the least significant in terms of impact on other components. The model is then used as the basis for developing change strategies.

2. *Developing change strategies.* Since different components of the model will probably have different impacts, client members are in a position to determine potential levers for change. ''For instance, if a model included a category called formal structure which contained such items as authority structure, reward system, and formal communication structure, the category might be considered a good leverage point if changes in this category produced desirable changes in a number of other categories'' (Tichy, Hornstein, and Nisberg 1977, p. 372). Thus, the strategy is a statement of a plan for what is to be changed, the method of change, and the sequence of events comprising the change steps.

3. *Developing change techniques.* This phase consists of exploring potential techniques, determining which are most appropriate, and then matching the selected techniques with each organizational component that has been designated for change.

4. *Assessing the necessary conditions for assuring success.* The final selection of change techniques is based on criteria developed in this phase. These criteria usually stem from such conditions as the system's readiness for change, the available resources, budget considerations, and the system's history regarding change, especially whether OD has been attempted before.

5. *Evaluating the change strategies.* For this final phase, criteria are developed for evaluating the success or failure of the overall change strategy, and measurement procedures are developed.

The emergent pragmatic approach to organizational diagnosis is based on two assumptions: (1) that most managers and consultants have intuitive theories about how organizations function, rather than well-formulated conceptual frameworks; and (2) that many consultants impose their models and theories on client organizations, regardless of how appropriate they may be for the particular client. Hornstein and Tichy advocate a collaborative model of diagnosis to avoid the potential negative consequences of operating on the basis of these two assumptions.

The two models described earlier—Weisbord's six-box model and the Nadler-Tushman congruence model—are generic frameworks and do not fall prey to the problems of Hornstein and Tichy's two premises. When the consultant and the client do not find the Weisbord, Nadler-Tushman, or other formal models to their liking, however, the emergent pragmatic approach offers a clear alternative. It is a do-it-yourself model, and, if both consultant and client are willing to spend the time required to do it right, a mutually satisfying and appropriate model for the client organization is likely to result.

The three models described may all be categorized as *contingency* models; they do not specify directions for change prior to diagnosis. What needs to be changed emanates from the diagnosis. None of the models advocates a particular design for an organization's internal structure, a certain style of behavior, or a specific approach to management. The inventors of these models do have biases, however. Weisbord says the boxes should be in balance, Nadler and Tushman argue that the various dimensions of their model should fit with one another, and Hornstein and Tichy state that consultant and client should collaborate toward the emergence of a model that is appropriate for the given organization. These biases have more to do with the best way to diagnose than with the most important dimension to change.

Lawrence and Lorsch's Contingency Theory

Lawrence and Lorsch—early contingency advocates—specify neither a best way to diagnose nor a particular direction for change. They do emphasize certain dimensions of organization, however—particularly structure and intergroup relationships. They consider other dimensions, but these two take priority in their view of organizations.

Lawrence and Lorsch do not have a model of organizations as such, and thus they may be classified more appropriately as contingency theorists. They argue (or hypothesize) that there is a cause-effect relationship between how well an organization's internal structure matches environmental demands and how well the organization performs—that is, accomplishes goals and objectives. Their research in the 1960s provided support for their argument (Lawrence and Lorsch 1967).

A brief explanation of Lawrence and Lorsch's contingency theory was provided in Chapter 2. For our purposes here, we want to understand the use of their contingency theory for diagnosis. Keep in mind that the two primary concepts of the Lawrence and Lorsch contingency theory are differentiation and integration. These two concepts represent the paradox of any organization design—that labor must simultaneously be divided and coordinated or integrated. Within the Lawrence and Lorsch framework and for diagnostic purposes, therefore, we want to examine our client organization along the dimensions they consider to be important. The methodological appendix of their book provides considerable detail concerning these dimensions and the questions to ask for obtaining the relevant information (Lawrence and

Lorsch 1967). We shall summarize these dimensions and some of the related questions.

Environmental Demands

1. On what basis does a customer evaluate and choose between competing suppliers in this industry (price, quality, delivery, service, and so forth)?
2. What are the major problems an organization encounters when competing in this industry?
3. Have there been significant changes in the market or technical conditions in this industry in recent years? What is the current situation?

Differentiation

1. Regarding structure, what is the average span of control? How important is it to have formal rules for routing procedures and operations?
2. Regarding the time span of feedback, how long does it take for employees to see the results of their performances? (In sales, for example, the time lag is typically short, whereas in R&D it may take years.)
3. Regarding interpersonal relationships, how important are they, and how much interaction is necessary?
4. Regarding goal certainty, how clear-cut are the goals? How are they measured?

Integration

1. How interdependent are any two units: high (each depends on the other for survival), medium (each needs some things from the other), or low (each functions fairly autonomously)?
2. What is the quality of relations between units?

Conflict Management

1. What mode of conflict resolution is used: forcing (top-down edicts), smoothing (being kind and avoiding), or confronting (exposing differences and solving problems)?
2. How much influence do employees have on the hierarchy for solving problems and making decisions?

Employee-Management Contract

1. To what extent do employees feel that what is expected of them is appropriate?

2. To what extent do employees feel that they are compensated and rewarded fairly for their performance?

Summary

These five dimensions represent the organizational domains that Lawrence and Lorsch believe most important for effective diagnosis. Based on their research findings, the organizational diagnostician would be looking for the degree of match between environmental demands and complexities and the internal organizational structure. The greater the environmental complexity, the more complex the internal design should be. If the organization's markets change rapidly and are difficult to predict and forecast, and if the environment in general fluctuates considerably, the organization's internal structure should be relatively decentralized so that many employees can be in touch with the environment and can act quickly as changes occur. Under these conditions, differentiation may still be high, but a premium is placed on integration. There must be sufficient integrating mechanisms so that communication flows adequately across and among the many subunits and so that superiors in the hierarchy are kept well informed. The plastics industry represented this type of organization in the Lawrence and Lorsch research study. When the environment is relatively stable and not particularly complex—the container industry in their study—a fairly simple and straightforward internal structure may be best, with functional division of labor and centralized authority.

The issue is not whether one organization should be highly differentiated and another highly integrated but that they should be highly differentiated *and* integrated. High integration seems to be important regardless of environment, and differentiation may be somewhat lower for organizations with stable environments. The paradox remains in any case: both are needed, but they are antagonistic—the more the organization is differentiated, the more integration is required.

The organizational diagnostician should also seek the mode of conflict resolution. Lawrence and Lorsch found that, the more organization members and units confront their differences and work to resolve them, rather than smoothing them over or squashing them with edicts from on high, the more effective the organization tended to be.

Finally, it is necessary to know the degree of employees' satisfaction with their psychological contract with the organization. There is apparently a positive relationship between clarity of employees' understanding of what is expected of them—their perceived satisfaction with the rewards they receive for performance—and overall organizational performance.

Although Lawrence and Lorsch are contingency theorists, particularly with respect to organizational structure, they too have their biases. They stress interfaces—between the organization and its environment, between and among units within the organization, and between individual employees and the organization as represented by management.

Normative Theories

Unlike contingency theorists, normative theorists argue that, for organization development, there is one best way to and direction for change. Major proponents of normative theory are Likert (1967) and Blake and Mouton (1968, 1978).

Likert's Profiles

Likert categorizes organizations, or systems in his terms, as one of four types: System 1—autocratic, top-down, exploitative management; System 2—benevolent autocracy (still top-down but not as exploitive); System 3—consultative (employees are consulted about problems and decisions but management still makes the final decisions); and System 4—participative management (key policy decisions are made in groups by consensus).

Likert's approach to organizational diagnosis is standardized. The mode used is a questionnaire, the "Profile of Organizational Characteristics," with six sections: leadership, motivation, communication, decisions, goals, and control. Organization members answer questions in each of these sections by placing the letter N at the place on a twenty-point scale that best represents their opinion now and a P at the place that indicates their previous opinion—how they experienced their organization one or two years ago. Sometimes the consultant asks organization members to use an I instead of a P, to indicate what they would consider ideal for each of the questions. Exhibit 9.7 is the short version of Likert's profile. Notice that the questionnaire is divided vertically by four lines. Each division represents the four Likert systems, with System 1 at the left and System 4 at the right. Thus, a profile of the organization can be determined by averaging organization members' responses to each of the questions.

Organizational profiles typically range in the System 2 or 3 categories. If the ideal response is used, its profile will usually occur to the right of the now profile—toward or within System 4. In such cases, the direction for change is established—toward System 4. Exhibit 9.8 gives an example of such a profile.

When one declares that there is one best way—in this case System 4 management—others usually demand evidence. Is System 4 management a better way to run an organization than System 3 or 2 or 1? Contingency theorists, of course, would say no; it depends on the type of business the organization is in, the nature of the environment the organization faces, and the technology involved. Likert contends that, regardless of these contingen-

185

EXHIBIT 9.7

Likert's Profile of Organizational Characteristics: Short Form

		SYSTEM 1	SYSTEM 2	SYSTEM 3	SYSTEM 4
LEADERSHIP	How much confidence is shown in subordinates?	None	Condescending	Substantial	Complete
	How free do they feel to talk to superiors about job?	Not at all	Not very	Rather free	Fully free
	Are subordinates' ideas sought and used, if worthy?	Seldom	Sometimes	Usually	Always
MOTIVATION	Is predominent use made of 1) fear, 2) threats, 3) punishment, 4) rewards, 5) involvement?	1, 2, 3 occasionally	4, some 3	4, some 3 and 5	5, 4, based on group set goals
	Where is responsibility felt for achieving organization's goals?	Mostly at top	Top & middle	Fairly general	At all levels
COMMUNICATION	How much communication is aimed at achieving organization's objectives?	Very little	Little	Quite a bit	A great deal
	What is the direction of information flow?	Downward	Mostly downward	Down and up	Down, up and sideways
	How is downward communication accepted?	With suspicion	Possibly with suspicion	With caution	With an open mind
	How well do superiors know problems faced by subordinates?	Know little	Some knowledge	Quite well	Very well
DECISIONS	At what level are decisions formally made?	Mostly at top	Policy at top	Broad policy at top, more delegation	Throughout but well integrated
	What is the origin of technical and professional knowledge used in decision making?	Top management	Upper & middle	To a certain extent, throughout	To a great extent throughout
	Are subordinates involved in decisions related to their work?	Not at all	Occasionally consulted	Generally consulted	Fully involved
	What does decision-making process contribute to motivation?	Nothing, often weakens it	Relatively little	Some contribution	Substantial contribution
GOALS	How are organizational goals established?	Orders issued	Orders, some Comment invited	After discussion, by order	By group action (except in crisis)
	How much covert resistance to goals is present?	Strong resistance	Moderate resistance	Some resistance at times	Little or none
CONTROL	How concentrated are review and control functions?	Highly at top	Relatively highly at top	Moderate delegation to lower levels	Quite widely shared
	Is there an informal organization resisting the formal one?	Yes	Usually	Sometimes	No - same goals as formal
	What are cost, productivity, and other control data used for?	Policing, punishment	Reward and punishment	Reward - some self-guidance	Self-guidance problem-solving

From *The Human Organization* by Rensis Likert. Copyright © 1975 by Rensis Likert. Used with the permission of McGraw-Hill Book Company.

186

EXHIBIT 9.8

Example of a Summary of Organization Members' Responses According to Likert's Profile of Organizational Characteristics

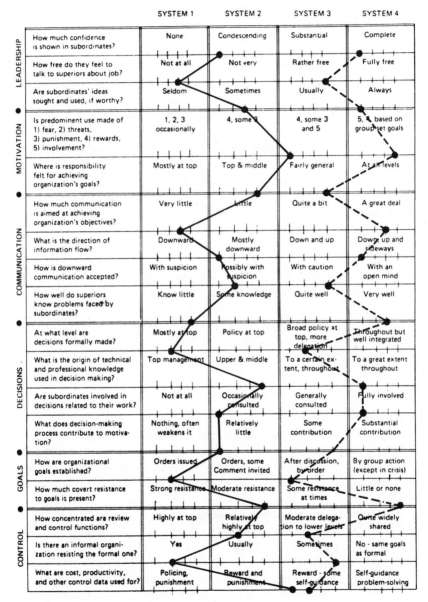

The solid line represents current perceptions, and the dotted line represents the ideal

From *The Human Organization* by Rensis Likert. Copyright © 1975 by Rensis Likert. Used with the permission of McGraw-Hill Book Company.

cies, System 4 is best. Likert's (1967) own research supports his claim, and so does research done by others. A longitudinal study of perhaps the most systematic change to System 4 management—conducted in the Harwood-Weldon Company, a manufacturer of sleepwear—is a noteworthy example (Marrow, Bowers, and Seashore 1967). Changes were made in all dimensions of Likert's profile as well as in work flow and organizational structure. The durability of these changes was supported by a later study conducted by Seashore and Bowers (1970).

A System 4 approach was also used as the change goal for a General Motors assembly plant (Dowling 1975). As a result of these deliberate change efforts toward System 4, significant improvements were accomplished on several indices, including operating efficiency, costs, and grievances.

In summary, Likert's approach to organizational diagnosis is structured and directional. It is structured by use of his questionnaire, the "Profile of Organizational Characteristics," and of later versions of his profile (J. Taylor and Bowers 1972), and it is directional in that the data that are collected are compared with System 4. The survey feedback method (to be explained in the next chapter) is used as the main intervention; that is, the data from the questionnaire (survey) are reported back to organizational members in a set manner.

In order to use Likert's approach, the consultant should feel comfortable with the questionnaire method as the primary mode for data gathering and with System 4 management as the goal for change. Although participative management may feel comfortable as a change goal for many consultants and clients, the relatively limited diagnosis by profile characteristics only may not be so comfortable.

Blake and Mouton's Grid Organization Development

The other normative approach to OD is based on the managerial grid model developed by Blake and Mouton (1964, 1978). Like Likert's System 4 approach, the grid method of OD is structured and involves a high degree of packaging. Blake and Mouton also argue that there is one best way to manage an organization. Their label is 9,9, which also represents a participative style of management.

Blake and Mouton also depend on questionnaires, but grid OD (Blake and Mouton 1968) goes far beyond an initial diagnosis with a questionnaire. In some respects, regardless of organization, Blake and Mouton start from an initial, general diagnosis. In a cross-cultural study of what managers consider the most common barriers to business effectiveness and corporate excellence, Blake and Mouton (1968) found that communication topped the list of ten, and a lack of planning was second. These two barriers were selected by managers much more frequently than the remaining eight (74 percent noted communication and 62 percent mentioned planning); morale and coordination, for example, the next most frequently mentioned barriers, were noted by less than 50 percent. Blake and Mouton further pointed out that communication and planning were the top two mentioned regardless of country, company, or characteristics of the managers reporting. These two major barriers, and the other less prevalent ones, are symptoms of organizational problems, not causes, according to Blake and Mouton. The causes lie deeper in the system. Faulty planning, for example, is a result of an organization's not having a strategy or having a strategy that is based on unsound rationale. Communication problems derive from the nature of the supervision practiced in the organization.

For addressing these underlying causes, Blake and Mouton have developed a six-phase approach to organization development that considers both the organization's strategic plan, or lack thereof, and the style or approach to supervision and management. They contend that, to achieve excellence, an organizational strategic model should be developed and the supervisory style should be changed in the direction of participative management. Organization members should first examine managerial behavior and style and then move on to develop and implement an ideal strategic organizational model. Before explaining the six phases of their OD approach in more detail, we should consider Blake and Mouton's managerial style model, the managerial grid, because most of their normative rationale is based on this model.

Building on earlier research work on leadership (see Chapter 7), in which the dual functions of a leader were variously labeled as initiation of structure and consideration, task and maintenance, and task and socioemotional behaviors, Blake and Mouton (1964) simplified the language by using terms closer to managers' understanding—production and people. They did more, however; the creative aspect of their work was to conceptualize each of the two leader functions on a continuum—one for the manager's degree of concern for production and one for his or her concern for people—and to put the two together in the form of a graph, a two-dimensional model.

As noted in Chapter 7, Blake and Mouton (1981) contend that they have done more than merely simplifying the language and creating nine-point scales. They argue that the original dimensions—initiation of structure and consideration—and those that followed, especially Hersey and Blanchard's situational leadership model, were conceptualized as independent dimensions. Blake and Mouton's dimensions—production and people—are interdependent, however, and represent attitudes more than behavior. They note that leadership is not possible without both task and people. We shall now consider Blake and Mouton's model in more detail.

Any manager will have some degree of concern for accomplishing the organization's purpose—producing products or services—that is, a concern

189

for production, results, or profits. A manager will also have some degree of concern for the people who are involved in helping to accomplish the organization's purpose. Managers may differ in how concerned they are with each of these managerial functions, but how these two concerns mesh for a given manager determines his or her *style* or approach to management and defines that manager's use of power.

Blake and Mouton chose nine-point scales to depict their model and to rank the manager's degree of concern for production and people; 1 represents a low concern and 9 indicates a high concern. Although there are eighty-one possible combinations, Blake and Mouton realistically chose to consider only the four more or less extreme positions, represented in the four corners of the grid, and the middle-of-the-road style, position 5,5 in the middle of the grid. Exhibit 9.9 illustrates the managerial grid.

Blake and Mouton describe the five styles as follows:

9,1. In the lower right-hand corner of the Grid a maximum concern (9) for production is combined with a minimum concern (1) for people. A manager acting under these assumptions concentrates on maximizing production by exercising power and authority and achieving control over people through compliance.

1,9. Here a minimum concern (1) for production is coupled with a maximum concern (9) for people. Primary attention is placed on promoting good feelings among colleagues and subordinates.

1,1. A minimum concern for both production and people is represented by 1,1 in the lower left corner. [This] manager does only the minimum required to remain within the organization.

5,5. This is the "middle of the road" theory or the "go-along-to-get-along" assumptions which are revealed in conformity to the status quo.

9,9. Production and people concerns are integrated at a high level . . . This is the team approach. It is goal-oriented and seeks to gain results of high quantity and quality through participation, involvement, commitment, and conflict-solving. (Blake and Mouton 1978, p. 12)

As noted earlier, Blake and Mouton contend that communication problems in the organization stem from the nature of supervision. Most supervision—the predominant style in United States organizations today—can be characterized as 5,5 (Blake and Mouton 1978). A recent popular book, *The Gamesman* (Maccoby 1976), is a description of Blake and Mouton's 5,5 manager. In an unpublished study a colleague, Barry Render, and I also found 5,5 to be the predominant style of middle managers in a large government agency ($N = 400$). This style, according to Blake and Mouton, is bureaucratic and mechanistic, thus less than effective. They posit, therefore, that communication problems come from such less-than-effective supervision and management approach. The three styles labeled 9,1, 1,9, and 1,1 are even poorer, causing similar if not worse communication problems. The 9,9

EXHIBIT 9.9

The Managerial Grid

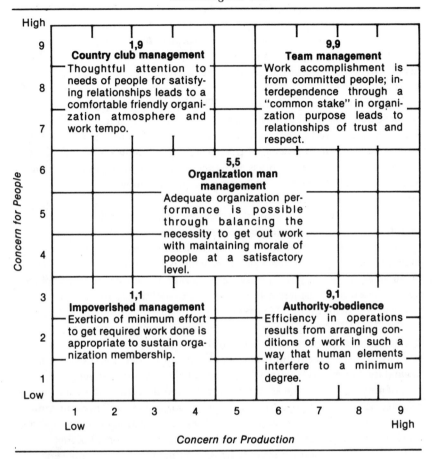

Source: R. R. Blake and J. S. Mouton, *The New Managerial Grid* (Houston: Gulf, 1978). Reprinted by permission.

style, then, is best and when practiced consistently will assure significantly fewer problems of communication. Training managers to adopt a 9,9 style will therefore lead to significantly fewer barriers to organizational effectiveness.

The six phases of grid organization development begin with a one-week seminar at which participants assess their present styles and learn the behaviors associated with the 9,9 style. Participants also receive feedback on their styles from their fellow group members.

Phase 2 of grid OD is teamwork development. Assessment again takes place—identifying the norms and working characteristics of all managerial teams in the organization, starting with the top team and moving downward in the hierarchy to include the others. Team members also receive feedback regarding their interpersonal styles in the team. The teams work on actual problems and practice team behavior according to the participative management model. Thus, openness is encouraged, trust is stressed, exposing and dealing with conflict is emphasized, and consensual decision making is practiced.

Phase 3 is intergroup development. The objective of this phase is to reduce win-lose patterns of behavior between groups in the organization. Thus, the behaviors associated with competition and cooperation are examined. Ideal models are generated—each group separately developing a model of an ideal relationship—and these models are exchanged between groups. Finally, action steps are planned for facilitating the groups' move toward what they jointly decide is an ideal relationship.

Phase 4 is development of an ideal strategic corporate model. This phase is essentially what is called corporate strategic planning. It begins with the development of an ideal strategic organization, usually done by the top management team. This team practices what Blake and Mouton call "strict business logic" as they (1) specify minimum and optimum financial objectives, (2) describe business activities to be pursued in the future, (3) define markets for penetration, (4) create an internal structure for synergistic results, (5) delineate policies to guide future decisions, and (6) identify development requirements for sustaining the model.

Phase 5 is implementation of the ideal strategic model. This phase, similar to what Beckhard and Harris (1977) later called transition management, consists of moving toward the ideal model in a carefully managed, evolutionary manner while continuing to run the organization as before. This continuing-to-run process gradually changes, so that the organization begins to operate more and more within the policies and procedures of the ideal model.

Phase 6 is systematic critique. During this final phase, the change effort is evaluated and so-called drag factors are identified—specific barriers that still exist and must now be overcome.

Phases 1, 2, and 3 are thus designed to deal with communication barriers to organizational effectiveness, and Phases 4, 5, and 6 deal with the planning barriers.

It is interesting that not until Phase 6 do Blake and Mouton begin to deal with an organization diagnostically in terms like those of the other diagnostic models we have considered. Blake and Mouton have evidently decided that all fairly large organizations that are not already involved in organization development have serious communication and planning barriers to effectiveness. These two primary barriers must be reduced first, and grid OD will do the job. At Phase 6 we will see how effectively the first five phases have progressed and we will know, *in particular* and *in detail,* what barriers must now be tackled.

Blake and Mouton never state it, but they apparently assume that, unless an organization learns how to communicate more effectively (practice 9,9 management) and plan more logically and systematically (build an ideal strategic model and begin to implement it), its management will never be able to deal optimally with the specifics of running a business. Phase 6 in the grid OD sequence gets to the specifics.

Blake and Mouton refer to their book *Corporate Excellence Diagnosis* (1968b) as "the Phase 6 Instrument." It is based on their diagnostic model, "The Corporate Excellence Rubric," and consists of seventy-two windows—elements that are used to diagnose corporate behavior, performance, and results. The model, or rubric, is composed of three major dimensions. The first dimension consists of the organizational *functions* that are typical of most business or industrial organizations—human resources, financial management, operations, marketing, research and development, and corporate (headquarters). Three *perspectives* comprise the second major dimension: effectiveness—ratings of present behavior, performance, and results; flexibility—the ability of the organization to adapt quickly to unanticipated changes; and development—ratings of potential for growth and adequacy of long-term strategies. Four *orientations*—the third major dimension—are assessed within each of the eighteen (six functions by three perspectives) major windows of the overall model: (1) internal—actions under the direct control of the organization; (2) external—outside environmental forces; (3) aggressive—thrustful actions, such as being opportunistic and challenging the competition; and (4) defensive—eliminating weaknesses, reducing restraints, and warding off threats. Thus, internal aggressive assessments consider how well the organization can take advantage of opportunities from the standpoint of internal resources; internal defensive assessments concern management's efforts and ability to solve internal weaknesses; external aggressive assessments deal with how well the organization takes advantage of opportunities in the external environment, such as potential markets; and external defensive assessments diagnose how aware the organization is of competitors' activities and other external forces.

The rubric consists of these three major areas, six functions, three perspectives, and four orientations, which combine to produce seventy-two windows. For use in diagnosis, each window consists of nine-point rating scales. Each scale begins with a paragraph description of the management issue to be rated. In the human resources function, for example, "top level leadership" is an issue. The description states: "The character of a company, whether dynamic, forceful, initiating, and risk-taking or mechanically repetitive, dull, aimless, or backward-looking, is established at the top" (Blake and Mouton 1968b, p. 22). The organization member then

193

rates top leadership on the scale, with the option of rewriting the issue somewhat to fit his or her situation better before rating it. Next, the person provides examples and seeks causes and improvement steps.

Blake and Mouton's (1968) book has more than four hundred pages of various issues and scales. Phase 6 is obviously time-consuming, detailed, structured, and tedious but very thorough. Although it is highly structured, there is some flexibility in that respondents may rewrite issues to suit their own situations better.

Levinson's Clinical-Historical Approach

As discussed briefly in Chapter 2, Levinson's theory of organization behavior is grounded in psychoanalytic theory and views organizations in familial dimensions: "An organization is composed of persons in authority and 'siblings' who relate to these authorities" (Levinson 1972a, p. 23). Because it is so closely aligned with psychoanalytic theory, it is not surprising that Levinson's approach to organizational diagnosis (Levinson 1972a) (1) is very detailed, (2) emphasizes history, and (3) generally relies on clinical methods (Levinson 1972b). Using Levinson's approach, the consultant does a workup on a client organization—much as a physician would do with a patient—and obtains as complete a history as possible, especially in terms of how the organization fits into its environment. In the search for information, Levinson (1972a) suggests:

> Most newspapers have morgues, or files of clippings, filed by subject. Historical societies often have much information on file. Large organizations will frequently be the subject of articles in trade or professional magazines which may be located through libraries . . . . The sheer availability of various kinds of information is a datum of diagnostic value. (p. 26)

Physicians collect historical information about their patients and then, in addition to taking such measurements as blood tests, observe their patients and thump here and there to determine what the patients "feel like." Levinson also stresses observation, especially initial impressions of the organization. Levinson (1972a) notes: "Since the consultant is his own most important instrument, he should begin [his tour of the organization by using] his antennae for sensing subtleties" (p. 18). Levinson argues that the consultant should request a tour of as much of the organization as time and practicalities will permit so that initial impressions can be made and recorded. "The consultant will find it helpful to keep a diary of his experiences in the company, to record events and observations which will not likely be reported in interviews or questionnaires" (Levinson 1972a, p. 19). Levinson (1972a) relies on six categories of data for diagnosis:

194

1. *Consultant observations and feelings:* how the consultant experiences the organization, especially initial impressions. These are recorded and become a set of information for later diagnosis.

2. *Factual data:* recorded policies and procedures, historical data on file in the organization, annual reports, job descriptions, personnel statistics, and former consultant or task force reports. Collecting this information is not enough, according to Levinson; how the data may interrelate is important, as is the type of language used. The language will convey attitudes toward people and assumptions about what motivates employees.

3. *Outside information:* information collected, primarily through interviews, from the organization's suppliers and competitors, cooperating organizations, agents, professional associations, and the like. This information will help the consultant understand the organization's environment in general and the impact it has on the client.

4. *Pattern of organization:* primarily the organization chart and the authority-responsibility structure of the organization. Levinson stresses a holistic approach rather than a view of the interaction of just one or two subsystems.

5. *Settings:* according to Levinson (1972a), "First overall organizational purposes and then how these purposes are subdivided into specific functions performed by definable groups within definable temporal and physical space . . . The consultant must learn where and by whom essential functions of the organization are carried out" (p. 28). Levinson refers to Bennis (1959) for a further breakdown of these settings into more specific organizational functions: service activities—support functions; problem-solving settings—collecting and analyzing information, such as production planning; production activities—the primary throughput between input and output, such as manufacturing; indoctrination settings—formalized training programs; and control activities—goal setting, monitoring, and evaluating progress. Levinson also notes in this context what Rice (1958) has called the time dimension: "temporal boundaries within which the setting's central purpose is accomplished . . . such as factory shift work . . . or . . . planning activities in a management group" (Levinson 1972a, p. 29).

6. *Task patterns:* group-level variables that exist in each setting. Levinson cites four such patterns: complementary activities—contributions of each work group member toward some common goal; parallel activities—group members performing essentially identical tasks; sequential activities—group members performing some phase of the overall group task; and individualized activities—unique functions performed by each person. These patterns constitute a setting, and the consultant attempts to learn the setting boundaries by analyzing the task patterns.

It is important to note that, although Levinson's theoretical base is

195

psychoanalytic and his method of diagnosis is patterned after the clinical model, he does not become absorbed in pieces of the system. His approach is systemic and holistic. Although he is biased toward a Freudian view, he does not lose himself in the analytics but rather looks for systemic issues and considers how the organization influences and is influenced by its environment, how subparts of the organization relate, and how work flows from one setting, activity, and function to another. Thus, being an organizational diagnostician of the Levinson school would require a thorough grounding in psychoanalytic theory, an understanding of the clinical method of diagnosis, and a systems view of organizations that highlights patterns of relationships and work flow.

Summary

In this chapter we have considered the diagnostic phase of organization development consultation in some depth by examining certain models. These models—Weisbord's six-box model, Nadler and Tushman's congruence model, Hornstein and Tichy's emergent pragmatic model, Lawrence and Lorsch's contingency model, the normative models of Likert and Blake and Mouton, and Levinson's historical-clinical approach—are not the only ones available. For organization development purposes, however, they are the most relevant ones and they demonstrate the diversity of the field. There is considerable choice for the OD practitioner-consultant. I have my biases, of course, as demonstrated in Chapters 5, 6, and 7, but I have also occasionally used elements of many of the models examined in this chapter.

I do not often have the time required for using Levinson's approach, although I like his thoroughness and the systemic-flow perspective. When time is short and my client is naive about systems, Weisbord's six-box model works well. Nadler and Tushman's model is appealing for some of the same reasons Levinson's is, but it is easier to work with and easier to communicate to a client. Hornstein and Tichy's approach is very useful for clients who are concerned that a consultant might impose something on them, and it is useful for setting the stage for in-depth diagnosis. Lawrence and Lorsch's contingency model is currently the most popular one among OD practitioners, and with good reason—it emphasizes organizational structure, which was overlooked by OD people in the early days, and shows how the organization's environment has an internal impact. Likert's and Blake and Mouton's theories are appealing because they clearly show the way, but if their approaches are chosen, they must be followed completely; a partial application will not work. Their high degree of structure and their normative view turns away some OD practitioners. Under certain circumstances, however, I have found both to be useful—Likert's profile for providing an outside, more objective questionnaire assessment of an organization, and Blake and

196

Mouton's grid for providing a framework for examining managerial style in the organization.

An OD practitioner's choice from among these models should be based primarily on two considerations. First, it is important to know the models as thoroughly as possible. It is impossible to use a model effectively if one does not understand it. Second, the practitioner should feel comfortable with the model and its approach. If one does not really believe in participative management, using Likert's or Blake and Mouton's approach is not likely to be successful.

CHAPTER 10

Diagnostic Techniques
and Feedback

In the previous chapters we have covered the phases of OD practice and several organizational models for diagnosis. Now that we have some conceptual frames of reference for diagnosis, we are in a position to examine actual techniques. With our models in hand we now know *what* to look for, but we must learn *how* to look for it, *how* to analyze what we find, and *how* to inform the client organization about our findings. In more technical terms, this chapter will cover (1) the process of collecting data about a client organization, (2) techniques for data collection, (3) techniques for data analysis, and (4) the process of data feedback.

First, however, a brief clarification of language is necessary. I have been using the terms *information* and *data* interchangeably, but the words are not exact synonyms. When consultants enter client systems in the initial phase of diagnosis, they collect information and facts about the organization. Later, as they analyze and reduce the array of information and facts to more understandable and workable terms, preferably within the context of some model, they begin to have *data*—a basis for reasoning, for making inferences, and for taking targeted and focused action. This is perhaps a minor, academic point, but it is important to be clear about the phases of OD practice and about where the points of departure are between phases—from seeking and collecting information to data analysis and diagnosis.

The Process of Data Collection

As noted in the previous chapter, when a consultant enters an organization to collect information, he or she is already intervening in the system, even though the intervention phase of OD practice comes later in the sequence. This intervening process may be considered from both the client's and the consultant's viewpoints.

198

The Client

Data collection in OD practice is anything but innocuous and innocent. The consultant asks questions not only about the organization in general but also about the people—how they feel about their jobs, the quality of supervision, barriers to motivation or better performance, and so forth. Thus, the client becomes involved at the very beginning, and certain impressions are made and expectations raised. Regardless of how good a first impression the consultant makes, he or she is an outsider, an intruder, and the client is being asked to reveal some things that outsiders do not normally know. The consultant is usually perceived as a professional, however, and is expected to help, so client organization members may be very willing to open up. Sometimes they eagerly await the consultant's visit or questionnaire as an opportunity to contribute to the improvement of their organization or simply to unload.

When a client is asked questions, he or she wants to know *who* the consultant is, *why* the consultant is there, *what* the consultant wants to know, *how* the consultant is going to use the information, and, fundamentally, whether the consultant can be trusted.

The Consultant

The consultant must be prepared to respond to the client's questions and must be sensitive to the fact that he or she is making an impression on the client during this initial phase of data collection that may affect the data collected—a first impression that may last.

Nadler (1977) suggests that the consultant has three goals in the data collection process. First, the consultant must strive to collect *valid information*. The data collected should reflect the organization's reality—how things really are, how they actually operate. Being conscious of and sensitive to the organization members' questions should help the consultant obtain accurate information—provided, of course, that he or she takes the time and effort to give answers to each member.

A second goal is to create and direct *energy*. Assuming that the data are valid, they may then serve as a focal point for action and change in the organization. The data collected may serve a consciousness-raising purpose, thereby generating energy. Data collection may also create expectations that someone (usually higher management) cares and that change is possible. With these kinds of expectations, energy can be created and focused.

There is a potential problem here. When data are collected, the typical reaction from organization members is raised expectations—that their opinions must count and that some things are going to be changed, or these questions wouldn't be asked. If those expectations are not realized, problems in the organization are likely to become worse than if data had never been col-

199

lected in the first place. Action must follow data collection. Follow-through of all seven phases of OD practice helps assure that raised expectations will be addressed.

The third goal of data collection is to build *relationships* between the consultant and members of the client organization. During the data collection process, the consultant has the opportunity to convey messages about his or her goals, values, and methods. How the consultant responds to client concerns reveals something about his or her values and priorities. Thus, the data collection phase can be used to begin the process of building relationships, or it can result in suspicion, disappointment, and an early demise of an OD effort. The consultant must recognize that interactions of human beings are involved during the data collection process and that relationships will begin or not depending on how well the consultant presents himself or herself.

Techniques for Data Collection

There are four major techniques for data collection in OD practice: interviews questionnaires, observations, and documents or records—what Nadler (1977) refers to as secondary data or unobtrusive measures.

Interviews

The interview is the most popular technique for data collection in organization development practice and may be the most useful, depending on the skill of the practitioner. Potentially, the interview can be best in accomplishing all three goals of data collection—acquiring valid information, creating and directing energy, and building relationships—because, compared with the other three techniques, it is the most flexible and adaptable. The structure of an interview can vary from very little structure—the practitioner simply encouraging the client to talk—to a high degree of structure—the practitioner asking a limited number of questions that are designed to elicit limited answers, such as questions that require only a yes or no answer or multiple-choice questions for which the client simply answers with one of the alternatives. Most interviews are somewhere in between, and whether questions are open-ended or have limited responses depends on a number of contingencies, such as how far along the OD effort is—and therefore how much trust in the process has been established—or how specific and targeted the diagnosis is intended to be—total system or subsystem, management and operations in general, or specific programs or projects.

At the beginning of an OD effort, I prefer to interview with some degree of structure, but leaving a fair margin of open-endedness as well. I usually rely on four primary questions:

200

1. What is going well in the organization; what are strengths, the positive qualities?
2. What is not going well; what are the problems, concerns, and issues?
3. What factors of your job provide satisfaction?
4. What are the barriers and hindrances that prevent you from doing the kind of work you feel you should and want to be doing?

I ask the client to keep a system perspective when responding to the first two questions, and to respond in terms of his or her job itself for the other two. I also make sure that the client understands that with the first and third questions I am looking for positives and with the second and fourth questions for negatives—problems that need attention. By emphasizing both the organization and the person, these questions provide an opportunity for diagnosing interface problems—the difference between organizational objectives and individual goals and needs. By asking both positive and problem-focused questions, the message conveyed is that OD is not a process of change for the sake of change. We are also looking for the aspects of the organization that are pluses and therefore should be affirmed, and maintained, and strengthened rather than changed. Our change emphasis will focus on client responses to the second and fourth questions.

These four questions are not the only ones asked. After explaining the reason for my being there (preferably in the client's office, since that environment provides additional information for diagnosis, such as position of the desk, pictures, and so on), I usually ask the client to explain his or her current job and job history with the organization. This is easy for the person to talk about and helps to break the ice as well as providing me with some useful information—especially the job history. Other secondary, probing questions are asked during the course of the interview so that a complete response to the four primary questions can be obtained.

Some examples of other useful interview questions are:

If you had complete power (or if you were the boss), what would you do to change things?

What's it like to work around here? Is it fun, frustrating, challenging? Do you like the people with whom you work? How do you feel about your boss?

What are the purposes (missions, goals, objectives) of the unit (organization) to which you belong? Are they clear?

What do you have to do to get ahead in this organization? What does it take to get promoted?

How does your job affect others in your organization?

201

Most organizations have a formal system and an informal one. How would you characterize your informal organization? How wide would you say the gap is between the formal and the informal organization? More specifically, who *really* makes the decisions?

How are differences among people typically handled? When people have differences of opinion or different points of view, for example, are these differences discussed or do they rarely surface? If they are discussed, do differences get resolved in ways that are reasonably satisfactory to the people involved, regardless of differences in status and hierarchy?

What attracts people to work and stay with this organization? Is there anything in particular that causes those who leave to change organizations?

Interviews may be conducted with one individual at a time or in small groups. Conducting interviews with groups saves time, of course, but people might be more inhibited in a group situation and therefore might reveal less than they would otherwise. In a group situation, however, the potential for more information and greater perspective increases as a result of individuals' responding further to one another's comments.

Deep sensing, an approach to collecting data from groups that was developed at TRW, Inc., several years ago, is a group interview technique. The technique involves assembling a group of employees for a meeting, usually a one-time event, with a manager or an OD practitioner. The employees are usually a mixed group, representing various functions and levels in the organization. The group is rarely larger than fifteen people. If a manager attends, he or she is from a higher level in the managerial hierarchy than the employees assembled in the group and may be from a different function than that represented in the group. If most of the employees come from such functions as manufacturing, employee relations, engineering, and sales, for example, the manager may be from finance or corporate planning. The mixture of people is thus heterogeneous. The meeting itself is relatively unstructured. The manager is there specifically to listen. The manager or the OD practitioner may ask questions but usually does not comment on people's responses except to seek further understanding and clarification.

The purpose of a sensing meeting is for higher management to obtain a sense of the organization from levels that are normally inaccessible to them. The OD practitioner facilitates these meetings by seeing that a comfortable climate is established so that people will speak up. At the beginning, for example, the manager stresses the importance of higher management's need to know what is on people's minds so that appropriate action for improvement can be taken.

It is rare for a first meeting of this kind in an organization to result in a

202

trusting atmosphere and valid information. As more meetings are conducted and as employees realize that they can speak their minds without fear of retribution, the deep sensing technique can provide a highly useful pulse-reading on the health of the organization. This type of meeting is somewhat similar to quality control circles, a Japanese technique now being employed more and more in the United States for diagnosing and working on problems of quality (see Chapter 13).

Interviewing, whether one-on-one or in a group, is a particularly useful technique for obtaining the kind of diagnostic information the practitioner may want and for building relationships. By being a good listener and demonstrating, by paraphrasing, that he or she understands, the practitioner can show empathy during the interview, especially with respect to the problems discussed.

The limitations of the interview technique concern potential bias on the part of both the practitioner and the client. By asking leading questions or by limiting the questions to one model or frame of reference, the practitioner may overlook other information that is just as critical to an effective diagnosis. The client may provide limited or inappropriate information because he or she feels threatened, suspicious, competitive, or angry, for example.

A final problem with interviews is the need to summarize and interpret all the data. Coping with this problem will be considered later in the analysis section.

In summary, the interview may be the most useful technique for data collection because it comes closest to accomplishing all three goals, but the burden of achieving the technique's optimal effectiveness rests on the practitioner's skills in establishing rapport, asking the right questions at the right time, being an active listener, and making sense of all the data collected.

Questionnaires

The major advantage of a questionnaire is that it is not dependent on the interviewer, who may have biases, and it saves time and perhaps money. As Nadler (1977) points out, a questionnaire "allows simultaneous data collection from many people in an organization. With fixed responses quantitative analysis can be done in a short period of time, allowing for a relatively short turnaround time" (p. 125).

Questionnaires come in various sizes, shapes, and forms. Some are standardized, such as Likert's "Profile of Organizational Characteristics" and the later, more thoroughly developed instrument based in part on Likert's original profile, the *Survey of Organizations* (Taylor and Bowers 1972). Some are custom-made for a particular organization, such as General Motors' questionnaire on quality of working life (Carlson 1980). For examples of various questionnaires, see Appendix B in Nadler's (1977) book.

203

The advantages of a questionnaire for data collection are that the answers may be easily quantified and therefore are subject to quick interpretation and that the comparative cost of the technique is low. Questionnaires are not useful for building relationships, however, and responses are limited to the questions asked in the instrument. Thus, probing and clarification are not possible, and interpretation, though quick, is also limited.

Perhaps the major advantage of a questionnaire is that it can be used more than once, and thus the technique remains standard over time and usage. This feature permits diagnosis to be coupled with the last phase of OD practice—evaluation.

Observations

This technique is perhaps the most obvious one, but its value may be overlooked. Practiced systematically, observations may provide more overall information than any of the other techniques. According to Nadler (1977): "Observation is particularly valuable because it removes one possible source of bias, the report of the respondent" (pp. 132–33). The fundamental and most obvious problem with observations as a technique for data collection is the bias of the observer. To compensate for this bias, observations can be highly structured, such as simply counting the number of times a person speaks directly to a particular individual in a group.

There is a paradox in this technique, according to Nadler (1977):

> The basic strength or weakness of observation as a tool is that the observer is the data-collection instrument (as opposed to the questionnaire as the observation instrument). A sensitive observer making use of an effective structure for observation can be an effective data-collection tool. An observer who has little sensitivity and no guiding structure may spend hours observing, see nothing, and report no usable data. (p. 133)

Even if the observer is highly skillful and sensitive, his or her presence may have an effect on the data collected. As Rosenthal (1976) has demonstrated, a person collecting data, as opposed to a questionnaire, for example, will often cause the results to be different.

Setting aside for the moment the limitations of and problems associated with the observation technique, the best instrument for data collection and analysis is the consultant. Knowing these limitations and problems and being sensitive to them should help the consultant make effective use of the most available and potentially beneficial resource in OD practice. For more on the consultant as a person and as an instrument of practice, see Chapter 17.

204

Secondary Data and Unobtrusive Measures

Most organizations keep records. These sources of information, such as records of turnover, absenteeism, grievances, work performance, and costs, annual reports, and profit and loss statements, provide rich and varied data for diagnosis. Minutes of key meetings and recent task force or committee reports are also valuable sources. Several years ago, in my consultation with a state medical college and its various associated schools, my job was to help them make a new organizational structure work. I found an invaluable source of diagnostic information in reading the task force report of the planning and rationale for the new structure.

The major advantage of this form of data collection is the absence of bias, but there can be built-in bias in the data. Sometimes organization members record information according to what they think management wants or what they may be rewarded for, rather than just the facts. Access to records also may be a problem, as might the quality of the data.

Perhaps the main consideration regarding this technique of data collection is as Nadler (1977) states:

> In general, archival data and unobtrusive measures are underused by consultants. There is a tendency to rely on one type of data, usually [from] interviews or questionnaires, and sometimes observations, and to ignore the existence of data that have already been collected by the organization. (p. 139)

Exhibit 10.1 compares the four techniques for data collection.

Techniques for Data Analysis

Once the information is collected, the OD consultant must help the client not only to understand all the facts and perceptions but also to be in a position to use the information. As I mentioned at the beginning of the chapter, this is the phase in which information and facts become data. There are certain techniques that may help the OD consultant make this transition.

Analyzing Interviews

One technique for analyzing interviews is very simple. Looking at all interviewees' responses to a particular question, the practitioner consolidates statements that make essentially the same point and then puts a number in parentheses at the end of the consolidated statement to represent the number of people who said it. This was done with the interviews conducted in the case

205

EXHIBIT 10.1

A Comparison of Different Methods of Data Collection

Method	Major advantages	Major potential problems
Interviews	1. Adaptive—allows data collection on a range of possible subjects 2. Source of rich data 3. Empathic 4. Process of interviewing can build rapport	1. Can be expensive 2. Interviewer can bias responses 3. Coding and interpretation problems 4. Self-report bias
Questionnaires	1. Responses can be quantified and easily summarized 2. Easy to use with large samples 3. Relatively inexpensive 4. Can obtain large volume of data	1. Nonempathic 2. Predetermined questions may miss issues 3. Data may be overinterpreted 4. Response bias
Observations	1. Collects data on behavior rather than reports on behavior 2. Real time, not retrospective 3. Adaptive	1. Interpretation and coding problems 2. Sampling is a problem 3. Potential validity 4. Costly
Secondary data and unobtrusive measures	1. Nonreactive, no response bias 2. High face validity 3. Easily quantified	1. Access and retrieval possibly a problem 2. Potential validity problems 3. Coding and interpretation problems

Source: D. A. Nadler, *Feedback and Organization Development: Using Data-Based Methods,* © 1977, Addison-Wesley Publishing Company, Inc., Chapter 7, page 119, Table 7.1, "A Comparison of Different Methods of Data Collection." Reprinted with permission.

example of Ron, the regional manager, and his senior management group (see Chapters 8 and 9). Consolidated statements are listed in descending order as a function of how many people made essentially the statement or response. These statements are then typed and duplicated for the feedback session. The interview data might look like the following:

Summary of interviews conducted with ten (10) managers, April 1–15

1. What is going well; what are the strengths of the organization?
   —We have talented and competent people. (8)
   —Our capital financing is in good shape. (7)
   —Our people are committed and loyal. (5)
   —The boss provides clarity about goals. (2)
   —We now have a better handle on some of our energy problems and how to correct them. (2)
   —Etc., etc.

206

2. What is not going well; what are some problems and issues that need attention?
   —Our turnover rate among the sales force is entirely too high. (9)
   —The new organization structure is not working. (9)
   —There is too much friction between R&D and marketing. (7)
   —Our quality of service is not up to par. (6)
   —The bonus system is bad. (3)
   —Etc., etc.

A feedback report in such a summarized form, which might take no more than two pages, reflects only what two or more people stated in their interviews. Statements made by only one interviewee are not reported, since the content of the statement might reveal the identity of the person. Usually the consultant promises anonymity for the people being interviewed so that more openness and candor is likely during the interview itself. During the feedback session, any member of the client group may add statements to the list of responses. The choice of whether to add a statement, even if it is unique to and perhaps directly associated with the individual, is then with that person.

Analysis of the interview data by this technique is thus a consolidation effort. If specific words from the interviews capture several individuals' similar point, those words should be used in the report so that the consultant does not risk filtering out some of the tone, if not the meaning, in the consolidation process.

A second technique for analyzing interview data is relating the collected information to some model, to some organizational, systemic frame of reference. As noted earlier, one goal of the OD process is to help organizational members think about their organization as a system—a series of dimensions and functions that interact yet are humanly derived and humanly operated. Selecting a model to assist with the data analysis is therefore an important step. See Chapter 9 for an example of this analysis technique in using Weisbord's six-box model.

Analyzing Questionnaires

Analysis of questionnaire data is more straightforward, since the questionnaire itself provides much of the conceptual frame of reference. This is especially true of Likert's "Profile of Organizational Characteristics." Assuming that the questionnaire's form is a Likert-type scale—that is, a continuum for each item, ranging from strongly agree (or highly characteristic) to strongly disagree (or highly uncharacteristic)—it would be best to summarize the data in at least two ways: an average for each item and the variability for each item. Sophisticated statistical procedures are usually not necessary. For the variability analysis, a simple count of how many people

207

chose each of the points on the continuum is sufficient—that is, how many respondents to each questionnaire item chose "strongly agree," how many chose "slightly agree," and so on throughout the scale.

If the questionnaire is not based on an organizational model, then categorizing the responses according to some model, as illustrated with the interview data, is highly desirable.

Analyzing Observations and Secondary Data and Unobtrusive Measures

These data are typically less suitable to model classification and, in any case, should be used as support for major points to be made from the interview or questionnaire data. The analysis should be relatively simple—either a summary count or a percentage, such as the rate of absenteeism or the number of times the boss's recent memo had the word *urgent* in it.

Many of the consultant's observations may be more subjective and qualitative than objective and quantitative. These observations should clearly be labeled as such so that organization members can be clear about the consultant's potential biases. An incident from my consulting experience may help to illustrate this point.

For about a year I served as an outside consultant to a manufacturing corporation's organization development department, which consisted of eight professionals. After I had conducted interviews with each of them, we had an off-site meeting to diagnose and work on internal problems of the department and to plan strategies for various consulting projects. Our meeting was held at the corporation's conference center, which happened to be the corporate founder's former estate. The current chairman of the corporation was a descendant of the founder and still owned a major portion of stock. The meeting was held in the library of the mansion, and the feelings I experienced when I first entered the room were almost overwhelming. I felt a sense of heaviness, even oppressiveness, and a sense of some depression. The physical characteristics of the room contributed to these feelings. The windows were lattice-type, with heavy dark draperies that allowed little outside light to enter the room. The walls were covered with floor-to-ceiling bookshelves, and almost all the shelves contained old, dark-spined books. A dingy, wine-colored oriental rug covered the floor, and the furniture consisted of heavy stuffed chairs and sofas, which were also dark-colored.

At the beginning of the meeting I remarked to the group that I didn't think I could proceed with the meeting effectively until I could briefly explain my feelings to them. They told me to go ahead, and so I stated what I felt. They laughed and said, "Oh, we're used to this place, and eventually you'll get used to it too"; so we proceeded with the meeting.

Midway through the morning I asked the department manager to explain his perception of how power was used in the corporation. He responded by drawing the organization chart and explaining the difference between it and the informal system. I was struck with the Machiavellian manner in which the top management group seemed to operate. There was considerable oppression and heavy-handedness in the way decisions were made and implemented. The manager fully agreed with my analysis, adding that he had never quite seen it that way before. I also wondered to myself if I would have seen the management of the organization the way I did had I not been in touch with my feelings when I entered the meeting room. My observations were obviously highly subjective, and perhaps there was no connection between my earlier feelings and what I later perceived and analyzed. What I said made sense to the manager and his group, however. The important point is that one's feelings as a consultant, subjective though they may be, are useful categories of information for potential data analysis and diagnosis.

The Process of Data Feedback

After the data collection and analysis have been done, there are three primary objectives for the consultant in the feedback session with the client organization members:

1. To help the client understand the data
2. To transfer the ownership of the data from the consultant to the client
3. To energize the client to use the data for action planning

The best way to help the client *understand* the data is to be adequately prepared and organized for the feedback session. This means having the data summarized and analyzed as simply as possible without sacrificing the client's ability to grasp the systemic meanings of the information. This is easier said than done, of course, and it is important to avoid data overload. Giving the client too much information is more likely to assure misunderstanding rather than understanding. Data overload also relates to the third objective—energizing the client. Too much data may create overwhelmed feelings, and may thus immobilize the client.

One other step that will help the client's understanding of the data is making sure that the data that come from interviews, questionnaires, or secondary and unobtrusive sources are distinguished from the consultant's subjective observations, feelings, and impressions. Some OD experts argue that the consultant's impressions should not become a part of the feedback, that as much objectivity as possible should be achieved and valued. In my experience, clients want to know what I think about them, what my impressions are, whether or not they ask for it directly. Rather than fencing and avoiding the issue, I include my impressions in the feedback process. I take special

209

care, however, that clients understand when I am giving impressions as opposed to summarized and analyzed data collected through interviews or questionnaires.

This last point relates to the transfer of ownership issue and objective. When the consultant collects data from the client, the data become the consultant's to some extent. Regardless of how cooperative the client may have been and how objectively the consultant has recorded the information, the mere collection and summary process causes the client to perceive that the data belong to the consultant. Taking the aforementioned step—distinguishing between consultant observations and other categories of data—helps but is not sufficient.

An incident from my experience illustrates the point. I had interviewed all members of a department in a school of medicine, had summarized the data according to the questions asked, and had prepared for the feedback and action planning session, which was held at an off-site location. After some preliminaries, I began the feedback process by handing each department member a two-page copy of my summary of the interviews. In the process of discussing the data, it became quickly apparent that the group disagreed with my summary, even though I argued that what was on the two sheets of paper was essentially what they had told me and that I had merely categorized their responses according to the questions asked during the interviews. I then suggested that they discuss in small groups the possibility of somehow reorganizing the data and changing whatever errors I might have made or biases I might have shown. The small-group discussions took an hour, at the end of which they decided that my summaries and categories were as good as any they could think of. The problem had been a matter of their not owning the feedback. After the small-group discussions, the department members were very willing to move on to further clarification, interpretation, and action planning. Working with the data themselves for a period helped transfer the ownership of the information from me back to them.

It is critical to keep in mind the psychological process of a client who is about to receive feedback. Although the organization members may believe that their anonymity will be protected, they feel a part of their group and the organization, and so there is a degree of personalization, especially for the leader. Nadler (1977) suggests that organization members enter a feedback session with some if not all of the following four feelings:

1. Anxiety: Such feedback sessions are not common events in organizations, so there is a degree of uncertainty, of not knowing exactly what to expect.
2. Defensiveness: It is possible that some people may hear something negative about themselves, and it may feel like an attack.
3. Fear: If some individuals were critical of the boss in their interviews or in

responses to a questionnaire, for example, they could feel that some retribution may occur.

4. Hope: This meeting is, after all, a chance to take action, to improve matters.

Where there are feelings, there is energy, so the consultant needs to work in such a way that organization members become *energized* to take the data and use them for action planning. The key is to raise expectations that something can be done and that there is potential for improvement. To help channel energy in the client group toward a problem-solving and action-planning mode, the consultant must be highly sensitive to the group's process (E. H. Schein 1969). As I have already stated, it is important to allow enough time for the group to discuss their understanding of and feelings about the data before moving toward action planning. If some individuals are still feeling fearful or defensive by the action-planning stage, not much corrective action will take place. Second, the consultant can provide considerable help with interpretation of the data. By keeping the client focused on systemic issues, using the model, and by emphasizing that any problem is likely to have multiple causes, the consultant can keep the problem-solving process oriented properly, rather than toward individual members. To be avoided are such statements as, "If we could only get rid of Clyde, things would be so much better." Finally, providing a structure for problem solving will facilitate the focusing effort. The best ways of providing structure are following logical steps of problem solving and using such techniques as a force field analysis (Fordyce and Weil 1971, p. 106).

Summary

Once the entry and contracting phases have been completed, the consultant begins diagnosis. The goals of the consultant during this diagnostic phase are (1) to collect valid information and later provide it to the client, (2) to energize the client for action toward organizational change and improvement, and (3) to build a good working relationship with the client—open, trusting, and collaborative. For data collection, the consultant may use interviews, questionnaires, observations, and secondary data and unobtrusive measures. Since no single technique is optimum, using two or more is best.

For the feedback phase of the OD effort, the consultant must be well-prepared and sensitive to the client group's process. During the feedback session the consultant serves in multiple roles—probably teaching a little, managing the meeting, at least initially, and facilitating the group's understanding of the feedback and how to use it constructively. By the time the group begins to discuss the data interpretively, as a prelude to action planning, the consultant has begun to turn the leadership of the meeting back over to the boss.

Although there are a number of techniques for data collection and feedback, the fundamental instrument is the consultant. The key to effective diagnosis is being sensitive not only to the client but also to oneself. What the consultant experiences and feels, even as an outsider, may reflect what many people inside the organization experience and feel.

Survey feedback is a technique that encompasses in a structured way much of the process discussed in this chapter, but since the technique of survey feedback constitutes a major intervention as well as diagnosis, we will defer coverage of it to Chapter 15.

PART IV

INTERVENTIONS

In Part IV we shall consider the next two phases of organization development practice: planning change and intervention. As stated earlier, the planning phase may be the second half of the feedback phase—to be understood and digested more thoroughly. The planning phase and the intervention phase are more distinct from one another, however; that is, a plan is made and then implemented. The intervention phase is the implementation.

As in diagnosis, in order to plan a change process adequately, a theoretical or conceptual frame of reference is necessary. Chapter 11 covers intervention theory—the concepts and models that provide a basis or rationale for planning organizational change. This initial chapter thus considers the planning phase in OD practice.

The remaining four chapters in this part—Chapters 12, 13, 14, and 15—examine OD interventions in four categories: (1) interventions that have the individual as their focus or target for change, (2) interventions that deal with groups, (3) interventions with intergroup focuses, and (4) interventions that are associated more directly with large, systemwide change.

Our ultimate goal in OD practice is to effect change in the total system. This goal is addressed directly in Chapter 15. The preceding chapters consider the interventions at various levels that help promote and provide support for the ultimate goal. There is nothing sacred about the order of my coverage of these interventions. The arrangement simply reflects my need to have some logical way of proceeding; thus, it is from individual to group to intergroup to total system.

CHAPTER 11

Intervention Theory and Models

Once a diagnosis has been made and feedback has been provided to the client, it is time to plan the appropriate steps to take so that problems identified in the diagnostic phase are addressed and an ideal future state for the organization can be determined. Guiding this planning phase should be a set of coherent and interrelated concepts—a theory, a model, a conceptual frame of reference.

In this chapter we shall first consider the definition and nature of an intervention, then the criteria for choosing a particular intervention or stages of several interventions. Finally we shall explore several different methods for categorizing interventions in organization development practice. Understanding more precisely what an OD intervention is, examining criteria for making choices from among an array of interventions, and exploring a number of different models of interventions should help in planning the specific steps for organizational change more effectively. The purpose of this chapter, therefore, is to provide an understanding of interventions in general, not to explain them in any detail nor even to define any of them in particular. The remaining chapters in this part of the book cover the specifics.

We shall first define intervention and then cover the planning phase in more detail. An intervention is the planned change activity of an OD effort. Chris Argyris (1970) gives a more technical and specific definition:

> To intervene is to enter into an ongoing system of relationships, to come between or among persons, groups, or objects for the purpose of helping them. There is an important implicit assumption in the definition that should be made explicit: the system exists independently of the intervenor. (p. 15)

According to Argyris, collecting data from an organization is intervening, which supports our earlier claim that the phases of OD are not discrete. For

215

this phase of organization development, however, we shall think in terms of some specified activity, some event or planned sequence of events that occurs as a result of diagnosis and feedback. The process of moving from a functional way of organizing to a project form, for example, regardless of how long it takes—and it might take months—could constitute an OD intervention. Another example of a possible OD intervention would be a two-day workshop on performance appraisal. In this case the intervention would be a singular event and would take a comparatively short period of time. Either type of activity could serve as an OD intervention, provided the event:

1. Responds to an actual and felt need for change on the part of the client
2. Involves the client in the planning and implementing of the change (intervention)
3. Leads to change in the organization's culture

Criteria for an Effective Intervention

Argyris (1970) has specified similar criteria for what he considers the primary tasks of an interventionist (OD practitioner). His three criteria are valid and useful information, free choice, and internal commitment. By *valid and useful information,* he means "that which describes the factors plus their interrelationships, that create the problem for the client system" (Argyris 1970, p. 17). According to Argyris, the information the OD practitioner has collected from and about the client accurately reflects what people in the organization perceive and feel, what they consider to be their primary concerns and issues, what they experience as complexities and perhaps accompanying frustrations of living within and being a part of the client system, and what they would like to see changed. Argyris goes on to specify that, if several independent diagnoses lead to the same intervention, the data the practitioner has gathered are valid.

For all practical purposes this first primary task of an interventionist—obtaining valid and useful information—is similar to my first criterion for intervention—responding to an actual and felt need for change on the part of the client. If valid information is obtained by the practitioner, it will reflect a need. If the practitioner responds to that need, he or she will have done so by providing valid and useful information.

By *free choice,* Argyris (1970) means that "the locus of decision making [is] in the client system" (p. 19) and that the client is provided alternatives for action. No particular or specified action is automatic, preordained, or imposed. Argyris (1970) states:

A choice is free to the extent the members can make their selection for a course of action with minimal internal defensiveness; can define the path (or paths) by which the intended consequence is to be achieved; can relate the choice to their central needs; and can build into their choices a realistic and challenging level of aspiration. Free choice therefore implies that the members are able to explore as many alternatives as they consider significant and select those that are central to their needs. (p. 19)

By *internal commitment,* Argyris means that the client owns the choice made and feels responsible for implementing it. Organization members act on their choice because it responds to needs, both individual and on behalf of the organization.

These latter primary tasks of the practitioner—choice and internal commitment—will be accomplished if he or she involves the client in the planning and implementing of the intervention—my second criterion for an OD intervention. Argyris does not specify cultural change, my third criterion. He implies that, if the practitioner accomplishes the three primary tasks, the organization's culture will be changed. This is only an implication, however; he does not specify it.

Although there are similarities between Argyris's criteria and mine, the primary difference is that I am expressing processes or means while he is stating end states or outcomes. Either way of expressing these criteria makes sense.

Planning the Intervention or Change

There are at least three considerations in planning an intervention: (1) determining the client's readiness for change, (2) making certain that the change is tied to the power points in the organization, and (3) arranging for internal resources to help manage, monitor, and maintain the change process. The broad planning steps are as follows.

1. Determine the client's readiness for change. Argyris (1970) states this determination in terms of the system's being open to and capable of learning. What Argyris and Schön (1978) call "double loop learning" means essentially that organization members not only learn how to fix existing problems (single loop learning) but they also learn a new problem-solving process so that old problems do not reappear to be fixed again. This extra loop of the learning process occurs as members go about changing their organization's culture so that the new norms, values, and reward and authority structures are supportive of behaviors such as confronting issues directly and openly, expressing feelings , taking risks, collaborating, and exercising individual and group responsibility.

The diagnostic phase will help determine the client's readiness for change to some extent—but not entirely. When organization members respond to the interview or questionnaire with problems they believe need attention, the

217

consultant can assume that some readiness (motivation) exists to do something about them. Readiness and the energy to move toward change also derive from organization members' awareness of a difference, a gap, between the current status of their organization and what they would like it to be—their idea of some improved state. How much readiness there is cannot be fully determined until it is time to plan and implement action steps for change, to decide on an intervention or series of interventions and assign the various responsibilities for implementation. It is at this stage that any existing resistance will become apparent. A recent consulting experience illustrates this point.

I was asked by the president of a medium-sized manufacturing company to help conduct a three-day off-site OD meeting. The president was relatively new to the organization, having been in his position for only a year, and he wanted to spend time with his vice-presidents and key staff people to assess this first year, to bring problems to the surface, to work on solutions, and to organize themselves through better processes for more effective problem solving in the future. I contracted with the president to conduct individual interviews with each person scheduled to attend the meeting. In the interviews, although not everyone was in favor of the off-site meeting, most clearly expressed a need and enthusiasm for it. Many problems were identified, building a sufficient agenda for the meeting. The president started the meeting by expressing his hopes and purposes for the meeting and then turned it over to me for feedback of the interview data. The feedback went fairly smoothly; questions were raised, discussion followed, and the information was deemed valid. The next morning we began discussing the problems identified in the interviews more thoroughly—to begin to identify causes and eventually to move on to action planning. For the better part of that day, the people talked, but rarely to one another; they discussed problems, but rarely agreed on whether these problems were from the past or still existed; and they made speeches, but rarely spoke to any point that was considered a purpose of the meeting. The president became agitated, frustrated, and eventually angry. In my role of process consultant, I finally called attention to a number of counterproductive behaviors in the group and pointed out that it felt like resistance to me. No one disagreed with my observation, but neither did anyone do anything differently. It also became apparent to me that much of the resistance was toward the president. He was trying something new on them; they had never before held such an off-site meeting. Moreover, the president had been brought in from the outside by the parent company, passing over some of the vice-presidents and the executive vice-president. By the end of the second day, it was clear to me that this group was not ready for change. As far as they were concerned, change had already occurred a year earlier, and that was enough. My advice to the president was to forget for the

218

time being any further effort toward what both he and I clearly saw as a need, to move the organization's top management toward a more collaborative mode of operating with one another, and to operate more as a group. I further advised him to consider a rearrangement of some of his top managers—not necessarily firing anyone but reorganizing in such a way that the team became his, rather than an aggregate of individuals that he had inherited. I added that I was not willing to help him with this reorganization if he chose to do it, since I did not consider that within my purview as an OD practitioner. Thus, we parted ways, agreeing to touch base again in the future if and when reorganization had occurred.

2. Link the change process to the power points in the organization. Change will not occur unless power is exercised by someone or by some group. If the client system is hierarchical in its authority and decision-making structure, the change process should be managed by the top manager of the system and by his or her key subordinates. Regardless of structure, the intervention should be linked for implementation to the individuals who are central to the main problems identified in the diagnostic phase. Referring once again to Weisbord's six-box model, if the leadership box is loaded with problems, the intervention should be tied directly to the leadership of the organization. If the rewards box is loaded with problems, however, then the human resource specialists should be directly linked with the intervention, with top management a second direct link in sponsoring and supporting the human resource specialists' plans and actions.

Linkage to points of power in the organization is absolutely necessary (see Chapter 7). To illustrate, we refer again to the case example of change in a medical school, summarized in Chapter 3. The effort to change the school's curriculum was linked to the hierarchical positions of power. The chairman of the curriculum committee was the associate dean, who was accountable directly to the dean. (The fact that they were good friends also helped.) Just as important for purposes of linkage, moreover, was a key member of the committee, the chairman of the department of medicine. He had to be directly involved in the planning of change, because the department of medicine was the largest and most powerful unit within the school—as is frequently the case in medical schools. Without the endorsement of the head of this unit, our plan for change would have suffered if not failed. We not only sought his endorsement but arranged for him to have a significant role in the planning of how the curriculum change would be implemented. Directly involving him undoubtedly contributed to the strong, positive vote from the entire faculty.

3. Arrange for internal resources to help manage the change process. If the primary consultant is from outside the organization, an internal consultant should be assigned to the change effort as early as possible, preferably at the very beginning. This was done in the medical school consultation. The in-

ternal consultant monitored progress and helped with committee, departmental, and administration concerns when I was not present. He helped to insure that the momentum we had begun would continue.

Managing the change process is difficult, generally following Murphy's law—if anything can go wrong, it will. The internal resource people are there to monitor and maintain the change process, continually to collect data on how things are going, and to help with the conduct of such subinterventions as team-building sessions, training programs, further data analysis, and the like. As Hornstein, Bunker, Burke, Gindes, and Lewicki (1971) have pointed out, these internal consultants are guardians of the new culture; they help *regulate* the process of OD.

In the planning change phase of OD practice, the consultant tests the client system's readiness for change, helps to insure that the change process is linked to power sources, and helps to arrange for support and maintenance people as well as support mechanisms, such as additional questionnaires to assess the effectiveness of team-building activities.

A most important function of the OD consultant during the planning phase is providing alternative interventions. The consultant may suggest possibilities, may confirm or argue against suggestions made by the client, and generally helps the client move toward a decision. The decision may be to choose one major intervention and begin to implement it or to choose a series of interventions—some to occur simultaneously, others according to certain priorities. We are now in a position to examine the range of interventions consultants have at their disposal.

General Types of Intervention

Argyris (1970) states that there are three general types of intervention activity. First are the more common interventions—the tried and true. There are problems that are endemic in most organizations—communication and planning (Blake and Mouton 1968) and lack of trust, poor communication, and lack of internal commitment to certain organizational policies (Argyris 1970)—and a body of knowledge and practice exists to deal effectively with many of these common problems. Some examples are Likert's "Profile of Organizational Characteristics," the survey feedback method (Mann 1957), Beckhard's (1967) confrontation meeting, team building, and intergroup conflict resolution. The outcome and consequences of these interventions are generally predictable, and they do not usually require much time to implement.

The second type of intervention is creative arrangement of existing knowledge. By this, Argyris means creating an intervention that is based on existing knowledge yet is planned and conducted in such a way as to be unique. No two team-building sessions are exactly alike, of course, but the

220

general process and flow of events is similar from one time to the next or from one team to the other. Using a technique from some other domain in a team-building session might be unique, however, such as using image exchange, typically employed in an intergroup activity, with two subgroups in the team. Another example might be taking the experimental design of a research project and replicating it within the organization as an intervention.

Argyris (1970) states: "The danger of too strong an emphasis upon this type of activity is development of a compulsiveness to find a new twist, a new intervention technique in every client relationship" (p. 32). It is also possible that consultants who may become weary of helping to conduct yet another team-building effort may then try something new, whether the team needs it or not, just to break the boredom and weariness, whereas the tried and true process of team building may be just what is needed.

Regardless of how much experience may be associated with an intervention, most interventions need some adjusting and fine-tuning for each new client; thus, some degree of creativity is always possible.

The third general type of intervention is the addition to basic theory. Although it is exceptional and rare, some interventions simultaneously help the client and add to existing knowledge—development of a new model, new theory, or new methodology. As Argyris points out, this kind of intervention activity is especially demanding, since it requires that the practitioner be both a consultant and a researcher. According to Argyris (1970):

> An outstanding example of an individual who preferred this type of activity was Kurt Lewin [see, for example, Marrow (1969)]. He was able to relate such practical problems as inducing people to drink orange juice, eat liver, buy bonds, and produce higher quality pajamas to basic conceptual issues. (p. 32)

This general type of intervention should be a goal for some practitioners, especially those—such as Argyris and myself—who are academically based and active as consultants. Achieving such an intervention would be rewarding both as a consultant and as an academician.

Choosing the Depth of an Intervention

In considering the degree of a client's readiness for change, the consultant is also attempting to discern just how far he or she can go with that client—whether the intervention should be biased toward structure and largely systemic matters or toward some personal confrontations, toward more emotional and perhaps value-laden issues. Roger Harrison has developed a way to think about these questions. His model differentiates interventions according to depth—how much a given intervention requires the emotional involvement of the client and to some extent of the consultant, too. By *depth*, Harrison

(1970) means "how deep, value-laden, emotionally charged, and central to the individual's sense of self are the issues and processes about which a consultant attempts directly to obtain information and which he seeks to influence" (p. 181). The deepest type of intervention is intrapersonal analysis; a less deep type—involving surface characteristics and processes—might be a change in the organization's structure or an activity such as open-systems planning (see Chapter 4).

Harrison also defines depth according to how accessible the data are—private versus public—and according to individuality—the degree to which the intervention is directed toward the individual organizational member rather than the organization itself. The deeper the intervention is, the more likely it is to involve private, personal information.

On the basis of Harrison's model, Huse (1980) has developed a list of types of interventions according to depth. His list helps clarify and illustrate the utility of Harrison's model (see Exhibit 11.1). With the possible exception of grid OD, the interventions classified in Huse's list as systemwide approaches

EXHIBIT 11.1

Typology of Change According to Depth of Intervention

Systemwide approaches
Contingency theories of organization design
Survey feedback and development
Organizational confrontation meeting
Collateral organization
Quality of work life programs
Grid organizational development (The six-phase grid OD program covers almost every level but is placed here for the sake of convenience and clarity, since it involves a total systemwide effort.)

Individual-organizational interfaces
Job design
Decision centers
Role analysis
Management by objectives

Concern with personal work style
Process consultation
Third-party intervention
Team building
Managing interdepartmental and intergroup relationships

Intrapersonal analysis and relationships
Life and career-planning interventions
Laboratory training
Encounter groups
Personal consultation

---

represent interventions with the least depth according to Harrison's criteria, and those labeled intrapersonal are interventions with the greatest depth. The two intermediate categories—individual-organizational interfaces and concern with personal work style—are between the two extremes of intervention depth, with personal work style having more depth than Interfaces.

On what basis, then, does the consultant help the client make a choice? Harrison offers two criteria for choice. The consultant should intervene at a level no deeper than (1) that required to produce enduring solutions to the problems at hand and (2) that at which the energy and resources of the client can be committed to problem solving and to change. Harrison also points out that some consultants prefer to push, to confront the client's resistance directly, and other consultants prefer to deal with the client's actual, felt needs, whatever they may be, and to intervene accordingly. Harrison favors the latter approach, because he believes that consultants who prefer to deal more directly with resistance will choose interventions at a level deeper than the client is comfortable with. The consequences of choosing an intervention that is too deep is likely to cause the client to resist even more and withdraw.

How can the consultant tell? Resistance may take a variety of forms, but it rarely comes out as a simple no. More often, it consists of the client's directing challenging, skeptical questions at the consultant, or arguing that the consultant's suggestions will not work, or expressing deep concern about how long the OD process will take.

How the consultant should respond depends on the activity, of course, and on whether the consultant has suggested a specific intervention that has met with resistance. If the consultant has suggested an intervention that he or she genuinely believes is appropriate, but the client resists, the consultant should withdraw the suggestion and make another one that is less threatening (less depth, according to Harrison's criteria) but still within the nature or essence of the originally suggested intervention. If the consultant suggested an off-site meeting to deal with a management team's interpersonal problems, for example, and some members thought the suggestion highly appropriate but a majority thought otherwise, an alternative intervention would be to suggest that the consultant observe some of their regular meetings for a stated period of time and occasionally make suggestions for improving their meeting effectiveness, specifying that these suggestions would be more procedural than interpersonal (see Chapter 13 for details).

As we shall see in the next section, there are many types and categories of interventions from which to choose. Guiding our choice so far are the general types according to Argyris (1970)—going with what usually works, inventing something new, or conducting research along with whatever intervention we choose—and Harrison's depth model. We shall now examine some of the schemes for categorizing interventions.

Categories and Typologies of Interventions

Early attempts at classifying OD interventions were fairly superficial. My colleague Harvey Hornstein and I were among the first to attempt such a classification, albeit a very simple one (Burke and Hornstein 1972). We listed six categories: team building, managing conflict, survey feedback, technostructural, training, and miscellaneous—giving ourselves room to grow by including the miscellaneous category.

Schmuck and Miles (1971) devised a more complex scheme, with more dimensions—the "OD cube" (see Exhibit 11.2). Their dimensions provided a basis for classifying interventions in a more sophisticated manner, and their model more accurately represented the growing complexity of the field. Their three classifiers are (1) diagnosed problems, (2) focus of attention, and (3) mode of intervention. Thus, a diagnosed problem of role definition—the first dimension of the cube—within a team—the second dimension—might lead to any one of the eight categories of interventions.

EXHIBIT 11.2

The OD Cube: A Scheme for Classifying OD Interventions

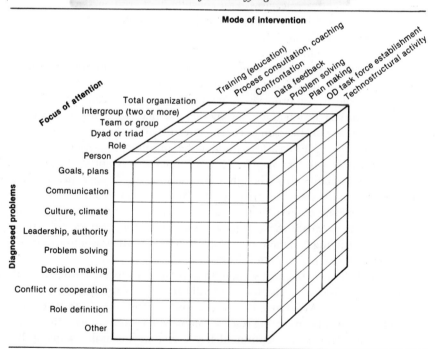

Source: Reprinted from Richard Schmuck and Matthew Miles (Eds.), *Organization Development in Schools.* San Diego, Ca: University Associates, 1976. Used with permission.

Blake and Mouton (1976) also developed a cube for classifying interventions and their accompanying dimensions. Their Consulcube (see Exhibit 11.3) is dissimilar to Schmuck and Miles's scheme with respect to the characteristics of two of their dimensions: (1) focal issues, which are social and psychological, and (2) kinds of interventions, which vary from acceptant —the least form of intervening—to theory and principles—requiring advice and direction from the consultant.

Bowers, Franklin, and Pecorella (1975) also have devised a cube as have Lippitt and Lippitt (1975) and White and Mitchell (1976). Although some of these models are clearer and more useful than others, it should be obvious that the field of OD is blessed with many typologies for classifying interventions.

Although the cube schemes are relatively coherent and *look* like models, W. L. French and Bell (1978) and Huse (1980) have categorized OD interventions more usefully. French and Bell categorize interventions by target group, type of intervention, and hypothesized change mechanism (see Ex-

EXHIBIT 11.3
The Blake and Mouton Consulcube Model

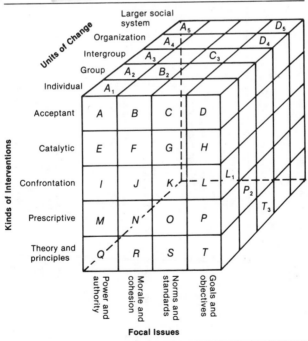

Source: R. Blake and J. Mouton, *Consultation* (Reading, Mass.: Addison-Wesley, 1976), p. 7. Reprinted by permission of Scientific Methods, Inc.

EXHIBIT 11.4

Typology of OD Interventions by Hypothesized Change Mechanisms and by Target Group

Intervention typology based on principal emphasis of intervention in relation to different hypothesized change mechanisms

Hypothesized change mechanism	Interventions based primarily on the change mechanism	Hypothesized change mechanism	Interventions based primarily on the change mechanism
Feedback	Survey feedback T-group Process consultation Organization mirroring Grid OD instruments Gestalt OD	Confrontation and working for resolution of differences	Third-party peacemaking Intergroup interface sessions Coaching and counseling individuals Confrontation meetings Collateral organizations Organizational mirroring Gestalt OD
Awareness of changing or dysfunctional sociocultural norms	Team building T-group Intergroup interface sessions First three phases of Grid OD	Education through: (1) new knowledge (2) skill practice	Career and life planning Team building Goal setting, decision making, problem solving, planning activities T-group Process consultation Transactional analysis
Increased interaction and communication	Survey feedback Intergroup interface sessions Third-party peacemaking Organizational mirroring Some forms of management by objectives Team building Technostructural changes Sociotechnical systems		

Intervention typology based on target group

Target group	Types of interventions	Target group	Types of interventions
Interventions designed to improve the effectiveness of *individuals*	Life- and career-planning activities Role analysis technique Coaching and counseling T-group (sensitivity training) Education and training to increase skill, knowledge in areas of technical task needs, relationship skills, process skills, decision making, problem solving, planning, goal-setting skills Grid OD phase 1 Some forms of job enrichment Gestalt OD Transactional analysis	Interventions designed to improve the effectiveness of *intergroup relations*	Intergroup activities Process directed Task directed Organizational mirroring (three or more groups) Structural interventions Process consultation Third-party peacemaking at group level Grid OD phase 3 Survey feedback
Interventions designed to improve the effectiveness of *dyads/triads*	Process consultation Third-party peacemaking Grid OD phases 1, 2 Gestalt OD Transactional analysis	Interventions designed to improve the effectiveness of the *total organization*	Technostructural activities such as collateral organizations Confrontation meetings Strategic planning activities Grid OD phases 4, 5, 6 Survey feedback Interventions based on Lawrence and Lorsch's contingency theory Interventions based on Likert's Systems 1–4 Physical settings
Interventions designed to improve the effectiveness of *teams and groups*	Team building Task directed Process directed Family T-group Survey feedback Process consultation Role analysis technique "Start-up" team building activities Education in decision making, problem solving, planning, goal setting in group settings Some forms of job enrichment and MBO Sociotechnical systems		

Source: Wendell L. French and Cecil H. Bell, Jr., *Organization Development: Behavioral Science Interventions for Organization Improvement*, 2nd ed. © 1978, pp. 112, 114. Reprinted by permission of Prentice-Hall, Inc., Englewood Cliffs, N.J.

227

hibit 11.4). Their model shows the multiple emphases found in several of the activities, but, as Huse (1980) points out, "A weakness of the model is that it does not consider some of the newer structural approaches to OD" (p. 108):

Huse's summary of interventions may be the best, since his typology is based on a comprehensive review of the literature and is more current. He groups OD interventions into ten basic classifications:

1. Individual consultation: counseling and any coaching activities, including career development and behavior modification.
2. Unstructured group training: sensitivity training and team building (Huse places team building in more than one category.)
3. Structured group training: management development and related training activities, such as training in management by objectives (MBO), managerial grid phase 1, and assertiveness. Team building is also an activity within this category.
4. Process consultation: "any intervention used with small groups or work teams to identify and solve common problems" (Huse 1980, p. 112). Team building is also included here.
5. Survey-guided development: methods that use data collection in a fairly formal way, followed by feedback and action planning. According to Huse, three survey-guided development designs can be delineated, according to increasing effectiveness:

   —data handout (information is collected by the practitioner and reported back, but with no further involvement of the practitioner);
   —action research, data feedback, and action planning (the more typical form of OD practice); and
   —concepts training, data feedback, and action planning (OD is conducted within a structured workshop or training setting).

6. Job redesign: changing tasks, shifting responsibilities, or modifying the technical and physical environment—the work itself. Examples include job enrichment, quality of work life (QWL) programs, flex-time, autonomous work teams, and the like.
7. Personnel systems: changes in such areas as the reward system, the process of performance appraisal, selection and promotion, and manpower planning.
8. Management information and financial control systems: such activities as MBO, performance evaluation, and human resource accounting.
9. Organizational design: changes in the organizational structure.
10. Integrated approaches: Huse's "final catchall category of interventions which include more than one of the methods described above" (Huse 1980, p. 113).

Summary

In this chapter we have discussed Argyris's criteria for an effective intervention: valid information, free choice, and internal commitment. These criteria represent the goal of an intervention, whereas the criteria I prefer—responding to actual client needs, involving the client in planning and implementing, and leading to cultural change—deal more with the means for achieving such goals.

In planning an intervention, the consultant must assess the client's readiness for change, link the intervention to the sources of power in the organization, and arrange for internal resources to serve as consultants and as guardians of the new culture.

Argyris's three general types of intervention—the tried and true ones that fit many organizations, newly created interventions that fit the uniqueness of a particular client situation, and interventions that both help the client and contribute to research and theory—introduced us to the various ways of categorizing OD interventions. We saw that there are many ways and many people involved in classification. Harrison's (1970) depth scheme may prove to be the most useful technique for a consultant in choosing the type of intervention to use with a client.

In the remaining four chapters of this part of the book, we shall examine in more detail many of the interventions mentioned or briefly discussed in this chapter. These are the OD practitioner's tools—what he or she uses to fix or constructively change organizations, with fortitude, tenacity, patience, skill, intelligence, and some luck. The first interventions to be considered are those that are individually focused (Chapter 12); next will be group interventions (Chapter 13), then intergroup interventions (Chapter 14), and finally interventions that are targeted toward the organization as a whole (Chapter 15).

CHAPTER 12

Individually Focused
Interventions

Many people in organizations believe that changing a system means changing people—their behavior, their attitudes, and perhaps even their values. They believe that, if we change certain people, especially managers, the organization thereby will be changed. Some OD practitioners make the same assumptions or hold values that are primarily, if not exclusively, individually focused (see Chapter 5). The tendency to focus on the individual as the target for organization change may still be paramount. From Lewin's research and theory we know, however, that, for systematic change to occur at the group or organizational level, the strategy for change must be focused at that level, not toward the individual. In Chapter 2 we discussed Fleishman's research at International Harvester, which showed that trying to train first-line supervisors to behave toward their subordinates differently from the ways they were treated by their bosses had no long-term payoff. The culture of the existing organization did not support the objectives for change of the training program. The culture, not the individuals involved, needed changing. Thus, focusing on the individual puts the cart before the horse (Burke 1971).

Culture implies behavior, however, and it is people who behave, not organizations. It is true that people's behavior in an organization must change for the organization to change, but staying with Lewin's premise, the behavior to be changed is in patterns of conformity, not individual personalities. It is the organization's personality that changes with organization development, not the individual's.

Individually focused interventions are nevertheless important and highly relevant in OD practice. Once the direction of organization change—the "desired state" (Beckhard and Harris 1977)—has been determined, individually focused interventions may then be used to facilitate the overall change effort in general, and perhaps to enhance movement within the "transition state" (Beckhard and Harris 1977) in particular.

Categories of individually focused interventions include recruitment and selection, training and development—particularly management development—counseling, career development, interventions associated with a reduction in force, and interventions that are focused on jobs or roles. We shall consider these categories by defining each one and by explaining its role in organization development.

Recruitment and Selection

Recruiting and then selecting appropriate people for the organization are the most important individually focused actions and decisions made by managers. Appropriate performance by these people in the organization is a function of both their competence (ability) and their motivation: Performance = Ability × Motivation (McGregor 1967). One can work on developing people's motivation for months and years, but if they are basically incompetent or if their talents are inappropriately matched for the job to be done—that is, their ability equals zero—their performance will also be at least zero (or negative for a highly motivated person doing the wrong things). It is far more important for managers to spend time, effort, and money on recruiting and selecting the right people than for them to try to develop people who never should have been selected or people in inappropriate assignments—the wrong match of talent and job.

Recruiting is the process of seeking out individuals who might be interested in and qualified for working for the organization. It may involve advertising available positions in the organization in the public media, interviewing prospects on college campuses or in local communities, or interviewing on the organization's premises as interested people respond to advertisements about the available positions. Selections are then made from these prospects. It is often difficult to determine exactly where recruitment ends and selection begins. Selection is the process of reaching a final decision regarding a job offer, but the offer may be made or implied in the recruitment phase. For final selection purposes, the process may amount to no more than an interview and perhaps a letter or two of reference, or it may be very elaborate and sophisticated. A certain manufacturing organization, for example, in selecting its first-line supervisors: (1) conducts individual interviews with each applicant; (2) administers a battery of psychological tests, including measures of aptitude, interests, and personality; (3) conducts a test of the applicant's ability to differentiate between effective and ineffective supervisory practice, using videotaped vignettes of certain supervisor-subordinate relationships; and (4) provides a one-day conducted tour of one of its plants. The final job offer depends on the applicant's interview responses, test scores, responses to the videotaped vignettes, and reactions to the plant visit. This example of an elaborate form of selection is similar to and

231

based largely on the assessment center technique (Bray, Campbell, and Grant 1974; Byham 1970), to be explained in more detail later in this chapter.

For OD purposes, helping with recruitment and selection may be a key intervention, particularly in start-up situations, such as building a new plant, creating a new department, starting a new venture, and the like. The most widely known and perhaps best example of selection for OD purposes was the start-up situation in a General Foods food-processing plant in Topeka, Kansas, some years ago. As reported by King (1972), the plan was to design this new manufacturing organization according to the criteria of Likert's (1967) System 4 (see Chapters 2 and 10). This meant that major tasks would be accomplished by teams and that first-line supervisors would be team leaders rather than operating more traditionally as supervisors, giving close individual supervision. Status differences among all employees were to be minimized. There would be no executive dining room, for example, but one cafeteria for all; and a participative approach to management was to be practiced. The top management group for the plant, the general manager and three operating managers (operations service, manufacturing, and technical), had been selected by corporate headquarters according to the new plant design criteria; that is, these individuals were compatible with and committed to managing their organization according to the participative management premises of System 4. The objective of the selection process, therefore, was to find people who were also compatible with a participative approach. Team leaders would be expected to manage participatively.

The selection process was managed by the top team with the assistance of an OD consultant. The principles that guided their work were as follows:

1. All selection decisions would be made by the people who were to work with those selected.
2. Decisions would be based on how applicants behaved in collaborative and conflicting group situations.
3. All applicants would receive feedback from the decision makers regarding why they did or did not receive a job offer.
4. The selection process would reflect as much as possible the types of tasks and relationships that would be characteristic of work in the plant; that is, status differences were minimized, the process was personalized, there was a growth and development emphasis for all employees, communication was two-way, and considerable activity took place in small groups.
5. Psychological tests would be used, but only as secondary information, and the results would not become a part of an individual's employee file.
6. Contact between those who were already members of the organization and those who were strong prospects would gradually become more extensive and open as the selection process progressed.

King has described in detail the two-day process for the selection of team leaders. The process included a plant visit, a detailed description of the new organization, role-play exercises, a battery of psychological tests, group decision-making tasks, and simulation exercises of plant work. As King (1972) points out:

> The selection decision makers must obtain an accurate indication of whether or not the candidate is likely to function well in a participative organization. At the same time, prospective employees need accurate information to assist them in deciding whether or not it is advisable for them to join such a new system. (p. 201)

King's report was written about nine months after the start-up of the plant. During that time only two people had left the organization, absenteeism was less than one percent, and productivity had exceeded original expectations. This early success was sustained (Walton 1975), but the managerial and change process associated with it did not spread into the overall parent company. Walton (1975) has hypothesized several reasons for this lack of diffusion within General Foods and within six other similar situations of organizations in the United States, Canada, the United Kingdom, and Norway. An eighth organization, Volvo of Sweden, was an exception. The success of an initial pilot effort there was effectively diffused into other parts of the overall organization (Gyllenhammar 1977).

The opportunity to select people for a new organization in a planned, systematic way is rare. The advantages of such an opportunity are clear:

> Many difficult problems in overcoming resistance to change are obviated. New norms, different from traditional norms in industry, can be developed. Rather than the problem of changing established roles and role expectations about how supervisors or employees "should" act, roles are established anew. The newness of the physical setting and technology is congruent with the institution of a new approach to organization and interpersonal relationships. (King 1972, p. 201)

Although new plant start-up situations such as the one in Topeka are rare, many of the selection processes described by King can be applied to other similar situations, such as creation of a new unit within an organization or significant expansion of a department that already exists. In the latter case, care must be taken to alleviate the potential for a "we-they" conflict between old employees and new ones (Porter, Lawler, and Hackman 1975, p. 441).

Selection is important not only for finding people with particular abilities and matching those abilities with the appropriate jobs but also for aligning people's values and needs with the organization's culture. This latter purpose is usually not realized or even considered by most organizations (Schneider 1976). A lack of this consideration can have undersirable consequences for an organization, however, especially for service organizations, as Schneider's (1980) research has shown.

To some extent, certain types of people are attracted to certain types of organizations. Those who are attracted to service organizations tend to be more people-oriented than the general population; they seem to enjoy and perhaps need other people more. These people tend to be more outgoing, gregarious, and extroverted, particularly those who are attracted to jobs that require direct contact with the public, such as sales, bank work, nursing, and so forth. The extent to which these kinds of people will be effective as employees apparently depends on how they are managed.

In a study of one type of service organization, a bank, Schneider (1980) has shown that service organizations (1) tend to attract employees who are people-oriented and value service behavior; (2) typically have bosses who are oriented more toward costs, profits, procedures, and efficiency than toward customer service; (3) experience a gap between employee values and orientations and those of management; and (4) are susceptible to poor customer service when management's and employees' orientations and values differ considerably. Schneider has defined two different types of managements in service organizations: the service *enthusiasts* and the service *bureaucrats*. Managers who are service enthusiasts are concerned with the organization's clients and customers, while managers who are service bureaucrats are more internally focused—concerned with system maintenance and conformity to policies and procedures.

The results of Schneider's research show that, the more service enthusiasts an organization has among its managers, (1) the more satisfied both its employees and its customers are likely to be, (2) the more the employees are likely to remain with the organization, (3) the less employees experience frustration in their work, and (4) the less employees experience role conflict and ambiguity. Thus, Schneider's study demonstrates that when a service organization's managers are oriented toward the client, the employees will feel more congruence about their work and value orientations and there will be a higher degree of customer satisfaction. Schneider also believes that this customer satisfaction index is just as important a criterion of organizational effectiveness as so-called bottom line results.

There are many aspects of recruitment and selection. For OD purposes, it is important to concentrate on two objectives: (1) matching the right person to the right job and (2) matching personal preferences and values with appropriate organizational climate or, where a mismatch may occur, attempting to change the organizational climate toward more congruence. Assessment center techniques may be highly useful for the person-job match, and both the King (1972) and the Schneider (1980) studies show not only a relationship between management and organizational climate (participative-team management in the former and customer orientation or service enthusiast climate in the latter) but also positive performance consequences for the organization when there is congruence of personal preferences and organizational climate. It is the OD practitioner's responsibility to watch for incongruencies.

Training and Development

The primary target of interventions in training and development is management. Training programs and job rotation are typical. Much current OD begins with management training, usually with development of professional skills but sometimes with a personal focus as well. This latter focus has been significant in the growth of OD. Many of OD's roots are associated with individually focused interventions, T-group or sensitivity training, Maslow's hierarchy of needs theory, and individual assessment (see Chapter 2). In the early days of OD (late 1950s and early 1960s) it was difficult to distinguish what was beginning to be called organization development from sensitivity training, because the people who are considered the pioneers of OD—such as Chris Argyris, Richard Beckhard, Warren Bennis, Robert R. Blake, Lee Bradford, Paul Buchanan, Sheldon Davis, Charles Ferguson, Murray Horwitz, Douglas McGregor, Herbert Shepard, and Robert Tannenbaum—were all heavily involved in sensitivity training at the time. Some are still very involved. For early OD, the T-group was the primary intervention. This type of training evolved into what we now know as team building. I hasten to add, however, that team building is *not* a team T-group (see Chapter 13).

Sensitivity Training

Sensitivity training may still be considered an OD intervention, but it is rarely used as such today. The change in emphasis over two decades has been considerable. When sensitivity training was brought into organizations as a developmental technique and conducted with family units—a boss and the subordinates who reported directly to him—the developmental objective became background and internal politics became foremost. It is difficult to tell people exactly what you may think and feel, especially about them, when you know (1) that you will have to continue working with them after the training, and (2) that people, particularly bosses, tend to remember the feedback they receive, especially when it is considered negative. It is only natural to fear retribution. Organization development is still a taboo term in some organizations today because of bad experiences with sensitivity training fifteen or more years ago.

The place of sensitivity training in organization development now is marginal. Most OD practitioners who recommend sensitivity training to their clients suggest that the people involved go to a public program away from the organization, with program members who are strangers at the outset. The risks are thus lessened, of course, and the individual can feel freer to experiment with his or her behavior and to learn therefrom. The T-group learning experience should be treated as self-development without a requirement that it *prove* to be useful for the organization. Such an outcome cannot be proved anyway (J. P. Campbell and Dunnette 1968). Whether sensitivity training will make better managers of people is yet to be determined. There is evidence, however, that it does make an individual difference (Beer 1976a; Bunker 1965; Bunker and Knowles 1967; J. P. Campbell and Dunnette 1968; Lieberman, Yalom, and Miles 1973). People learn, for example, (1) to listen to others more actively and with empathy, (2) to express their feelings more clearly, (3) to be more sensitive to other's feelings and needs, and (4) to understand more about their impact on other people.

For OD purposes, then, sensitivity training can be used to increase peoples' general level of interpersonal competence. This *may* have value organizationally where people must work together more collaboratively; where potential for conflict is high, such as in a matrix organization, and creative use of conflict is needed; where team building will become a major intervention for a number of people, in that prior experience with sensitivity training can expedite the objectives of team building (Crockett 1977, 1970); and where employees must deal sensitively with customers, the general public, or fellow employees—for example, airline ticket agents, health care delivery specialists, recruiters, and counselors.

In addition to sensitivity training, some other training or educational modes and techniques may accomplish many of these same objectives for self-development. These other techniques include Gestalt therapy and training, transactional analysis, the Managerial Grid Seminar, and Tavistock training. A brief explanation of these four alternatives follows. (There are others, of course, such as Erhard Seminar Training (est), the Managerial Effectiveness Program of the American Management Association, the Levinson Institute's program, and leadership training at the Menninger Foundation and at the Center for Creative Leadership, to name a few. These programs provide some variation on one or more of the themes that comprise sensitivity training or the four alternatives listed here.)

Gestalt Therapy and Training

I have designated this approach to self-development both therapy and training because the distinction is not clear. Sensitivity training also encompasses both aspects, as there is not much difference between "getting better" and learning something new about oneself. The roots of sensitivity training are in education, however, whereas the basis of Gestalt training is both in Gestalt psychology and in a particular approach to therapy. *Gestalt* is a German word that translates roughly as "wholeness" or "totality". Since there is no precise translation, the word has been retained in English usage. Gestalt also implies the notion that a whole is something more than the sum of its parts. In Gestalt therapy, therefore, the patient is treated as a total person, a total entity, rather than by a singular analysis of his or her parts—personal history, current physical condition, attitudes about sex, or relationship with father or mother. These parts are important only as they relate to the whole—for example, how the personal history affects the person's functioning less than optimally today.

The Gestalt approach to self-development emphasizes, among other things, (1) integration of mind and body; (2) increased clarity about one's personal wants, values, and goals; (3) greater awareness of self, especially one's feelings and impact on others; and (4) resolution or completion of unfinished business. One is not whole until past experiences—an interpersonal conflict that continues to nag, the death of a friend or relative that continues to hurt, a past failure that one fears might be repeated—are resolved in some way. For more detailed discussion of Gestalt therapy, see Polster and Polster (1973) and some of the writings by the founder of this approach, Fritz Perls (Perls, Hefferline, and Goodman 1951; Perls 1969).

The person who has been most active in relating Gestalt therapy to organization development is Stan Herman. He has advocated that OD practitioners help their clients resolve core personal and organizational problems by encouraging them (1) to accept and experience the full range of behavior—good and bad, positive and negative, love and hate, dominant and submissive—so that behavior will be based more on reality than on symptoms of problems and unauthenticity; (2) to become more aware of how they stop themselves from getting what they want (curbing their power); and (3) to stick with difficult personal or interpersonal problems until they have been resolved in some fashion (Herman 1972). Herman argues that, the more OD practitioners help their clients with these kinds of issues, the more effective they will be as employees and managers and the more effective the organization will be (Herman 1977; Herman and Korenich 1977).

The value of the Gestalt approach to self-development is that it emphasizes the total person. Whether this self-development pays off for the organization, as Herman argues, is yet to be determined. Many practitioners in OD are nevertheless attracted to the Gestalt approach because it treats the person as a total system in much the same manner as OD considers the organization a total system (Burke 1980c), and because it emphasizes personal growth and development—a strong value underlying OD.

Transactional Analysis

Although training in transactional analysis (TA) is not as popular as it was in the early 1970s, it is still available as a technique for increasing one's self-awareness and development. The training focuses both on the person and on the nature of transactions the person has learned to conduct with others. Eric Berne, the father of TA, theorized that each individual's personality is composed of three ego states, analogous to Freud's superego, ego, and id, and that, as a result of life experiences, especially childhood experiences, we are programmed to behave in certain ways (Berne 1964, 1961). Berne's *parent* ego state is the program instilled by parents and other authority figures. The extent to which one acts parentally with others is a function of how strongly this program was instilled. The *child* ego state, again programmed from birth, is a result of our impulses and basic needs. When a person is thought to be acting childishly, this ego state is the predominant one. The *adult* ego state is the rational one. When a person sizes up a situation, determines that action must be taken, considers alternative action steps, makes a choice, and acts accordingly, he or she is behaving in the adult ego state.

In TA training, interactions between people are analyzed as transactions between ego states. These transactions are classified as complementary, crossed, or ulterior. *Complementary* transactions are usually the most effective for communicating and understanding. These transactions may occur between the same ego states—as adult to adult—such as an exchange between boss and subordinate (*Boss:* "Your decision about Project X was the appropriate one in my opinon. Nice work!" *Subordinate:* "Thanks. I felt good about it myself.") or between different ego states—as parent to child or the reverse (*Boss:* "Fortunately, your decision about Project X turned out to be the appropriate one, but I was worried since you are so inexperienced and naive about these kinds of projects." *Subordinate:* "Yeah, I was lucky, all right. I certainly did not know much about it, but I had a certain amount of comfort knowing that you were around to rescue me if things went wrong."). The two examples are depicted graphically in Exhibit 12.1.

Complementary transactions may also occur between child and child when both are in a playful state, but they rarely occur between two parent states, since the parent typically attempts to dominate the other party.

Crossed transactions occur when a message is sent from one ego state but responded to from an inappropriate ego state. Again using a boss-subordinate interaction to illustrate, such a transaction might be: *Boss:* "I would appreciate your tackling the X Project for our department. It's a tough one but I think you can do it." *Subordinate:* "You always pick on me for the tough ones. Why don't you lay off me for awhile!" This transaction is depicted in Exhibit 12.2.

238

EXHIBIT 12.1

Examples of Complementary Transactions

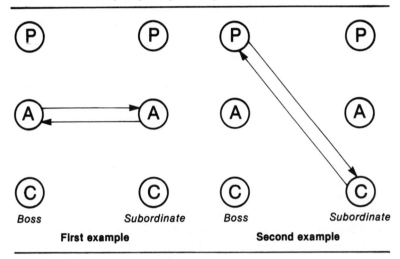

P = parent ego state; A = adult ego state; C = child ego state.

EXHIBIT 12.2

Example of a Crossed Transaction

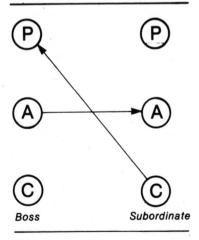

P = parent ego state; A = adult ego state; C = child ego state.

Crossed transactions are usually emotionally charged and rarely result in effective communication and understanding between people.

Ulterior transactions involve more than two ego states. The usual ulterior transaction occurs when a person sends a message in words from one ego state but sends his or her intentions from another. These intentions may not be readily apparent—they are ulterior—but they embody the real message. An example would be a boss saying to a subordinate, "I want you to tackle this project because I think you're capable," while in practice the boss never lets the subordinate decide to take any action alone for fear that he would make a mistake. The boss may be expressing an adult message in words but conveying a parent to child transaction in action. This transaction is depicted in Exhibit 12.3.

Ulterior transactions are obviously ineffective because of the incongruence between the message sender's words and actions or intentions.

The core of TA training is analyzing transactions according to these categories and helping people understand them and appreciate the greater effectiveness of complementary transactions as opposed to crossed and ulterior transactions. There are also other aspects of TA training: time structuring and script analysis—the analysis of the games people play in their interactions and of the programs that have been instilled from life experiences. It should be clear that the underlying assumption of the training is that greater self-awareness about one's tendencies regarding these ego

EXHIBIT 12.3

Example of an Ulterior Transaction

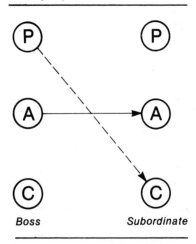

Boss   Subordinate

P = parent ego state; A = adult ego state; C = child ego state.

240

states—using the parent state excessively, for example—and practice in complementary transactions will lead to increased interpersonal competence.

There is little hard evidence that TA training does result in greater interpersonal competence—more use of complementary transactions—but there is at least some indirect evidence (Jongeward and Contributors 1973). Many organizations use this type of training (Rush and McGrath 1973) in an attempt to improve interpersonal relationships in general and those between boss and subordinate, agent and customer, and management and labor in particular.

The Managerial Grid Seminar

Based on Blake and Mouton's (1978) model of managerial styles, the managerial grid, the seminar is a five-day training program, usually residential, that (1) teaches the model as a way of conceptualizing various managerial styles, with the emphasis on five primary ones; (2) provides opportunities for participants to receive feedback from questionnaires and from fellow participants about their relative use of the five primary styles; and (3) advocates one style, the 9,9 participative approach, as best. See Chapter 9 for a description of the managerial grid model.

The grid seminar is similar to sensitivity training and Gestalt therapy in that participants give and receive feedback from one another in the training group. The seminar differs from the other two training programs in that it is a more structured approach, relying heavily on the model, a tight design schedule, and questionnaires and other learning instruments, such as film. The grid seminar is also similar to TA training in that the training format follows one model exclusively.

The grid seminar is individually oriented (the training group is more of a vehicle for learning than a learning objective itself) and provides an opportunity for self-development in that a participant may learn how far he or she is from being a 9,9 manager and can plan personal change objectives accordingly.

For OD purposes, a grid seminar may be used as Phase 1 of an overall grid organization development effort (see Chapter 9), as a preliminary step in general team building that is not grid-focused, as a training intervention for management development in general, or as an intervention to facilitate an organization's movement toward participative management.

The Tavistock Approach

The Tavistock approach to training, like sensitivity training, emphasizes the small group. The Tavi method, as it is sometimes called, is different from sensitivity training in some significant ways, however. In a Tavistock group there is more emphasis on authority and leadership as the primary focus of learning, and the role of the trainer differs considerably from that of T-group trainers.

The Tavistock approach gets its name from the institute in London where its creators—Eric Trist, A. K. Rice, C. Sofer, and their colleagues—were located at the time it was developed in the late 1950s. The first training conference of its kind was held in England by the Tavistock Institute and the University of Leicester in September 1957 (Trist and Sofer 1959). Influenced by the theories of Kurt Lewin and Wilfred Bion, as well as by the training methodology of the National Training Laboratories (NTL) Institute in the United States, the primary emphasis at that time was on group behavior. Over the next decade, Rice (1965) gradually shifted the learning focus to issues of authority and leadership and to organizations, not just small groups. Bion's (1961) theory about the task group and the basic assumption group also became more influential.

Whereas, in sensitivity training, the trainer sits in with the group and interacts personally with group members (some more than others, of course), the Tavi "educator," as he or she is called, does not become a part of the group. The educator often sits outside the group as an observer and outside commentator. This role outside the boundary of the group, whether the boundary is physical or psychological, causes a vacuum of authority and leadership within the group. How group members react to this vacuum becomes the prime focus of activity and learning. "The leader or leadership in a group can be thought of as representing or embodying the function of the group, expecially its major function or primary task . . . [that is] that task which an organization or institution must perform in order to survive" (Rioch 1975, p. 7).

The A. K. Rice Institute in the United States is the major organization providing this type of training on this side of the Atlantic. The Rice Institute educators have patterned their approach after A. K. Rice's work at the Tavistock Institute. Each year educators from both institutes work together to insure consistency and cross-fertilization.

This type of training obviously can be used to help people learn more about leadership, especially in the context of authority issues. The training is also useful for helping group members differentiate behavior that facilitates task accomplishment from behavior that impedes. For more information on this form of education, see *Group Relations Reader,* edited by Colman and Bexton (1975).

Summary of Self-Development Programs

The four types of training I have covered so far in this training and development section are by no means all that is available. They represent, in my opinion, the primary programs for self-development. Other programs that might

242

be considered in the same domain are more specific to organizational tasks or functions, such as training in management by objectives (MBO), which may aid in self-development but only as a by-product, not as the primary objective.

The programs covered so far typically exist outside the organization; managers usually must go away for these types of training. I shall now turn to programs that are internal to the organization and that are tailor-made or specifically designed for the people of a given organization—usually the managers.

Tailor-made Training and Development

Many large organizations, particularly those in business and industry, design and conduct their own training and development programs. These programs may consist of supervisory or sales training, for example, and rely exclusively on the training staff of the organization, or they may be for middle management, conducted by both the organization's staff trainers and outside, contracted trainers. The more the training concerns managers and executives, the more likely it is that outside instructors will be used. These in-house training and development programs take a variety of forms, ranging in length from a day to two or three weeks and covering a wide array of topics. Some companies' training departments publish annual catalogs of their program offerings. AT&T, for example, spends over a billion dollars a year on training, most of which is conducted by their own training staff. The variety of training in organizations is thus considerable, and the resources devoted to training are immense, particulary in some large corporations.

The kind of training and development most relevant for organization development is that conducted for managers and executives, especially the programs that concentrate on topics concerned with the management of people. These programs have usually been designed as a result of a needs analysis. The training staff conducts interviews with a sample of managers in the organization, asking them about their needs and preferences regarding their further development as managers or executives. After summarizing and analyzing these interview data, the training staff designs a program based on the needs and preferences mentioned most frequently. The resultant program typically consists of such topics as communication skills, performance appraisal, group dynamics or team development, managing meetings, business strategy and policy, delegation, time management, management by objectives, motivation, leadership, finance for the nonfinancial manager, and stress management. These topics are loosely coupled for the program design, and learning methods usually include combinations of lecture, case study and discussion, role-play, group problem solving, films, and perhaps a management simulation game.

A few organizations recently have taken a different approach to the design

243

and conduct of management training and development. One such organization, Citicorp, the second largest banking institution in the United States—with worldwide operations—launched a unique training program, "Managing People," early in 1977. Although a formal needs analysis was not conducted, the corporation's top management was concerned that, along with their rapid growth in the late 1960s and early 1970s, the increasing strain on managers to continue to produce profits and adapt to rapid change had caused mounting people problems in the organization. More and more people were feeling like cogs in a (money) machine. Since it was accepted by top management that people were the organization's most important resource, particular attention had to be paid to managing this resource more effectively. William Spencer, president of the corporation at that time, publicly stated in a filmed introduction to Citicorp's program: "The management of people is probably a greater skill mandated than individual brilliance. Even the most brilliant person, if there is little or no ability to manage people, is a lost cause in our operation."

Using the Forum Corporation of Boston as outside consultants, particularly George Litwin, the education and research division of Citicorp, headed by Henry Brenner, conducted a study (1) to identify the best management talent within the organization, (2) to determine the specific set of management practices that seemed to distinguish them from average managers, and (3) to design a training program based on these superior practices. A criterion group of managers was thus established by asking senior executives to identify subordinate managers within their respective groups who were outstanding and would most likely be taking their places as senior executives within the next decade. Thirty-nine such managers were identified. The researchers then asked these same senior executives to identify thirty-nine additional managers within their groups who were satisfactory managers but not as effective as the first group. The researchers next arranged for 353 subordinates of these seventy-eight managers (thirty-nine in the A group—outstanding—and thirty-nine in the B group—satisfactory) to rate their bosses on fifty-nine management practices culled from a list of hundreds. The ratings were done with five-point Likert scales. Some of the practices rated were

> Your manager communicates high personal standards informally—in conversation, personal appearance, and so forth.
>
> Your manager tries to make the best use of staff members' skills and abilities when making assignments.
>
> Your manager works with staff members (subordinates) to reach mutual agreement on their performance appraisals.

Your manager uses recognition and praise—aside from pay—to reward excellent performance.

The work-group meetings your manager conducts serve to increase trust and mutual respect among the work-group members.

The A group was rated significantly higher than the B group on twenty-two of the fifty-nine practices—regardless of their management situation in the corporation. Another eight practices differentiated between the two groups, but only under structured conditions of management, such as in a back-office operation of check processing. The A group practices were then used as the basis for design of the training program. Since this A group had been identified as outstanding managers, and since subordinate ratings had further identified some of the specific practices that these managers did exceptionally well, it followed (at least to Citicorp's top management) that the larger population of managers should be trained to adopt this special set of people-management practices. Prior to participation in the program, managers are rated by their subordinates on the selected practices. The five-day program then consists of training on clusters of these practices, with each training day devoted to one cluster. The five clusters are (1) getting commitment to goals and standards, (2) coaching, (3) appraising performance, (4) compensating and rewarding, and (5) building a team for continuity of performance. Training techniques include case method, role practice, group problem-solving and decision-making exercises, and occasional short lectures. For each day of the program, the managers receive a computer printout of their ratings by their subordinates on that day's cluster of practices. This feedback for the manager is the most powerful part of the training program, as managers focus their learning and improvement objectives on the practices that received the lowest ratings. In its first three years, some 2,000 Citicorp managers went through the program. It continues to be popular and highly valued among Citicorp managers.

Other companies, such as Firemen's Fund Insurance, have designed management training programs along the same lines as Citicorp's. Yet other organizations, such as the National Aeronautics and Space Administration, have designed and conducted successful management development programs and then later launched studies to determine profiles of their most competent administrators and managers. In such cases, the results of the competency studies are used (1) to refine the already existing training program, (2) to modify the performance appraisal system, and (3) to improve existing human resource planning systems, especially those for managers.

In this section on training and development we have explored development activities that consist of training and education, but we should not lose perspective. By far the most popular and widely used management development activity is job rotation (Digman 1978). Providing a variety of managerial experiences across the primary functions of an organization is still considered the most important activity for developing general managers and executives. Career development is the human resource management function that facilitates and integrates employees' development, particularly in the areas of job rotation and education.

Career Development

Systematic career development does not really exist in most organizations. One's career develops more as a result of random opportunities—being in the right place at the right time and having someone higher in the organization, a mentor, looking out for you—than through a systematic process through a planned sequence of jobs, progressing up the rungs of a clearly defined ladder. Some organizations do make a conscious effort to provide the right mix of learning opportunities through a series of job changes, so that those who have the greatest ability to gain from such opportunities can progress upward in the organization, gradually acquiring more experience and wider responsibilities. IBM and AT&T are examples of major United States organizations that practice this sort of career development. Typical developmental activities remain within an organization's regular activities. Employees within the marketing function may rotate through a variety of jobs, for example, typically alternating from line to staff positions but for the most part remaining within marketing. This form of career development helps significantly in maintaining an organization's specialties, but it begins to reach a point of diminishing returns when a person reaches the general management level, when the next move upward in the organization means that he or she will be managing functions other than or in addition to marketing.

The most important decision for an employee in a large organization, both from the person's perspective and for the good of the organization, may be whether the individual should remain a specialist or should move toward general management. An aid in this decision is the so-called assessment center, perhaps the primary technique for career development other than job rotation.

The Assessment Center

The assessment center, originally developed and used by the U.S. Office of Strategic Services (OSS) during World War II, is now a popular method of screening and selecting employees for future management positions. Under the leadership of Douglas Bray, AT&T has been the primary developer and user of the assessment center since World War II (Bray, Campbell, and Grant, 1974). The method usually requires two to five days of a person's time

246

at a location away from work—either a hotel or the organization's training center. The assessment center typically involves *psychological testing*—questionnaires measuring aptitudes and personality characteristics; *simulation techniques,* such as the in-basket exercise, which confronts the individual with typical managerial problems that need action; and *leaderless group activities,* in which problems need to be solved or decisions made within a group. A team of assessors, composed of experienced managers in the organization and human resource specialists with backgrounds in psychology and the behavioral sciences, observe and record the assessment center participants' behavior, discuss among themselves their individual assessments of the participants, and provide feedback to the participants. The participants also give and receive feedback from one another. Decisions regarding the participants' career futures are then made on the basis of these assessments. Who makes these decisions and how they are made creates a dilemma for both the assessed individual and the organization's management. This dilemma stems from the larger issue for any employee and employing organization—the interface between individual needs and goals and the organization's objectives. A question arises regarding the extent to which the assessment center is used purely for development of the individual, with the results remaining exclusively within the person's prerogative, or for evaluation, with the results belonging only to management. Although the purpose of an assessment center does not have to be described in such either-or terms, the results usually belong more to management than to the individual and are used more for evaluation than for development. This tendency creates problems for organizations that are attempting to become more humanistically oriented and more involved in organization development. A few organizations have successfully used the assessment center method purely for individual development purposes (Goodstein 1980).

As already noted, the development-evaluation question does not necessarily have to be in opposition. To assume opposition is to assume that individual needs and goals and organizational needs and goals cannot become integrated. From an organization development perspective, however, effective integration of these two sets of needs and goals is the primary mission of any OD effort. Organization development practitioners sometimes serve as human resource specialists for assessment centers. In this role, they are in a perfect position to facilitate the integration process. How these sets of needs and goals integrate, of course, depends on the particular individual and organization involved.

The assessment center method is a proven asset. Studies have shown that people selected for management positions or promoted further on the basis of assessment center results perform significantly better than individuals who are selected and promoted by other means (Huck 1977). Therefore, although the assessment center method creates an individual and organizational

247

dilemma, that is insufficient reason to reject the process as a technique for both helping individuals to reach their career goals and helping the organization to achieve its mission.

There are other career development processes and techniques. Some organizations provide career development workshops (Brynildsen 1974) in which participants may take psychological tests, assess their current career status against aspirations, and test with peers and workshop leaders the reality of their abilities and needs relative to their career aspirations. Many books and workbooks have also been published recently to help people individually to achieve greater clarity about their abilities and interests and to plan their futures on a more informed, realistic basis (Kotter, Faux, and McArthur 1978; Crystal and Bolles 1974; Hagberg and Leider 1978). Career development activities, especially workshops, have also been designed and conducted within the context of life changes and transitions (Gould 1978; Levinson et al. 1978; Vaillant 1977). This context adds significantly to the individual's perspective regarding the match of personal needs and career status and aspirations in his or her life.

Career development as an integral part of human resource planning and development has come into its own only in recent years. This recent upsurge in popularity and increased legitimacy as a necessary function within organizations is undoubtedly a result of several factors:

> Highly talented candidates (particularly minorities and females) often give preference to employers who demonstrate that career advancement opportunities exist.
>
> Women who are employees in midcareer and college recruits are asking for career-planning assistance. Popular publications have raised their awareness of the need for career planning.
>
> Affirmative action programs and court-approved settlements of discrimination suits frequently require companies to set up career development programs for protected classes.
>
> Company growth and changing staffing requirements necessitate individual career development to help assure that needed talent will be available. (Walker 1980, p. 334)

For more information on how to integrate career development within an overall human resource planning and development function, see E. H. Schein's (1978) recent synthesis.

An essential component of any career development effort is counseling, and OD practitioners are often placed in the role of counselor. We shall now briefly explore this aspect of organizational responsibility and its role within organization development.

248

Counseling

As noted in Chapter 2, counseling was recognized as a tool for individual development and organizational improvement approximately fifty years ago, when the Hawthorne studies were conducted. The counselors at the Hawthorne plant were not consultants and therefore did not act as intervenors into the system (Dickson and Roethlisberger 1966). When counseling is used for purposes of furthering organization development, we again have the problem of integrating individual needs and organizational goals. This is not an easy problem to solve,

> since the requirements of system-wide change may not be in the interest of the individual, and vice-versa. However, if the counselor [OD practitioner] can relate equally to the demands of organization change and to the needs of the individual, he is in a unique position to help the individual and the organization renegotiate a new psychological contract. (Beer 1980, p. 190)

The OD practitioner frequently takes the role of counselor. Most of the time this is an informal role—carried out during lunch conversations, brief and spontaneous talks with the client before or after an intense meeting, phone conversations with the client about scheduling the next time together in which a current problem is discussed incidentally, and so forth. One of the most important times is when the OD practitioner-counselor is helping his or her client (usually a boss) deal with feedback that is experienced by the client as negative (Crockett 1970). Defensive feelings are the most common ones, and the more the OD practitioner-counselor can help the client talk about those feelings, the more the client will be able to move on to a problem-solving mode of behavior.

There are several different approaches to counseling, and it is important for the OD practitioner to be familiar with them and therefore be able to choose the one that is most comfortable for him or her. Any of the accepted approaches will work if the counselor is particularly knowledgeable about a particular approach, experienced in its use, personally comfortable with it, and consistent in using it. One of the early approaches is nondirective or client-centered counseling, as developed by Rogers (1951). Another is transactional analysis, discussed earlier in this chapter as a technique for training and development. I have found Gestalt therapy the most effective approach to counseling in my consulting practice. I prefer a Gestalt approach because of its emphasis on the whole person, its relationship to general system theory (Burke 1980c), its focus on the present rather than on the past, and its immediate applicability to problem solving. Gestalt therapy also forces the client to deal with reality, as does any good approach to counseling. Exploring fan-

249

tasies and wishes may be part of the counseling process, but usually only as a vehicle for helping the client deal with reality more effectively.

Reality is the prime concept of reality therapy (Glasser 1965), and its method is to deal directly with reality. The ultimate objective of this approach to therapy is to help individuals learn how to meet their needs better while not depriving others in their pursuits of need fulfillment. This is how Glasser defines responsibility. According to Beer (1980): "In organizational terms, this would mean that an individual must balance his needs with those of the organization and the people who depend on the organization to maintain its efficiency and effectiveness (other employees, stock-holders, management, etc.)" (p. 190). Beer advocates reality therapy as particularly suitable for organization development, in that it focuses on behavior rather than on attitudes. Beer (1980) argues that "changing behavior leads quickly to a change in attitudes and in turn leads to fulfilling needs and further changes in behavior. Since most managers and consultants have neither the time or skill for more traditional forms of psychotherapy, this approach makes sense for organization development" (p. 191).

Regardless of the counseling approach chosen, to be effective it is imperative that OD practitioners (1) be genuine in their relations with the client; (2) respect the client; (3) care for if not actually like the client as a person; (4) be prepared and able to confront the client; and (5) be self-aware—know their own needs and how these needs might help or hinder the counseling process.

Job Design

When modifications are made in the design of a job, the individual is not usually the direct focus of the change, but the change *effort* is most often individually focused. This is why I have included job design in this chapter on individually focused interventions. Although groups of jobs may be changed at the same time, as is frequently the case, our focus is on a single job or on a single job type.

The Job Characteristics Model

In the Job Characteristics Model, Hackman and Oldham (1975) hypothesize that five core job dimensions—skill variety, task identity, task significance, autonomy, and feedback—create three critical psychological states—experienced meaningfulness of work, experienced responsibility for outcomes of work, and knowledge of work results—and that these states lead, in turn, to certain personal and work outcomes (see Exhibit 12.4). The model further states that the links between the job dimensions, the psychological states, and the outcomes are mediated by an individual's need for growth.

As can be seen from Exhibit 12.4, three of the core job dimensions con-

EXHIBIT 12.4
The Job Characteristics Model of Work Motivation

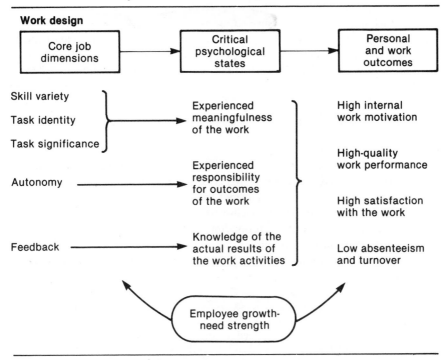

Source: J. R. Hackman, "Work Design," in *Improving Life at Work,* ed. J. R. Hackman and J. L. Suttle (Santa Monica: Goodyear, 1977), p. 129. Reprinted by permission.

tribute to the psychological state of work meaningfulness and one each to the remaining two states. The three that contribute to a job's meaningfulness are defined as follows:

Skill variety. The degree to which a job requires a variety of different activities that involve the use of a number of different skills and talents

Task identity. The degree to which the job requires completion of a whole and identifiable piece of work, that is, doing a job from beginning to end with a visible outcome

Task significance. The degree to which the job has substantial impact on the lives or work of other people, whether in the immediate organization or in the external environment. (Hackman 1977, p. 130)

The fourth dimension, autonomy, is the degree to which the job provides discretion and freedom in determining how it will be implemented, and feedback is the degree to which the outcome of the job activities provides the employee with direct information about the effectiveness of his or her performance.

The degree to which these five core job dimensions combine determines what Hackman (1977) calls a motivating potential score (MPS). According to the Job Characteristics Model, a job high in MPS must be high in at least one of the dimensions contributing to experienced meaningfulness and also high in autonomy and feedback. Hackman depicts this part of the model as follows:

$$MPS = \frac{skill\ variety \times task\ identity \times task\ significance}{3} \times autonomy \times feedback$$

The multiplication signs signify that a zero or near-zero degree of autonomy or feedback will reduce the overall MPS to zero or near-zero; that is, a near-zero on one of the three job dimensions associated with meaningfulness will not, in itself, cause the MPS to decline to near-zero.

The model also accounts for individual differences in the need for growth. These differences among individuals affect the model at two points: the link between job dimensions and psychological states and the link between psychological states and the personal work outcomes.

> The first link means that high growth need individuals are more likely (or better able) to *experience* the psychological states when their objective job is enriched than are their low growth need counterparts. The second link means that individuals with high growth need strength will respond more positively to the psychological states, when they are present, than will low growth need individuals. (Hackman 1977, p. 132)

The Job Diagnostic Survey

Hackman and Oldham (1975) developed the Job Diagnostic Survey (JDS), based on their Job Characteristics Model, to be the applied arm of their model. With the survey one can determine the MPS for a given job or set of jobs from the perspective of those who hold the jobs being surveyed. The JDS is a self-administered questionnaire or a Job Rating Form, an instrument used to observe a given job or set of jobs and records these observations according to the dimensions of the Job Characteristics Model. Hackman (1977) explains the steps to follow in using the model by these instruments. Briefly, these steps involve the following five questions:

1. Are motivation and satisfaction really problematic? The real problem may lie somewhere other than in the design of a job, such as in the equipment or technology of the job.
2. Is the job low in MPS? If so, the practitioner would move on to question 3.

If not—if MPS is high—the practitioner would search for other factors that might be causing the motivational problems, such as supervisory practices or the compensation system.

3. What specific aspects of the job are causing the difficulty? The job or set of jobs is examined on each of the five core job dimensions.
4. How ready are the employees for change? This step involves examination of employees' growth-need strengths, which are provided by the JDS.
5. What special problems and opportunities are present in the existing work system? The larger organization unit and context should be examined for potential barriers or hindrances to job changes, such as employees' feelings about their job security, support from higher management, and the like.

Job Enrichment

Hackman and Oldham have contributed significantly to our understanding of human motivation and the design of work. Herzberg's earlier motivator-hygiene theory, discussed in Chapter 2 (Herzberg, Mausner, and Snyderman 1959), and its application—job enrichment—had set the stage. Herzberg has explained job enrichment in a number of places (Herzberg 1968), and the most significant application, in AT&T, has been documented by Ford (1969). Herzberg claims that work motivation can be affected only by changes in the work itself. Jobs are changed and enriched through horizontal loading (also known as job enlargement)—increased responsibility laterally in the work unit—and vertical loading—increased authority for decision making within the job itself.

As Herzberg has conceptualized and applied it, job enrichment is based on several assumptions. One assumption, already noted, is that only job changes that affect motivators will enhance motivation. Another is that individual job holders who will be directly affected by the job change should *not* be involved in the decision-making process for planning and implementation. Both of these assumptions have been challenged, the latter by Sirota and Wolfson (1972). They point out that where job enrichment has failed, a likely cause for the failure has been the *lack* of involvement in the decision-making process on the part of the job holders. As implied by Hackman and Oldham's Job Characteristics Model and its application, motivational problems may be explained by factors other than Herzberg motivators. As Beer points out, moreover, Herzberg's approach does "not specify the job characteristics that might be manipulated to increase motivator need satisfaction" (Beer 1980, p. 170).

Hackman and his colleagues have expanded or enriched the implementation process of job enrichment by suggesting five principles to follow in designing jobs (Hackman, Oldham, Janson, and Purdy 1975):

253

1. *Form natural work units*—group tasks toward some meaningful whole.
2. *Combine tasks* so that skill variety and task identity may be maximized.
3. *Establish client relationships*—provide direct contact between worker and client as well as criteria and procedures for how the client can judge the quality of the product or service.
4. *Load the job vertically*—give the worker, as much as possible, direct responsibility for and control over the way the job is to be done.
5. *Open feedback channels*—give the workers as much direct information as possible about his or her performance.

Exhibit 12.5 shows how Hackman has combined these principles with the core job dimensions of the Job Characteristics Model. It illustrates the effect these principles have on the core job dimensions and suggests appropriate design modifications. If the diagnosis showed that autonomy was low, for example, then following the principles of *client relationships* and *vertical loading* would be appropriate. As Hackman (1977) has explained, these principles and the Job Characteristics Model can be followed in designing work for individuals as well as for teams. Team design is appropriate, for example, in situations where, for efficiency reasons, work cannot be combined into meaningful wholes for a single worker. An automobile assembly line is perhaps the best example of this type of situation. Volvo, has experimented, apparently successfully, with team assembly, however, there, the team has a meaningful whole with respect to task—assembling an entire engine together (Gyllenhammar 1977; Tichy and Nisberg 1976).

To summarize this discussion of job design and job enrichment, consider the seven issues that Beer (1980) raises for the OD practitioner who is involved in planning and implementing changes in jobs:

EXHIBIT 12.5
The Effects of Design Strategies on Core Job Dimensions

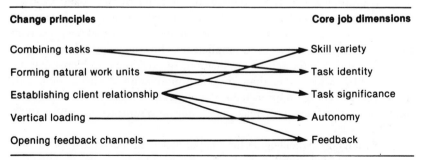

Change principles		Core job dimensions
Combining tasks		Skill variety
Forming natural work units		Task identity
Establishing client relationship		Task significance
Vertical loading		Autonomy
Opening feedback channels		Feedback

Source: J. R. Hackman, "Work Design," in *Improving Life at Work,* ed. J. R. Hackman and J. L. Suttle (Santa Monica: Goodyear, 1977), p. 136. Reprinted by permission.

1. Dealing with individual differences: Not all people are interested in enriched jobs and not all people are equally adaptable to some of the complexities of work redesign.
2. Effects on interpersonal relations: Changes in jobs usually affect interpersonal relations. There is more strain on relationships, for example, with the greater complexity and responsibility of an enriched job.
3. Management-worker relations: These relations are affected, especially in a unionized organization. If trust does not exist, well-intended changes will be met with suspicion.
4. Fit with organization culture: The types of job design changes considered here will succeed far more easily in an organization that rewards collaboration and a management approach that emphasizes delegation and participation than in an organization that is strictly hierarchical and competitive internally.
5. Fit with personnel systems: This fit is particularly important for the reward system—including compensation, of course—but it is important for performance appraisal and job evaluation as well.
6. Workers' participation in planning change: participation is important because involvement leads to commitment and thus less resistance to change, and because the job holders themselves are likely to know the most about the details of potential design changes.
7. Confronting difficult problems early: An OD practitioner may not want to raise issues before the change for fear that an intervention may never occur, but the more these issues are discussed ahead of the change itself, the more likely it is that the practitioner will have credibility with the client when problems of implementation do arise later.

Layoffs, Reductions in Force, and Firings

With recessions every six or seven years becoming a stable part of United States society, organizations expand and shrink more frequently than they did during the post–World War II boom period. Thus, employees come and go, and not just hourly or most recently hired employees. Top level managers also occasionally must go elsewhere. Organization development practitioners have been called on by management to help with these reduction problems.

These problems are obviously difficult even to address, much less to handle efficiently and humanely. They are particularly difficult for OD people, because OD activities and values are usually associated with development and growth, especially growth that comes with increased challenges from expanding business. Dealing with people who know that they soon may be unemployed is not simple.

Because of more rapid changes within organizations regarding expansion and shrinkage and the typical management approach during times of shrinkage to let people go, consulting organizations that specialize in outplacement, as it is called, have emerged in recent years. These firms help former employees, usually managers, find other employment when their company has decided to cut the work force. The company placing the manager out pays the consulting firm's fee for relocating the recently departed employee. During times of recession, these consulting firms usually do very well financially.

Whether for outplacement as such or for dealing with people involved in a reduction in force (RIF) condition, there are steps that OD practitioners can take to help individuals cope with their situations realistically and effectively. Lehner (1972), for example, designed and conducted various workshops for engineers who were suddenly out of jobs because of the severe cutbacks in the United States aerospace industry during the late 1960s and early 1970s. In addition to providing specific data about the job market in other industries—where to go for certain information and assistance—Lehner helped his client organizations and their cutback victims through three types of workshops. The income development workshop helped participants "to explore how they might generate income by means not necessarily involving their technical specialties" (Lehner 1972, p. 219). The job search workshop assisted participants with searching activities and helped them learn how to present themselves in writing—their resumes—and in person—interview procedures. The career optimization workshop was essentially a career development activity, with emphasis on considering related but different careers or different careers altogether, such as starting their own businesses.

In a related OD activity, helping individuals to cope with a recent demotion (not being fired or laid off), Golembiewski and his colleagues demonstrated the effectiveness of a sensitivity training intervention for reversing feelings of anxiety, depression, and hostility (Golumbiewski et al. 1972). This reversal of feelings helped the people involved to move more quickly into a productive mode of working. Another way in which an individual can lose his or her job is through retirement. Many people do not consider retirement as a process of *losing* their jobs, of course, but look forward to *gaining* a different life-style. Many people, however, do experience a loss when they retire, because they are not prepared. Work and living have not been separate activities for them, so not working is more closely associated with dying than with living. This is an appropriate arena for OD work. Since most organizations do not have an established process for assistance, OD practitioners are frequently in a position to take initiative in helping employees who are about to retire to prepare for the change more adequately than they might have otherwise. Combining his own experience with retirement and his knowledge and expertise in OD, Bradford (1978) has provided some useful guidelines for OD practitioners working with people who are about to retire.

The social technology that OD practitioners have available to them for dealing with these loss problems is limited, but helpful things can be done both for the individual and for the organization. Usually very little is done, and people who suddenly find themselves without a job or about to retire have to fend for themselves. These areas of consultation are highly appropriate for OD practitioners, and the likelihood is small that these kinds of problems—opportunities, perhaps—will diminish in the immediate future.

Summary

In this chapter we have considered a number of individually focused activities in organizations that fall within the realm of organization development. These activities have been presented in a sequence similar to a career in an organization: first we considered the recruitment and selection process, then training and developing the individuals selected, counseling them when necessary, providing them with opportunities for career guidance, designing jobs that would be stimulating, challenging, and motivating for them, and finally dealing with the possibility that some of them might lose their jobs.

The coverage of individually focused interventions was not exhaustive. It did not include, for example, interventions concerned with organizational role, but brief explanations of two such interventions—the role analysis technique (Dayal and Thomas 1968) and the job expectation technique (Huse 1975)—were provided in Chapter 5.

Another individually focused activity for an OD consultant is coaching—both a manager and another OD practitioner. In this latter role, called shadow consultation, one consultant coaches another from behind the scenes. The shadow consultant acts as a sounding board, gives suggestions, and generally provides support for his or her client—in this case, another OD consultant (see Chapter 17). More frequently, however, the OD consultant coaches a client manager—providing suggestions, perhaps conducting a practice session before a significant event, planning a meeting and coaching in some steps for conducting the meeting, helping the manager mediate conflict between two subordinates, and so forth. One-on-one work between consultant and client may be the most important individually focused intervention in OD practice.

From an OD perspective, it is important to remember that organization development is a process of *system* change—focusing on the organization as a social and technical system, not on the individual—but that there are numerous individually focused interventions that will promote readiness for change, provide new competencies for system change efforts, and provide better linkages or matches between individual values and the organization's culture.

CHAPTER 13

Group Interventions

A few years ago I was contacted by the president of a medium-sized chemical company to help him with a two-and-a-half-day off-site meeting with his operational and staff executives—his top management group. Having been president for almost a year, he was interested in gaining a clearer assessment of (1) where he stood as the relatively new leader of this group (especially since he had been brought in from the outside), (2) what some of the critical business problems were, and (3) how the group felt about their effectiveness as a top management team. After an initial meeting with the president (the entry phase), he and I reached an agreement about what we would do (the contract) and then implemented the agreement. I conducted individual interviews with each member of his top management team (diagnosis), and we met at a resort for two and a half days to discuss the interview results (feedback), to problem solve as a team (a team building intervention), and to plan follow-up steps. In elaborating on this consulting example, I shall use the case to illustrate (1) some salient and relevant points about groups, especially within the context of organization development, and (2) the typical steps and characteristics of team building.

In this chapter we shall also consider process consultation, perhaps the most important skill of an OD practitioner; group theory that is relevant to organization development; team building as an OD intervention, including various approaches; and special uses of groups in organization development, such as semiautonomous work groups and quality control circles. In the following chapter we shall consider conflict between and among groups and what to do about this conflict from an OD perspective.

It should be noted that two concepts from previous chapters are especially pertinent to the discussion in this chapter: groups have norms and values, and their members usually occupy certain roles (see Chapter

258

5); and groups also have leaders, formal or informal, and thus matters of control and power are always present (see Chapter 7).

A Case Example of Team Building

The issues and substance of this case are presented as they actually existed at the time of the consultation but names and certain identifying factors have been changed. As already mentioned, the president of Acme Chemical Company, J. J. Armstrong, contacted me as a consultant to help him assess the current state of his top management team.

Background

THE COMPANY   Acme Chemical Company was a medium-sized manufacturing and sales organization with annual sales of about $100 million. A goal of the company at the time of the consultation was to become a $500 million business within the next five years. Acme was a completely owned subsidiary of a larger conglomerate that consisted of diverse companies, all in manufacturing or processing of such products as heavy machinery, agricultural chemicals, specialty machine parts, petroleum chemicals, plastics, and the like.

Founded in the 1930s, Acme was a small company for about thirty years and then began to grow fairly rapidly. The parent company has held a tight financial rein on Acme. Acme management has had little opportunity to capitalize the business further, to diversify, or to acquire other smaller companies. The parent company has used Acme as a "cash cow"; that is, the high Acme profits have been used by the parent company to finance other operations rather than to provide Acme with any discretionary funds.

THE PRESIDENT   Armstrong was hired from the outside by the parent company to replace the former president of Acme, who was a technical expert in chemistry but a tyrannical boss. He was uncooperative, argumentative, and generally difficult in his dealings with the parent company. Armstrong, in contrast, was a professional manager, a generalist with a strong financial background. He had considerable managerial experience having left a divisional vice-president position with a large manufacturing organization a year earlier to assume the position as Acme's chief executive officer. His previous position had actually been larger in scope and responsibility than the Acme presidency, but he made the move because he wanted "to run his own company."

Behaviorally, Armstrong was relatively low key in expressing himself; he was smooth and polished, with excellent interpersonal skills. He had been educated in organizational behavior and was familiar with the ideas

259

of McGregor, Maslow, Blake and Mouton, Herzberg, and Likert. On a few occasions prior to joining Acme he had used an organization development consultant for team building purposes.

Armstrong faced some general problems at Acme:

1. There was tight budgetary control by the corporate parent.
2. He was an outsider who had been brought in by the parent company with no involvement by Acme management in the decision.
3. He inherited the entire present management of Acme, some of whom he felt positively about, some not.
4. His management style differed significantly from his predecessor's. The former president of Acme was autocratic and authoritarian, whereas Armstrong's style was far more participative—approximating at least a System 3 approach on Likert's profile. Armstrong's subordinates at Acme were finding it difficult to make the adjustment.
5. At the time, Armstrong was still learning about the Acme business. He had made some financial-reporting changes so that he (1) could understand the numbers—the accounting information—better and (2) could hold his key line managers more responsible and accountable (although he gave them considerable autonomy in running their own domains). These changes had naturally caused problems—misunderstanding and resistance by some.

THE TOP MANAGEMENT STRUCTURE   Acme Chemical was structured functionally; each key operation in the organization had a single boss, who reported to the executive vice-president or to the president. Exhibit 13.1 depicts the top management structure of Acme. As is typical of many manufacturing and sales organizations, the line operations vice-presidents report to the executive vice-president, who serves as a chief operations officer, and the staff vice-presidents report directly to the president, the chief executive officer (CEO). At the time of the consultation, a year after he had taken the CEO position, Armstrong had made only one executive change. He had elevated the personnel director's position to vice-presidential status and made the occupant an officer of the company. Thus, Armstrong had attempted to work with the organization largely as it had been. His managerial style, however, was significantly different from his predecessor's.

The Consultation

PREPARATORY STEPS   Before talking with me, Armstrong had discussed with his management group his idea about and desire for an off-site meeting to take "a reading on where we are as top team" and to identify

260

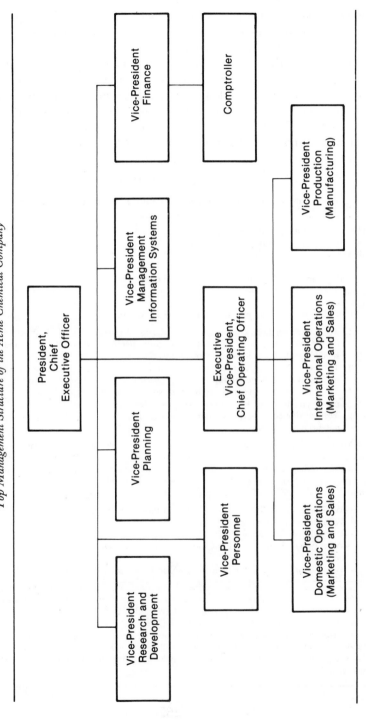

EXHIBIT 13.1

Top Management Structure of the Acme Chemical Company

problems that needed addressing. Although his management group was not very enthusiastic about the idea, they were not opposed, at least as Armstrong perceived the situation. He and I agreed to proceed with my interviews with each of the eleven people occupying the positions shown in Exhibit 13.1, including Armstrong. We also agreed that, if I discovered in my individual interviews that most of the executives were opposed to an off-site meeting, we would cancel the idea. I then helped Armstrong with the wording of a memorandum that he sent to each of his ten executives. The memorandum is shown in Exhibit 13.2.

EXHIBIT 13.2

Memorandum to Top Management Group of Acme Chemical Company

TO: Officers, Acme Chemical
FROM: J. J. Armstrong, President
SUBJECT: Off-Site Meeting

The purpose of this memo is to follow up on our recent officers' meeting and, therefore, to confirm the off-site management team meeting. Further, I will provide more specific information.

Our objectives for the meeting include the following:

1. To determine more clearly the goals we should pursue as a top management team. Other than, in general, developing a more effective and profitable company, what specific goal(s) should we as a team have?
2. To determine what further clarity we may need regarding our individual roles and responsibilities as we attempt to work together more effectively as a team.
3. To consider the effectiveness of our working procedures and processes as a top management team. Do we need to change some or create new ones?
4. To consider our working relationships as people, how we handle our differences and potential agreements.

More specificity regarding our meeting agenda will evolve as interview data from each of you is collected by our outside consultant. I have contracted with W. Warner Burke (see attached bio) to help us with this meeting. Prior to the meeting he will be coming to our offices to interview each of us individually for about an hour. The interview will be fairly open-ended, with Warner's asking such questions as:

—What is going well with Acme Chemical these days?
—What is not going well?
—What do you like about your job?
—What prevents you from doing the kind of job you would like to do or think you should be doing?
—What would you like for us to accomplish in our meeting off-site?

The first part of our off-site meeting will be devoted to hearing from Warner regarding his summary of these interviews. His summary will be just that—a consolidation of all interviews, not what any one of you per se may have said. Thus, you should feel free to express yourself to Warner as openly as you wish.

I am personally looking forward to this meeting since the timing of it will mark fairly closely the end of my first year with Acme Chemical. Thus, we'll use the time for some review as well as for planning how we can make our future years together more productive and satisfying.

DATA COLLECTION   The eleven interviews took two days. I spent about an hour with each officer and asked the five questions mentioned in the memo (see Exhibit 13.2). These were not the only questions asked, of course; more specific, probing questions were raised within the framework of each of the five more general questions. I began each interview with a brief explanation of why I was there, to see if the executive's understanding was the same as mine. I also repeated the points made in the memo—that all interviews would be treated confidentially and that only information given by two or more people would be reported back to the whole group. No information that could specifically identify one of the officers would be reported. Next, primarily to establish rapport, I asked each person about himself, his background—particularly his job history—and his current responsibilities. I took notes in plain view so that, if the interviewee wanted to see what I was writing, he could. The executives were cooperative but fairly cautious in the interviews. My further impressions were that almost all of them were ambitious and that they were somewhat more suspicious than open, yet that there was a general desire for improving things—even their relationships. There was considerable diversity among the group in managerial style. The one common style characteristic was their tendency to manage one-on-one rather than dealing with their subordinates in a group arrangement. Armstrong was respected for his professionalism but not respected, by some, for his desire to move the management approach of the company—particularly at the top—more toward team work and collaboration. It was also clear, even from the interviews, that the group had little if any experience working together as a top management team.

A summary of the eleven interviews appears in Exhibit 13.3. Although it is somewhat abbreviated, the summary in Exhibit 13.3 is basically the one that was distributed to each officer at the opening session of the off-site meeting.

EXHIBIT 13.3

Summary of Eleven Interviews at Acme Chemical Corporation

I.   Strengths, positives of the organization

Enthusiasm of our people; motivated, dedicated (6)
Flexibility of organization—small, can move rapidly, responsive to customers, can get product marketed quickly (4)
Strong product line (4)
A people company (3)
Many entrepreneurs; aggressive (3)
Exciting business (2)
Strong technical image (2)
Worldwide distribution system; strong field sales force (2)
Positioned well for growth (2)

(continued)

EXHIBIT 13.3 *(continued)*

II. Problems and issues of the organization

Being a subsidiary—restrictions of parent company (10)
Carryover from the old regime (6)
Too much infighting among division heads (3)
Lack of trained managers, especially in business skills (3)
Too much CYA (3)
Short-term objectives over emphasized (2)
Need for more systematic and systemic management (2)
Very competitive marketplace (2)
Compensation poor and uneven (2)
Need for clearer definition of total organizational structure (2)
Need clearer decision-making process (2)
Lack of conceptual overview (2)

III. Satisfaction with your job

Many areas of opportunity and challenge (4)
The job itself (2)
The greater emphasis on planning (2)
Having a voice in company direction (2)
Autonomy (2)

IV. Dissatisfactions with your job

Paperwork (3)
Have to be more competitive than I prefer (3)
Understaffed (2)
Some working relationships I have (2)
Not enough autonomy (2)

V. The off-site meeting

Worthwhile endeavor (4)
We must work together more rather than blaming one another (4)
Meeting should emphasize job responsibility of each of us in terms of our contribution
  to the team effort (2)
Mostly preventive (2)
Key thing is right organizational structure (2)
Most of meeting will be self-serving (2)
I have high hopes (2)
Could be accomplished without going off-site and without a consultant
If clearer directions are a result, then meeting will have been worthwhile—no need for
  interpersonal relations work
Neutral, wait and see
Establish priorities
Hope we can express more openly our conflicts and problems
No burning need for meeting
Must learn together how to get at our problems more effectively
Hope we can be more respectful of "what is on one another's plate"
Off-site aspect is important—need to relax with one another
Primary objective is the process

Note: The number in parentheses following each phrase indicates the number of individuals out of the total of eleven who made the statement summarized by the phrase. No number indicates that only one person's remarks are summarized by the phrase.

DIAGNOSIS   The interview data, combined with my observations, led me to conclude the following:

1. An off-site meeting was warranted.
2. Although all officers were not enthusiastic and highly committed, enough were, and no one was unalterably opposed—or at least no one voiced strong opposition.
3. Problems and issues existed that needed work by the group as a group—such problems as

   —addressing the issues of change in managerial style and approach;
   —addressing the infighting issue and the apparent need of some officers to cover themselves—to be overly cautious and protective and to be sure that, if decisions have to be made, they are thoroughly documented and conform precisely to corporate policy and procedures; and
   —some lack of clarity about overall direction and organizational structure.

4. There was considerable pride and ambition among the officers, and thus motivation to perform well must be high.
5. The parent company's restrictions were indeed a problem, but the focus for problem solving needed to stay with what they as a management group could control.
6. Although Armstrong's managerial style and direction for change certainly fit with my values and biases, full implementation, even if it were possible, was going to take a long time.
7. The fact that the group had practically no experience in working as a team could create problems at the off-site meeting.

INTERVENTION   The design of the off-site meeting was fairly simple. The meeting consisted of four phases, the first of which was the opening session on Wednesday evening. This session was devoted entirely to data feedback and discussion, not debate or problem solving. After Armstrong's opening remarks, I distributed the summary of the interviews, and we discussed the data in terms of their validity, meaning, and implications for needed action. There was agreement that the interview results accurately reflected the state of affairs and that "we should get on with it." The next phase, taking most of Thursday, was devoted to (1) establishing priorities regarding the problems to be worked on and (2) identifying underlying causes to these most pressing problems. This second phase continued through to Friday and consisted of problem solving—generating alternative solutions to the problem causes that had been identified.

The third phase, Friday evening, was a change of pace. When there is enough time in such meetings, when doing something different may renew group members' energy and commitment to working together, and, most important, when further diagnosis of themselves as a group may help them learn how to work together more effectively, I like to use a questionnaire that will provide (1) a conceptual structure for learning about interpersonal group behavior, (2) greater self-insight for individuals, and (3) further group data for diagnosis and greater understanding. For these purposes, I frequently use Will Schutz's questionnaire, the FIRO–B—Fundamental Interpersonal Relations Orientation-Behavior (Schutz 1967). The three fundamental behavioral dimensions of the FIRO–B are inclusion, control, and affection; occasionally, coverage of these aspects of behavior can become somewhat threatening to people. A similar but potentially less threatening questionnaire is the one developed by Atkins and Katcher (1967), LIFO—life orientations. Their questionnaire has four dimensions of interpersonal relationships or ways that we orient ourselves toward others: supporting, controlling, conserving, and adapting behaviors. I used the LIFO questionnaire with Acme executives. From this session we learned that the highest score of six of the officers was on the controlling dimension, which meant that more than half of the group had a tendency to want to control others. The tendency to seek and enjoy control is not unusual for managers, but this particular orientation can certainly militate against collaborative behavior and teamwork. Additional insight into this individual tendency among group members helped the officers understand some of the difficulties they were having in trying to work together as a team.

The final session and phase, Saturday morning, was devoted to planning action steps for follow-up.

As it turned out, the off-site meeting was more a diagnostic effort than a team building activity. Armstrong had to face the fact that his officers as a group were not as ready for collaborative teamwork as he had hoped. They were used to competitiveness, and they were far more accustomed to one-on-one management than team-orientation management. Thus, several of the officers found Armstrong's behavior to be puzzling, at best, or untrustworthy, at worst. Armstrong, in turn, considered these officers resistant to change. One officer, eventually became so resistant to Armstrong's directions and desires for change that his behavior evolved into rebellion. Six months after the off-site meeting, Armstrong finally fired him. During this six-month period, and thereafter, Armstrong continued to move toward a team orientation, but at a slower pace and more patiently. His next effort was to provide some training for the top group in conflict management, group decision making, and group problem solving. He also planned to have another off-site meeting a year after the original one.

266

This case, which illustrates a group intervention in OD practice, is both typical and atypical. It is typical in terms of design and type of consultation. It is not typical in that most organizational groups that enter into such activities, whether they are labeled team building or not, are more prepared or amenable to working together as a group than these Acme managers were. Regardless of its unique characteristics, however, the case is a good example of the key aspects of group consultation in OD practice. I shall therefore refer to this case periodically as we proceed through the chapter.

Groups in Organizations

The primary work group—whether a top management team, a packaging unit at plant level, or a district sales team—is the most important subsystem within an organization. The work group serves as the context and locus for (a) the interface between the individual and the organization; (2) the primary social relationships and support of the individual employee, whether or not he or she is a manager; and (3) a determination of the employee's sense of organizational reality. The extent to which members of a group work well together and the extent to which they as a group work well with other groups in the organization will determine, in part, the overall effectiveness of the organization.

Work groups have always been important for organizational effectiveness. We first recognized this importance systematically in the Hawthorne studies (see Chapter 2). This importance is increasing. The single individual who knows many of the functions and specialities within an organization is becoming a rarity. Groups of various specialists attempting to produce something that is greater than the total of their individual specialities are becoming more the rule than the exception. Newer organizational structures, such as the matrix design, require an increase in group activities. In spite of such experiences as the Acme Chemical case, more and more meetings in organizations are occurring in groups larger than two people. The success of Japanese management and its extensive reliance on groups has also accentuated the importance of and need for effective work groups.

Most large organizations have a variety of work groups. Whether an OD intervention such as team building is appropriate for a group depends on how dependent the individual members are on one another for accomplishing their work. The greater the interdependence, the more likely it is that a team building activity will prove useful. In the Acme case, there was some interdependence between functions, such as between marketing-sales and production and between these two functions and R&D, but in terms of a total management team effort, there was no interdependence. The managers previously had looked to the president to take care of any necessary coordination or interdependence. Armstrong believed that, for the company to make the big jump from a $100 million company to five times that size, a certain amount of synergy within the top team was absolutely necessary. He simply did not believe that he alone could do all that was required for optimum coordination. For a team building intervention to be effective, a need for interdependence is a prerequisite.

Usually a team building activity involves at least two levels of management: a boss and his or her immediate subordinates. In the Acme case three levels were represented, but all the executives were company officers, thus composing the top management group. The semiautonomous work group is an exception to the requirement for two or more levels of management since this type of work group operates without a formal leader. More will be explained about this special kind of group later in the chapter.

In summary, then, work groups are becoming increasingly important for achieving overall organizational effectiveness, especially in large, complex organizations. Whether OD consultation in the form of team building activities is appropriate for a work group is a function of how interdependent the group members need to be for accomplishing their work objectives and how important it is to consider issues of leadership and control within the group.

Team Building

When a work group has at least one goal that is common to all members, and when accomplishment of that goal requires cooperative interdependent behavior on the part of all group members, team building may be an appropriate intervention. Dyer (1977) has developed three checklists to help team members determine whether they need team building. These three lists are presented in Exhibit 13.4. Studying the lists will help clarify the purposes and the nature of team building.

Using Beckhard's (1972) succinct statement of the four primary purposes of team building and Plovnick, Fry, and Rubin's (1975) elaboration as a guide, I shall now provide a more thorough explanation of team building. We shall assume that a work group has responded to Dyer's checklists (Exhibit 13.4) and has determined that team building is needed. According to Beckhard (1972), there are four purposes of team building:

1. To set goals or priorities
2. To analyze or allocate the way work is performed according to team members' roles and responsibilities
3. To examine the way the team is working—its processes, such as norms, decision making, communications, and so forth
4. To examine relationships among the team members

268

EXHIBIT 13.4
Dyer's Team Building Checklist

I. Problem identification: To what extent is there evidence of the following problems in your work unit?

	Low evidence		Some evidence		High evidence
1. Loss of production or work-unit output	1	2	3	4	5
2. Grievances or complaints within the work unit	1	2	3	4	5
3. Conflicts or hostility between unit members	1	2	3	4	5
4. Confusion about assignments or unclear relationships between people	1	2	3	4	5
5. Lack of clear goals, or low commitment to goals	1	2	3	4	5
6. Apathy or general lack of interest or involvement of unit members	1	2	3	4	5
7. Lack of innovation, risk taking, imagination, or taking initiative	1	2	3	4	5
8. Ineffective staff meetings	1	2	3	4	5
9. Problems in working with the boss	1	2	3	4	5
10. Poor communications: people afraid to speak up, not listening to each other, or not talking together	1	2	3	4	5
11. Lack of trust between boss and member or between members	1	2	3	4	5
12. Decisions made that people do not understand or agree with	1	2	3	4	5
13. People feel that good work is not recognized or rewarded	1	2	3	4	5
14. People are not encouraged to work together in better team effort	1	2	3	4	5

Scoring: Add up the score for the fourteen items. If your score is between 14–28, there is little evidence your unit needs team building. If your score is between 29–42, there is some evidence, but no immediate pressure, unless two or three items are very high. If your score is between 43–56, you should seriously think about planning the team building program. If your score is over 56, then building should be a top priority item for your work unit.

II. Are you (or your manager) prepared to start a team-building program? Consider the following statements. To what extent do they apply to you or your department?

(continued)

EXHIBIT 13.4 (*continued*)

	Low		Medium		High
1. You are comfortable in sharing organizational leadership and decision making with subordinates and prefer to work in a participative atmosphere.	1	2	3	4	5
2. You see a high degree of interdependence as necessary among functions and workers in order to achieve your goals	1	2	3	4	5
3. The external environment is highly variable and/or changing rapidly and you need the best thinking of all your staff to plan against these conditions.	1	2	3	4	5
4. You feel you need the input of your staff to plan major changes or develop new operating policies and procedures.	1	2	3	4	5
5. You feel that broad consultation among your people as a group in goals, decisions, and problems is necessary on a continuing basis.	1	2	3	4	5
6. Members of your management team are (or can become) compatible with each other and are able to create a collaborative rather than a competitive environment.	1	2	3	4	5
7. Members of your team are located close enough to meet together as needed.	1	2	3	4	5
8. You feel you need to rely on the ability and willingness of subordinates to resolve critical operating problems directly and in the best interest of the company or organization.	1	2	3	4	5
9. Formal communication channels are not sufficient for the timely exchange of essential information, views, and decisions among your team members.	1	2	3	4	5
10. Organization adaptation requires the use of such devices as project management, task forces, and/or ad hoc problem-solving groups to augment conven-					

	Low		Medium		High
tional organization structure.	1	2	3	4	5
11. You feel it is important to surface and deal with critical, albeit sensitive, issues that exist in your team.	1	2	3	4	5
12. You are prepared to look at your own role and performance with your team.	1	2	3	4	5
13. You feel there are operating or interpersonal problems that have remained unsolved too long and need the input from all group members.	1	2	3	4	5
14. You need an opportunity to meet with your people and set goals and develop commitment to these goals.	1	2	3	4	5

Scoring: If your total score is between 50–70, you are probably ready to go ahead with the team building program. If your score is between 35–49, you should probably talk the situation over with your team and others to see what would need to be done to get ready for team building. If your score is between 14–34, you are probably not prepared at the present time to start team building.

III. Should you use an outside consultant to help in team building? (Circle appropriate response.)

1. Does the manager feel comfortable in trying out something new and different with the staff?	Yes	No	?
2. Is the staff used to spending time in an outside location working on different issues of concern to the work unit?	Yes	No	?
3. Will group members speak up and give honest data?	Yes	No	?
4. Does your group generally work together without a lot of conflict or apathy?	Yes	No	?
5. Are you reasonably sure that the boss is not a major source of difficulty?	Yes	No	?
6. Is there a high commitment by the boss and unit members to achieve more effective team functioning?	Yes	No	?
7. Is the personal style of the boss and his or her management philosophy consistent with a team approach?	Yes	No	?
8. Do you feel you know enough about team building to begin a program without help?	Yes	No	?
9. Would your staff feel confident enough to begin a team building program without outside help?	Yes	No	?

Scoring: If you have circled six or more "yes" responses, you probably do not need an outside consultant. If you have four or more "no" responses, you probably do need a consultant. If you have a mixture of yes, no, and ? responses, you should probably invite in a consultant to talk over the situation and make a joint decision.

Source: W. E. Dyer, *Team Building: Issues and Alternatives,* © 1977, Addison-Wesley Publishing Company, Inc., Chapter 4, pp. 36–40, Figure 4.1, "Team Building Checklist." Reprinted with permission.

Beckhard points out that all these purposes are likely to be operating in a team building effort, ''but unless *one* purpose is defined as *the* primary purpose, there tends to be considerable misuse of energy. People then operate from their own hierarchy of purposes and, predictably, these are not always the same for all members'' (Beckhard 1972; p. 24). From a combination of responses to Dyer's checklists and individual interviews with group members, a diagnosis can be made that should indicate the primary purpose for an initial team building session. If the team building effort is the first one for the group, the OD practitioner should determine if the focus of the first session should be setting goals or establishing priorities among team goals. If the goals and their priorities are clear, the OD practitioner should determine if roles and responsibilities among team members are clear. If so, then the practitioner determines if working procedures and processes are clear. It is important and beneficial for the OD practitioner to use Beckhard's four purposes in the order that they are listed. The reason for this ordering of the purposes is as follows: *interpersonal* problems could be a consequence of group members' lack of clarity regarding team goals, roles and responsibilities, or procedures and processes; problems with *procedures and processes* could be a consequence of group members' lack of clarity regarding team goals or roles and responsibilities; and problems with *roles and responsibilities* may be a result of group members' lack of clarity about team goals. To begin a team building effort with work on interpersonal relationships may be a misuse of time and energy, since it is possible that problems in this area are a result of misunderstandings in one of the other three domains. Clarifying goals, or roles and responsibilities, or team procedures and processes may eliminate certain interpersonal problems among team members; clarifying roles and responsibilities may in itself eliminate some of the problems with the team's working procedures and processes; and clarifying team goals and their priorities may in itself eliminate certain problems team members may have with their roles and responsibilities.

We shall now consider case examples of team building interventions for each of these four purposes.

Setting Goals and Priorities

In the course of an OD effort with a medical school, the school's internal consultant and I, as an outside consultant, were asked by one of the clinical department chairmen to help with some departmental team building. In our interviews with the department members my colleague and I diagnosed that there was a pervasive sense of no direction for the department as a whole. In a subsequent meeting with the chairman, the three of us designed an off-site session for one evening and the following day for the fifteen members of the department. Briefly, the design of this off-site meeting was as follows. The fifteen members, including the chairman, were initially divided into three groups of five people each, heterogeneously grouped. Their common tasks were (1) to determine what they believed the departmental goals should be and (2) to select two of their members to represent them in a later plenary session. Having developed their goal statements, the three groups then assembled in the large room and the two representatives from each group met together in the center while the remaining nine department members were positioned around them as observers. Exhibit 13.5 depicts this arrangement of a small group of six persons working together in the center, with their colleagues gathered around them and observing.

The task for this six-person temporary executive committee was to communicate what each group had developed and to consolidate their three lists of statements into one, which would then become the statement of objectives for the department. An empty chair was provided within this inner circle of six so that, if any of the observers believed that what his or her group had developed was not being represented or thought that this temporary executive committee was going astray, the person could occupy the empty chair, state his or her position or raise an issue, wait for and

EXHIBIT 13.5

*Configuration of the Second Phase of an Off-Site Meeting
to Set Departmental Goals*

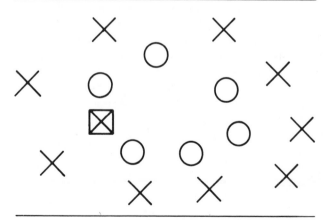

The circles represent the inner group, a temporary executive committee, and the X's are the remaining members of the department, who only observed during this phase. The X within a square symbolizes an empty chair, which could be occupied temporarily by an observer, who could then participate with the inner executive group.

possibly deal with the reaction of the executive group, and then return to observer status.

Once the executive group had consolidated the three lists into one, the total group individually ranked the statements (fourteen in this case) according to priority of importance for the department. Next, the total group individually selected their first and second choices of objectives they wished to develop into action steps for implementation. The fifteen people were then regrouped into three groups of five, according to their choices of an objective. These three groups met periodically after the off-site meeting to plan action steps for implementing the three most important objectives.

At the conclusion of the off-site meeting, each person was asked to respond to two questions, with responses arranged according to a five-point Likert scale: (1) How pessimistic or optimistic are you at the moment about the state of the department? (The 1–5 response ranged from "highly pessimistic" to "highly optimistic.") (2) To what extent do you believe positive change will occur as a result of this meeting? (The 1–5 response ranged from "not at all" to "to a great extent.") I like to ask these two questions toward the end of an off-site meeting because they provide a relatively simple way to consider the process of the meeting—people's feelings—and an opportunity to examine the degree of an individual's motivation to follow through on the steps planned for future implementation. In this case the departmental members' ratings were uniformly optimistic and positive.

The rationale for such a team building design has several elements. For such a short period of time (in this case, only slightly more than one day), it is important to have as much member participation as feasible and to use the allotted time as efficiently as possible. The smaller group of six obviously could work more efficiently than the total group of fifteen, but some degree of total participation was maintained by employing the empty chair. Selecting representatives and then being able to see what they do, and also having a chance to influence their decision making, helps to assure the involvement of all department members and therefore their commitment to implementing the goals they identified. The follow-up groups did indeed meet periodically to plan action steps. A year later, in a brief interview, my colleague and I were pleased to learn that the departmental chairman continued to be satisfied with the progress of his department. He attributed much of this progress to the success of the off-site meeting.

Allocating Work According to Roles and Responsibilities

As mentioned in Chapter 5, ambiguity regarding one's role and conflict between what is expected of an individual in a particular role and what that individual believes is appropriate can cause considerable confusion within a work group and anxiety for its members (Katz and Kahn 1978). There are various techniques for gaining greater clarification of roles and responsibilities within a team. These techniques typically involve team members' (1) presenting their perceptions and understandings of their roles to one another, (2) discussing these perceptions and understandings, and (3) modifying roles as a function of increased agreement about mutual expectations. One such technique is the role analysis technique (see Chapter 5 for an explanation), developed by Dayal and Thomas (1968). Another similar one is the job expectation technique, which is particularly useful when there is a need to integrate a new member into a team (Huse 1980).

A technique that is particularly suitable for situations of role conflict is Harrison's (1972) role negotiation technique. Although it is most suitable for this second purpose of team building, the approach also may be used with either of the remaining two purposes, since role is not limited to formal position. According to Harrison (1972), his role negotiation technique "intervenes directly into the relationships of power, authority and influence within the group" (p. 92). Each group member lists for each other member the things these other members (1) should do more or better, (2) should do less or stop, and (3) should continue as now. Agreements about changes are negotiated among the members and then finalized in the form of a written contract.

A technique that emphasizes the responsibilities aspect of this second purpose of team building is what Beckhard and Harris (1977) refer to as *responsibility charting*. Using a grid format, the types of decisions and actions that need to be taken are listed along the left side and those who should have some part in the decision-making process are listed across the top of the grid. Exhibit 13.6 shows this type of grid. The process consists of assigning an action to each of the team members whose names appear opposite an issue or decision. As the exhibit shows, there are four types of actions: R, the *responsibility* to insure action, to insure that the decision is implemented; A–V *approval* required or the right to *veto;* S, provides logistical *support* and resources; and I, must be *informed* about the decision or action. As Beckhard and Harris point out, there can be only one R on any single horizontal line. Either a consensus is reached by the team, or the boss determines who takes the responsibility.

Responsibility charting is particularly useful for new teams and for start-up situations. The process can also be used for problem solving in an ongoing team. Beckhard and Harris describe a case in which the top management team of a regional headquarters of an oil company had been having difficulty for several years in working out a new franchise relationship with some of the company's gas station owners:

275

EXHIBIT 13.6
Responsibility Chart

	Code:	R	Responsibility (initiates)
		A-V	Approval (right to veto)
		S	Support (put resources against)
		I	Inform (to be informed)

Actors ⟶ Decisions ⟶																	

Source: Beckhard/Harris, *Organizational Transitions: Managing Complex Change,* © 1977, Addison-Wesley Publishing Company, Inc., Chapter 6, page 78, Figure 6.1, "Responsibility Chart." Reprinted with permission.

The problem was complex, and there had been all sorts of misunderstandings, conflicts, slow-downs, and differences of emphasis between staff areas. The top management—the managing director, director of marketing, director of operations and director of finance—were concerned about this issue because it was a matter of significant investment and cost, but they had been unable to resolve it. . . . It was suggested that they do a responsibility charting exercise on the problem, which they did. As a result, they discovered that they did not have a consensus about the location of the different types of responsibilities and behaviors. This problem was relatively easy to work through. (Beckhard and Harris 1977, p. 82)

Examining Team Procedures and Processes

The third purpose of team building is to establish working procedures and processes for a newly formed team or to examine and look for ways of improving these procedures and processes if the team has already been operating as a group for some time. By *processes,* Beckhard (1972) means

276

such things as group norms (see Chapter 5) and leadership style. *Procedures* are the processes that are more directly related to goal (task) accomplishment, such as type of decision making, problem-solving technique, communication, and team structure for dealing with different agenda. The team building activity therefore involves (1) identifying the norms that are hindering effective teamwork and (2) changing them to different norms that will facilitate teamwork. The activity may be examining a particular team procedure that doesn't seem to be working very well. Exhibit 13.7 is a brief report of a case in which the communication procedure within a team was vastly improved by first examining the nature of the problem and then planning and implementing a new procedure for internal communications.

Examining Relationships Among Team Members

This fourth purpose of team building concerns identifying interpersonal problems that exist among team members and working toward some res-

EXHIBIT 13.7

The Case of the Misunderstood Memo

Recently, a vice president in a large U.S. corporation was having trouble with his division managers occasionally responding inappropriately to his memos. The vice president had the choice of (a) sending his subordinates to a communications course, (b) attending a communications course himself, (c) both (a) and (b), (d) trying to live with the problem, or (e) working on the problem directly. He chose the last alternative. An external OD consultant and an internal consultant from the Employee Relations Division worked on the problem with the vice president in a team development session. They designed a work session to be held from 9:00 a.m. to lunch on a regular work day in the staff meeting room. Before the meeting, several memos from the vice president to the division managers were selected and prepared on a glass slide which could then be shown on a screen via a projector. With the vice president and consultants present, all division managers considered several of the memos according to a certain procedure. After reading the memo on the screen, they were asked three questions: (1) What do you think the message says? (2) What priority would you give to the message: (a) HIGH, take care of the matter immediately, (b) MEDIUM, take care of the matter relatively soon, or (c) LOW, take care of it when I can get to it. (3) What action would you take?

After everyone responded to the three questions by writing their answers, each manager was asked to read his response to the total group. Considerable differences occurred among the managers. Later, the vice president explained what he meant the memo to say, what priority he desired, and what action he wanted. As might be expected, a number of misunderstandings were corrected and learning resulted, both learning on the vice president's part, as well as the division managers'.

An interesting side effect resulted later in time; the vice president's memos decreased in number by 40 percent. Also, after a year of collecting relevant data, a considerable monetary saving amounting to approximately twenty thousand dollars was realized as a result of changes in communications procedures.

Source: Reprinted with permission from the *Journal of Applied Behavioral Science* ''Improving Communication within a Managerial Workgroup'' by J. B. Harvey and C. R. Boettger, 7(1971): 164–79. Copyright 1971, NTL Institute.

olution of these problems. A case example of this form of team building concerned the top management group of a high-technology business organization. The climate within the group was open and spontaneous, particularly in their discussions of ideas and technical problems. They expressed a desire to be open with one another about their feelings and interpersonal relationships, but their individual styles and the patterns of interaction among them blocked this desire. They conformed to a nonconfronting norm when it came to interpersonal issues. This norm was reinforced by the president, who was highly analytical, rational, and sensible and was greatly admired by the subordinate team members. Eventually, a subgroup within the team emerged and began to push for facing up to the team relationship issues. They suggested that an extended meeting be held so that the group could examine their interpersonal relationships. The suggestion was agreed to by all group members and the meeting took place.

> At this meeting each individual received some feedback from all of his colleagues about his strengths and weaknesses as they perceived them. What bothered or pleased them about his behavior. Each individual could use this feedback any way he wished—there was no requirement for change. The feedback surfaced some historic issues that had been affecting the work of the group; for example, two people who had been competing throughout their careers maintained this competition in the group. They were perceived by all the others as sometimes robbing the group of their technical resource capability on the tasks because of their interpersonal relationship. It was agreed that the group would try to draw this to their attention whenever it arose in the future. The feedback to the president by the team was accepted and generally understood by him. . . . however, the main benefit . . . was that it freed the group to produce this kind of information in the future as needed. This became a norm of the group and was perhaps the single most significant result. (Beckhard 1972, p. 31)

As illustrated in this case, when the purpose of team building is to work on relationships, a critical dimension of the process is interpersonal feedback. Anderson (1970) has provided a useful summary of the most important rules to follow when giving and receiving feedback. Anderson's summary is presented in Exhibit 13.8.

Criteria for an Effective Team

Regardless of the purpose we may be emphasizing in a team building effort, our ultimate goal is to improve the overall effectiveness of the team as a group. It is appropriate, therefore, for us to consider at this point some of the criteria for and characteristics of an effective group.

Douglas McGregor observed and worked with many groups, especially in a managerial context. Based on his research, his observations, and his

EXHIBIT 13.8

Guidelines for Giving and Receiving Feedback

Giving feedback	Receiving feedback
Helps	*Turns On*
Providing specific behaviors—what was said or done	Paraphrasing what you have heard
	Requesting clarification of feedback
Providing recent examples	Checking other's perception of the feedback
Conveying feelings of concern—intend to be helpful	Summarizing what several people have said
Conveying equal power in relationship— you control the exchange as much as I	Speculating about examples of your own behavior that might have led to feedback
Being descriptive; not evaluating other person	Exploring the feelings created by the feedback
Describing own feelings as consequence of other's behavior	*Shuts Off*
Revealing your underlying assumption	Justifying your actions
Hinders	Building a case for why you do what you do
Giving general or vague feedback	Apologizing
Providing old examples	Promising not to do it again
Using power to drive feedback home	Overinternalizing feedback
Evaluating and judging other person	(assuming it is all true)
Attributing negative motives	
Fault finding, accusations, blaming	
Bringing up behaviors that the others can't change	

Source: M. Beer, *Organization Change and Development: A Systems View* (Santa Monica: Goodyear, 1980), p. 145. Reprinted by permission.

consultation with these different groups, he listed what he considered the unique features of an effective managerial team (McGregor 1967):

1. *Understanding, mutual agreement, and identification with respect to the primary task.* Team members have clarity about their ultimate purpose or mission and are committed to its accomplishment.

2. *Open communications.* Team members express their ideas, opinions, and feelings openly and authentically. For further discussion of authenticity, see Herman and Korenich (1977). McGregor also points out that being *absolutely* open, regardless of situation, is not the criterion for effectiveness. Openness is related to the task at hand.

3. *Mutual trust.* Trust and openness go hand in hand, and openness is practically impossible to achieve without trust among team members. McGregor's (1967) definition of trust is worthy of quotation:

> Trust means: "I know that you will not—deliberately or accidentally, consciously or unconsciously—take unfair advantage of me." It means: "I can put my situation at the moment, my status and self-esteem in this group, our relationship, my job, my career, even my life, in your hands with complete confidence." (p. 163)

279

McGregor notes, further, that trust is a delicate aspect of relations, influenced more by actions than by words. Trust can be destroyed quickly and easily—one act can do it. Trust is a feeling influenced by needs, expectations, guilts, anxieties, and the like, and it is based on peoples' perceptions of others and their behavior, not on objective reality.

4. *Mutual support.* This feature of an effective team is characterized by the absence of hostility or indifference among members and by the presence of care, concern, and active help toward one another.

5. *Management of human differences.* Group creativity typically comes from an open exchange of different ideas, opinions, and intuitions, and from an active process of integrating these differences into an outcome that represents the best of the individual contributions. Research has clearly documented that the more groups uncover and deal with their differences, the higher the quality of their decisions will be (J. Hall 1971; Hall and Watson 1970; Hall and Williams 1966). Managing differences successfully within a group is easier said than done, of course. The key is to maintain a balance between fostering conflict of ideas and opinions and controlling these differences.

6. *Selective use of the team.* Being discriminatory about when and when not to use the team in a group endeavor for consensual decision making will help insure time efficiency and a wise use of member energy. Effective teams know when they should meet, and they know how to use their time.

I have found the following guidelines useful in deciding when to use the team for consensual decision making:

> When you do not know who has the most expertise regarding the decision to be made
>
> When implementation of the decision will require several people—most if not all members of the team
>
> When the facts are few—when judgment and opinion are required

These guidelines are very similar to Vroom and Yetton's (1973) more elaborate and detailed decision tree for managers' use in determining how participative to be in decision making.

7. *Appropriate member skills.* The effective team has among its membership—not just with the leader—the variety of skills that are needed for performance of the task and for maintenance of the team as a viable group. It is absolutely necessary that there be an adequate level of technical knowledge among the team's membership for task accomplishment. Just as necessary are the skills required to elicit that knowledge and integrate the various elements of it into a decision whole. These skills are of two types—task and maintenance. From the earlier work of Benne and Sheats

(1948) and Bales (1950), Bennis and Shepard (1961) assembled a composite, representative list of these important skills and functions:

Task Functions	Maintenance Functions
Initiating activity	Encouraging
Seeking information	Gatekeeping
Seeking opinion	Standard setting
Giving information	Following
Giving opinion	Expressing group feeling
Elaborating	Testing for consensus and commitment
Summarizing	Mediating
Testing feasibility	Relieving Tension
Evaluating	

The more all members of the team can develop these two sets of skills, the more effective the team is likely to be.

8. *Leadership*. The leadership function of an effective team is managing and integrating the other seven characteristics. It is unreasonable to assume that the leader alone can set direction, be open, trust and support team members, manage individual differences, always know when to use the team as a group, and provide all the necessary task and maintenance functions. In the effective team these characteristics become the responsibility and concern of all members. The team leader's job is to see that these characteristics are first identified and then become group norms. In addition, the team leader is the prime coordinator, seeing that the various responsibilities for effective teamwork are shared among members and differentiated according to subtask requirements and member talent.

Prior to McGregor's list of eight features, Likert (1961) had proposed twenty-four "performance characteristics of the ideal highly effective group." There is considerable overlap between the two lists, but four from Likert's list are different enough to be worth mentioning:

1. The values and goals of the group are integrated with and express the relevant values and needs of the members. Since the group members help to shape these values and goals (analogous to McGregor's first feature), they will be committed to and satisfied with them.

2. Group members, including the leader, believe that they as a group can accomplish the impossible. This kind of expectation stretches and challenges group members and establishes the potential for growth and development. This characteristic of an effective group is reminiscent of Vaill's (1978) "high performing systems."

3. The group understands the nature and value of constructive conformity and knows when to use it and for what purposes. Likert (1961) clarifies this characteristic:

> Although it [the group] does not permit conformity to affect adversely the creative efforts of its members, it does expect conformity on mechanical and administrative matters to save the time of members and to facilitate the group's activities. The group agrees, for example, on administrative forms and procedures, and once they have been established, it expects its members to abide by them until there is good reason to change them. (p. 166)

Actually, this characteristic of Likert's helps amplify McGregor's management-of-differences feature—the process of maintaining a balance between fostering conflict and controlling it.

4. There is mutual influence among group members and especially between the members and the leader.

Likert used the word *ideal* in the preface to his list of twenty-four characteristics of an effective group. McGregor's list also can be labeled ideal. Striving for these characteristics may be idealistic for a team, but it is not necessarily unrealistic. Even approximating these ideals can improve teamwork. For team building purposes, having a standard for evaluating effort toward a more effective team is critical, not only for direction but also for motivation as well.

By way of summary, we can define team building as an activity whereby members of a work group (1) begin to understand more thoroughly the nature of group dynamics and effective teamwork, particularly the interrelationship of *process* and *content,* and (2) learn to apply certain principles and skills of group process toward greater team effectiveness.

Process Consultation

In my definition of team building, the terms *process* and *content* are emphasized. We should now clarify these terms within the context of group work and then consider the role of the consultant—the *process* consultant.

According to Steiner (1972), how well a group performs a task depends on three factors: task demands, resources, and process.

Task demands specify the requirements for satisfactory accomplishment of the task itself.

> Such requirements determine whether a particular resource (knowledge, ability, skill, or tool) is relevant, how much of each kind of resource is needed for optimal performance, and how the various relevant resources must be combined and utilized in order to produce the best possible outcome. . . . Whether, and how well a group can perform a task depends in part upon the nature of the task it is asked to perform. (Steiner 1972, p. 7)

Resources include all the relevant knowledge, abilities, skills, or tools possessed by individual group members.

282

Process, according to Steiner's definition, consists of the actual steps taken by a group in undertaking a task.

> [Process] includes all those intrapersonal and interpersonal actions by which people transform their resources into a product, and all those non-productive actions that are prompted by frustration, competing motivations, or inadequate understanding. . . . Unlike task demands and resources, process cannot be measured or evaluated before work begins. Process is a series of behaviors, one following another, each determined to some degree by those that have gone before and each, in turn, influencing those that will come later. To the extent that the total sequence of behaviors corresponds to the pattern demanded by the task, actual productivity will approximate potential productivity. (Steiner 1972, pp. 8–9)

Steiner adds that the adequacy of the resources available to the group determines its potential productivity and that the appropriateness of the processes determines how well the group's actual productivity approximates its potential productivity. Thus:

$$\text{Actual productivity} = \text{potential productivity} - \text{losses due to faulty process}$$

Referring to the Acme Chemical case again, the diagnosis of that top management group suggested that their potential productivity as a team was fairly high. They seemed to be clear about the demands of their tasks, and they apparently possessed more than adequate resources. Their process, however, to use Steiner's term, was woefully "faulty." The fault in this case was primarily caused by a lack of skill and experience in working together as a group.

Content and Process

Content and process are the primary dimensions of group activity: content is *what* and process is *how.* What Steiner refers to as the task demands and the resources comprise the *content* of a group work. How the group goes about this work is the *process.* In a team meeting, for example, agenda items are content; the problem to be discussed or solved and the decisions to be made are content. The resources the group has to work with are content; the extent to which the group uses these resources and the way in which it accomplishes the task are elements of process. For purposes of organization development in general and team building in particular, our concern is with process.

For a greater understanding of process and in order to relate process consultation to Beckhard's four purposes of team building, we shall analyze this dimension of group activity further. We can subdivide process

283

into two categories: procedure and maintenance. Procedural processes are the activities within the group that relate directly to task accomplishment, including the following:

1. *Organization*—how the group organizes itself to accomplish the task. For some tasks the group may stay together; for other tasks the group may subdivide into subgroups, each of which would work on different aspects of a larger task. The off-site meeting with the medical school department, which was described earlier as an example of team building associated with Beckhard's first purpose, goal setting, illustrates different forms of organization for task accomplishment.

2. *Leadership*—a group function that can be handled in various ways. Regardless of agenda item, the team leader may lead the meeting throughout its duration. Alternatively, leadership may rotate according to expertise—the group member having the most expertise on certain agenda items leading the meeting when that item is being discussed. In this latter case, the team leader deals more with the process and sees that the content leadership is coordinated among the members.

3. *Decision making*—which can be done in a variety of ways. Five methods come to mind: (1) unilateral—the group discusses the problem, but the team leader alone makes the final decision; (2) minority control—a group consisting of seven members, for example, discusses the problem, but only three of the members finally decide; (3) majority rule—a vote is taken before or after discussion and, if and when a majority agrees, the decision is made; (4) consensus—all members of the group influence the final decision (the *minimum* criterion for a consensual decision being when *all* members can at least partially agree to live with the final decision); and (5) unanimity—all members agree completely (not partially) to the final decision. Among these five alternatives, unanimity is rarely possible. Although consensus often takes considerable time, it is the most effective and practical method if the situation calls for a group decision. Refer to the three guidelines summarized under McGregor's sixth feature, selective use of the team, for help in determining the appropriate situation.

4. *Problem solving*—groups can solve problems in various ways. The rationale steps developed by Kepner and Tregoe (1965) are one way. Another is to use the nominal group technique or the Delphi method (Delbecq, Van de Ven, and Gustafson 1975).

These four examples of procedural processes represent some of the more salient ones for group work, but they are by no means exhaustive.

Maintenance processes are the activities within the group that help to hold the group together as team, that facilitate a cohesiveness among the members, ensuring that the group is maintained and doesn't splinter or fall apart. Examples of maintenance processes include openness of communication, mutual trust, mutual support, gatekeeping (providing oppor-

284

tunities for members to participate), tolerance of differences, and relieving tension when needed. This set of processes obviously concerns the interpersonal relationships among group members.

Procedural and maintenance processes are similar to and overlap to some extent the task and maintenance functions listed previously under McGregor's seventh feature, appropriate member skills. The primary difference between the two sets of categories is a matter of perspective. The Bennis and Shepard lists of task and maintenance functions refer to team member skills, while the procedural and maintenance processes represent the domain of process consultation—the concern of the OD practitioner. The OD practitioner's interventions are behaviors that are directed toward facilitating and improving the team's procedures and maintenance activities.

The relation of process consultation to the four purposes of team building is as follows: when OD practitioners help team leaders design meetings for goal setting, they are serving procedural needs; when they facilitate a session by use of a technique such as responsibility charting, they are serving procedural needs; when they help with decisions about the form of decision making to use, they are serving procedural needs; when they facilitate interpersonal understanding and collaboration, they are serving maintenance needs. Actually, maintenance needs may be served by OD practitioners within any of the four primary team building purposes, since these needs are ongoing regardless of meeting objectives.

When OD practitioners consult with team leaders about goal-setting sessions or meetings concerned with members' roles and resonsibilities, their interventions are largely structural and procedural—the design for the meeting, when each activity will occur, who will be primarily involved for what activity, and so forth. Prior planning is of paramount importance. The more team building approaches a maintenance purpose, the less structured the meetings will be and therefore the less prior planning is appropriate.

To summarize quickly, we shall refer to the foremost source book for process consultation and consider its definition of process consultation: "a set of activities on the part of the consultant which help the client to perceive, understand, and act upon process events which occur in the client's environment" (Schein 1969, p. 9). It should be apparent that this definition coincides with my definition of team building. Thus, for team building purposes, the OD practitioner serves as a process consultant. In the early stages of team building, particularly if the purpose is one of Beckhards' first three, the types of process interventions are structured and procedural. Over time, particularly if the team building purpose is to emphasize member relationships, the types of process interventions are less structured and procedural and deal more with events as they occur. Timing is critical, therefore, for the ultimate effectiveness of these latter interventions, and consultants must be neutral regarding the issues of the conflicting parties but empathetic to their feelings.

Process consultation may be structured or unstructured, planned or spontaneous, mostly intellectual or mostly intuitive. Whatever the form may be, the consultation is facilitative. The intervention helps the client (1) to achieve a better understanding of the dynamics and characteristics of what is happening behaviorally within an interpersonal, group, or intergroup setting, and (2) to act on that increased understanding in such a way that work will be improved and productivity increased.

Related Theory

As emphasized in Chapters 8 and 10, it is necessary for effective OD practice that OD consultants' diagnoses and interventions be grounded in one or more theories, or at least tied to a coherent conceptual frame of reference. In working with groups, there are several conceptual groundings.

Stages of Group Development

The work of Will Schutz and Bennis and Shepard is particularly useful for understanding the psychological phases or stages through which groups seem to move as they progress from start-up situations to greater maturity. These two theories are particularly helpful in understanding the behavior of relatively new groups.

Schutz (1958) contends that, in the initial stages, group members are fundamentally concerned with issues of inclusion and membership. Their implicit questions are: "Do I belong in this group?" "Am I accepted?" "Do I want to be a member?" "Who are these other people, really, and will I like them?" "Will they like me?" When these issues are resolved to some extent, the group then evolves to a second stage—the control phase. During this stage, the paramount concern, whether voiced or not, is who is in charge. If there is a formal leader, will he or she really run the show, or will informal leadership emerge? The implicit questions then are: "Where will I as a member be with respect to the issue of control?" "If there is no formal leader, who will emerge?" "Will I?" "If not, will I be happy with the one who does?" The third and final stage concerns affection and intimacy. This stage is reached, according to Schutz, only after the issues within the previous two stages have been resolved, at least to some extent. In the final stage, members are concerned with how close they want to be with one another, how much they want to be cared for and care about others in the group, and how deeply affectionate they want to be with one another. This stage may wax and wane, but it is likely to last for the life of the group.

Bennis and Shepard's (1956) theory is similar and consists of two stages—the first concerning issues of power and authority and the second concerning issues of intimacy and interdependence.

Interpersonal Competence

Argyris (1962) developed criteria for interpersonal competence (experimenting, openness, and owning—see Chapter 2) and later (Argyris 1971) integrated these criteria within a broader theoretical framework in which he posited that there is a particular pattern (Pattern B) of behavior that manifests the assumptions of McGregor's Theory Y and another pattern (Pattern A) that reflects McGregor's Theory X assumptions about human behavior. Pattern B represents behavior associated with the dimensions of interpersonal competence, and Pattern A represents the opposite forms of behavior. Thus, the goal of an OD effort, in this case team building, is to move from XA to YB. Argyris further contends that competent behavior is congruent with beliefs and attitudes. As a consultant, he helps the client understand Theory Y assumptions and, if the client believes in and values these assumptions, Argyris then intervenes in such a way that discrepancies between beliefs and behavior are confronted. Change, therefore, is behavioral, reducing the discrepancy between beliefs and action.

In team building, Argyris's theory can be helpful to the OD practitioner during any phase, but it is particularly useful for maintenance purposes.

The Group Unconscious

Chapter 2 provided a brief description of Bion's (1961) theory of group dynamics. The theory focuses on issues of authority, claiming that group members unconsciously reject authority in one or sometimes two of three ways—by fight or flight, by dependency, or by pairing. Bion's theory is particularly helpful for understanding and dealing with issues of control and leadership. In my work with Acme Chemical, for example, it became clear to me that the group of executives reporting to Armstrong, the president, was more a basic assumption group than a work group. The primary modes of the basic assumption group were flight and pairing. The Acme group tended to flee from the primary task of the meeting, and a subgroup eventually formed (pairing) under the informal leadership of the executive vice-president. The basic assumption group was so predominant that little work was accomplished at the off-site meeting. In as diplomatic a way as I could manage, I suggested to Armstrong that he would have to break up the subgroup if he wished to remain president. He later took this action by

287

changing some of the vice-presidents' roles. As I mentioned earlier, he also eventually fired one of his vice-presidents, who happened to be a strong member of the subgroup—the primary person paired with the executive vice-president.

Whether or not the interventions I made in this case were the most effective, it is clear that I would have had little understanding of what was occurring or not occurring between Armstrong and his group without a knowledge of Bion's theory.

Group Research

Although it is not theoretical as such, Steiner's (1972) work in summarizing considerable research done with groups and applying this knowledge to group process and productivity can be very useful to the team consultant. Steiner analyzes and categorizes group tasks and shows how different tasks place different demands on group performance. He also provides information about the effects of group size and composition as well as member motivation. The usefulness of Steiner's work is that he approaches group process from a perspective different from that of most OD practitioners, and he clearly shows the relationship between process and productivity.

In a different but related way, Delbecq, Van de Ven, and Gustafson (1975) have summarized numerous group research studies, particularly those concerned with face-to-face interaction, and have argued on the basis of this summary that certain group procedures are likely to be more successful than others. They point out that, in face-to-face interacting groups, the problem of individual status and perceived power significantly affects group performance. In these kinds of groups, the relative quantity and quality of ideas is low, one or two people typically dominate, and conflict resolution is usually ineffective. They show that the nominal group technique and the Delphi process are more effective for generating a greater quantity and quality of ideas. This knowledge and these alternative group techniques can be particularly helpful to OD practitioners in their attempts to relate procedural process more efficiently and effectively to task demands.

Team Building Applied to Special Groups

The aspects of team building that we have covered in this chapter are also applicable to groups other than managerial teams. Much if not all of what we have considered is applicable to ad hoc groups, committees, task forces, and the like. Team building is also applicable to semiautonomous work groups and quality control (QC) circles.

The semiautonomous work group originally developed in Western Europe and was an application based on Bion's theory. Since groups have such problems with leadership and authority, as Bion's theory contends, a logical action is to minimize these issues. Semiautonomous work groups, therefore, typically determine their own goals, work schedules, and job assignments. Within limits (thus the prefix *semi*), these groups exercise the traditional management prerogatives that deal with planning, decision making, and controlling. Team building that concentrates on procedures that facilitate shared leadership and participation should be particularly useful.

Quality control circles have existed for more than two decades in Japan but are of recent vintage in the United States. Briefly, a QC circle is a voluntary group of workers who share a common area of work responsibility. They typically meet for about an hour each week to discuss problems of quality, to investigate causes, to generate solutions, and to take the necessary actions. The supervisor of these employees serves as the QC circle leader, but he or she functions more as a group member than as a boss. Group training is usually a necessity for QC circles to work effectively. Elements associated with team building are frequently incorporated within this training—communication processes, problem-solving techniques, leadership skills, and adult learning techniques. The group also receives training in technical matters—the use of the various measurements and quality strategies, including cause-and-effect diagrams, Pareto diagrams, histograms, and various types of checklists and graphs (Yager 1979). Since QC circles are ongoing, there is a clear need for periodic team building sessions.

Summary

We began this chapter with a case example of team building. The Acme Chemical case was typical of the flow of events in an initial team building effort but was somewhat atypical with respect to the groups' readiness and ability to work together as a group. Although this top management group was neither experienced nor skilled in group work, the trend today—and in the future—is toward more utilization of groups for work and for problem solving.

Dyer's checklists for determining the need for team building comprise a highly useful first step. If team building is appropriate, the OD practitioner should plan the diagnosis and intervention according to Beckhard's four purposes: setting goals and priorities, analyzing and allocating the way work is performed with respect to roles and responsibilities, examining the working procedures of the team, and dealing with issues of interpersonal relationships within the team.

Regardless of the purpose of team building, it is beneficial to maintain certain standards for what constitutes an effective group. Both McGregor and Likert have provided criteria for and characteristics of an effective group.

In team building, the OD practitioner is a process consultant. In this role, the practitioner is concerned with procedures that will facilitate group productivity and with processes that will help to maintain the group as a cohesive and viable entity.

As emphasized in Chapters 9 and 11, it is imperative that OD practitioners diagnose team behavior and intervene in the life of the team according to some relevant theory or conceptual frame of reference.

CHAPTER 14

Intergroup Interventions

In the previous chapter I described an off-site problem-solving and goal-setting meeting for a department in a medical school. Later in my consulting effort with that medical school, my colleague (the internal consultant) and I worked with another department, the department of clinical pathology. What began as a team building effort eventually became an intergroup conflict resolution session among three subgroups of the department. I shall briefly describe the department, discuss what my colleague and I did as consultants, and then cover some of the theory and practice associated with intergroup work.

A Case Example

The Department of Clinical Pathology

This department, like most departments of its kind in medical schools, had the dual mission of performing laboratory work and training students—future M.D.'s, residents, research scientists (Ph.D.'s) and medical technicians. The department's laboratory work consisted of providing testing services—blood tests, tissue analysis, and so forth—for the university hospital, for a nearby VA hospital, for various clinics, and for faculty members' clinical practices. Members of the department also conducted classes and laboratory sessions for medical students, trained future medical technicians, provided graduate training for Ph.D. candidates and for M.D.'s seeking advanced training, and supervised some aspects of residency training for M.D.'s.

My colleague and I were asked by the department chairman to help him with some departmental team building. We began, as usual, by conducting interviews with department members, and we administered a brief (eight items) questionnaire, asking the members to assess their department's effec-

291

tiveness in working together as a group. We soon discovered that what we had first considered a fairly routine team building intervention was more like dealing with a house divided into three parts, with each part having cohesive membership but with thick walls between the parts. In our initial interview the chairman had led us to believe that his department was splintered because of the multiple, varied demands placed on its members; they had to serve too many constituents within the university medical complex. This diagnosis appeared valid to us, but as we interviewed further we discovered a deeper cause—well *within* the department.

The three membership parts of the department consisted of medical doctors, Ph.D. pathologists, and medical technicians. Although the parts overlapped, each of the three subgroups had distinct roles to play and responsibilities to carry out. The pecking order was even more distinct, however: the M.D.'s were kings and queens of the hill; the medical technicians were the workers—maintaining the hill and serving the M.D.'s; and the Ph.D. pathologists were somewhere in between. They had status because of their education and expertise but were clearly second-class citizens within the department. Each group held resentful feelings toward the other two groups. The medical technicians resented both of the other groups—the M.D.'s for their arrogance and demands and the Ph.D.'s for their unrealistic expectations and for their arrogance as well. The Ph.D. pathologists also considered the M.D.'s arrogant and believed that this arrogance was unwarranted because, in their opinion, the M.D.'s were doing scientific work and were not adequately trained for it. The pathologists viewed the medical technicians as uncooperative and believed they catered to the M.D.'s too much. The M.D.'s considered the Ph.D. pathologists no more than highly trained technicians and believed the medical technicians were sullen, resistant, and even rebellious at times.

The Intergroup Intervention within a Group

We usually begin an off-site team building session with feedback, and my colleague and I did so with the department of clinical pathology. We normally would begin with goal-setting activities or perhaps with some specific team problems to be solved. In this case, after the feedback, we questioned the department members about the validity of our diagnosis—whether we were correct about the resentful feelings among the three subgroups of the department. They were reluctant to agree with our diagnosis at first, but gradually, after one or two members risked expressing their feelings and opinions openly, the entire membership finally admitted that three subgroups existed, with thick walls between them. At that point my colleague and I were prepared to suggest an action step.

292

We proposed the following activities. First, each of the three groups—the medical technicians, the Ph.D. pathologists, and the M.D.'s—would meet separately as a subgroup and generate three lists. These lists would be responses to the following three questions: (1) How do we see ourselves as a group? (2) How do we see the other two subgroups (a list for each subgroup)? (3) How do we think the other two subgroups see us (separate lists for each subgroup)? Second, each of the three subgroups would present its lists to the other two subgroups and seek questions of clarification but not debate the issues at that time. Third, each subgroup having presented its lists and having heard from the others, would separate again and develop a list of what they believe to be the most pressing problems existing among the three subgroups. Fourth, the total group would reconvene, and the three subgroups would present their respective lists to one another. Again, only questions of clarification could be raised; no debating would take place just yet. Fifth, representatives from each of the three subgroups would meet together to consolidate the three lists of identified problems. Sixth, temporary cross-subgroup task forces would be formed to work on the high-priority problems. These newly constituted groups would have equal representation from each of the three subgroups. Finally, after the problem-solving groups had done their work, they would present their ideas to the total group. Under the leadership of the chairman, action steps would then be planned for follow-up.

The chairman and the department members agreed to our proposal, and we spent the next two days systematically working through the seven phases. Although all resentful feelings did not vanish and all problems become solved, progress was made toward these ends, and follow-up did indeed occur.

For all practical purposes, this off-site meeting with the department of clinical pathology was a team building activity. The goal—building the department into more of a team—was accomplished to some extent. The methodology used, however, was more like the intervention employed in organization development practice when two separate organizational groups are in conflict than like the team building activities described in Chapter 13. Such conflict situations include differences that frequently exist between labor and management, sales or marketing and manufacturing, accounting and computer services, and those between larger subsystems, such as the school of nursing and the school of medicine within the same university.

Another colleague of mine and I worked with this latter intergroup conflict situation in another university medical complex and found that the perceived differences and feelings were not only conflicts between the two schools but stemmed from male (medical school) versus female (nursing school) issues and from degree differences—M.D. versus Ph.D. and R.N. The intergroup conflict resolution meeting between the top groups of both schools was indeed complicated. For a more detailed description of how to conduct such an intergroup conflict resolution session, see Burke (1974).

Intergroup Conflict Resolution

Now that we have covered some of the ways OD practitioners deal with inter-group conflict, we shall broaden our perspective by considering some of the underlying theory and research and by exploring other dimensions of conflict within organizations.

Conflict between groups that are normally dependent on one another—such as in the foregoing case and between headquarters and field, R&D and marketing, and so forth—is very common and natural. Each group has its own mission but, for that mission to be accomplished, each group occasionally must rely on the other. This mutual dependence, or interdependence, is a natural setting for conflict.

Theory and Research

The original research in intergroup conflict, which set the stage for how we deal with it in OD practice, was conducted by Sherif and his colleagues in the late 1940s and early 1950s (Sherif et al. 1961). In a series of studies with groups of boys at summer camp, Sherif and his colleagues demonstrated how to develop strong in-group feelings with two separate groups and then how these feelings translated into competitive behavior when the two groups were placed in a win-lose situation. Experiments were also conducted in reducing the conflict and in establishing a cooperative attitude between the two groups. These experiments also were conducted over a period of years with adults in industrial organizations (Sherif and Sherif 1953). Blake, Shepard, and Mouton (1964) summarized Sherif's work and demonstrated refinements of the processes in work done with actual groups in conflict—such as staff and line, headquarters and field, sales and operations, and management and union. Alderfer (1977) has provided an overview and summary of intergroup relations, as has E. H. Schein (1980). Relying on these sources and on my experience as a consultant in these situations, I shall review the steps in an intergroup conflict resolution event and provide the rationale from research, theory, and practice for each activity or phase.

Before an off-site meeting, the OD practitioner conducts interviews with selected or all members from each of the two (or three) conflicting groups. Interviews can be supplemented by a brief questionnaire for additional information if desirable. During this data collection and analysis phase—the diagnostic step—the OD practitioner determines if real conflict exists between the two groups. It is possible that so-called phony conflict (Harvey 1977a) is the phenomenon to be diagnosed, not actual conflict. According to Harvey (1977a), the difference is that real conflict involves substantive differences—one party says, "The research project is technologically feasible," while the other says, "not according to my understanding of the data."

294

Phony conflict, however, consists of negative, even hostile, blaming behavior that occurs when *agreement is mismanaged*—one party says, "I told you the project wouldn't work. Look at the mess you've got us in," while the other says, "Don't blame me. It would have worked if you had done your job." Harvey argues that conflict is a symptom, not a generic process. As a symptom, conflict may be reflected as real differences or it may be symptomatic of agreement that people are not willing to acknowledge. Harvey (1977a) further argues that when consultants fail "to distinguish between real and phony conflict they collude with maintaining the problem they are attempting to solve" (p. 166). In a phony conflict situation, all members—regardless of group—know what the problem is and what solution is required. They are reluctant to act because of action anxiety, negative fantasies, fear of separation, real risk, and psychological reversal of risk and certainty (Harvey 1974a). Confronting reality, recognizing and acting on the implicit agreement, may require more risk than people in the situation feel like taking. Thus, there is an underlying agreement, but it is not being exposed and managed. According to Harvey, it is the consultant's job to bring this agreement to the surface and to help the boss manage it toward action.

Real conflict between groups involves substantive issues, and the two (or more) groups express competitive behavior—not merely blaming one another. Within each group, the OD practitioner is likely to find that members are close and loyal to one another—their internal differences are submerged; group climate is formal, serious, and task-oriented, rather than informal, playful, and oriented toward members' psychological needs; the group leader is more directive and less participative; activities are structured and organized; strong norms exist that demand loyalty to the group from each member; and there is considerable energy to resist the other group.

The Conflict Resolution Session

Once it has been determined that real conflict exists and that there is motivation within both groups to work on the problems, an off-site conflict resolution session is warranted. The following seven phases comprise the sequence of events:

PHASE 1   Separate the groups and have each group work on their perceptions of themselves and of the other group. When groups are competing and in conflict, each group (1) sees the other group more as an enemy than as a group whose help they may need at times; (2) perceives the other group far more negatively than they do themselves—perceptions are distorted, and weaknesses within one's own group tend to be denied while the worst aspects of the other group are emphasized; (3) increases its negative feelings and stereotypes over time while actually communicating with the other group less and less; (4) tends to see and hear only what it wants—not what is objective and not the broader picture; and (5) usually has a sense of how the other group feels about them, although these perceptions are rarely discussed within the group.

Since these behaviors within and between conflicting groups are highly predictable, Phase 1 is devoted to a process that will demonstrate it. Thus, each group is asked to make three lists of perceptions—one about themselves, one about the other group, and one about how they think the other group perceives them as a group. Burke (1974) describes a conflict resolution session between an engineering design group and a manufacturing group in an industrial organization. A sample of the two groups' lists is as follows:

Engineering	*Manufacturing*
How We See Ourselves	
Stable	Competent
Cooperative	Error-prone
Creative	Hard-working
How We See Them	
Unstable	Error-prone
Not creative	No sense of urgency
Conscientious and industrious	Unified as a group
How We Think They See Us	
In an ivory tower	Constantly changing
Error-prone	Error-prone
Intrusive	Inflexible

As can be seen from these abbreviated lists (about a quarter of the total), the predictions about how conflicting groups behave are confirmed.

PHASE 2   Each group presents its lists to the other group in an exchange of perceptual images. The purpose of this phase is to demonstrate that perceptions are both distorted and accurate—"We are superior to them, yet we know fairly accurately what they think or us." Once the groups see the respective lists and have a change to understand them, they are in a better position to distinguish between real differences and overblown perceptions. The ground rule for Phase 2 is that only questions of clarification may be exchanged between the two groups, not debate about who is right. Since distortions are rampant and selectivity of what one sees and hears during conflict is normal, it is critical that mutual understanding begin at this stage. There is likely to be continuing disagreement about some issues, but at least distorted perceptions can be reduced.

PHASE 3   The groups separate again and generate their lists of problems and issues that they now believe to exist between them. It is important to keep the competing groups intact during these first three phases (1) to accomplish the early tasks required for the off-site meeting, (2) to maintain the integrity of each group, (3) to insure that each group's interests are adequately and fairly represented, and (4) to insure that the conflict is real and worthy of work toward resolution.

PHASE 4   Each group presents its list of issues and problems to the other group. Again the ground rule of only clarifying questions is maintained to insure that each group really hears and understands the other group. This phase typically demonstrates that there is considerable agreement about what the problems actually are between the two groups. Overlap occurs, but priorities may differ.

PHASE 5   Representatives from each group meet to consolidate the lists into one. The total group (both groups together) rank-orders the consolidated list, from most important issue or problem to least important.

Research has shown that several techniques can help reduce or resolve intergroup conflict. Three such techniques support this fifth phase: (1) having a common enemy; (2) developing a superordinate goal; and (3) bringing leaders or subgroups from the competing groups together for task accomplishment.

In some respects, the consolidated list of problems and issues represents a common enemy because it was generated by both groups, a superordinate goal is established because neither group can resolve the issues or solve the problems without the other group. When representatives from each of the groups meet to consolidate the two lists, the third technique for resolving the conflict has been applied. This technique is then fully actualized during the next phase.

PHASE 6   Cross-groups are formed for problem solving. Temporary problem-solving groups or task forces are created with half of their membership from each of the competing groups. If the total for both groups was twenty-four people, for example (and assuming that there were equal numbers in each competing group—a key assumption), then four task groups might be formed with three people each from the two competing groups. These task groups would each choose a separate problem to work on, and their tasks would be to generate lists of possible solutions to the problem and to rank-order the solutions according to feasibility of implementation. The

297

superordinate goal for each task force is to defeat the common enemy, a problem that neither competing group can solve alone.

PHASE 7   In this phase, each task force explains to the others its solutions to the problem it tackled and invites questions and criticism. Finally, the meeting concludes with plans for follow-up activities to insure that the problem solutions are implemented.

The OD practitioner's role in all of this is largely that of meeting manager. He or she sees to it that the design elements of the meeting are understood and carried out and also insists that the ground rules are followed. The practitioner thus facilitates the management of the process of the meeting, not the content. To manage this process well, it is imperative that the practitioner understand the rationale for each of the phases and elements of the meeting design.

Other Intergroup Interventions

Another intervention for intergroup problems is called the organization mirror. The intervention is so named because some central group within an organization receives feedback—reflections—from several other groups with which it interacts and has some degree of interdependence. The technique was developed by OD practitioners at TRW, Inc., during the 1960s. Two of these practitioners, who have written about a number of OD interventions, define the organization mirror intervention as

> A particular kind of meeting that allows an organizational unit to collect feedback from a number of key organizations to which it relates (e.g., customers, suppliers, users of services within the larger organization). The meeting closes with a list of specific tasks for improvement of operations, products, or services. (Fordyce and Weil 1971, p. 101)

The organization mirror is a useful intervention for helping an organizational unit that is having difficulties with the groups it serves or receives services from to understand the nature, if not the causes, of some of these difficulties. Prior to the meeting, an OD practitioner interviews members of the central unit (the unit to receive the feedback) and representatives from each of the outside but related units. The purposes of the interviews are to obtain a sense of the intergroup difficulties and to prepare the participants for the meeting. There may be two, three, or as many as six of these outside, related units. It is important that those giving the feedback balance the membership of the receiving, central group. Thus, if the central group has six members and feedback is to be received from three other units, two representatives from each of these other "reflecting" groups would be sufficient. Balance should also be maintained with respect to organizational hierarchy; the out-

298

side groups' representatives should occupy organizational positions comparable to those of the central group's membership.

The meeting usually begins with remarks from the manager of the central group, including an outline of the meeting's objectives and activities, and the manager begins to establish the tone or climate for the meeting. Next, the OD practitioner provides a summary of the interview results. Following the summary, representatives from the outside groups meet together in the center of the room to discuss and interpret the interview results. The central group forms a circle around the outside group representatives to observe, listen, and take notes, but they do not intervene or ask questions at this point. The central group then moves to the inner circle to discuss among themselves what they heard and to identify issues and problems that need further clarification. During this period, the outsiders only observe and listen. In the next phase, all participants meet as a total group to discuss and clarify the issues and problems.

Once the issues and problems have been identified and clarified, the total group is reorganized into problem-solving groups, each comprised of both central group members and outside group members. These new subgroups report to the total group when they have identified changes that need to be made. The total group discusses these proposed changes and endorses or modifies them. The subgroups meet a second time to develop plans and specific action steps for the proposed changes. The meeting ends with a summary of the subgroups' work, a review and critique of the meeting, and individual assignments for the action steps.

As an OD intervention, the organization mirror process has proven itself as a useful technique (Fordyce and Weil 1971) for communicating effectively across unit boundaries; converting critics into helpers; moving criticism toward corrective action; and improving overall effectiveness.

Another form of consultation with conflicting parties involves the OD practitioner's serving as a third party between two individuals. In OD practice this form of consultation has been called "interpersonal peacemaking" (Walton 1969). Some of the same dynamics that occur between groups also transpire between two individuals—competition for resources, recognition, power, and the like, and frustration with perceived negligence, indifference, or hostility from the other party. A neutral third party—the OD consultant-practitioner—can help the two parties (1) identify more clearly their issues and problems with one another, (2) deal with one another more constructively about these issues and problems, and (3) develop ways to interact with one another more productively in the future. This interpersonal peacemaking process will only have such outcomes, of course, when the two parties are mutually dependent to some extent and when they both can see that it is in their mutual interest to improve their relations.

There are many examples of interpersonal conflict in organizations.

Sometimes it is simply referred to as a personality conflict—the two people just cannot seem to work together. Other conflicts arise as a result of pressure felt by each of the two parties—pressure to complete critical projects when resources are scarce, resulting in completion. What is sometimes referred to as a personality conflict is as much a result of job history as it is of differences in interpersonal styles. In a consultative experience involving two conflicting managers, it became clear to me early in the process that the previous boss-subordinate relationship between these two individuals, who were managerial peers at the time, was exacerbating the current conflict. There was residual bitterness on both individuals' parts about "the way I was managed as a subordinate—treated like a kid" and "your lack of appreciation for all I did for you when I was your boss."

The interpersonal peacemaking intervention came about as a result of previous team building activities. It reached a point at which team building could not proceed any further until these two team members resolved some of their continuing competitiveness and interpersonal problems. The two managers eventually agreed to meet with me, as a third-party consultant, to work on their interpersonal conflict. The following steps were followed:

1. We met on neutral territory—in a conference room for the first session and in another manager's office for the second session.
2. I asked them to begin with a discussion of their previous working relationship and what it was like.
3. Next they gave one another feedback, primarily in terms of how each feels (or felt) when he perceives that the other is doing (or did) something.
4. I then asked each of them to tell the other what each now wanted from the other.
5. Finally, they contracted with one another about what each would do differently in the future.

These five steps took seven hours—two three-and-a-half-hour meetings, with a two-week interim period. Following the two sessions, we resumed the team building activities with the total group.

My role in this interpersonal process was (1) to structure the meeting to some extent; (2) to manage the interchange between the two managers by encouraging them to exchange feelings and by ensuring that they heard and understood one another (which involved my asking occasional clarifying questions, occasionally suggesting that one party paraphrase what the other had said, and giving one of the individuals feedback when he seemed to be unable to hear it from the other person); (3) to maintain calmness and stability in my behavior, especially when the two managers were being highly confrontive and emotional; and (4) to see that a balance was achieved at the end, when the two expressed what they wanted from each other and began to contract with one another.

Although the content of each conflict situation differs for the OD practitioner, the process of consultation should follow certain guidelines. In the interpersonal peacemaking consultation just described, I operated from moment to moment, on an ad hoc basis, attempting to respond to what the situation seemed to demand at the time. Overall, however, I followed many of the steps suggested by Walton's (1969) theory and guidelines for serving as a third-party consultant. His chronological list of specific consultant interventions has been summarized by Beer (1980):

1. Initiating agendas for the meetings of the two parties
2. Structuring the setting of meetings to facilitate constructive exchange
3. Helping the parties provide each other with honest and constructive feedback about their reactions to each other
4. Suggesting specific ways in which discussions between the parties might proceed
5. Restating views of the parties—making sure they are heard and heard accurately
6. Refereeing the interaction between the parties and sometimes even providing mild rewards (and punishments) for productive (and counterproductive) behavior by the participants
7. Helping parties diagnose the reasons for their conflict
8. Diagnosing (and sometimes attempting to change) the conditions that have caused poor dialogue between the parties
9. Obtaining agreement for changes in behavior and periodic review and follow-up

Summary

When problems of apparent conflict exist within and between groups, it is critical to diagnose whether the conflict is genuine or merely a symptom that masks underlying agreement. This implicit agreement may exist but not be made explicit because individuals fear retribution if they reveal their true opinions and feelings. If the conflict is a symptom of implicit agreement, the OD practitioner's function is to facilitate the surfacing of the agreement. If the conflict is real, the OD practitioner function is to facilitate clarification of the differences and management of their resolution. Both approaches— managing agreement and managing conflict—are grounded in sound theory and research, the former tied to Bion (1961) and Harvey (1977a, 1974a) and the latter related to the work of Sherif (Sherif 1958; Sherif et al. 1961; Sherif and Sherif 1953).

301

An OD intervention that is related to intergroup conflict resolution is the so-called organization mirror technique. This intervention is also based on intergroup feedback and problem solving as a function of the feedback.

Finally, the principles and techniques used to help resolve conflict between groups can also be applied to two individuals in conflict. Walton's (1969) interpersonal peacemaking model and his methods of application are very useful in helping to establish peace between two parties who are at war with one another.

CHAPTER 15

Large System Change

Providing consultation for an individual can be complex, but intervening within a group of individuals is even more complicated, and attempting to resolve conflict between groups is a formidable task. The ultimate goal in organization development, however, is to bring about change throughout an entire system. If the system for change is a very large one, the task is extremely complex, but we begin nevertheless.

An organizational change effort rarely if ever begins all at once with the total system, especially in a large organization. Beginnings typically involve an individual, a group, a program—such as management training—or an already recognized need to make a significant change—in the organization's structure, for example. The previous chapters in this part have dealt with much of the groundwork that either leads to large system change or facilitates it. In this chapter we shall consider some of these previously considered interventions in the context of an attempt to change a large organization—a system composed of multiple groups, functions, and processes. In examining large system change, we shall consider briefly the business of beginning, then the orders or levels of change, the phases of large system change, and finally selected interventions.

Where to Begin

Early definitions of organization development, particularly Beckhard's (1969), stated or implied that an organization development effort begins at the top, usually with the top team itself. Later writings on OD practice have indicated that OD may begin in places or with groups other than the top management team (Beer and Huse 1972). In later writings Beckhard himself broadened his viewpoint about where to start. He and Harris have provided a useful list of alternative places to start a change effort:

1. The top management or top of the system;
2. Management-ready systems—those groups or organizations known to be ready for the change;
3. "Hurting" systems—a special class of ready systems in which conditions have created acute discomfort in a previously unready system;
4. New teams or systems—systems without a history and whose tasks require a departure from old ways of operating;
5. Staffs—subsystems that will be required to assist in the implementation of later interventions;
6. Temporary project systems—those systems whose existence and tenure are problem-defined and whose task is to achieve a specific goal. (Beckhard and Harris 1977, pp. 42-43)

As can be seen from this list, the initial effort is with a subsystem. Although this first subsystem may be a group of strategic planners—and change will come later—the focus for change is more often with the initial subsystem itself.

The initial effort can thus begin in various places. The primary criterion is that, regardless of where the change starts, beginning with an individual or group that has power gives greater likelihood of early success. When in doubt, start at the top.

Orders of Change

Because change within large systems is so complex, it is useful to think strategically about different orders of change. Kimberly and Neilsen (1975) have suggested three orders of change. (Order refers to the level of the ultimate target for change.) For *first-order* changes, the target is the subsystem of initial focus. The change would occur as a result of an intervention in a particular unit (subsystem) within the organization. The unit might be a management team and the intervention could be team building, with a change objective of developing more collaborative, consensual decision-making behavior. First-order change, then, is with a subsystem, and although change in that unit will have some consequences for the larger system, the likelihood is that, unless other complementary and supplementary changes are also occurring in related parts of the total system, the change within the initial subsystem will be short-lived. For an excellent example of this point, see the Hovey and Beard case (Whyte 1955).

Second-order change means that the target is a subsystem or process that is beyond the initial focus but that will be affected if the initial effort is successful. The focus is frequently a category or a particular set of subsystems within the organization. An intervention might take place with one group or set of employees—first-line supervisors, for example, when the ultimate objective for the change effort is to affect all workers below these supervisors in the organizational hierarchy. If we want to decrease absenteeism and turn-

304

over among the workers who are accountable to these supervisors, our initial effort might be a training program for the supervisors in which they would have the opportunity to learn more about human motivation, the consequences of certain kinds of rewards and punishment, and effective ways of providing feedback on worker performance. With proper application of this learning, the supervisors would help reduce absenteeism and turnover—our ultimate target for change.

Third-order change eventually influences some organizational process or outcome that is affected by multiple factors. Wherever the interventions or series of interventions are made, the ultimate objective of the change effort is larger—to increase productivity, for example.

As Golembiewski (1979) points out, "first order change due to OD interventions is well established, both in concept and research" (p. 267), but there is little evidence in the literature regarding second- and third-order changes. The process of total system change, however, is third-order change.

Change Phases

Beckhard and Harris (1977) have written most definitively about large, total system change. They have taken the steps of an OD effort that we have considered already (see Chapter 8)—entry, contracting, diagnosis, feedback, planning change, intervention, and evaluation—and placed them within their framework for large system change. Their six phases are as follows:

1. Diagnosis—determining the present condition and the need for change;
2. Goal setting—defining the new state or condition after the change;
3. Transition state—defining the new state or condition between the present and the future;
4. Strategy for change—developing action plans for managing the transition from present to future;
5. Evaluation—evaluating the effort;
6. Stabilization—stabilizing the new state and establishing a balance between stability and flexibility.

Once a need for change has been established, the new, future state (the new culture) is defined, a plan for getting to the future state is established, the implementation occurs, the effort is evaluated, and stabilizing factors are put into place to maintain the new state or culture. The process can be depicted simply as follows:

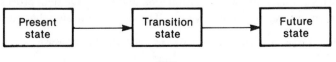

Beckhard and Harris state that the most difficult part of any organizational change effort is managing the process of moving from the present state to the future one. This *transition* phase, then, is critical. The important issues to be considered for effective transition management, according to Beckhard and Harris (1977) are:

> Determining the degree of choice about whether to change: this determination can be made by examining the number and intensity of outside or inside forces pushing for change.

> Determining what needs changing: considerations are (1) cultural aspects (norms, values, and so on); (2) mission, goals, objectives, and the like; (3) structure of the organization; and (4) working procedures such as a management information system.

> Determining where to intervene: a list of six alternatives was provided at the beginning of this chapter.

> Choosing intervention technologies: the choice should be the one that will best move the transition forward. Later in this chapter we will examine some of the major alternatives.

It is useful for the consultant to keep in mind the seven phases of consultation, from entry to evaluation. To help the client maintain perspective, the consultant should provide a map or flow of events that represents the three phases of change—present to transition to future. It is relatively easy to determine the present state and the desired future state. What is difficult is moving from one to the other.

As I have done in other chapters, I shall present a case example from my consulting experience that illustrates large system change.[1]

A Case Example

A colleague and I were recently invited by a pharmaceutical firm to explore the possibility of our consulting with them as an organization. Approximately a year prior to our initial visit, a morale survey had been conducted throughout the company. All employees, including management, were surveyed—about 3,000 people. An outside opinion research firm was hired to conduct the survey. The results of the survey showed clearly that there was considerable dissatisfaction throughout the company, especially among the rank and file. The major problem concerned managerial style and the general approach various levels of supervision took in the management process, particularly in the management of people. The survey indicated that most man-

[1] Adapted from my pages 193–196 in Michael *et al.* (1981) by permission.

agers were perceived as autocratic, rather rigid in their approach and style, and unilateral (top-down) in the decision-making process. Another serious problem was the perception by the employees that the company lacked a sense of mission and purpose or that there was a lack of clarity regarding the organization's mission. Other problems were identified, but these two were the primary ones and reflected the general nature of the organization at that time.

In their final report, the opinion research firm recommended that the pharmaceutical company hire an outside consultant—they used the term *change agent*—to help them deal with the major problems identified in the survey. The opinion research firm suggested that change was in order and that the company could use some help in bringing it about. The president of the pharmaceutical company followed this advice and appointed a top management committee to interview potential change agents and make a recommendation to him.

Entry

My colleague and I met with this management committee for about three hours. We were shown the survey results and then asked what we might do as change agents. We asked many questions and learned, for example, that, since the survey results had been reported to all employees (several months), each department within the company had conducted a series of peer group meetings. The groups were composed of selected representatives from within each department who had roughly similar status within the company—thus, peers. The purpose of the meetings was to discuss the survey results in more detail and to determine the degree and appropriateness of the results for their particular departments. We stated that we would want to conduct a further and continuing diagnosis of the organization, since surveys usually reflected symptoms, not causes, of problems. We also stated that we would design a process or flow of events that would facilitate development of a conceptual framework for change—a sort of roadmap that would clarify directions, targets, and priorities for change. We explained that this roadmap would also help us determine exactly which action steps to take at what particular time. Finally, we said that we would be particularly interested in studying in some depth the effectiveness of the human resource management function of their organization—such aspects as the compensation and reward systems, training programs, the design of any career development efforts, and so forth.

After meeting with the committee, we had lunch with the president and summarized what we had just discussed and recommended. Our perception of the president was that he definitely wanted to take corrective action in response to the survey. He also impressed us with the scope of his understanding of what was needed and with his commitment to starting a significant

307

change effort. In both meetings, with the management committee and later with the president, we explained that we believed organizational change was a management responsibility and that the managers of the company were the real change agents. We stated further that we saw our function as primarily facilitative, that the direction we would provide would be in terms of *how* to determine what needed changing and *how* to implement the change, not necessarily *what* to change. Later, a supervisor in the production area said that he saw us as catalysts, a term that is very familiar to people who work with chemicals and that my colleague and I agreed was as accurate as any to describe our role and function. Our official designation eventually became, simply, organization consultant.

Approximately one month following our entry meeting with the management committe and the company president, we were contacted again and told that they had selected us to consult with them. When they asked if we were still interested, we confirmed that we were and immediately arranged a meeting with the president.

Contract

In our second meeting with the president, we had two primary agenda items. We wanted him to understand and agree to what we intended to do, and we wanted him to take certain steps. Fortunately, we agreed to terms quickly and easily. Following this meeting, we sent the president a letter that summarized and specified what we had discussed. He responded in writing and, though the process was relatively informal, we had established a consulting contract. (The specifics of the contract will be covered as I proceed with the description of this case.) The length of time for the initial contract was six months, with my colleague and I agreeing to a range of consulting days—a minimum number of days we thought would be required but not to exceed a specified maximum number.

Data Collection and First Action Steps

Our initial step was to establish an advisory committee for the change effort. The committee was composed of the president, as chairman, and a vertical cross-section of the company: a member of the top management team—a department head who reported directly to the president—a representative from the next level of management but from another department, a first-line supervisor, a nonsupervisory administrator, two nonexempt employees, and a person from the personnel department, who served not only as a member of this advisory committee but also as internal consultant for the company for the OD effort. The committee thus consisted of ten people—eight from the company, including the president, and the two of us as external consultants.

The committee met once a month and had the following purposes: (1) to monitor the change effort; (2) to advise the president and the consultants about the efficacy of our plans; (3) to keep us informed and on track regarding the consequences of the various activities within the overall change effort; (4) to help with the overall communication process; and (5) to suggest additional plans and activities.

Our next step was to conduct individual interviews with each member of the top management team, including the president. Exhibit 15.1 is an organizational chart showing the members of this management group. Our purposes for these interviews were (1) to determine more thoroughly the views of these top managers regarding their sense of need for organizational change—whether they agreed with the survey results; (2) to determine their individual degree of motivation for and commitment to a change effort, especially as each of them would be closely involved, both personally and in the role of managerial change agent; and (3) to establish some rapport between them and us as consultants—to begin the process of building interpersonal trust. The questions we asked in the interviews were as follows:

1. What are your reactions to the outcome of the survey?
2. What are the major managerial strengths of the company?
3. What are the major managerial weaknesses of the company?

EXHIBIT 15.1

Organization Chart: Top Management Team of a Pharmaceutical Company

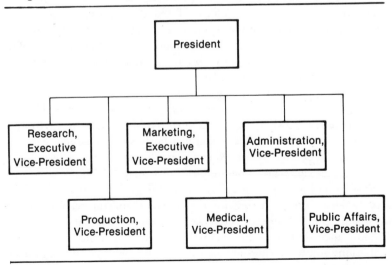

4. What are your hopes for the organizational change effort?
5. What are your fears regarding the organizational change effort?

We didn't start the interviews by immediately launching into the questions. We began with some getting-to-know-you comments and questions and then asked each one to describe his job and scope of responsibility. We then asked the five basic questions, with additional, more specific questions concerning each of the five areas. Since there were two of us, my colleague and I divided the seven interviews between us. The ground rules that we established with each manager at the outset of the interview were (1) that the information we collected would become public among the seven of them at a later feedback session but would go no further; (2) that no person would be identified as the author of any specific statement, and the control regarding who said what would be with each person; and (3) that the information would be used to clarify the top management team's view of the current state of the company, and as a basis for planning action steps for the change effort.

Diagnosis

After the interviews were conducted, my colleague and I met to categorize and analyze the information we had collected and to plan the session at which we would report back to the seven members of the group the results of the interviews and what seemed to be indicated. We categorized the interview data two ways, first according to each of the five basic questions. Although we summarized the interview responses, we attempted to stay as close to their actual words and phrases as possible. We listed the responses to each question according to how many of the seven people mentioned a particular topic, rank-ordered from most frequently mentioned topic down to the one noted by only two persons. In some cases we listed a response that had been made by only one individual if the topic did not obviously identify the person who said it. As it turned out, all the managers admitted their single responses.

The second way we categorized the data, thereby analyzing their interview responses somewhat, was according to Weisbord's (1976, 1978) six-box model (See Chapter 9). This model is a fairly simple, largely descriptive representation of what Weisbord considers the primary dimensions of any organization. There are other models, of course (Nadler and Tushman 1977; Kast and Rosenzweig 1976), but in this case Weisbord's model sufficed, because it provided a quick and easy way of tying interview responses to an organizational frame of reference, thereby enabling the managers to diagnose their situations for themselves in system terms, and a way of establishing some priorities for the parts or dimensions of the organization that needed the most or immediate attention. Thus, if a predominance of the

310

weaknesses or fears identified in the interviews could be categorized (with all seven managers agreeing) within the leadership box, which was the case in this company, then direction and priority would become clearer.

In addition to the Weisbord model, we used the transition model of Beckhard and Harris (1977). This model was presented to the client at the end of the feedback phase for the purposes of guiding the overall change effort and bridging over to the next phase—intervention.

Feedback

Approximately one week following our interviews, my colleague and I arranged a meeting with the top seven managers of the company. The agenda for this half-day session included the report (feedback) to the team of seven—our summary of the one-hour interviews—and presentation of the two models we wished to follow for diagnostic purposes (Weisbord's six-box model) and for planning purposes (Beckhard and Harris's transition stages model). The report or feedback portion of the meeting had two parts. First, we gave them our summary of the seven interviews, organized simply and straighforwardly, as noted earlier, according to the five interview questions. The second part of our feedback was the reorganization and categorization of the interview data according to Weisbord's six-box model. We took their responses to the weaknesses and fears questions and assigned them to one or more of the six boxes. This categorizing indicated which boxes showed the most "blips on the radar screen" and therefore which of the organizational dimensions needed the most attention. During the meeting the managers indicated whether we had categorized their interview data appropriately, and some changes, mostly additions, were made accordingly.

Intervention

Having obtained agreement with the top management team that (1) their interview data were summarized accurately, (2) our way of analyzing those data (Weisbord's six-box model) was useful, and (3) our plan for the steps to take in moving toward a more desired state for the company was appropriate (the transition model), we then began the process of intervening more directly into the routine of the organization. This intervention process consisted of steps 2, 3, and 4 of Beckhard and Harris's change model—defining the new state, defining the transition state, and developing strategies for managing the transition. Specifically, the following steps were taken. A one-day meeting was held with the top management team in which the president and his six department heads defined their desired state for the organization. A

311

two-day meeting was then held in which the top forty managers of the company, including the president and his six executives, defined the desired state. The previous work by the top team provided an overall picture and a lead for the next level of management to become more specific regarding the desired state for their respective organizational units. The design for these meetings, which were held away from company premises at a local tennis club to minimize interruptions, was highly participative and involving. At the beginning of the meeting we used the nominal group technique (Delbecq, Van de Ven, and Gustafson 1975) to insure equal and potentially maximum participation for everyone. This technique is a highly structured way of generating many ideas in a short period without having to cope with some of the typical problems of face-to-face, interacting groups, especially status differences. In a hierarchically structured organization, such as our pharmaceutical company, status differences are part of the daily routine. We therefore wanted to insure that maximum participation would occur and that ideas for the future state of the organization would be prolific, not stifled. Following the definition of the desired state, we began the harder work of planning specific action steps required for each organizational unit to reach that future state, step 4 in the Beckhard and Harris transition model.

Following the initial off-site meeting of the top managers, my colleague and I began working with each of the six primary units of the company (see Exhibit 15.1) We helped them plan action steps for implementing the transition phase for their particular functions. We also continued to meet with the advisory committee, which eventually served two primary purposes: (1) communication—helping to design various ways for us to keep all members of the organization informed about the change effort; and (2) management and monitoring—serving in many respects as the transition management team, monitoring progress and planning actions to rectify problems that arose during the transition.

The overall plan called for reaching the desired state in two years. Some clarification is necessary regarding this desired future state for the organization—and it involves a paradox. Although organization members involved in a change process should describe and plan for a desired state, for success as an organization that plan or desired state should never be completely realized. It is critical, of course, to have a direction for change—the desired state—but this future outcome is defined in terms of the present. With change in our society and the world at large occurring at such an accelerated rate, it is impossible for any group of managers to be able to predict two years in advance exactly what their organizational needs and the precise nature of the organization's environment will be. A general direction for organizational change is a necessity, but just as critical is a transitional plan that allows for modifications in the original plan for the desired state.

312

Evaluation

How to know when and if the desired state has been reached is the purpose of evaluation in the organization development effort. In the pharmaceutical company case, my colleague and I recommended to the president that essentially the same survey that had been administered approximately a year before we began our consultation should be administered again two years later. The following summarizes what I mean:

Year 1: survey conducted

Year 2: change effort (OD) begins

Year 3: survey conducted again

Year 4: organization reaches desired state

By Year 4 we may recommend that the survey be administered for yet a third time. A number of large companies in the United States routinely conduct annual surveys of their employee's opinions, attitudes, and general morale, so our recommendation, though atypical for this company, would not necessarily be out of the ordinary. Other comparative data should also be collected to determine if the company is performing better in such areas as net profit, return on investment, number of new products in the works and recently introduced into the marketplace, and relative standing among its competitors—the company's percentage share of the market.

Summary

Our activities as consultants to the pharmaceutical company generally followed the flow of events outlined by Beckhard and Harris (1977). We placed particular emphasis on establishing processes and mechanisms for managing the transition state between diagnosing the present state of the organization and defining the desired future state. Three steps were key to this transitional management. First, we established an advisory committee, which represented all hierarchical levels of the organization, to help with the communication process and generally to keep us on track. Second, we conducted a two-day, off-site meeting with the top forty managers of the organization to define the desired state for their organization and to plan the specific and necessary steps for reaching that future condition. This was followed by assisting individual units in planning and implementing activities that helped them determine more specifically what their desired state should be. During the transitional period, it is often wise to try a new plan on a pilot basis—a different incentive system, for example—to see how

313

workable and appropriate it will be before actually making a permanent change. This is one of the primary purposes for having a transitional period—to try things before making a more permanent move. Finally, we insisted that we be referred to as organizational consultants, not change agents. Although reference is occasionally made to *change agent* as synonymous with *OD consultant* in the organization development literature (Tichy 1974), my colleague and I wanted to be sure the president understood that he was the primary agent of change and the one most responsible for managing the overall organization development effort. Our role was to help him and others in the organization to plan and bring about the change. Thus, our expertise was primarily for *process*. We provided (1) models for mapping the organizational terrain and for facilitating an orderly management of change; (2) design and structure for meetings and events that would insure involvement of organization members in making decisions that would directly affect them, thereby gaining commitment to change rather than resistance; and (3) a plan, which was gradually acted on, for developing in-company expertise in the type of consultation we represented. Although it was somewhat secondary to the activities just described, we also provided *substantive* expertise in the domain of human resource management, such as ideas or plans for career development, management education and development, changes in the reward system, assessing managerial talent, and appraising manager performance. Since the company was unionized, we also offered suggestions for working with the union more effectively.

In this consulting effort with the pharmaceutical company, my colleague and I used several interventions, some that established the directions for change and others that facilitated movement in those directions. Two interventions that helped to establish directions were (1) a phased planning process that was based on the transition model, and (2) a variation of Beckhard's (1967) confrontation meeting, which will be described later in the chapter. This latter intervention was the off-site meeting conducted with the top forty managers of the company. These two interventions actually were used in conjunction with one another. Interventions that helped to promote and support the overall change effort were coaching (see the summary at end of Chapter 12), process consultation, and some elements of team building (see Chapter 13).

We shall now consider interventions that are more directly related to large system change.

Interventions for Large System Change

There are at least two types of interventions associated with large system change—those that are primarily part of and facilitative of the change regardless of the direction and those that establish a particular direction for

314

the change. In the former category, the ones to be considered are open-systems planning, the confrontation meeting, and structural interventions. Interventions that determine direction are grid organization development, survey feedback—when based on Likert's Systems 1, 2, 3, and 4—and quality of work life.

Open-systems Planning

In Chapter 4 I explained open-systems planning in the context of considering an organization from an open system perspective. The model described followed that of Jayaram (1976). Beckhard and Harris (1977) also have a version of open-systems planning. They describe seven phases, which are broader than those of Jayaram's and, of course, are more closely associated with their transition model. The seven phases or steps in open-systems planning according to Beckhard and Harris are:

1. Determine the core mission. This step involves defining the organization's reason for being—a statement or series of statements that goes beyond the organization's goals and objectives.
2. Map the demand system. This step involves listing the groups (such as stockholders) and other organizations (such as government agencies) that make demands on the organization.
3. Map the current response system. This step involves determining the organization's response to each of the demands identified in the previous step.
4. Project the future demand system. This step involves making 3- or 4-year projection of the probable demands on the organization if management does nothing significant in response to current demands.
5. Identify the desired state. This step involves identifying what would be desirable in three or four years.
6. Plan activities for achieving the desired state. This step involves determining the types of activities it will be necessary to carry out in order to reach the desired state.
7. Define cost-effectiveness. This step involves analyzing the social and economic costs of the action plans determined in the previous step.

The process outlined by Beckhard and Harris is similar to the one provided by Jayaram. The difference lies in how the core mission is determined. Beckhard and Harris advocate a process of defining it at the outset—as the first step. In the process outlined by Jayaram, the core mission as currently defined is determined first by mapping the external and internal demands. The organization's reason for being is determined by its responses to these demands. The core mission in the desired state may be the same or different,

315

depending on how the organization members react to their thoughts, opinions, and feelings about the current mission. In the case example described in Chapter 4, the members of the food-management company were surprised and appalled at what their core mission turned out to be (efficient production of garbage) when they had gone through the demand-identification process. Their core mission determination for the desired state was very different. The advantage of identifying the organization's core mission by the Jayaram process is that, once dissatisfaction with the current mission is clearly illustrated, motivation is generated to do something about changing it. Beginning by identifying the desired core mission will establish the direction for change but runs the risk of not being clear about the dissatisfaction organization members are experiencing with the current state. Regardless of this relatively minor difference, an open-systems planning intervention can be highly useful for the initial stages of an OD effort.

The Confrontation Meeting

This intervention, developed by Beckhard (1967), is a relatively brief (one-day) meeting designed for an entire management group, regardless of size, to come together to *confront* problems. It follows a six-step format:

1. Climate setting
2. Information collecting
3. Information sharing
4. Priority setting and group action planning
5. Immediate follow-up by top team
6. Progress review

The series of activities provides a quick and reliable way for the organization to identify problems and develop corrective action. My colleague and I used a version of the confrontation meeting in our work with the top forty managers of the pharmaceutical company.

Structural Interventions

For total system change, structural modifications are the most common interventions. Most often these changes in structure are not within an overall OD effort. When a structural change is planned as part of an OD effort, however, the new design is more likely to work because many people are involved in planning the change.

Structural change may be the most important intervention for affecting organizational behavior, because such important dimensions of organizational dynamics as authority, control mechanisms, and reward and com-

316

munication systems are tied directly to structure. Kanter (1977) has argued persuasively that organizational power lies within structures.

Structure is manifested in various forms. The most common form, of course, is the design of the organization's authority and responsibility structure. Another form involves the organization's physical settings. Steele (1973) has shown the relationship between an employee's physical environment in the organization—work flow layout in a plant, office arrangements, and the like—and the person's behavior. He has also provided the OD practitioner with ways of diagnosing and intervening in the physical aspects of organization members' environments.

Most changes in organizational design concern the authority and responsibility structure. The rule of thumb for changing structure is that form follows function, that the nature of the work should determine the structure for authority and responsibility. Since different organizations perform different work, it follows that there is no single, best way to design an organization—although the prevailing design for centuries has been the hierarchical form based on that used by military organizations and the Catholic Church.

Three primary forms of organizational design have evolved (Chandler 1962). The *functionally designed* organization operates according to the organization's major functions, such as production, R&D, marketing, personnel, and finance. The organizational case explained in Chapter 1, the Acme Chemical case described in Chapter 13, and the pharmaceutical company example used earlier in this chapter all illustrate functionally designed organizations.

A second major form of organizational design is a *product-, program-,* or *mission-based* structure. When an organization has a variety of products, programs, or missions, it tends to organize accordingly. Instead of managers of functions, there are managers of products, and so forth. Authority is usually more decentralized in this form of organization than in the functional form.

The third major form, the *matrix* design, is a combination of the other two in which an attempt is made to capitalize on the advantages of both—the efficiency and maintenance of specialties within the functional design and the decentralized authority to respond quickly to market demands that is inherent within the product design. Thus, the matrix design is both a centralized and a decentralized structure. As Exhibit 15.2 shows, in a matrix design, organization members belong to a product-, program-, or mission-oriented subsystem and also to a functional organization. As the exhibit illustrates, some individuals have two bosses. Davis and Lawrence (1977) have depicted the matrix in the shape of a diamond to show that functional heads and product heads have equal power. With authority simultaneously decentralized and centralized, overall power in the organization is more diffuse than it is in the other two designs, and conflict is more common in the matrix organization. Beer (1980) has summarized the strengths and weaknesses of these three

317

EXHIBIT 15.2
A Matrix Organization Structure

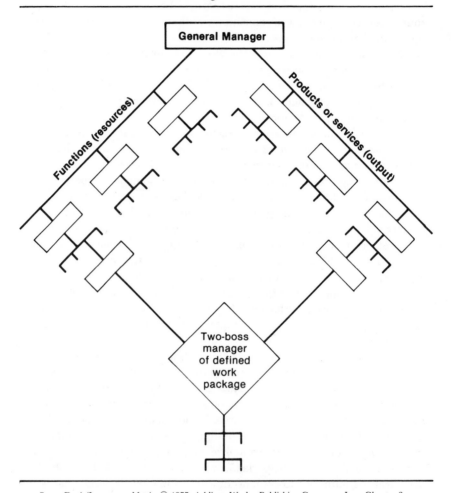

General Manager

Functions (resources)

Products or services (output)

Two-boss
manager
of defined
work
package

Source: Davis/Lawrence, *Matrix,* © 1977, Addison-Wesley Publishing Company, Inc., Chapter 2, page 22, Figure 2.1, "Example of a Matrix Design." Reprinted with permission.

designs succintly by comparing and evaluating them across six different variables: environment, strategy, information-processing capacity, capacity for shared resources, capacity for diversity in mission focus, and difficulties in implementation. Exhibit 15.3 gives his summary of these strengths and weaknesses.

Lawrence and Lorsch (1969) and Galbraith (1977) have expanded the notion of form following function and have provided considerable detail about the functional and environmental contingencies for determining the ap-

318

EXHIBIT 15.3

Strengths and Weaknesses of Different Organizational Forms

Organizational form	Environment	Strategy	Variables to be considered in evaluating alternative forms			
			Information-processing capacity	Capacity for shared resources	Capacity for diversity in mission focus	Difficulties in implementation
Functional	Effective in certain and stable routine	Defend through cost-effectiveness	Low	Not applicable	Not applicable	Low
Decentralized product organization	Effective in uncertain or dynamic complex	Grow through diversification (prospector)	Moderate	Low	High	Moderate
Matrix	Effective in uncertain or dynamic complex	Mix of efficiency and growth strategies	High	High	High	High

Source: M. Beer, *Organization Change and Development: A Systems View* (Santa Monica: Goodyear, 1980), p. 163. Reprinted by permission.

319

propriate form. (Lawrence and Lorsch's ideas and framework are summarized in Chapter 2.)

Other forms of structural intervention are the collateral organization (Zand 1974) and the parallel organization, developed by Carlson at General Motors (Miller 1978) and further elaborated by Stein and Kanter (1980). These forms of organization are supplemental structures that coexist with the formal organization. They are created to deal with problems that the formal structure is not designed to handle or is too cumbersome or conflict-prone to deal with efficiently and effectively. In these collateral and parallel organizations, which may be temporary or fairly permanent, different norms about authority and decision making usually prevail. Although these supplemental forms have not been used widely (the QC circle may be a special case), there is evidence that they affect performance positively.

Grid Organization Development

This form of intervention was explained in Chapter 9. It was covered in that chapter because grid OD encompasses all phases of a change effort, not just intervention (Blake and Mouton 1971). It is mentioned again here because it is a total system approach.

Beer (1980) has provided an excellent evaluation of grid OD. He cites nine strengths and six problems. According to Beer, some of grid OD's most important strengths are as follows:

1. It provides a theory of behavior—the managerial grid.
2. It integrates individual and group development through the grid seminar and the team development phase.
3. Intergroup interventions follow group development; that is, skills within groups have a chance to be developed before intergroup conflict is dealt with.
4. Organization development starts at the top.
5. Diagnosis is emphasized.
6. Strategy and structure are examined.
7. Involvement leads to commitment, and organization members share in the decisions for change.
8. It reduces dependence on consultants.
9. Multiple interventions are used.

The six problems that Beer identifies are as follows:

1. Beer questions the normative stance that one culture is best for all organizations. He believes that "a company's approach to management should depend on the nature of its business, tasks, and people" (Beer 1980, p. 209).

320

2. Beer questions the assumption that all organizations should develop adaptive human resources for two reasons:

> First, not all organizations can expect the same rate of change in their future environment. Investment in organizational health should be dependent on a forecast of the need for it as well as on a conscious choice that organizational growth rather than decline is desirable. Second, adaptiveness may also be obtained by maintaining liquid financial resources which allow diversification through acquisition. This strategy for adaptation does not require adaptive human resources throughout the organization'' (Beer 1980, pp. 209–10).

3. Grid OD is based on a long-term educative strategy, but pressing problems in an organization may not wait for everyone to be educated. Significant change, even within an OD framework, can occur much more rapidly than is required for all phases of grid OD (Foltz, Harvey, and McLaughlin 1974).

4. Beer contends that, contrary to grid OD's assumptions, managers do not respond well to standardized, lock-step programs.

5. One sequence of intervention is not necessarily appropriate for all organizations, as grid OD maintains. Beer makes a case for organic, tailor-made programs of change, since early interventions are likely to cause unexpected consequences. The more flexible the OD program is, the more readily an intervention can respond to immediate need.

6. Grid OD assumes that organization change begins with attitude change. There is evidence to the contrary, or at least as strong a case can be made that behavioral change can precede attitudinal change (Porter, Lawler, and Hackman 1975).

The fundamental difference between grid OD and the kind of OD espoused in this book and in Beer's (1980) is the issue of standardization. Blake and Mouton (1971) argue that their standardized approach eliminates consultant bias and error, and they do have a point. A more organic approach, however, though relying heavily on the skill of an OD practitioner, can respond to client need more readily and flexibly.

Survey Feedback

This intervention is like the grid approach in that it encompasses both diagnosis and intervention and is standardized and follows a set pattern of activities. The survey feedback approach, developed by Likert and his colleagues, especially Floyd Mann, at the Survey Research Center of the University of Michigan in the 1950s, uses a standardized questionnaire for data collection. The collective responses to this questionnaire are reported back to work and managerial teams within the organization. These teams analyze and interpret the data and then plan action steps to deal with problems that have been identified. This approach was given support as an effec-

321

tive technique for organizational change when Mann (1957) found that more change occurred when employees received feedback on their responses to a survey than when they did not receive the results. He also found that the extent of change among those received feedback was mediated by the degree of involvement these employees had with their managers in planning the change; the more involvement there was, the greater the amount of change.

The steps in survey feedback are as follows:

1. Top management is involved. This is particularly important, since the questionnaire is based on Likert's model (Systems 1, 2, 3, and 4) and, if top management doesn't agree to the direction of change that is tied to the model, the approach will not work.

2. The questionnaire (Taylor and Bowers 1972) is administered to all members of the target organization.

3. The results of the questionnaire responses are analyzed by an outside source—the Institute for Social Research at the University of Michigan.

4. Data are reported back to individual managers, starting at the top. In a cascading fashion, the data are then reported back to each level of management.

5. After the managers are familiar with the data, they hold meetings with their subordinates to discuss the results, to interpret their own group's results, and to plan action steps for solving the identified problems. Finally, they make plans for introducing the data to the next lower level of organization members. An OD practitioner works with these groups to facilitate the process of their meetings. In addition to Mann's (1957) earlier findings, there is more recent evidence that the survey feedback approach is effective (Bowers 1973), and there are forms other than the one conducted by the University of Michigan people (Miles et al. 1969).

The major advantage of the survey feedback approach is that it is standardized and thus there is less room for consultant error. The major disadvantage is its relative inflexibility as a process of change.

It should be noted, however, that use of a survey feedback intervention does not have to be linked to a particular normative model or theory. The intervention can be used in a more open-ended, organic fashion (Miles et al. 1969).

Quality of Work Life (QWL)

This intervention is directional, in that the goal for change is to humanize the work place—to improve working conditions, such as physical facilities and equipment; to improve human relationships, especially those between boss and subordinate; and to give employees more voice in decisions that directly affect them.

At present, the so-called QWL movement is very popular in the United

States, particularly in manufacturing organizations. As an intervention, it is typically employed in a piecemeal manner and is rarely associated with large system change. One exception is the effort that has been taking place over the last decade in General Motors. As practiced in that organization, QWL approaches a systemwide change effort. Howard Carlson, an internal consultant and researcher at General Motors, with colleague D. L. Landen, has developed a model of QWL to guide their effort (Carlson 1980; Landen 1977).

Quality of work life was defined by Walton (1973) as a process for humanizing the work place. Carlson (1980) states that QWL is both a goal and an ongoing process for achieving the goal:

> As a goal, QWL is the commitment of any organization to work improvement: the creation of more involving, satisfying, and effective jobs and work environments for people at all levels of the organization. As a process, QWL calls for efforts to realize this goal through the active involvement of people throughout the organization. (p. 83)

Carlson also states that QWL is a philosophy of management with the active support of the union (Bluestone 1978).

In some respects, QWL is nothing more than an elaborate definition of organization development. In practice, there is hardly a difference. The value of QWL to OD has been its emphasis on the shop-floor level, not exclusively with management. The value of OD to the QWL movement has been the availability of social technology for organizational change.

In General Motors, the philosophy of QWL encompasses all levels of the organization, and a QWL survey is administered at least annually throughout all parts of the system. Changes in QWL survey results for the various subsystems are reflected in a manager's performance appraisal. Thus, the QWL effort in General Motors is tied directly to the managerial reward system. In this case, at least a second-order change objective is sought.

Although Carlson (1980) subsumes OD within his model for QWL, the similarities of the two are far greater than any of the differences. In some organizations QWL has become a new label for other activities because OD has fallen into bad repute. Whatever the label, the ultimate objectives of OD and QWL remain the same.

Summary

In this chapter we have considered orders, phases, and interventions for large system change. Beckhard and Harris's (1977) transition model provides the most reasonable and sensible approach. The pharmaceutical company example provided a case study of a consultative effort based on this model.

323

Interventions that fit nicely within the transition model and are therefore more organic include open-systems planning, the confrontation meeting, and some structural changes.

Grid organization development, survey feedback, and quality of work life are special cases of large system interventions, since they are highly standardized (at least the first two are) and are associated with a particular direction for change—toward more participative management and, in the case of QWL, toward more humanism in the work place. A QWL intervention may be a total system change effort, as in the approach at General Motors. Although there are some differences in roots and some practices of OD and QWL, for all practical purposes they are the same in terms of both objectives and methodology.

With this chapter we conclude Part IV, dealing with interventions in OD practice. We have considered these interventions first in terms of theories and models and then according to level of intervention—from individual to group to intergroup and finally to large system. Theories and models of interventions were examined to help establish criteria for intervening and choosing types of interventions. The various levels and orders of intervention all have their place in leading to and providing for eventual systemwide change.

PART V

THE FIELD OF
ORGANIZATION DEVELOPMENT

In the three remaining chapters we examine the final phase of an organization development effort—evaluation; the OD practitioner as a consultant and as a person; and, again, the field of OD. We considered organization development as a field of practice based on research and theory in Chapter 2. We will complete the book by considering OD as a field again, this time in terms of (1) what we know about its effectiveness as a technique for organizational change, (2) the people who serve as consultants in the field, and (3) an assessment of OD's present status and speculation about its future.

In Chapter 16 we consider issues involved in evaluating OD, guidelines for conducting an effective OD evaluation, and the status of OD from the perspective of research that has been conducted to determine its impact.

Chapter 17 is devoted to the OD practitioner both in terms of role and function and in terms of the personal aspects and characteristics of one who serves as an OD consultant. Different roles are considered according to how directive or nondirective the consultant might be. Being an OD consultant requires certain abilities and related personal characteristics, which are defined according to individuals' experience in the field. The chapter concludes with a discussion of how one might become an OD practitioner.

In the final chapter we attempt to gain some perspective on organization development by examining where the field has been, where it appears to be currently, and where it should be going. This concluding chapter is an attempt to assess the field of OD realistically and thereby to gain perspective.

CHAPTER 16

Evaluating Organization
Development Efforts

With this chapter we complete the seven phases of organization development consultation. We have considered each of the other six phases—entry, contracting, diagnosis, feedback, planning, and intervention. Evaluation is the final phase, but, as noted earlier, that does not mean that it begins only after an intervention has occurred. Ideally it should begin at the contract stage and then become a part of diagnosis, coupled with the data-collection process. Learning about how the OD effort is going can also become an intervention itself, in that as evaluative information becomes known, actions that might not otherwise occur may be taken. Most important is the fact that evaluative information provides data for determining the next steps in an OD effort.

We shall first cover evaluation as the seventh phase of OD and then consider evaluation in terms of research conducted on organization development as a technique for organizational change. The chapter is thus divided into two major parts. The first part, evaluation as a phase of OD practice, examines (1) some of the primary oppositions to conducting this phase, (2) arguments for conducting an evaluation, and (3) guidelines for conducting an evaluation. The second part consists of (1) an exploration of the central issues regarding research in the field of organization development and (2) some issues that must be addressed in order to increase research effectiveness.

Evaluation as a Phase of Organization Development

The evaluation phase of OD practice can be compared to an annual physical examination—everyone agrees that it should be done, but no one, except a highly motivated researcher, wants to go to the trouble and expense of making it happen. We shall examine the pressures opposed to evaluation and then some reasons and guidelines for going ahead with this phase.

Pressures Opposed to Evaluation

There are at least four sets of people involved in or related to OD evaluation: the manager or decision maker, the organization members who are directly involved in the OD process (the manager or decision maker may or may not be in this process), the OD consultant, and the evaluation researcher. There are pressures on each of these categories of people to ignore evaluation.

THE MANAGER OR DECISION MAKER   Managers want results. If interventions in an OD effort are accompanied by change in certain organizational areas that are important to managers—such as increased profits, decreased absenteeism, or increased morale—that is often all that is necessary for a manager to choose to continue with OD or to move on to other things. As Beer (1980) notes: "Unfortunately, managers typically assume that the effects of OD on these indices will be self-evident and they lose sight of the complexity of factors that might cause change in them" (p. 246). Managers want to know *if* it works, not *why* it works. Such managers are usually found in fast-moving, marketing-oriented organizations, where short-term results are rewarded. There are other types of managers, however.

Managers in highly technical, scientific organizations may take the opposite stance. They may demand proof—hard empirical evidence—before they will decide. For these managers, a quasi-experimental design, with perceptual data as the mainstay, may strike them as soft, lacking in objectivity and scientific rigor. These managers might argue that, unless you can measure the consequences of an organization development effort in a rigorous, scientific manner, an evaluation is not worth doing. They might even argue that OD itself is not worthwhile, since so much is dependent on techniques that are nonscientific.

Opposition to evaluation research from managers who are in key decision-making roles may take either extreme: evaluation research is not necessary because the outcomes are self-evident or because the effects of OD cannot be measured scientifically. Other reasons for opposition from managers could be (1) the cost involved, (2) the amount of extra time it will take, or (3) the undesirability of an outsider coming in to do research on them.

THE ORGANIZATION MEMBERS INVOLVED IN THE OD EFFORT   Opposition from those directly involved in the OD process may take the same forms as those mentioned with respect to the managers or decision makers. In addition to those possible if not highly potential forms of opposition, organization members may complain about the time it will take for them to answer the questionnaires, for example, when this time could be utilized more productively in getting on with further aspects of the OD effort. Stopping to fill out forms, to answer interview questions, or to document activities and events

328

not only takes valuable time, but it may reduce the potential momentum of the change that is being attempted. They also might argue that the research staff is likely to be more beneficial to the goals of the researcher than to the goals of the organization's change effort.

THE OD CONSULTANT   The OD consultant is likely to want an evaluation study but for reasons that differ from those of the manager or decision maker. Managers are interested in OD's impact on outcomes—profits, turnover, costs, productivity—whereas OD consultants may be more interested in process—the impact that OD may have on behavior, attitudes, organizational procedures, changes in authority relationships, and the like. A study by Porras and Wilkens (1980) indicates that many OD consultants may be disappointed with evaluation research on organization development. Porras and Wilkens found that OD in a large organization had a positive impact on outcomes, such as unit performance, but a negative consequence for attitudinal and behavioral variables that described organizational and individual processes. As Porras and Wilkens noted, these latter, unexpected negative findings may reflect a beta change, not an alpha change (Golembiewski, Billingsley, and Yeager 1976), since their measures of attitudes and behavior were through self-report questionnaires whereas their measures of unit performance came from company records. These different types of changes are covered in the second part of this chapter.

The point here is not that OD consultants are uninterested in or opposed to determining OD's impact on outcomes but that certain factors may be more important to the consultant as a professional. According to Beer (1980): "OD specialists are more interested in data that will help them intervene more effectively now and in the future" (p. 246). Thus, with this potential difference in priorities, OD consultants and managers may consider one another opposed to evaluation research, when in reality they may only have different priorities or values about the goals of a research effort.

THE EVALUATION RESEARCHER   The researcher is interested in both outcome and process measures, but his or her objectives for the use of the research results may differ from those of the other three groups of people concerned with an OD effort. The researcher is often more interested in contributing to the body of knowledge concerning organizations as changing systems or the effectiveness of organization development as a field than in providing information for the organization's decision makers. This difference in objectives or priorities can cause problems with planning and implementing an evaluation research effort, but opposition on the part of a researcher toward conducting an evaluation study is likely to occur for another reason. Most researchers are trained according to the traditional scientific method of research, which involves distancing oneself from and controlling the subjects of the research (client), not collaborating with them. Researchers are typically trained according to the mechanistic approach, whereas effective OD evaluation research calls for an organic approach.

Reasons for Conducting Evaluation Research

The forces that oppose evaluative research of an organization development effort are formidable and should not be dismissed lightly, but there are also compelling reasons for conducting evaluative research.

Briefly, the primary arguments for an evaluative research study of an OD effort are as follows:

1. An evaluation forces the definition of the change objectives.
2. An evaluation forces the clarification of the change outcomes that are expected.
3. An evaluation forces the clarification of how these change outcomes are to be measured.
4. An evaluation forces specificity with respect to how certain procedures, events, and activities will be implemented.
5. An evaluation helps to signal many of the problems and obstacles to be anticipated in the OD effort.
6. An evaluation facilitates planning for next steps and stages of organizational improvement and development.

As we know from system theory, particularly as applied to organizations, there may be no such thing as a single cause for a single effect. Systematic evaluation will provide many of the casual answers for what occurs and has occurred in organizations. Generally, but perhaps most importantly, evaluation forces clarity about what *effectiveness* is for an organization.

Guidelines for Conducting Evaluation Research

There are four general guidelines worthy of consideration in conducting an evaluation of an organization development effort. These guidelines are stated here in order of design and activity and in the form of admonitions for an effective evaluation.

First, the researcher should collaborate with all the parties involved (managers, organization members, and OD consultants) in the planning of the evaluative endeavor; otherwise, the needs of these respective groups will not be met (Alderfer 1977). This collaboration should begin at the contracting phase of the OD effort and be carried into the diagnostic phase so that the model for diagnosis will be the same as that for evaluation, or at least the two will be in agreement and will harmonize with one another. For an example of how an evaluative research project can be done collaboratively with the client, see Nadler, Mirvis, and Cammann (1976).

Second, The researcher should develop a clear research strategy, which will help to determine what should be evaluated. Referring to Beckhard and Harris (1977) as well as to his own work, Beer (1980) lists four possible strategies:

1. Evaluation of total system effectiveness, efficiency, and health—whether the organization as a whole has changed
2. Evaluation of attitudes toward the change process itself—how organization members feel about the way changes have been managed
3. Evaluation of a specific intervention—such as team building or some structural change
4. Evaluation of performance outcomes—profits, sales, turnover, productivity, and so forth

These strategies need not be mutually exclusive; one or more could be used. To help in the strategy decision, Beer provides a table that relates the four research strategies with the various goals of an evaluation (see Exhibit 16.1).

Beer's strategies and purposes of evaluation are oriented toward organization development per se, whereas other models for determining organizational effectiveness are broader (Cameron 1980). These differences should be considered in planning the research strategy, and joint decisions between the

EXHIBIT 16.1

The Relationship Between Strategy and Purpose of Evaluation

	Research strategies			
Purpose of evaluation	Evaluation of total system functioning	Evaluation of interventions	Evaluation of change process	Evaluation of performance outcomes
Assessing OD impact on the target unit	X			X
Modifying change strategy	X	X	X	
Selling OD to upper levels				X
Upgrading intervention skills and methods (professional practice)		X	X	
Scientific knowledge	X	X	X	X

Source: M. Beer, *Organization Change and Development: A Systems View* (Santa Monica: Goodyear, 1980). Reprinted by permission.

331

researcher and client should be made at the contracting stage. Part of the strategy is determining how pervasive the research effort should be—whether we are interested in overall organizational effectiveness, as in Beer's first strategy and Cameron's (1980) suggestions, some of the more specific aspects of OD as a change technique.

Third, the research design should be tied to the diagnostic model (see the first guideline) and should be realistic. By realistic, I mean that the evaluation research should be designed in light of organization contingencies. Control groups are difficult if not impossible to arrange, so, for adequate control, the design should be quasi-experimental, with a phased or time-series component. To learn more about evaluation research in general, consider the work of Weiss (1972); for more on research designs for organizational assessment in particular, recent works by Lawler, Nadler, and Cammann (1980) and Van de Ven and Ferry (1980) are noteworthy.

Fourth, the researcher should provide adequate methods for collecting and analyzing data. These methods should (1) help distinguish among alpha, beta, and gamma changes; (2) provide valid information; (3) be tied to a model or theory; and (4) be useful to the client in the final analysis.

In a broader context, Lawler, Nadler, and Camman (1980) have established a set of criteria that helps determine the adequacy of any organizational assessment effort. They include criteria for determining the adequacy of the methods for data collection, which makes their broader model worthy of coverage here. Lawler, Nadler, and Cammann note that the effectiveness of organizational assessment can be determined in terms of its *accuracy of description*—how well the data reflect the functioning of the organization—and in terms of its *usefulness* for the client. Accuracy of description has two parts: adequacy of the information-collection methods and adequacy of the organizational assessment models. Usefulness to the client is determined in terms of salience of the assessment domain and adequacy of the reporting process. Exhibit 16.2 summarizes their criteria, which we shall now briefly consider.

ADEQUACY OF INFORMATION-COLLECTION METHODS   This adequacy is determined by four subcriteria. *Sensitivity* is the extent to which measurement instruments are able to distinguish among objectives that are considered different. *Reliability* is the constancy and consistency of results from measurement instruments as they are used over time. *Convergent validity* is the extent to which different measurement instruments that are designed to measure the same thing do indeed produce similar results under similar conditions. *Discriminant validity* is the extent to which measurement instruments that are designed to measure different things do indeed produce different results. The more the researchers' measurement instruments meet the criteria for sen-

EXHIBIT 16.2

Criteria for Effectiveness of Organizational Assessment Efforts

Accuracy of description		Usefulness to client groups	
Adequacy of information-collection methods	Adequacy of organizational assessment models	Salience of assessment domain	Adequacy of reporting process
Sensitivity	Predictive ability of models	Identification of potential clients	Method of reporting
Reliability			
	Comparative power of prediction relative to other models	Creation of mutual influence between clients and researchers	Completeness of reporting
Convergent validity			
Discriminant validity			Acceptance of results

Source: Organizational Assessment: Perspectives on the Measurement of Organizational Behavior and the Quality of Work Life by E. E. Lawler III, D. A. Nadler, and C. Cammann, copyright © 1980 by Wiley-Interscience. Reprinted by permission of John Wiley & Sons, Inc.

sitivity, reliability, and ability, the more effective the evaluation is likely to be.

ADEQUACY OF ASSESSMENT MODELS   Lawler, Nadler, and Camman (1980) note that "the collection of valid information does not, by itself, suffice to ensure accurate descriptions of an organization. Assessors must also know what information to collect and how different pieces of information relate to each other" (p. 15). By *predictive ability,* they mean how well the model will predict observed relationships among the characteristics of organizational functioning that are assessed both at the time of evaluation and for the future. By *comparative power,* they mean how well the model will predict relationships as compared with other models that have already proved their predictive abilities. See Chapter 9 for coverage of some of these models.

USEFULNESS OF ASSESSMENT RESULTS   Lawler, Nadler, and Cammann refer to *salience of assessment domain* and *adequacy of reporting process.* By the former criterion, they mean the degree of importance of the factors assessed for the client. The more the client is involved in the decision-making process for determining these factors at the outset, of course, the more salient they will be. Adequacy of reporting is simply the effectiveness with which the evaluation results are communicated to the client, including the method chosen, the completeness of the report, and the degree of acceptance of the results by the client.

333

Summary

These criteria for measurement instruments, models, and usefulness to the client should prove useful for the researcher in planning the details of the evaluation effort. The four overall guidelines for (1) relationship with the client, (2) research strategy, (3) research design, and (4) adequacy of methods should also prove useful for general planning. These guidelines and criteria should be considered by the researcher before the initial meeting with the client, but this consideration should be for providing the client with knowledge and expertise about choices to be made, not for imposing a plan and method of research on the client.

We now turn from considering evaluation as a phase of an OD effort to evaluating organization development as a technique for organizational change—that is, does it work?

Evaluating the Effectiveness of Organization Development

Our objective in this second part of the chapter is to evaluate OD as a technique for organizational change and to explore some of the major issues regarding OD research.

From a survey of sixty-three organizations regarding their knowledge and use of organization development, Heisler (1975) found, among other things, that the major criticism of OD efforts was the difficulty in evaluating their effectiveness. There is evidence, however, that OD does indeed work. French and Bell (1978), for example, selected nine studies that they considered supportive of OD's effectiveness:

1. "Breakthrough in Organization Development" (Blake et al. 1964);
2. *Management by Participation* (Marrow, Bowers, and Seashore 1967);
3. "Short- and Long-Range Effects of Team Development Effort" (Beckhard and Lake 1971);
4. "Eclectic Approach to Organizational Development" (Huse and Beer 1971);
5. "Participative Decision Making: An Experimental Study in a Hospital" (Bragg and Andrews 1973);
6. "OD Techniques and Their Results in 23 Organizations" (Bowers 1973);
7. "Expectation Effects in Organizational Change" (King 1974);
8. "Effects of Organizational Diagnosis and Intervention on Blue-Collar Blues" (Hautaluoma and Gavin 1975); and
9. "Organization Development and Change in Organizational Performance" (Kimberly and Nielsen 1975).

Other studies could be included, such as Golembiewski, Hilles, and Kagno (1974); perhaps these ten are proof enough that there is supportive evidence for the efficacy of OD.

There are problems, however, and much has been written about them (King, Sherwood, and Manning 1978; Morrison 1978; Porras 1979; Porras and Patterson 1979). We shall now consider the nature of some of these problems.

Research Issues in Evaluating OD Efforts

The overriding issue in OD evaluation is purpose—whether the research effort is evaluation or knowledge generation, whether it is for the benefit of the client or the social scientist. Since we are discussing *evaluation,* that should be the obvious concern, not scientific generation of knowledge; but the assessment methodology—how we collect and analyze our information for evaluative purposes—is based on the traditional scientific method. We control and manipulate some independent variables, make some interventions, and see if any difference occurs with respect to some dependent variables. We decide to use team building as an intervention, for example, and we collect information (dependent variable) to see if it made any difference. We might use a questionnaire to ask team members if they feel more satisfied with and committed to the team, and we might determine if the team's work performance increases after the team building effort has occurred. Even if our data showed increased satisfaction, commitment, and work performance, it would be difficult to demonstrate that the team building intervention had *caused* these outcomes unless we had also collected data from a matched control group—a similar team for which no team building had been done—unless we had collected data from both teams before *and* after the team building effort, and unless we had collected these two sets of data at essentially the same time. Another critical factor in this evaluation effort would be the people who collect and analyze the data. Numerous studies have shown that the researcher can affect the outcome (Rosenthal 1976). This brings up the question of objectivity. To be scientific, or objective, the researcher should be someone other than the team building consultant or the organization members involved. Argyris (1970) has argued, however, that, the more scientific the evaluation is, the less it is likely to be relevant to and therefore used by the client. He states that traditional scientific methods of evaluation (his term is "mechanistic") "tend to create primarily dependent and submissive roles for the clients and provide them with little responsibility; therefore, the clients have low feelings of essentiality in the program (except when they fulfill the request of the professionals)" (Argyris 1970, p. 105). To overcome these problems of evaluation research, Argyris argues that an organic approach is required, one that involves the client more directly in decisions about what

335

data to collect and how to collect them. Exhibit 16.3 is Argyris's summary of the contrast between a mechanistic and an organic approach to evaluation research.

If the research to be done is evaluative, and if the data are to be used by the client for further decision-making purposes, then the client should be involved in the research process itself, since this involvement will lead to more valid data and increased likelihood that the data will be used. This involvement is not scientific in the strict sense of the word, but our major concern and purpose is the collection and analysis of valid information. So-called scientific

EXHIBIT 16.3

A Comparison of Mechanistic and Organic Research

Mechanistically oriented research	Organistically oriented research
1. The interventionist takes the most prominent role in defining the goals of the program.	1. The subjects participate in defining goals, confirming and disconfirming, and modifying or adding to those goals defined by the professionals.
2. The interventionist assumes that his relationship of being strictly professional cannot be influenced by the clients. He maintains his power of expertise and therefore keeps a professional distance from the clients.	2. The interventionist realizes that, in addition to being a professional, he is a stranger in the institution. Subjects should be encouraged to confront and test their relationship with him. His power over the subjects, due to his professional competence, is equalized by his encouraging them to question him and the entire program.
3. The amount of client participation in the entire project is controlled by the interventionist.	3. The amount of participation is influenced by the subject and the interventionist.
4. The interventionist depends upon the clients' need to be helped or need to cooperate as being the basis for their involvement. He expects clients to be used as information givers.	4. The interventionist depends upon the clients' need to be helped for encouraging them to control and define the program so that they become internally involved and feel that they are as responsible as the interventionist.
5. If participation is encouraged, it tends to be skin-deep, designed to keep the subjects "happy."	5. Participation is encouraged in terms of instrument design, research methods, and change strategy.
6. The costs and rewards of the change program are defined primarily by the interventionist.	6. The costs and rewards of the change program are defined by the clients and the interventionist.
7. The feedback to subjects is designed to inform them how much the diagnostician learned about the system, as well as how professionally competent the diagnosis was.	7. The feedback to subjects is designed to unfreeze them, as well as to help them develop more effective interpersonal relations and group processes.

Source: C. Argyris, *Intervention Theory and Method: A Behavioral Science View,* © 1970, Addison-Wesley Publishing Company, Inc., Chapter 5, pp. 104–105. Reprinted with permission.

336

research in an organizational setting may generate invalid data (Argyris 1968).

To be more specific, we shall now examine some primary research issues and problems associated with the evaluation of an organization development effort. The issues and problems are addressed in the form of six questions, which are not necessarily mutually exclusive.

1. WHAT IS ORGANIZATIONAL EFFECTIVENESS?   In general, the goal of an OD effort is to improve the organization, to make it more effective, whether the effort is with a large, total system or with a division—a subsystem of a larger organization. It is not a simple matter to define effectiveness (Goodman and Pennings 1980) or to get people to agree on a definition. Cameron (1980) points out that there are at least four different criteria for organizational effectiveness and that these criteria differ significantly from one organization to another. The differences are particularly apparent when comparing profit-making with nonprofit organizations. The four criteria or models are as follows:

> The goal model: Organizational effectiveness is defined in terms of the extent to which the organization accomplishes its goals.
>
> The system resource model: Effectiveness is equated with the ability to acquire needed resources.
>
> The process model: Effectiveness is defined in terms of how smoothly the organization functions, especially the degree of absence of internal strain in the organization.
>
> The strategic constituencies model: Effectiveness is determined by the extent to which the organization satisfies all its strategic constituencies—special interest groups.

As Cameron notes, these models or definitions of effectiveness may be useful or inappropriate, depending on the type of organization and the public or market it tries to serve. The goal model may be best when organizational goals are clear and consensual, the system resource model when inputs are clearly tied to outputs, the process model when there is a clear connection between internal organizational processes and primary tasks, and the strategic constituencies model when external special interest groups have considerable influence on what the organization does or is supposed to do. Not all organizations fit neatly into one or more of these models, however. Cameron suggests, therefore, that evaluative researchers raise six critical questions. He contends that answers to these questions will help in determining the right criteria for evaluating an organzation's effectiveness. Cameron's six critical questions for the organizational evaluative researcher are as follows:

1. What domain of activity is the focus? Effectiveness in one domain may militate against effectiveness in another. A high degree of effectiveness in marketing, for example, could have negative consequences for manufacturing or for R&D.

2. Which constituencies' points of view are being considered? Effectiveness for one group may be ineffectiveness for another. In a university, for example, effectiveness for students is excellent teaching and learning conditions. For the faculty who provide this excellence, however, the time required may decrease their research effort and thus militate against their effectiveness as scholars—yet another critical dimension of a university's effectiveness.

3. What level of analysis is to be used? Effectiveness on the individual or team level, for example, may produce ineffectiveness on the organizational level.

4. What time frame is to be used? Effectiveness criteria change over time; short-term and long-term effectiveness are not necessarily the same. Short-term criteria for a business may be profits, but long-term criteria could be something else, such as becoming a multinational corporation, that might reduce short-term effectiveness.

5. What types of data are to be used? Organizational records may provide different results for effectiveness than perceptual data gathered from organization members or constituencies (Porras and Wilkens 1980).

6. What referent is to be used? There are at least five available referents: comparative evaluations (Is the organization better than its competitors?); normative evaluations (Is the organization effective compared with some ideal model?); goal-centered evaluation (Did the organization reach its goals?); improvement evaluation (Did the organization improve over past performance?); and trait evaluation (Does the organization possess traits that are indicative of effective organizations?).

It should thus be apparent that determining organizational effectiveness is not simple. Obtaining answers to Cameron's six questions would certainly help.

2. WHAT IS OD IN THE ORGANIZATION DEVELOPMENT EFFORT? As illustrated in this book, OD is many things, and there are seven major phases in an OD effort. For evaluative research purposes, do we consider all these phases or just the intervention phase? Kahn (1974) stated accurately that at least in the scientific sense, OD is not even a concept: "It is not precisely defined; it is not reducible to specific, uniform, observable behaviors; it does not have a prescribed and verifiable place in a network of logically related concepts, a theory" (Kahn 1974, p. 490). Different OD interventions will also result in different outcomes (Porras 1979). For the practice of OD, the fact that the concept of OD lacks precision is not necessarily a problem unless we consider evaluation a part of the practice. In my opinion, evaluation is part of the prac-

tice, and we do indeed have a problem. Overcoming this problem involves being more precise. The more specific and precise we can be in defining the variety of activities coming under the rubric of OD, the more we will be in a position to evaluate the effectiveness of these activities. A way of increasing this precision is to achieve greater clarity about the remaining four questions.

3. WHAT IS THE INDEPENDENT VARIABLE? In an examination of thirty-eight research studies conducted on various aspects of OD, Pate, Nielsen, and Bacon (1977) reported that they had considerable difficulty in categorizing variables from the studies. They could not be sure whether the independent variable was the OD intervention itself or whether OD was only instrumental in the manipulation of some other independent variable. They took the view that OD is instrumental but does not constitute the independent variable as such. "For example, one might expect introduction of participative decision making (OD intervention) to facilitate worker awareness of the rationale for organizational actions (independent variable), which in turn may increase support for and commitment to those actions (dependent variables)" (Pate, Nielson, and Bacon 1977, pp. 450–51). Their emphasis of this issue is helpful because we can now be clearer about what activities to evaluate specifically. Perhaps one more example will be useful for clarifying this point. Suppose that, as a result of an OD diagnosis, a need for a new organizational structure is determined. Suppose further that a new structure is planned and implemented (OD intervention). This new structure changes authority relationships in that managers lower in the hierarchy now have more delegated authority for decision making. This changed relationship in authority would be the independent variable, and the differences in work performance, such as net profit and turnover, would be the dependent variables.

4. HOW CAN WE CONTROL VARIABLES? As organizations are dynamic systems, this is a question of causal attribution—determining whether the consequences of a change can be attributed to organization development. As noted earlier, the more we can control our research conditions—by having a control condition or control group for comparison, for example—the more we will be able to state with confidence what is cause and what is effect. In dynamic, changing organizations, however, this is almost impossible to do. It is difficult, for example, to persuade a manager to subject his or her organization to a series of time-consuming data-collection activities for the purpose of providing a control group. The manager is likely to ask, "What's in it for us?" It is even more difficult to find an appropriate control group. There are rarely two subsystems within an organization, much less two distinct organizations, that do the same things, have the same types of people, and are managed the same way.

With so much going on in the organizational world and with most of this

339

array of activities being impossible to control, we have what D. T. Campbell and Stanley (1966) refer to as a problem of internal validity—determining whether what we did by way of change made a measurable difference. In the absence of pure control group conditions—the true experimental design for research purposes—Campbell and Stanley have provided what they call quasi-experimental designs. These designs, though not perfect from a research perspective, provide ways for controlling certain conditions so that validity will be enhanced. Their time-series design is a good example. In this design several measures are taken at certain intervals *before* the intervention and several measures are taken at essentially the same intervals *after* the intervention. They diagram this design as follows, where O is the observation (measurement) and X is the experimental treatment or intervention:

$$O_1 O_2 O_3 O_4 \quad X \quad O_5 O_6 O_7 O_8$$

If it can be shown (1) that there are no significant differences among the first four observations, O_1–O_4, (2) that there are significant changes from the first four to O_5, and (3) that there are then no significant differences among O_5–O_8, then the differences that occurred between O_1–O_4 and O_5–O_8 must be a result of X, not merely the passage of time or other variables. Berkowitz (1969) has elaborated on this design in the context of evaluating organization development. The Pate, Nielsen, and Bacon (1977) study showed that most evaluation studies had used a quasi-experimental design for evaluating OD efforts. Thus, Campbell and Stanley's work is highly relevant and useful for OD evaluation.

5. WHAT CHANGED?   Golembiewski, Billingsley, and Yeager (1976) drew distinctions among three types of change, which they labeled alpha, beta, and gamma. *Alpha* change concerns a difference that occurs along some relatively stable dimension of reality. This change is typically a comparative measure before and after an intervention. If comparative measures of trust among team members showed an increase after a team building intervention, for example, then we might conclude that our OD intervention had made a difference. Golembiewski, Billingsley, and Yeager assert that most OD evaluation research designs consist of such before-and-after self-reports.

Suppose, however, that a decrease in trust occurred—or no change at all. One study has shown that, although no decrease in trust occurred, neither did a measurable increase occur as a consequence of team building intervention (Friedlander 1970). Change may have occurred, however. The difference may be what Golembiewski, Billingsley, and Yeager call a *beta* change—a recalibration of the intervals along some constant dimension of reality. As a result of a team building intervention, team members may view trust very differently. Their basis for judging the nature of trust changed, rather than their perception of a simple increase or decrease in trust along some stable continuum.

340

A *gamma* change "involves a redefinition or reconceptualization of some domain, a major change in the perspective or frame of reference within which phenomena are perceived and classified, in what is taken to be relevant in some slice of reality" (Golembiewski, Billingsley, and Yeager 1976, p. 135). This involves change from one state to another. Staying with the example, after the intervention team members might conclude that trust was not a relevant variable in their team building experience. They might believe that the gain in their clarity about roles and responsibilities was the relevant factor and that their improvement as a team had nothing to do with trust.

Thus, selecting the appropriate dependent variable—determining specifically what might change—is not as simple as it might appear. This is especially important when self-report data are used.

6. WHO WILL CONDUCT THE RESEARCH AND WHO WILL USE THE RESULTS? The last issue to be addressed is the people involved in the evaluation effort. To avoid the possibility of a Pygmalion effect and to increase the probability of objectivity, it is best that the researcher be someone other than the OD consultant. Both the researcher and the consultant are interveners into the organization, however, and therefore it is imperative that they collaborate. The researcher needs to know not only the consultant's overall strategy—change goals, targets, and so forth—and what interventions might be used, but also what the consultant's predictions are concerning what should change as a result of the OD effort. The researcher is both a data gatherer and analyzer and a consultant, in the sense that he or she must work directly and collaboratively with the client. In using Argyris's (1970) organic approach, the researcher involves the client in (1) defining research goals, (2) determining research methods and strategy, and (3) interpreting the results. Involving the client (the research subject) in the research effort requires many of the same skills and abilities needed by the OD consultant (See Chapter 17).

The people who will make decisions as a result of the evaluation research must be involved. These people may or may not be directly involved in the OD process itself, but the decision makers need to be involved by the researcher in much the same way that the organization members who are directly involved in the OD process would be participating in the research goals, methods, and interpretation. This involvement of the decision makers helps insure that the research results will be valid and will be utilized for further decision making.

Summary

Evaluation is the seventh phase of OD consultation, but it should begin early in the change process, preferably at the contract stage. Although some people emphasize the importance of conducting an evaluative effort, there are certain pressures against or forces that oppose evaluation. These forces were

341

considered for each of four groups involved in an OD evaluation: the manager or decision maker, the organization members, the OD consultant, and the evaluation researcher. Finally, a case was made for conducting this final phase of OD, and guidelines were provided for making the effort effective. The four broad guidelines for the researcher concern (1) collaboration with the client, (2) development of a research strategy, (3) development of a research design that is tied to the diagnostic model and is realistic, and (4) provision of effective methods for data collection and analysis.

In this chapter we also considered issues involved in the process of evaluating an OD effort. The most important issue to be resolved is the purpose of the evaluation. The next issue of importance is how the evaluative research will be conducted. For this type of research it is critical that the approach be more organic than the mechanistic (Argyris 1970). More specific issues that were considered concerned responses to the following questions:

1. What is organizational effectiveness?
2. What is OD in the organization development effort?
3. What is the independent variable?
4. How can organizational variables be controlled enough to determine what is cause and what is effect?
5. What changed (the issue of alpha, beta, and gamma changes)?
6. Who will conduct the research and who will use the results?

Now that we have completed our seven phases of organization development, it is time to consider OD consultants as skilled and competent helpers and as people—the subject of our next chapter.

CHAPTER 17

The Organization
Development Consultant

To be seen as a consultant is to have status, and thus many people aspire to the label and the role. A consultant is one who provides help, counsel, advice, and support, which implies that such a person is wiser than most people.

Although the label *consultant* usually conveys an image of one who provides help, there are obviously many different types of consultants. The purposes of this chapter are (1) to provide a context for the unique role and function of an OD consultant, (2) to consider the different roles and types of consultation within the field of organization development, (3) to explore the kinds of personal characteristics that are needed for OD consultation and the types of people who are in the field, and (4) to suggest ways for those who want to become OD consultants to do so.

Context for Roles and Functions

There are various ways of considering an OD consultant's role. We shall consider first the places one may find an OD consultant; next we shall look at the consultant's role with a client and the multiple roles of OD consultants with one another; and then we shall examine the OD consultant's role as compared with other types of consultants or change agents. The purpose of this first section is to provide a context for understanding and clarifying the OD consultant's role. The next section will examine the specifics of the role itself.

Where OD Consultants Are Located

Organization development consultants are found either inside an organization, as full-time or part-time employees, or outside organizations, with those organizations considered as clients. Internal consultants are usually located within the human resources, personnel, or employee relations function; they may be part of an OD department and serve exclusively in an OD capacity, or they may combine OD consultation with other duties, such as training, counseling, research, or career assessment and development. Thus, internal OD consultants are usually in a staff function, and they serve line managers throughout the organization.

External OD consultants may be employed by a consulting firm, may be self-employed, or may have academic appointments and consult only part of the time. In the past, external OD consultants usually came from colleges and universities. Now they are more likely to come from consulting firms or work on their own as full-time independent consultants.

Multiple Roles of the OD Consultant

Organization development consultants may serve managers or one another. The following diagram, suggested by Lundberg and Raia (1976) provides a quick picture of these different roles:

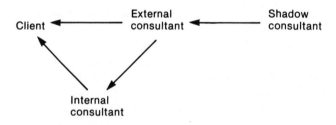

A shadow consultant (Schroder 1974) serves as a sounding board, an advisor, and a confidant for the consultant who is working directly with a client. The external consultant may serve as a shadow consultant for the internal consultant or as a direct consultant to the client. If the organization employs more than one OD consultant, they can serve as shadow consultants to one another.

Comparisons of the OD Consultant with Other Types of Consultants

E. H. Schein (1969) contrasts the process consultant role (a primary but not exclusive role and function of an OD consultant) with the *purchase model* and the *doctor-patient model*. According to Schein, the purchase model is the most prevalent form of consultation, essentially consisting of the client's purchase of expert services information. A client's employment of a consultant to conduct a market research study is an example of purchasing both expert service and information. The doctor-patient model consists of the client's (1) telling the consultant what is wrong with the organization, usually in the form of symptoms ("Our turnover is too high." "We're losing market share with respect to product X." "Our management information system is a mess.") and then (2) expecting the consultant to prescribe a remedy for the problem.

Schein contrasts these two models with the process consultant—one who helps the client organization (1) diagnose their own strengths and weaknesses more effectively; (2) learn how to see organizational problems more clearly; and (3) share with the consultant the process of diagnosis and the generation of a remedy. Schein (1969) also states: "It is of prime importance that the process consultant be expert in how to *diagnose* and how to *establish effective helping relationships* with clients. Effective (process consultation) involves the passing on of both these skills" (p. 8).

Thus, the primary though not exclusive function of OD consultants is to help clients learn how to help themselves more effectively. Although consultants occasionally provide expert information and may sometimes prescribe a remedy, their more typical mode of operating is *facilitation*.

In a study of congruence of values, cognitions, and actions among agents of planned social change, Tichy (1974) helped clarify the role of an OD consultant. He compared four types of change agents:

1. Outside pressure (OP) type—one who advocates certain changes, plans strategies for such advocacy, and implements the strategy by various techniques, such as published consumer reports, mass demonstrations, civil disobedience, and perhaps even violence.
2. Analysis for the top (AFT) type—one who conducts a study for the client organization and provides a report of such a study for the top management of the organization. This type is essentially the same as Schein's purchase model.
3. People change technology (PCT) type—one who provides a service for individuals in the organization through such techniques as training, education, behavior modification, and job enrichment. The target for change is thus the individual, not necessarily the organization.
4. Organization development (OD) type—Tichy uses the statement of an external OD consultant to describe this type. Although the statement is not an entirely adequate description in my opinion, it comes fairly close, and I shall quote it again here:

> I work on the human side of the enterprise. That is, I help people, mostly top executives, work out their problems of interpersonal relationships and communications, conflicts of interest, etc. I get involved in planning and implementing procedures of goal setting, decision making, conflict resolution, and the delegation of authority. In this way I help an organization develop and modify its governmental (self governance) and problem-solving mechanisms as well as help key executives work with each other within these ground rules. (Tichy 1974, p. 169).

From Tichy's comparisons we can see that the OD consultant facilitates change of the total system by working within it and by collaborating with the client in the process. Tichy's data help clarify these differences further. Exhibit 17.1 shows that OD consultants' primary change goal is improved system problem solving, whereas other types of consultants had different goals or different priorities.

Tichy's study also indicated that the outside pressure types were the most congruent in values, cognition, and action; that is, these change agents took action that was consistent with their stated values and with their models of how to bring about change (the cognition component of the study). The OD consultants, however, were consistent with respect to their model for change—facilitation—and their action—team development through process consultation; but they were inconsistent regarding values—democratic participation in decision making—and action—helping to improve efficiency within the organization. The paradox for the OD consultant, unlike that for the outside pressure type, "is that they (OD consultants) have a value-oriented change approach as reflected in their goals, but they are generally employed by organizations not for these values, but to help with problems effecting efficiency and output." (Tichy 1974, p. 179). Tichy suggests that, for OD consultants to become more congruent, they must deal more adequately

EXHIBIT 17.1
Primary Goals of Change Agents

Primary goal	OP (N = 27)	PCT (N = 17)	OD (N = 17)	AFT (N = 28)
Improved system efficiency and increased output	11%	35%	26%	57%
Improved system problem solving	4	18	58	32
Equalization of power and system responsibility to social welfare	67	23	5	7
Improved satisfaction of members	4	6	0	4
Improved interpersonal relations	4	6	5	0
Increased range of individual choice and freedom	0	6	5	0
Develop new system	11	0	0	0
No answer	0	6	0	0

Source: Reprinted from "Agents of Planned Change: Congruence of Values and Actions" by N. M. Tichy · published in *Administrative Science Quarterly* 19(1974): 164–82 by permission of the Administrative Science Quarterly. Copyright © 1974 by Cornell University.

Abbreviations for types of change agents are as follows: OP = outside pressure; PCT = people change technology; OD = organization development; AFT = analysis for the top.

with their apparent internal conflict with power figures. We shall discuss this conflict further later in the chapter.

Roles and Functions

The Lippitt and Lippitt Model

Using a continuum from directive to nondirective, Lippitt and Lippitt (1975) have devised a descriptive model of eight different roles for a consultant. They do not use OD as their frame of reference but it is clearly implied, since their advocate role, the one closest to the directive end of the continuum, is within the context of helping and working with the client rather than in opposition, like the OP type from Tichy's (1974) research. By *directive,* Lippitt and Lippitt mean that the consultant's behavior assumes a leadership posture and that he or she initiates activities, whereas at the opposite extreme—nondirective—the consultant merely provides data for the client to use or not. All along the continuum the consultant is active; what varies is how directive or nondirective this activity becomes. Lippitt and Lippitt also note that these roles are not mutually exclusive. The consultant may, for example, serve as a trainer and educator and as an advocate at the same time. Exhibit 17.2 summarizes the Lippitt and Lippitt model, and the following are brief descriptions of the identified roles.

EXHIBIT 17.2

Eight Consultant Roles

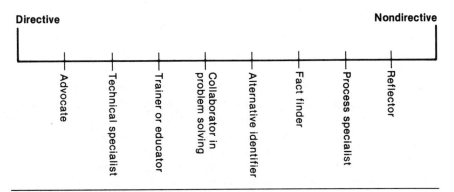

Source: Adapted from G. L. Lippitt and R. Lippitt, *Consulting Process in Action.* San Diego, Ca: University Associates, 1978. Used with permission.

ADVOCATE   In this role, the consultant attempts to influence the client. The advocacy may take either of two different forms: content advocacy—attempting to influence the client to select certain goals or to ascribe to particular values—or methodological advocacy—attempting to influence the client to use certain methods of problem solving or change management.

TECHNICAL SPECIALIST   In this role, the consultant provides a particular expertise. Again, the form could either be content, such as providing information about how to compose work groups for a particular task or about the effectiveness and validity of assessment centers, or methodological, such as designing an off-site meeting.

TRAINER OR EDUCATOR   An OD consultant is frequently cast in the role of teacher or manager and implementer of some learning activity. It is imperative that the OD consultant know about the process of adult learning and about designing and conducting learning activities.

COLLABORATOR IN PROBLEM SOLVING   In this role, the consultant helps the client (1) to discern problem symptoms from problem causes, (2) to generate alternative solutions, and (3) to plan and implement corrective action steps. In general, the consultant raises many questions and issues, so that useful working data are generated, and joins the client in the decision-making function.

ALTERNATIVE IDENTIFIER   In this role, the consultant performs all the activities associated with the previous role but does not collaborate with the client in making decisions.

FACT FINDER   The consultant in this role is essentially serving as a researcher, through interviewing, observing, or conducting a questionnaire survey.

PROCESS SPECIALIST   For this role, Lippitt and Lippitt describe the same activities as E. H. Schein (1969) describes for process consultation.

REFLECTOR   The role of the consultant as a reflector involves asking questions that will help clarify or perhaps change a situation. The consultant may serve as a facilitator or catalyst for action in this role, but the action is merely a consequence of the questioning process and is totally in the hands of the client. Harvey (1977a) describes this role as using the Socratic method. He provides a description of this role within the context of helping a client manage agreement (see chapter 14), and he explains the method with a case illustration. The label *reflector* or *Socratic* may imply a passive role, but the opposite is true. The consultant not only is active but may also be very confron-

348

tive, depending on the types of questions asked. Harvey (1977*a*) states that the function of the Socratic consultant is:

> (1) to help the individual (client) articulate the reality-based solution s/he would like to pursue; (2) to help the individual assess the potential reality of the fantasies which are preventing his/her taking action; (3) to recognize the individual's fear of separation (e.g., getting fired); (4) to recognize the need for connection as partial protection from the real stress that inevitably accompanies separation; (5) to help the individual face the reality that despite his/her planning and intentions s/he may make a choice which results in an outcome he/she may not like (getting fired); and (6) to assist the individual in becoming committed to living with the consequences whatever decision s/he may make. (pp. 183–84)

SUMMARY   The eight roles that Lippitt and Lippitt have identified are not the only roles and, as noted earlier, they overlap in that a consultant may be serving in two or more of the roles simultaneously or may be acting as an advocate one moment and as a reflector in another. Their model, though fairly simple and straightforward, nevertheless helps us to become clearer about (1) the multiple roles in which an OD consultant may function and (2) the situations in which one of these roles will serve better than others.

Marginality

Margulies (1978) has described the consultant's role differently and more generically. He argues that the OD consultant role is a marginal one. *Marginal* implies in between or on the edge—the periphery—and, accordingly, another term that Margulies uses is *boundary*.

First, Margulies contrasts two models of consulting with which we are already familiar: the *technical* consulting model and the *process* consulting model. His technical consulting model is like Schein's purchase and doctor-patient models and like Lippitt and Lippitt's technical specialist role, and his process model is the same as Schein's process consultation model. Margulies makes an analogy of technical-process with rational-intuitive and with the idea of the two-sided person represented by the two hemispheres of the brain. The OD consultant's role, he argues, is to function between these two halves, in the margin, being neither too technically oriented nor too process-oriented. Both sets of consultant expertise are appropriate, but for the OD consultant neither should be emphasized to the exclusion of the other. The consultant operates within the boundary of these two models of consultation, totally endorsing neither yet accepting both.

Margulies includes two other boundaries: the activities boundary and the membership boundary. For both, the OD consultant should operate at the boundary, in a marginal capacity. With respect to change activities, particularly implementation, the consultant must help but not be directly involved. Suppose, for example, an off-site team building session for a manager and his subordinates was forthcoming. The consultant would help the manager with the design and process of the meeting but would not lead the meeting.

With respect to membership, the OD consultant is never quite in nor quite out. Although the consultant must be involved, he or she cannot be a member of the client organization. Being a member means that there is vested interest, a relative lack of objectivity. Being totally removed, however, means that the consultant cannot sense, cannot be empathetic, and cannot use his or her own feelings as data for understanding the client organization more thoroughly. Being marginal with respect to membership means that the consultant becomes involved enough to understand client members' feelings and perceptions yet distant enough to be able to see these feelings and perceptions for what they are—someone else's—rather than as an extension of oneself.

Being marginal is critical for both an external consultant and an internal consultant. The major concern regarding the internal OD consultant's role is that he or she can never be a consultant to his or her own group. If the group is an OD department, a member of this department, no matter how skilled, cannot be an effective consultant to it. It is also difficult for an internal OD practitioner to be a consultant to any group that is within the same vertical path or chain of the managerial hierarchy as he or she may be. Since the OD function is often a part of corporate personnel or the human resource function, it would be difficult for the internal OD consultant to play a marginal role in consulting with any of the groups within this corporate function, because the consultant would be a primary organization member of that function. Consulting with marketing, R&D, or manufacturing within one's organization, for example, would be far more feasible and appropriate, since the OD consultant could more easily maintain a marginal role.

It is understandable that an OD consultant's role can be a lonely one. The role can also create anxiety about one's accuracy of perception—no one to check it with but the client—and about one's choice of intervention—whether it is the right one for the moment. Joining in fully, being a member, helps alleviate this loneliness and anxiety. Staying removed, distant, and aloof can also relieve the anxiety, since feelings are not involved. Doing either, however, lessens one's effectiveness as a consultant significantly. An obvious way to alleviate the problems of loneliness and anxiety is to co-consult. Working as an external and internal consultant team is probably the best way.

Other Considerations

Another way to examine the OD consultant's role and function is to consider the degree of personal use of oneself as an instrument of facilitation, feedback, and change. The bias of this book is that the OD consultant should be a finely

350

tuned instrument. He or she should be interpersonally competent, a diagnostician, a storehouse of knowledge in applying behavioral science, and useful in a helpful and timely manner. As Beer (1980) has pointed out: "A tailor-made program developed to fit the problems of a given organization is likely to be the most efficient and effective" (p. 211). This means flexibility and being organic in one's consultative approach—able to change the program at a moment's notice to deal with current and changing organizational realities. To be flexible and organic in approach, the OD consultant must of course be flexible in behavior and able to deliver different kinds of help as situational changes may demand.

This is a tall order for an OD consultant, and some believe that it is unrealistic. Blake and Mouton (1971) have argued accordingly and therefore advocate a more structured, systematic, and programmatic approach to OD—the grid OD program, which relies on the ability of the instruments within the program rather than on the ability of a person, the OD consultant. They state:

> Where consultation is introduced, it is supplemental rather than primary. Through the use of learning and application instruments, the Grid OD approach is internally administered by line managers which means that those who are responsible for results are, in fact, responsible for the change effort. To the degree that the developmental approach is theory-based, programmatic and instrumented, to that degree, it is not only self-administering, but also self-catalyzing and self-correcting. . . . the consultant approach relies almost exclusively on the consultant as a catalyst. . . . This means that the values [of the consultant] are likely to be significantly influencing the developmental effort. To the degree that [these] values are not made explicit, or are at variance with those in the organization, the use of the [consultant] approach may be based more upon faith than upon factual understanding. (Blake and Mouton 1971, p. 414).

Although it is not quite as programmatic and structured as the grid approach, the survey feedback method also relies less on the skill of a consultant for diagnosis and intervention than does the so-called organic approach advocated by Beer (1980) and others (Golembiewski 1979) as well as by myself. Bowers (1973) has collected data to show that the survey feedback approach is superior to a purer consultant approach for bringing about organizational change. He compared survey feedback with three other consultant-based approaches: interpersonal process consultation, task process consultation, and laboratory training. There are problems with Bowers's comparisons (Golembiewski, Billingsley, and Yeager 1976), especially since comparatively few cases were used for some of the analyses, but for our purposes here, the more important point is that a truly organic approach is not represented. The kind of OD practice that Beer (1980) and others explain and that is represented in this volume is based heavily on diagnosis and relies on far more techniques for change than are cited by comparative writings and studies of those such as Blake and Mouton (1971) and Bowers (1973).

351

The organic approach is nevertheless significantly dependent on the ability of the consultant. In the next section we shall examine this ability and what is needed for effective OD consultation more carefully.

Abilities and Needs

Speaking to a group of aspiring OD consultants in December 1973, Sherman Kingsburg, a consultant and trainer in human relations, said "You can learn the technology of OD in 15 minutes." He meant that one could learn, for example, the specifics of how to conduct a confrontation meeting, an intergroup conflict resolution session, or an organization mirror exercise in a comparatively short time. Kingsburg went on to emphasize that what must be learned or dealt with is not technology but the nature of such human processes as trust, dependency, and conflict. His basic question was, "How can you learn a technique, design, method, tactic—that is, a technology—for dealing with dependency, for example?" Our needs as consultants to be wise and powerful may cause us to be overly vulnerable to a client's dependency pleas. How do we learn to meet our needs as well as the client's? Learning to balance these simultaneous but sometimes conflicting needs requires experience and self-insight as a consultant. Thus, the abilities an OD consultant needs to be effective are not so much specific skills but rather certain personal characteristics that can be used in a flexible manner.

Beer (1980) lists five role and person characteristics that he considers important for the OD consultant:

1. Generalist and specialist: The OD consultant "is generalist in his organizational administrative perspective and a specialist in the process of organizational diagnosis and intervention" (Beer 1980, p. 222).
2. Integrator: The OD consultant sees to it that key linkages are made between the client and needed resources, such as calling in a particular expert for a specific change objective, and between various subsystems within the client organization, particularly between top management and certain staff groups, such as those involved in planning and human resource management.
3. Neutrality: The OD consultant should have no career authority over members of the client organization, should have no particular ax to grind with respect to the solution of organizational problems, should have no desire to obtain a high position within the client organization, and should be neutral with respect to the organization's internal politics.
4. Credibility: The more OD consultants can demonstrate that they have knowledge of the organization and its functioning and the more they are associated with organizational successes rather than failures, the higher

their credibility will be. As Franklin (1976) has shown, credibility is a significant variable linked to OD success.

5. Marginality: Here Beer cites Margulies and supports the argument for a boundary role for the OD consultant.

Consultants' Abilities

As Beer (1980) notes, these roles are difficult to maintain, requiring people with considerable ability. We shall now examine what some of these required abilities are. I consider that ten primary abilities are key to an OD consultant's effectiveness. Most of these abilities can be learned, but because of individual differences in personality or basic temperament, some of them would be easier for some people to learn than for others. The effective consultant should have the following abilities:

The ability to tolerate ambiguity: Every organization is different, and what worked before may not work now; every OD effort starts from scratch, and it is best to enter with few preconceived notions other than with the general characteristics that we know about social systems.

The ability to influence: Unless the OD consultant enjoys power and has some talent for persuasion, he or she is likely to succeed in only minor ways in OD. We will consider this point in more detail later.

The ability to confront difficult issues: Much of OD work consists of exposing issues that organization members are reluctant to face.

The ability to support and nurture others: This ability is particularly important in times of conflict and stress; it is also critical just before and during a manager's first experience with team building (Crockett 1970).

The ability to listen well and empathize: This is especially important during interviews, in conflict situations, and when client stress is high.

The ability to recognize one's own feelings and intuitions quickly: It is important to be able to distinguish one's own sensations from those of the client's and also be able to use these feelings and intuitions as interventions when appropriate and timely.

The ability to conceptualize: It is necessary to think and express in understandable words certain relationships, such as the cause-effect and if-then linkages that exist within the systemic context of the client organization.

The ability to discover and mobilize human energy, both within oneself and within the client organization: There is energy in resistance, for example, and the consultant's interventions are likely to be most effective when they tap existing energy within the organization and provide direction for the productive use of the energy.

The ability to teach or create learning opportunities: This ability should not be reserved for classroom activities but should be utilized on the job, during meetings, and within the mainstream of the overall change effort.

The ability to maintain a sense of humor, both on the client's behalf and to help sustain perspective: Humor can be useful for reducing tension. It is also useful for the consultant to be able to laugh at himself or herself; not taking oneself too seriously is critical for maintaining perspective about an OD effort, especially since nothing ever goes exactly according to plan, even though OD is supposed to be a *planned* change effort.

In addition to these abilities, it is important, of course, for the OD consultant to have self-confidence and to be interpersonally competent (Argyris 1970). Finally, I think it is helpful for the consultant to have a sense of mission about his or her work as an OD practitioner. I do not mean to imply that OD consultants should be zealots, but rather that they should believe that what they are doing is worthwhile and potentially helpful to others. This belief helps to sustain energy, to lessen feelings of loneliness and anxiety, and it provides a reason for continuing to work on organizations that appear recalcitrant and impossible to change.

Consultants' Needs

Regardless of their abilities, OD consultants have personal needs. Like most people, we want to be competent and to be recognized for this competence. Although we may not be interested in winning popularity contests, we do not wish to be disliked. We like to achieve and we like to help. We also like to influence and we are attracted to power. We often face the dilemma, however, of wanting to facilitate and help and at the same time wanting to influence, to exercise power, and perhaps even to lead. Reconciling and integrating these often conflicting needs is very difficult. Exacerbating this dilemma is the probability that most people who are attracted to and who are currently in the field of organization development are individuals who have a higher than average need for power. What does this mean for OD consultation? What are the consequences?

POWER AND POLITICAL ENTRAPMENT[1] Organization development consultants who have above-average power needs are vulnerable to being trapped politically within a client's power escapades. It is reasonable to assume that most managers have at least average but more likely above-

---

[1] This section is taken from a previously published chapter (Burke 1980a).

average needs for power and control. Unpublished evidence that I have helped to collect from more than 400 managers in a major agency of the federal government shows, for example, that their expressed control scores from the FIRO–B instrument (Schutz 1967) are above average when compared with general population norms. Furthermore, most OD consultants probably have an above-average need for power or control. McClelland (1975), for example, has found that those in the helping professions, such as therapists and consultants, have power needs that are well above average. In recent years, I have administered the FIRO–B to more than 100 OD practitioners and have found that most score similarly to managers—above average on expressed control. As part of my presentation at conferences on OD here and in England during 1980, I administered the control scales from the FIRO–B and, with a show of hands from the audiences, demonstrated that a clear majority scored 5 or higher on the expressed control dimension of the questionnaire. The average range for this scale is 2 to 5.

Thus, if my relatively informal data are representative, most OD practitioners enjoy influence and control. This characteristic is not bad, of course. In fact, it is probably a good thing. It would be difficult to be an effective consultant without an interest in trying to influence others. At the same time, however, the OD consultant is vulnerable to being trapped, if not seduced, by powerful clients and by clients' attempts to exercise power.

A concept from Gestalt therapy may help elucidate this point about the potential for political seduction. As Polster and Polster (1973) define it, "Confluence is a phantom pursued by people who want to reduce difference so as to moderate the upsetting experience of novelty and otherness" (p. 92). Behaving in a confluent manner may serve as a defense mechanism toward reducing unpleasant feelings that one may experience when encountering someone who is perceived as very different from oneself. To avoid the negative feelings associated with this perceived difference, one may change his or her perception of the other person, regardless of reality, and believe that this other person is very much like himself or herself. In OD consultation, since there is a high probability that consultant and client will have like needs for power and control, the consultant may be vulnerable to confluent behavior, assuming more prevalent similarities between himself or herself and the client than is warranted. Confronting differences between consultant and client is difficult; assuming similarities is easier.

COUNTERDEPENDENCE   Another potential consequence of an OD consultant's above-average needs for power is what laboratory trainers and therapists call counterdependence—the tendency to counter or rebel against people in power and holding positions of authority (dependence) or to collaborate with them. Collaboration could even feel like submission and dependence for the person with high power needs. Individuals who rebel

355

against authority are likely to have high power needs themselves. For the OD consultant, the behavior would not be rebellious, of course, but would take the form of subtle disagreement with the boss or collusion with subordinates against the boss.

In the past, I and others have accused OD consultants of overlooking issues of power in organizations and of being naive about organizational politics. Organization development consultants now are more cognizant of power and certainly are not as naive about politics as they might have been in the past, but the needs for power are still there and are probably abundant. Vicariously enjoying our client's power, we may become seduced into organizational politics and as a result lose our effectiveness as consultants in attempting to move from a marginal role to a more central one; or we may unconsciously feel resentment toward the client for all the power that he or she may have and therefore may attempt to undermine our client.

Being aware of our needs, particularly with respect to power, should help us as consultants to be wary of our motives, but this awareness also will help us learn how to meet our needs and serve the client effectively.

Becoming an OD Consultant

I have been asked occasionally how one becomes an OD consultant. I have typically responded with such vague answers as ''Well, it depends,'' since the question is difficult. There simply is no clear and systematic career path for becoming an OD consultant. Experienced people in the field may suggest such paths as going to a training laboratory, taking some psychology courses, tagging along with an experienced consultant to learn by observing and gradually trying some consulting interventions, reading some books, or attending the National Training Laboratories Program for Specialists in Organization Development. In the next few paragraphs I will attempt to answer the question of how one becomes an OD consultant a little more systematically.

Like any other field that consists of applying skills and implementing a particular kind of practice, experience is the best teacher for OD practice—or rather, experience accompanied by related feedback is the best teacher. One can have numerous experiences, but unless one receives feedback about which experiences are more related to effective practice, then learning rarely occurs. Thus, one should try to obtain experience in and feedback on consultative activities.

The second-best way to become an OD consultant is by some combination of academic learning and nonacademic training.

ACADEMIC TRAINING   A number of universities offer a curriculum either in organization development or in related courses. I suggest the following

356

twelve courses, mostly at the graduate level, that will provide a good background for OD practice. These courses are fairly common—perhaps not all in a single university, but similar courses may be available. Obtaining an education in these twelve subjects would be most useful:

1. Organizational psychology or organizational behavior: The former is typically offered in a department of psychology, the latter in a school of business or management. Either course provides the necessary background for understanding human behavior in an organizational context.
2. Group dynamics: This kind of course is a must. Organizations are composed of subsystems, usually in the form of work groups or managerial teams. Understanding the theory, research, and conceptual aspects of group behavior as well as the applicability of this knowledge helps one understand the utility of groups in organizations.
3. Research methods: Field research methods are preferable since they are the most applicable for learning about data collection and analysis in organizations.
4. Adult learning: This type of course is useful for understanding how organization members may learn from their experiences on the job as well as for knowing more about the appropriate rationale for designing training programs.
5. Career development: Since OD consultants are frequently involved in designing career development programs and are involved in human resource planning, background in this subject area is important.
6. Counseling and interviewing: This kind of course can provide critical skills, not only for diagnosis in general but also for specific help to individual organization members.
7. Organization development: Many universities now offer a one-semester or even a two-semester course in OD. The course may not be called OD, so one may have to read course descriptions carefully to find the right one.
8. Training and development: This type of course provides useful information about design of programs and about how to conduct certain learning activities.
9. Action research and consultation: This course may be the OD course. It usually offers good experience in data collection for diagnosis, feedback, and planned change. If the specific skills associated with this aspect of consultation are also included, so much the better.
10. Human resource management: This course, usually offered in a school of management or business, provides the necessary grounding in the organizational function that is most related to OD.
11. Process consultation: A course with this title may not be available, but if there is one that provides experience in group observation and interven-

tion, it may be a sufficient substitute. It would be even better if the course also included some substance and practice on interpersonal and intergroup conflict.

12. Organization theory: This course should follow the basic course on organizational behavior or organizational psychology. Usually this kind of course helps one learn about organizational design, effectiveness (performance criteria), and the organization as a system.

I purposely limited myself to twelve courses, conforming to a typical master's degree program requiring thirty-six to forty credits. Pepperdine University's nonresidential master of science in organization development program is an example, although their curriculum and what I have outlined are not exactly the same. The twelve courses I have listed assume that one would already have an undergraduate degree in psychology, sociology, or anthropology.

NONACADEMIC TRAINING   Several professional development programs are offered by training organizations or by the continuing education divisions of universities. These provide useful training in both the knowledge and the skill appropriate to OD practice, but the weight is usually on the side of skill development. The following are ten avenues or programs for developing oneself toward becoming an OD practitioner:

1. Basic laboratory training program: This involves attending at least a five-day event devoted to improving one's interpersonal competence—a T-group, Gestalt group, a Tavistock group, or something very similar.
2. Personal growth laboratory: The first program listed emphasizes interpersonal development, whereas this one focuses on intrapersonal understanding. Since the primary instrument in OD work is the consultant practitioner, it is important that one know this instrument as well as possible.
3. Training theory and practice: This is the name of a program offered by the National Training Laboratories (NTL) Institute, and other organizations may offer a similar program. Attending such a program will provide an opportunity to learn about the design of training laboratories and the necessary skills for conducting them.
4. Consultation skills: Practice in consulting is imperative, and this type of program is ideal since it offers a safe environment for testing untried skills.
5. Organization development laboratory: This program usually provides an introduction to the field and may range from a one-week version to a four-week one. Universities such as UCLA and the University of Michi-

gan offer one-week programs, and organizations such as University Associates and the NTL Institute offer even more variety.

6. Team building programs: Organizations such as the University of Michigan and Block-Petralla Associates offer training in how to consult with teams.

7. Supervised experience: Sometimes such an experience is provided as part of a consultation skills training program; otherwise, one needs to consult with an actual client and arrange some form of supervision from an experienced OD consultant. Having a mentor is a related avenue for professional and personal development.

8. Internal consultant with large organization: An excellent way to get started in OD is to work for an organization that has an internal OD service for its managers. I emphasize *large* organization because the opportunities would be greater and more varied. One may not be able to join an internal OD group immediately, so the entry job should be at least closely associated with OD work, such as training, career development, or human resource planning. One can then make contacts, express interest, and arrange for an experience such as that suggested in number 7.

9. Professional associations: Belonging to and attending the meetings of certain associations devoted to OD can of course help one learn about and keep up with the field. Such organizations are the OD Network, the OD divisions of the American Society for Training and Development and the Academy of Management, and certain regional groups, such as those in New York, Philadelphia, Ohio, and the Bay Area in northern California.

10. Advanced programs for professional development: Programs such as Columbia University's "Advanced Organization Development and Human Resource Management" and Harvard's "Managing Organization Effectiveness" are designed for experienced OD practitioners and provide an opportunity for more advanced development.

Being an OD consultant means being a practitioner. We practice OD much as lawyers and physicians practice law and medicine, but there are no schools of organization development, no bar or boards to pass, and no licensing procedure. For a consideration of such matters, see Jones (1980). Certified Consultants, Inc. (formerly known as the International Association of Applied Social Scientists) accredits OD consultants—among other types of practitioners, such as laboratory trainers—but there is no systematic procedure or plan provided for how to become an OD specialist. Short of such a procedure or plan, I believe that some combination of academic training and professional development is the next best approach to becoming an OD consultant.

Part of the excitement of being involved in organization development is the fact that, as a field, it is not all "put together" or "cut and dried." A new person coming into OD can still influence the shape, the form, and the eventual synthesis the field may take in the future. Since many OD people have higher-than-average needs to influence, and since many of us tend to distrust if not rebel against too much authority, perhaps the fact that the field of OD is still in an emergent phase is healthy (Burke 1976; Friedlander 1976). Opportunity still abounds.

Summary

In this chapter we have considered the role and personal characteristics of the OD consultant. The OD consultant may behave in a directive manner, perhaps even as an advocate, or, at the opposite extreme, may behave very nondirectively, serving perhaps as a reflector, primarily raising questions. For the most part, however, the OD consultant serves in a facilitative capacity, helping clients learn how to solve their own problems more effectively.

We also considered the role of the OD consultant from another perspective. Remaining marginal, at the boundary or interface between individuals—especially bosses and subordinates—and between groups and subsystems, is critical to effective consultation, at least from the vantage point of organization development practice. In this marginal role, the consultant functions in an organic way, attempting to intervene in a timely manner and according to what the client needs at the time. Consulting organically means that the practitioner must use himself or herself as an instrument—sensing client need by paying attention not only to what may be observed but also to his or her own feelings and intuitions. This form of consultation is not easy and is highly dependent on the skills of the consultant and subject to bias according to the consultant's personal values and attitudes. This form of consultation has been criticized accordingly (Blake and Mouton 1971).

Using oneself as an instrument and remaining marginal can nevertheless be practiced in a systematic manner, as Ferguson (1968) has demonstrated. As a way of summarizing and consolidating our points about marginal consulting and using oneself as an instrument, we shall briefly review Ferguson's roles and functions of the OD consultant:

1. Capture data: Listen and capture the essence of the pictures presented; also listen for cause and effect, for discrepancies in stories, and for dissonance and symptoms of stress along subsystem boundary lines.
2. Scan for troubled interfaces: According to Ferguson (1968): "The consultant is a radar device addressed at the organization to pick up blips and cues and to make tentative working assessments as to which are normal,

acceptable cues and which deserve further investigation or treatment'' (p. 187).

3. Promote psychological bonding: Show where collaboration is appropriate and needed.

4. Act as linking agent: Point to where communication across subsystems should occur.

5. Serve as communications conveyor: Sometimes it is appropriate for the consultant to transport messages between individuals and subsystems.

6. Suspend animation and analyze process: At times the consultant should intervene and stop the action to consider what may be blocking more effective working processes. Ferguson (1968) states that the intervention ''is like stopping a film to examine a frame for greater detail'' (p. 188).

7. Clarify formulation of issues: Conceptualize problems for better understanding.

8. Release emotional pressures: Expose issues that, when vented and discussed, will facilitate better understanding and working conditions among organization members.

9. Make communication congruent: Confront incongruities of behavior, such as when a person states that he is not angry but outward signs indicate the opposite. Such confrontation facilitates openness and honesty among organization members.

10. Encourage feedback: Encouraging may take the form of gentle prodding or starting the process by providing some initial feedback.

11. Serve as plumber or obstetrician: Observe blocks in communication and nudge the passage of these blocks by such questions as, ''Why don't you tell her what you just told me?'' Give birth to ideas by assisting with communication flow.

12. Promote a spirit of inquiry: Understand what and why something is or is not happening in the organization and encourage people to learn from the ''why.''

13. Analyze ongoing process: Deal with ''momentum and thrust (energy in the system) that must be analyzed even as a navigator checks the route of an aircraft in motion or a pilot in flight monitors his instruments'' (Ferguson 1968, p. 191).

14. Coach and build teams: Ferguson uses the analogy of an athletic team and contrasts the amount of time these teams spend on preparation and development with that spent by work teams in organizations.

15. Assist in the management of conflict: According to Ferguson (1968), this involves ''questioning the effectiveness of norms that smother disagreement and . . . arranging situations where important disagreements can come into clearly focused confrontation'' (p. 192).

16. Promote a proper psychological climate: Ferguson argues that people

flourish in a climate of understanding, trust, consistency, mutual respect and support, openness, and clarity.

17. Take calculated risks: By being at the boundary and not vested within the client system, the consultant can confront issues that would be too risky for organization members.

Note that all seventeen of Ferguson's consultant functions begin with an active verb, implying that the effective consultant takes action by using himself or herself as an instrument of intervention.

All this requires certain skills and abilities. We examined some of these, such as being a good listener, using empathy, being able to tolerate ambiguity, and being an effective conceptualizer, confronter, diagnostician, and teacher, and we considered the needs of people who are attracted to this field, particularly the need for power and influence. A high degree of self-awareness is perhaps the most important ingredient for OD consultant effectiveness.

Finally, we examined some of the ways one can learn to become an OD consultant. We considered a combination of academic avenues and non-academic settings. Becoming an OD consultant can be exciting, since the field is still in the growth process; synthesizing and consolidating is still occurring. Those who enter now will have an opportunity to influence what the field will eventually become.

CHAPTER 18

Perspectives on
Organization Development as a Field

In concluding this book I want to examine once again (1) the organization—that social and technical system that sometimes seems impervious to change; (2) organization development—that special type of change and consultative practice that now has history and precedent yet is still in a formative stage as a field; and (3) the OD practitioner—that person with a certain set of abilities, motives, and values. In dealing with the organization, I shall use the perspective of the organizational imperative, a concept developed by Scott and Hart (1979) to explain what they view as a significant shift of values in our society. To set the stage for the remainder of the chapter, we shall first explore our prime focus of interest—the organization—from the perspective of how powerful and prevailing a force it is in our society. My purpose in this initial section is to draw our attention to what we in the field of organization development are confronting.

In my final consideration of organization development as a field, the second section of this chapter, I have chosen the bureaucracy, typically a very large and complex system, as the context. Since a bureaucracy is pehaps the most difficult organization to change, as a system it confronts us with whether OD is up to the challenge. Do we simply tinker with bureaucracies by helping to fix some of its units here and there, or do we change anything fundamentally about their culture? This question is at the heart of organization development, or what it was originally intended to be as a field. We shall review OD's past briefly and then examine its current dilemma: Is it a field that represents change in an active, planned sense or one that merely helps organizations adapt more effectively to changes that have already occurred—decisions the boss has already made, forces from the outside environment, and so forth.

Finally, we shall again consider the OD practitioner, particularly his or her role and function and how this role may be carried out in the future.

Although these three foci are explored in separate sections, they should not be considered discrete but rather as highly interrelated. Please keep this in mind as you read.

My overall intent in this final chapter is to provide some perspective on the current state of organization development, its future, and the role of the OD practitioner.

The Organizational Imperative

In these times, to do something of significance, to have an impact, to succeed is almost impossible without an organization. One either must belong to an organization and have access to its resources or must create one to realize goals. We no longer belong to an age of individuals; this is an age of systems. We serve organizations to meet our goals, but this serving is perhaps more for the good of the system than for the good of the individual, at least according to Hart and Scott. They argue that our society is now characterized by the "organizational imperative" (Hart and Scott 1975; Scott and Hart 1979). This imperative consists of two a priori value propositions: the primary one is, "Whatever is good for the individual can only come from the modern organization" and the secondary one, which derives from the first, is "Therefore, all behavior must enhance the health of such organizations" (Scott and Hart 1979, p. 43). From these propositions come three rules of ethical behavior for organization members, particularly managers. They must be (1) technically rational, (2) good stewards of other people's property, and (3) pragmatic, all for the purpose of maintaining their organization's health. Hart and Scott also make an unsettling but substantive case for their belief that our society has gradually shifted from an individual to an organizational base. Specifically, they state that our cultural values have shifted in five ways:

1. From individuality to obedience
2. From the indispensability of the unique individual to dispensability
3. From community to specialization
4. From spontaneity to self-conscious planning
5. From voluntarism to an organizational paternalism

In helping organizations to renew, improve, and become more effective, OD consultants may be doing nothing more than responding to and facilitating the organizational imperative. The client is the system. Golembiewski (1979) puts it this way:

> however noble the professed goals underlying OD interventions, some danger—or perhaps an absolute inevitability—exists that those values will be perverted by the inexorable demands of the organizational system. (p. 115)

Referring to Walton and Warwick (1973), Golembiewski (1979) also states:

> OD interventions may be tolerated only when they basically serve to stabilize the system, as in "cooling out" those members who develop antagonistic feelings toward some system. Human needs will be responded to, in this view of the world, only (or mostly) when they happen to coincide with the organizational imperative. (p. 115)

Golembiewski raises the issue that OD may be nothing more than a practice that helps organizations do what they already do, but better. We OD practitioners simply help to fine tune systems; we do not facilitate change. I also raised this issue earlier (Burke 1972).

The central issue for people in the organization development field, therefore, is whether we as practitioners facilitate problem solving, helping organization members "fix things"—what Argyris and Schön (1978) refer to as single-loop learning—or whether we facilitate change, helping organization members solve problems in a different way—what Argyris and Schön call double-loop learning.

OD in Bureaucracies

In the early days of OD (the 1960s), we thought we were in the business of organizational change. Perhaps we still are, but it doesn't sound the same. Let us contrast early writing of Warren Bennis (in the 1960s) with that of Virginia Schein and Larry Greiner (in the 1970s). Our context is the toughest of all systems to change—the bureaucracy.[1]

Although he was writing about bureaucracies, not specifically about organization development, Bennis nevertheless implied that activities such as OD would facilitate change in large complex systems, particularly bureaucracies. He was optimistic (Bennis 1967; Slater and Bennis 1964). He went so far as to predict "the coming death of bureaucracy," giving it another twenty-five years or so (Bennis 1966). Bennis believed that bureaucracy was vulnerable because of several factors:

1. Rapid and unexpected change: A bureaucracy could not cope with the accelerated pace of change.
2. Growth in size: Growth organizations were becoming more complex and not as amenable to the bureaucratic simplicities of division of labor, hierarchy, standardization, roles, procedures, and so forth, for effectively coping with their environments.
3. More diverse and highly specialized competence required: Increases in

---

[1] This section is taken substantially from a previously published article (Burke 1980b).

size and complexity of organizations require greater and different specializations, whereas bureaucracy demands standardization, common policy and procedures, routine, and well-defined jobs.
4. A change in managerial behavior: Rather than the impersonality in human relations characteristic of bureaucracies, a newer philosophy is emerging, based on changing concepts of the human being (more complex with recognized needs), power (collaboration and reason more highly valued than coercion and threat), and organizational values (based more on humanistic and democratic ideals than on the depersonalized mechanistic value system of bureaucracy).

Others shared many of these beliefs, especially with respect to changes in values (Tannenbaum and Davis 1969).

There was also pessimism (Bennis 1970). As a result of Bennis's experience as an academic administrator—certainly a bureaucratic situation—he came to the view that, human nature being what it is, bureaucracies were not amenable to the kinds of changes in organizational life that he had previously predicted. He reluctantly declared that, as a rule, people are more concerned with (1) power and personal gain than with openness and love, (2) clarity of organization than with ambiguity, and (3) self-interests than with the good of the organization or the public interest.

Pragmatism came later (Perrow 1977; V. E. Schein and Greiner 1977). Perrow has argued paradoxically that the efficient bureaucracy can centralize in order to decentralize. His ideas are not so far-fetched as this statement may sound. His argument is based primarily on the accepted and valid principle of management in any organization—delegation. Schein and Greiner have addressed more directly the applicability of OD to bureaucracies. They point out that the basic ideology of OD is that, in response to their changing environments, organizations should become more organic systems and therefore more capable of responding to rapid change. Schein and Greiner characterized organic systems as having structures, such as matrix or project, rather than functional designs and as having open communications, interdependence among groups, considerable trust, joint problem solving, and employees who take risks. They did not believe that many such organizations exist:

> Despite OD's preoccupation with organic practices, we contend . . . that the millennium of organic organizations is not on the horizon, which in turn causes us to question the relevance of the present OD movement for the great bulk of business and public organizations. The preponderance of evidence, by contrast, shows that bureaucratic structures are still the dominant organizational form, either for an entire firm or for product groups. (V. E. Schein and Greiner 1977, p. 49)

They assumed that different organizational structures develop unique and inherent behavioral problems and that "behavioral diseases" emerging from bureaucracies differ from those that emanate from organic structures. Accordingly, they argued for a contingency model of OD and proposed a fine-tuning approach in dealing with bureaucracies. By fine-tuning they meant using OD techniques as a way of sharpening "the operations of an organization" and freeing it from "dysfunctional behaviors" (V. E. Schein and Greiner 1977, p. 53). For bureaucracies, then, OD consultants should not attempt to bring about significant change but rather should work to improve or fine-tune the operations of the system.

Schein and Greiner were specific in their recommendations for fine-tuning bureaucracies. They used two criteria for the selection of OD techniques for fine-tuning: (1) that the quality of working life will be enhanced as a result but (2) that the situations bounded by the environmental and technological realities of the organization will not be the prime focus of change. They went on to specify four behavioral diseases of bureaucracies and suggested certain OD techniques as potential cures. The four diseases were:

1. Functional myopia and suboptimization: results from high division of labor and individuals' allegiance to their specialty;
2. Vertical lock-in and incompetency: promotions stay within a single function; emphasis is on rank and seniority;
3. Top-down information flow and problem insensitivity: authority, problem solving, plans, and objectives are defined at the top;
4. Routine jobs and dissatisfaction: results from bureaucratic need for economies of scale and labor being considered a variable cost.

Exhibit 18.1 is a summary of Schein and Greiner's behavioral diseases in bureaucracies, the associated behavioral symptoms, and the OD cures for fine-tuning the operations of the system. Their final recommendations were that OD consultants (1) adopt a more positive and accepting attitude toward bureaucratic organizations; (2) acquire a more thorough knowledge of bureaucratic operations; (3) adopt a more conceptual and realistic orientation for understanding bureaucratic behavior; and (4) develop a more versatile range of OD techniques that apply to bureaucracies.

Schein and Greiner suggest that the time has come for OD practitioners to become more realistic; bureaucracies are here to stay. Organization development is more appropriate for organic systems, and few of these exist; therefore, we should learn more about the nature of bureaucracies and go about the business of fine-tuning them.

EXHIBIT 18.1

Summary of Behavioral Diseases of Bureaucracies, Their Symptoms, and OD Cures

Critical behavioral diseases of bureaucracies	Behavioral symptoms	OD cures for fine-tuning
Functional myopia and suboptimization	Interdepartmental conflict Lack of planning coordination Lack of adequate communication across functions	Team building for top management groups Off-site meeting of top two or three levels of management for participative planning and budgeting session Limited structural intervention designed to facilitate goal integration (e.g., senior coordination group) Job rotation of high potential managers
Vertical lock-in and incompetency	Frustration Boredom Technical knowledge valued more than managerial ability	Assessment center Job posting Manpower information system Career counseling Management training
Top-down information flow and problem insensitivity	Lack of innovation Minor problems becoming major by the time they reach top management	Develop shadow structure • reflective (Greiner) • collateral (Zand) • parallel (Carlson) Junior board of middle managers Ombudsman
Routine jobs and dissatisfaction	Absenteeism Boredom First-line supervisors feeling caught between workers' problems and management's pressure for production	Job Enrichment Job rotation Vary work schedules Flexi-time Supervisory training Scanlon plan Salary instead of hourly wages Employee stock-ownership plans

Source: Adapted by permission of the publisher from "Can Organization Development Be Fine Tuned to Bureaucracies?" by V. E. Schein and L. E. Greiner, *Organizational Dynamics*, Winter 1977, pp. 48–61. © 1977 by Amacom, a division of the American Management Associations. All rights reserved.

The Current Dilemma

For those of us who entered the field of OD in the 1960s, this advice is hard to swallow. We may be experiencing a particular dilemma: Are OD practitioners merely repair people, or do we facilitate change? The problem is not really definition—we have more than enough definitions. This abundance of definitions does reflect the problem, however. These days OD can be almost anything—from assessment center to management consulting, from System 4 to sociotechnical systems or QWL, from stress management to holistic organic interventions.[2]

We believe inappropriate expectations are the cause of this dilemma. Our expectations that the values of humanization and egalitarianism would promote organizational change—change in the direction of more humanism, a higher quality of work life, and a greater decentralization of power—have been naive and inappropriate. Although it may be true that the more a manager shares his or her power with subordinates, the more he or she is likely to have a stronger power base in the organization, this precept is difficult to communicate and is pure fantasy to many managers. It is difficult for managers to see how delegation, a more humane treatment of people, and consensus decision making will contribute to cost-effectiveness and the bottom line. Moreover, whereas we behavioral scientists may sermonize, it is impossible, at least for the present, for us to *prove* that better treatment of people and more involvement of people in decisions that directly affect them will *cause* higher productivity and morale.

Although we cannot prove that what we do in OD leads to greater productivity and cost-efficiency, we still believe in what we do. We are not necessarily true believers in the religious sense—although OD has been viewed as a religious movement (Harvey 1974*b*)—but we are certainly enthusiasts, if not romanticists. Warren Bennis, a romanticist about the field, helped lead the way. Defining OD as "a response to change, a complex educational strategy intended to change the beliefs, attitudes, values, and structure of organizations so that they can better adapt to new technologies, markets and challenges, and the dizzying rate of change itself" (Bennis 1969, p. 2), he went on to state that OD practitioners share a social philosophy and a set of values. We "believe that the realization of these values will ultimately lead not only to a more humane and democratic system but to a more efficient one" (p. 13). Furthermore, we practitioners (he called us change agents) share a set of normative goals based on this social philosophy and values. According to Bennis the most commonly sought goals are:

---

[2] The remainder of this chapter is based largely on a previous publication (Burke and Goodstein 1980). The use of *we* means that the statements were made by both Goodstein and myself.

1. Improvement in interpersonal competence
2. A shift in values so that human factors and feelings become legitimate
3. Increased understanding between and within working groups so that tensions will be reduced
4. Development of more effective team management
5. Development of improved methods of conflict resolution
6. Development of organic as opposed to mechanical systems

Bennis (1969) concluded that the basic value underlying OD is choice. Organization development is a means of providing "more and better organizational choices in a highly turbulent world" (p. 17). He also stated: "Organization development practitioners rely exclusively on two sources of influence: truth and love. Somehow the hope prevails that man is reasonable and caring, and that valid data coupled with an environment of trust (and love) will bring about the desired change" (p. 77). Bennis was not so naive as it might seem from this latter quotation. He also wrote: "Unless models can be developed that include the dimensions of power conflict in addition to truth-love, organization development will find fewer and narrower institutional avenues open to its influence. And in so doing, it will slowly and successfully decay" (p. 79).

As already noted, we do not perceive the field to be in a state of decay; thus, we have confronted issues of power and politics in organizations over the past decade and have incorporated these dimensions into our models (Weisbord 1976). We are still romantics about organization development, however. The truth-love model continues to appeal to us, although the realities of dealing with economically difficult times and with power and politics have subdued our fervor—not extinguishing it, let us hasten to add. Perhaps it is accurate to express our feelings as a continued enthusiasm, tempered by reality, perhaps what we are experiencing is really the way it is when new movements become more mature. Organization development is no longer an adolescent (Friedlander 1976). We are almost grown up now, and what are we going to do with our lives?

Some evidence of the field's maturity is the fact that many formalizations now exist—job titles in organizations, academic respectability, associations for granting credentials, and several professional organizations. The field is even approaching bureaucratization in such areas as formalized steps for acquiring credentials and membership societies.

All is not well, however. Although we are older and perhaps somewhat wiser, we are still not completely clear about what we are going to do with our OD lives. If we are not experiencing an identity crisis as such, it is certainly safe to say that we are in the midst of some reexaminations.

As a result of attempting to deal more realistically with power figures and organizational politics, we OD practitioners have become confronted more

370

with the limitations of our field. We have learned along the way that, despite what Lippitt, Watson, and Westley (1958) told us early in the game and what Bennis (1969) wrote some ten years later, we are not the agents of change. Line managers are the change agents. We facilitate change rather than initiate it.

It is probable, too, that, in dealing more directly with power and politics and in turn becoming clearer about our limitations (Nord 1978) and about where most of the power for change is located—with the client manager—we have become somewhat disillusioned. Organization development is not, after all, a revolutionary movement. Change in organizations most often is evolutionary, coming about slowly and by degrees: compromises occur; the original change goal is no longer feasible; people move to other positions or organizations just when change was in the making; changes in the environment cause cutbacks, and our OD effort is temporarily if not permanently shelved; the diagnosis is too negative for the boss to handle and we must temper or delay matters somewhat; the boss is on board but key subordinates are not; and so on.

Our disillusionment takes two forms: (1) real organizational change seems to occur through processes other than OD—for example, drastic changes in the environment cause internal shifts, or the introduction of a new computer may precipitate an entirely different monitoring and control process; and (2) we feel that sometimes we are diffusing the human spirit in organizations rather than enhancing it. With respect to this latter characteristic, it is possible to achieve an outcome in the name of OD whereby people in the organization are simply less resistant to what the boss wants. We practitioners know that, when conflict arises—between boss and subordinates, for example—an important early step is to create conditions whereby those involved can ventilate their frustrations and other related feelings. With the feelings dissipated, the boss may then step in and resolve the conflict to his or her liking with considerable ease. In some instances, then, OD may be nothing more than a cooling-out process, so that the change the boss wants is no longer resisted. This more or less boss-directed change may not be bad, of course, but nagging the OD practitioner are such questions as: Who is the client? Is my assistance helpful to all involved or just to the boss? Is my job to help the boss or to facilitate system change? Are these two consultative objectives compatible or incompatible? How can I tell? Am I merely in the service of those in power (Ross 1971)? Do I say comply just as easily as those others who occupy the lily pads on the organizational phrog farm (Harvey 1977b)?

Although many of us experience disillusionment at times, more frequently we have been learning more and more about organizations, making adjustments in our thinking about OD as a field of practice based on the behavioral sciences, and maintaining our commitment to remaining OD consultants.

371

Causes of Organization Change
and the OD Practitioner's Role

Organization development practitioners rarely initiate or cause change in an organization. Managers cause change more often, but not much. Causes of organization change derive primarily from the organization's environment. External factors usually cause internal change in the organization—factors such as shifts in the marketplace, raw material shortages, government regulations, lack of certain technological resources, sudden and new competition, consumerism, and so forth. The job and role of the OD practitioner is to help organization members adapt to and cope with these externally derived factors.

Thus, we OD practitioners facilitate change; we do not initiate it. This is not to say that we cannot or should not provide direction regarding change. We can and should provide recommendations, suggestions, and advice (Argyris 1971; Burke 1976). More particularly, however, the unique facilitative service we can provide is helping the client articulate the direction of change (Tichy, Hornstein, and Nisberg 1977) and providing the client with a "cognitive map" (Argyris 1971)—pathways for that direction.

We OD practitioners help clients manage the human components of the change process. We help managers understand the nature of resistance to change, where and how it is likely to occur, and how to deal with it. We collaborate with the managers in planning action steps, but we also push for the involvement of all people who will be directly affected by the change in the decision-making process. In short, we work to convince the client manager that the way he or she manages the change is as important for success as are the substantive aspects of the change.

We OD practitioners help change organizational values in the direction of serving both individual needs and organizational goals. Our job—a unique service and role—is to help the client see and understand the relationship between patent behavior and underlying values. The OD practitioner confronts the client with discrepancies between stated goals and behavior that leads people in other directions. It may be that the OD practitioner's greatest strength is in this area. Organization members and the organization itself may be served best by the OD practitioner's resolute efforts to illuminate these discrepancies and to emphasize the fact that, when people perceive a high degree of congruence between organizational goals and managerial behavior, they feel a high degree of trust. By the examination of organizational values and related or unrelated behavior, the OD practitioner may be contributing not only to the well-being of organization members but also to the bottom line.

The role of the OD practitioner is to be aware of but not embroiled in the client manager's power issues or organizational politics (Burke 1980b). The

372

practitioner focuses more on values—first, on the degree of similarity between the client's apparent values and those of the OD practitioner and, second, on any discrepancies between what the client advocates and what he or she actually does.

The higher one goes in the managerial hierarchy, the more he or she is expected to articulate and model the organization's values. Assuming that the organization's values are compatible enough with the OD practitioner's values, then a primary role of the practitioner is to help the manager or executive (1) to clarify his or her personal values and how they are congruent or incongruent with the organization's values; (2) to examine his or her stated values and how certain ones may be incongruent with behavior; and (3) to incorporate stated or implied organizational values within the fabric of the system, as manifested in the structure, reward system, control system, and political process.

Thus, an important function of the OD practitioner is to facilitate value clarification in the organization. This function is useful for both the practitioner and the client organization—for the practitioner because the function is unique from the standpoint of consultation and helps clarify the practitioner's *raison d'être,* and for the client because, the greater the congruence between values and behavior, the more directional and motivated organization members will be.

Conclusions

Like the late adolescent or young adult, the field of OD may still be searching for its identity, its uniqueness. Some of the blush of youth is gone, and we are not everything we had hoped or thought we would be. Reality and experience have tempered dreams and enthusiasm. We are clearer about where we have been, however, and, within that backward-looking clarity, we should be able to predict the future better than we have done in the past.

In some respects, the future will be back to basics. Our unique skill, for example, is process consultation, which should be in every practitioner's repertoire. The skill is fundamental to what we do—helping to relate process to content, bringing group and organizational behavior issues to the surface, especially those concerning values, and resolving conflict. Also basic are action research and collaboration. We work from data that we feed back to the system, and we facilitate change by creating conditions whereby people are involved in making decisions that directly affect them.

A Delphi study conducted prior to the OD'80 conference sponsored by University Associates showed that experienced OD practitioners are more concerned with goals than technology—goals such as greater productivity and total system change (Spier et al. 1980). This outlook is appropriate, but concern is one thing, clarity another. Organization development practitioners are clearer about what they do (the social technology) than they are about ultimate outcomes. Our conclusion is that clarity about goals comes partially from the past. In retrospect, we know what works and we can perceive some of our uniqueness more clearly. Process consultation works, and it is our most unique skill. We are in the business of facilitating organization change through the use of the action research approach and the skill of process consultation. There are many other things that we can and will do in the future—such as putting more emphasis on value clarification and systemic approaches—but fundamental to all of our activities is consultation that is data-based, facilitative, process-focused, and collaborative. By sticking to our unique techniques, by pushing ourselves to be clear about values—ours as well as our client's—and by keeping in mind that ultimately we are attempting to humanize the work place, primarily by involving people in decisions that directly affect them, our ultimate goals, though not completely clear, will nevertheless take care of themselves.

Bibliography

Ackoff, R. L. 1974. *Redesigning the Future.* New York: Wiley.

Adams, J. D. 1978. "Improving Stress Management: An Action-Research Based OD Intervention." In *The Cutting Edge: Current Theory and Practice in Organization Development,* ed. W. W. Burke, pp. 245–61. La Jolla, Calif.: University Associates.

Alderfer, C. P. 1977. "Group and Intergroup Relations." In *Improving Life at Work: Behavioral Science Approaches to Organizational Change,* ed. J. R. Hackman and J. L. Suttle, pp. 227–96. Santa Monica: Goodyear.

Allport, F. H. 1962. "A Structuronomic Conception of Behavior: Individual and Collective. I. Structural Theory and the Master Problem of Social Psychology." *Journal of Abnormal and Social Psychology* 64: 3–30.

Allport, G. W. 1945. *The Nature of Prejudice.* Cambridge, Mass.: Addison-Wesley.

Anderson, J. 1970. "Giving and Receiving Feedback." In *Organizational Change and Development,* ed. G. W. Dalton, P. R. Lawrence, and L. E. Greiner, pp. 339–46. Homewood, Ill.: Richard D. Irwin and Dorsey Press.

Argyris, C. 1973. "The CEO's Behavior: Key to Organizational Development." *Harvard Business Review* 51(2): 55–64.

———. 1971. *Management and Organizational Development.* New York: McGraw-Hill.

———. 1970. *Intervention Theory and Method.* Reading, Mass.: Addison-Wesley.

———. 1968. "Some Unintended Consequences of Rigorous Research." *Psychological Bulletin* 7: 185–97.

———. 1964. "T Groups for Organizational Effectiveness." *Harvard Business Review* 42(2): 60–74.

———. 1962. *Interpersonal Competence and Organizational Effectiveness.* Homewood, Ill.: Dorsey Press.

———. 1957. *Personality and Organization: The Conflict Between the System and the Individual.* New York: Harper & Row.

Argyris, C., and Schön, D. A. 1978. *Organizational Learning: A Theory of Action Perspective.* Reading, Mass.: Addison-Wesley.

"At Emery Air Freight: Positive Reinforcement Boosts Performance." *Organizational Dynamics* 1(3): 41–67.

Atkins, S., and Katcher, A. 1967. *LIFO Survey.* Beverly Hills: Stuart Atkins.

Bachman, J.; Smith, C.; and Slesinger, J. 1966. "Control, Performance and Satisfaction: An Analysis of Structural and Individual Effects." *Journal of Personality and Social Psychology* 4: 127–36.

375

Bales, R. F. 1950. *Interaction Process Analysis.* Reading, Mass.: Addison-Wesley.
Beckhard, R. 1972. "Optimizing Team-Building Efforts." *Journal of Contemporary Business* 1(3): 23–32.
———. 1969. *Organization Development: Strategies and Models.* Cambridge, Mass.: Addison-Wesley.
———. 1967. "The Confrontation Meeting." *Harvard Business Review* 45(2): 149–55.
Beckhard, R., and Harris, R. T. 1977. *Organizational Transitions: Managing Complex Change.* Reading, Mass.: Addison-Wesley.
Beckhard, R., and Lake, D. G. 1971. "Short- and Long-Range Effects of a Team Development Effort." In *Social Intervention: A Behavioral Science Approach,* ed. H. A. Hornstein, B. B. Bunker, W. W. Burke, M. Gindes, and R. J. Lewicki, pp. 421–39. New York: Free Press.
Beehr, T. A. 1976. "Perceived Situational Moderators of the Relationship Between Subjective Role Ambiguity and Role Strain." *Journal of Applied Psychology* 61(1): 35–40.
Beer, M. 1980. *Organization Change and Development.* Santa Monica: Goodyear.
———. 1976a. "The Technology of Organization Development." In *Handbook of Industrial and Organizational Psychology,* ed. M. D. Dunnette, pp. 937–93. Chicago: Rand McNally.
———. 1976b. "On Gaining Influence and Power for OD." *Journal of Applied Behavioral Science* 12: 44–51.
Beer, M., and Huse, E. F. 1972. "A Systems Approach to Organization Development." *Journal of Applied Behavioral Science* 8: 79–101.
Belcher, D. W. 1974. *Compensation Administration.* Englewood Cliffs, N. J.: Prentice-Hall.
Benne, K. D., and Sheats, P. 1948. "Functional Roles of Group Members." *Journal of Social Issues* 4(2): 41–49.
Bennis, W. G. 1970. "A Funny Thing Happened on the Way to the Future." *American Psychologist* 25: 595–608.
———. 1969. *Organization Development: Its Nature, Origins, and Prospects.* Reading, Mass.: Addison-Wesley.
———. 1967. "Organizations of the Future." *Personnel Administration* (September–October), pp. 6–19.
———. 1966. "The Coming Death of Bureaucracy." *Think* (November–December), pp. 30–35.
———. 1959. "Leadership Theory and Administrative Behavior." *Administrative Science Quarterly* 4: 259–301.
Bennis, W. G., and Shepard, H. A. 1961. "Group Observation." In *The Planning of Change,* ed. W. G. Bennis, K. D. Benne, R. Chin, pp. 743–56. New York: Holt, Rinehart and Winston.
Berg, J. G. 1976. *Managing Compensation.* New York: Amacom.
Berkowitz, N. H. 1969. "Audiences and Their Implications for Evaluation Research." *Journal of Applied Behavioral Science* 5: 411–28.
Berne, E. 1964. *Games People Play.* New York: Grove Press.
———. 1961. *Transactional Analysis in Psychotherapy.* New York: Grove Press.
Bion, W. R. 1961. *Experience in Groups.* New York: Basic Books.
Blake, R. R., and Mouton, J. S. 1981. *Toward Resolution of the Situationalism vs. "One Best Style . . . " Controversy in Leadership Theory, Research, and Practice.* Austin: Scientific Methods.
Blake, R. R., and Mouton, J. S. 1978. *The New Managerial Grid.* Houston: Gulf.
Blake, R. R., and Mouton, J. S. 1976. *Consultation.* Reading, Mass.: Addison-Wesley.

376

Blake, R. R., and Mouton, J. S. 1971. "Grid OD: A Systems Approach to Corporate Excellence." In *Social Intervention: A Behavioral Science Approach*, ed. H. A. Hornstein, B. B. Bunker, W. W. Burke, R. S. Lewicki, and M. Gindes, pp. 401-20. New York: Free Press.

Blake, R. R., and Mouton, J. S. 1968a. *Corporate Excellence through Grid Organization Development*. Houston: Gulf.

Blake, R. R., and Mouton, J. S. 1968b. *Corporate Excellence Diagnosis*. Austin: Scientific Methods.

Blake, R. R., and Mouton, J. S. 1964. *The Managerial Grid*. Houston: Gulf.

Blake, R. R.; Mouton, J. S.; Barnes, L. B.; and Greiner, L. E. 1964. "Breakthrough in Organizational Development." *Harvard Business Review*. 42: 133-55.

Blake, R. R.; Shepard, H. A.; and Mouton, J. S. 1964. *Managing Intergroup Conflict in Industry*. Houston: Gulf.

Bluestone, I. 1978. "Human Dignity Is What It's All About." *Viewpoint* 8(3): 21-24.

Bowen, D. D. 1977. "Value Dilemmas in Organization Development." *Journal of Applied Behavioral Science* 13: 543-66.

Bowers, D. G. 1973. "OD Techniques and Their Results in 23 Organizations: The Michigan ICL Study." *Journal of Applied Behavioral Science* 9: 21-43.

——. 1964. "Organizational Control in an Insurance Company." *Sociometry* 27: 230-44.

Bowers, D. G.; Franklin, J. L.; and Pecorella, P. 1975. "Matching Problems, Precursors, and Interventions in OD: A Systemic Approach." *Journal of Applied Behavioral Science* 11: 391-410.

Bradford, L. P. 1978. "Retirement and Organization Development." In *The Cutting Edge: Current Theory and Practice in Organization Development*, ed. W. W. Burke, pp. 278-92. San Diego: University Associates.

Bragg, J. E., and Andrews, I. R. 1973. "Participative Decision Making: An Experimental Study in a Hospital." *Journal of Applied Behavioral Science* 9: 727-35.

Bray, D. W.; Campbell, R. J.; and Grant, D. L. 1974. *Formative Years in Business: A Long Term AT&T Study of Managerial Lives*. New York: Wiley.

Brehm, J. W. 1966. *A Theory of Psychological Reactance*. New York: Academic Press.

Brown, L. D. 1972. "Research Action: Organizational Feedback, Understanding, and Change." *Journal of Applied Behavioral Science* 8: 697-711.

Brown, W. 1960. *Explorations in Management*. London: Heinemann.

Brynildsen, R. D. 1974. "Motivation and Individual Career Achievement." In *New Technologies in Organization Development: 2*, ed. J. D. Adams, pp. 159-80. La Jolla, Calif: University Associates.

Bunker, D. R. 1965. "Individual Applications of Laboratory Training." *Journal of Applied Behavioral Science* 1: 131-48.

Bunker, D. R., and Knowles, E. S. 1967. "Comparison of Behavioral Changes Resulting from Human Relations Training Laboratories of Different Lengths." *Journal of Applied Behavioral Science* 3: 505-24.

Burck, G. 1965. "Union Carbide's Patient Schemers." *Fortune* (December): 147-49.

Burke, W. W. 1980a. "Is Your Client *Really* Involved in OD? In *Trends and Issues in OD: Current Theory and Practice*, ed. W. W. Burke and L. D. Goodstein, pp. 301-9. San Diego: University Associates.

——. 1980b. "Organization Development and Bureaucracy in the 1980's." *Journal of Applied Behavioral Science* 16(3): 423-37.

——. 1980c. "System Theory, Gestalt Therapy, and Organization Development." In *Systems Theory for Organization Development*, ed. T. G. Cummings. Sussex, England: Wiley.

——— 1979. "Leaders and Their Development." *Group and Organization Studies* 4(3): 273-80.

———. 1977. "Japanese Style OD." *Group and Organization Studies* 2: 395-98.

——— 1976. "Organization Development in Transition." *Journal of Applied Behavioral Science* 12: 22-43.

———. 1974. "Managing Conflict Between Groups." In *New Technologies in Organization Development: 2,* ed. J. D. Adams, pp. 255-68. San Diego: University Associates.

———. 1972. "The Demise of Organization Development." *Journal of Contemporary Business* 1(3): 57-63.

———. 1971. "A Comparison of Management Development and Organization Development." *Journal of Applied Behavioral Science* 7: 569-79.

———. 1965. "Leadership Behavior as a Function of the Leader, the Follower, and the Situation." *Journal of Personality* 33: 60-81.

Burke, W. W., and Goodstein, L. D. 1980. "Organization Development Today: A Retrospective Applied to the Present and the Future." In *Trends and Issues in OD: Current Theory and Practice,* ed. W. W. Burke and L. D. Goodstein, pp. 3-11. San Diego: University Associates.

Burke, W. W., and Hornstein, H. A., eds. 1972. *The Social Technology of Organization Development.* La Jolla, Calif.: University Associates.

Burke, W. W., and Schmidt, W. H. 1971. "Primary Target for Change: The Manager of the Organization?" In *Social Intervention: A Behavioral Science Approach,* ed. H. A. Hornstein, B. B. Bunker, W. W. Burke, M. Gindes, and R. J. Lewicki, pp. 373-85. New York: Free Press.

Burns, T., and Stalker, G. 1961. *The Management of Innovation.* London: Tavistock.

Byham, W. C. 1970. "Assessment Centers for Spotting Future Managers." *Harvard Business Review* 48: 150-67.

Cameron, K. 1980. "Critical Questions in Assessing Organizational Effectiveness." *Organizational Dynamics* 9(2): 66-80.

Cammann, C., and Lawler, E. E., III. 1973. "Employee Reactions to a Pay Incentive Plan." *Journal of Applied Psychology* 58: 163-72.

Campbell, D. T., and Stanley, J. C. 1966. *Experimental and Quasi-experimental Designs for Research.* Chicago: Rand McNally.

Campbell, J. P., and Dunnette, M. D. 1968. "Effectiveness of T Group Experiences in Managerial Training and Development." *Psychological Bulletin* 70: 73-104.

Carlson, H. C. 1980. "A Model of Quality of Work Life as a Developmental Process." In *Trends and Issues in OD: Current Theory and Practice,* ed. W. W. Burke and L. D. Goodstein, pp. 83-123. San Diego: University Associates.

Cartwright, D., and Zander, A. 1960. *Group Dynamics: Research and Theory,* 2nd ed. New York: Harper & Row.

Cass, E. L., and Zimmer, F. G., eds. 1975. *Man and Work in Society.* New York: Van Nostrand Reinhold.

Chandler, A. 1962. *Strategy and Structure.* Cambridge, Mass.: MIT Press.

Coch, L., and French, J. R. P. 1948. "Overcoming Resistance to Change." *Human Relations* 1: 512-32.

Collier, J. 1945. "United States Indian Administration as a Laboratory of Ethnic Relations. *Social Research* 12(May): 275-76.

Colman, A. D., and Bexton, W. H., eds. 1975. *Group Relations Reader.* Washington, D.C.: A. K. Rice Institute.

Crawford, M. P. 1962. "Concepts of Training." In *Psychological Principles in System Development,* ed. R. M. Gagne, Chapter 9. New York: Holt, Rinehart & Winston.

Crockett, W. J. 1977. "Introducing Change to a Government Agency." In *Failures in Organization Development and Change,* ed. P. H. Mirvis and D. N. Berg, pp. 111–47. New York: Wiley.

———. 1970. "Team Building—One Approach to Organizational Development." *Journal of Applied Behavioral Science* 6: 291–306.

Crystal, J. C., and Bolles, R. N. 1974. *Where Do I Go From Here With My Life?* New York: Seabury Press.

Davis, S. A. 1967. "An Organic Problem-Solving Method of Organizational Change." *Journal of Applied Behavioral Science* 3: 3–21.

Davis, S. M., and Lawrence, P. R. 1977. *Matrix.* Reading, Mass.: Addison-Wesley.

Dayal, I., and Thomas, J. M. 1968. "Operation KPE: Developing a New Organization." *Journal of Applied Behavioral Science* 4: 473–506.

Delbecq, A. L.; Van de Ven, A. H.; and Gustafson, D. H. 1975. *Group Techniques for Program Planning: A Guide to Nominal Group and Delphi Processes.* Glenview, Ill.: Scott, Foresman.

Dickson, W. J., and Roethlisberger, F. J. 1966. *Counseling in an Organization: A Sequel to the Hawthorne Researchers.* Boston: Division of Research, Harvard Business School.

Digman, L. A. 1978. "How Well-Managed Organizations Develop Their Executives." *Organizational Dynamics* 7(2): 63–80.

Donnell, S., and Hall, J. 1980. "Men and Women as Managers: A Significant Case of No Significant Differences." *Organizational Dynamics* 8(4): 60–77.

Dowling, W. F. 1975. "System 4 Builds Performance and Profits." *Organizational Dynamics* 3(3): 23–38.

Driscoll, J. W. 1979. "Working Creatively with a Union: Lessons from the Scanlon Plan." *Organizational Dynamics* 8(1): 61–80.

Drucker, P. F. 1971. "What We Can Learn from Japanese Management." *Harvard Business Review* (March-April), pp. 110–22.

Dunnette, M. D. 1969. "People Feeling: Joy, More Joy, and the Slough of Despond." *Journal of Applied Behavioral Science* 5: 25–44.

Dyer, W. E. 1977. *Team Building: Issues and Alternatives.* Reading, Mass.: Addison-Wesley.

Ferguson, C. K. 1968. "Concerning the Nature of Human Systems and the Consultant's Role." *Journal of Applied Behavioral Science* 4: 186–93.

Fiedler, F. E. 1974. "The Contingency Model: New Directions for Leadership Utilization." *Journal of Contemporary Business* (Autumn), pp. 65–80.

———. 1967. *A Theory of Leadership Effectiveness.* New York: McGraw-Hill.

Fleishman, E. A. 1953. "Leadership Climate, Human Relations Training, and Supervisory Behavior." *Personnel Psychology* 6: 205–22.

Foltz, J. A.; Harvey, J. B.; and McLaughlin, J. 1974. "Organization Development: A Line Management Function." In *Theory and Method in Organization Development: An Evolutionary Process,* ed. J. D. Adams, pp. 183–210. Arlington, Va.: NTL Institute.

Ford, R. N. 1969. *Motivation Through the Work Itself.* New York: American Management Associations.

Fordyce, J. K., and Weil, R. 1971. *Managing with People.* Reading, Mass.: Addison-Wesley.

Franklin, J. L. 1976. "Characteristics of Successful and Unsuccessful Organization Development." *Journal of Applied Behavioral Science* 12: 471–92.

French, J. R. P., and Caplan, R. D. 1972. "Organizational Stress and Individual Strain." In *The Failure of Success,* ed. A. J. Marrow, pp. 30–66. New York: Amacom.

French, J. R. P., and Raven, B. H. 1959. "The Bases of Social Power." In *Studies in Social Power,* ed. D. Cartwright, pp. 150–67. Ann Arbor: University of Michigan, Institute for Social Research.

379

French, W. L. 1969. "Organization Development: Objectives, Assumptions, and Strategies." *California Management Review* 12: 23–34.

French, W. L., and Bell, C. H., Jr. 1978. *Organization Development,* 2nd ed. Englewood Cliffs, N.J.: Prentice-Hall.

Friedlander, F. 1976. "OD Reaches Adolescence: An Exploration of Its Underlying Values." *Journal of Applied Behavioral Science* 12(1): 7–21.

———. 1970. "The Primacy of Trust as a Facilitator of Further Group Accomplishment." *Journal of Applied Behavioral Science* 6: 387–400.

Friedlander, F., and Brown, L. D. 1974. "Organization Development." *Annual Review of Psychology* 25: 313–41.

Frohman, M. A.; Sashkin, M.; and Kavanagh, M. J. 1976. "Action Research as Applied to Organization Development." *Organization and Administrative Sciences* 7: 129–42.

Galbraith, J. R. 1977. *Organization Design.* Reading, Mass.: Addison-Wesley.

Glasser, W. 1965. *Reality Therapy.* New York: Harper & Row.

Golembiewski, R. T. 1979. *Approaches to Planned Change.* New York: Marcel Dekker.

Golembiewski, R. T.; Billingsley, K.; and Yeager, S. 1976. "Measuring Change and Persistence in Human Affairs: Types of Change Generated by OD Designs. *Journal of Applied Behavioral Science* 12: 133–57.

Golembiewski, R. T.; Carrigan, S. B.; Mead, W. R.; Munzenrider, R.; and Blumberg, A. 1972. "Integrating Disrupted Work Relationships: An Action Design for a Critical Intervention." In *New Technologies in Organization Development: 1,* ed. W. W. Burke, pp. 224–40. La Jolla, Calif.: University Associates.

Golembiewski, R. T.; Hilles, R.; and Kagno, M. S. 1974. "A Longitudinal Study of Flex-time Effects: Some Consequences of an OD Structural Intervention." *Journal of Applied Behavioral Science* 10: 503–32.

Goodman, P. S., and Pennings, J. M. 1980. "Critical Issues in Assessing Organizational Effectiveness." In *Organizational Assessment: Perspectives on the Measurement of Organizational Behavior and the Quality of Work Life,* ed. E. E. Lawler, D. A. Nadler, and C. Camman, pp. 185–215. New York: Wiley-Interscience.

Goodstein, L. D. 1980. "Identifying and Developing Executive Talent: The Career-Development Center." In *Trends and Issues in OD: Current Theory and Practice,* ed. W. W. Burke and L. D. Goodstein, pp. 199–212. San Diego: University Associates.

Gould, R. L. 1978. *Transformations: Growth and Change in Adult Life.* New York: Simon and Schuster.

Gregerman, I. B. 1979. "Introduction to Quality Circles: An Approach to Participative Problem-Solving." *Industrial Management* (September–October), pp. 21–26.

Gyllenhammar, P. G. 1977. *People at Work.* Reading, Mass.: Addison-Wesley.

Hackman, J. R. 1977. "Work Design." In *Improving Life at Work,* ed. J. R. Hackman and J. L. Suttle, pp. 96–162. Santa Monica: Goodyear.

Hackman, J. R., and Oldham, G. R. 1980. *Work Redesign.* Reading, Mass.: Addison-Wesley.

Hackman, J. R., and Oldham, G. R. 1975. "Development of the Job Diagnostic Survey." *Journal of Applied Psychology* 60: 159–70.

Hackman, J. R.; Oldham, G. R.; Janson, R.; and Purdy, K. 1975. "A New Strategy for Job Enrichment." *California Management Review* (Summer) pp. 57–71.

Hagberg, J., and Leider, R. 1978. *The Inventurers: Excursions in Life and Career Renewal.* Reading, Mass.: Addison-Wesley.

Hall, D. T. 1976. *Careers in Organizations.* Santa Monica: Goodyear.

Hall, J. 1976. "To Achieve or Not: The Manager's Choice." *California Management Review* 18(4): 5–18.

———. 1971. "Decisions, Decisions, Decisions." *Psychology Today* 5(6): 51–54, 86, 88.

Hall, J., and Watson, W. H. 1970. "The Effects of a Normative Intervention on Group Decision Making Performance." *Human Relations* 23: 299–317.

Hall, J., and Williams, M. S. 1970. "Group Dynamics Training and Improved Decision Making." *Journal of Applied Behavioral Science* 6: 39–68.

Hall, J., and Williams, M. S. 1966. "A Comparison of Decision-Making Performances in Established and Ad Hoc Groups." *Journal of Personality and Social Psychology* 3: 214–22.

Hamner, W. C.; Ross, J.; and Staw, B. M. 1978. "Motivation in Organizations: The Need for a New Direction." In *The Applied Psychology of Work Behavior,* ed. D. W. Organ, pp. 224–49. Dallas: Business Publications.

Harrison, R. 1972. "Role Negotiation: A Touch-minded Approach to Team Development." In *The Social Technology of Organization Development,* ed. W. W. Burke and H. A. Hornstein, pp. 84–96. La Jolla, Calif.: University Associates.

———. 1970. "Choosing the Depth of Organizational Intervention." *Journal of Applied Behavioral Science* 6: 181–202.

Hart, D. K., and Scott, W. G. 1975. "The Organizational Imperative." *Administration and Society* 7(3): 259–84.

Harvey, J. B. 1977a. "Consulting During Crises of Agreement." In *Current Issues and Strategies in Organization Development,* ed. W. W. Burke, pp. 160–86. New York: Human Sciences Press.

———. 1977b. "Organizations as Phrog Farms." *Organizational Dynamics* 5(4): 15–23.

———. 1974a. "The Abilene Paradox: The Management of Agreement." *Organizational Dynamics* 3 (Summer): 63–80.

———. 1974b. "Organization Development as a Religious Movement." *Training and Development Journal* 28 (March): 24–27.

Harvey, J. B., and Boettger, C. R. 1971. "Improving Communication Within a Managerial Workgroup." *Journal of Applied Behavioral Science* 7: 164–79.

Hatvany, N., and Pucik, V. 1981. "Japanese Management: Practices and Productivity." *Organizational Dynamics* 9(4): 5–21.

Hautaluoma, J. E., and Gavin, J. F. 1975. "Effects of Organizational Diagnosis and Intervention on Blue-Collar 'Blues'." *Journal of Applied Behavioral Sciences* 11: 475–96.

Heisler, W. J. 1975. "Patterns of OD in Practice." *Business Horizons* (February), pp. 77–84.

Herman, S. M. 1977. "The Shadow of Organization Development." In *Current Issues and Strategies in Organization Development,* ed. W. W. Burke, pp. 133–54. New York: Human Sciences Press.

———. 1972. "A Gestalt Orientation to Organization Development." In *New Technologies in Organization Development,* vol. 1, ed. W. W. Burke, pp. 69–89. San Diego: University Associates.

———. 1970. "The Organization as an Iceberg." Paper presented at the Organization Development Network Conference, Vancouver.

Herman, S. M., and Korenich, M. 1977. *Authentic Management: A Gestalt Orientation to Organizations and Their Development.* Reading, Mass.: Addison-Wesley.

Hersey, P., and Blanchard, K. H. 1977. *Management of Organizational Behavior,* 3rd ed. Englewood Cliffs, N.J.: Prentice-Hall.

———. 1969. *Management of Organizational Behavior,* 1st ed. Englewood Cliffs, N.J.: Prentice-Hall.

Herzberg, F. 1974. "The Wise Old Turk." *Harvard Business Review* 52(5): 70–80.

———. 1968. "One More Time: How Do You Motivate Employees?" *Harvard Business Review* 46(1): 53–62.

——. 1966. *Work and the Nature of Man.* Cleveland: World.

Herzberg, F.; Mausner, B.; and Snyderman, B. 1959. *The Motivation to Work.* New York: Wiley.

Hetzler, S. A. 1955. "Variations in Role-Playing Patterns Among Different Echelons of Bureaucratic Leaders." *American Sociological Review* 20: 700–706.

Homans, G. C. 1950. *The Human Group.* New York: Harcourt, Brace.

Hornstein, H. A.,; Bunker, B. B.; Burke, W. W.; Gindes, M.; and Lewicki, R. J. 1971. *Social Intervention: A Behavioral Science Approach.* New York: Free Press.

Hornstein, H. A.; Callahan, D. M.; Fisch, E.; and Benedict, B. A. 1968. "Influence and Satisfaction in Organizations: A Replication." *Sociology of Education* 41: 380–89.

Hornstein, H. A., and Tichy, N. M. 1973. *Organization Diagnosis and Improvement Strategies.* New York: Behavioral Science Associates.

House, R., and Rizzo, J. 1972. "Role Conflict and Ambiguity as Critical Variables in a Model of Organizational Behavior." *Organization Behavior and Human Performance* 7(3): 467–505.

Huck, J. R. 1977. "The Research Base." In *Applying the Assessment Center Method,* ed. J. L. Moses and W. C. Byham. Elmsford, N.Y.: Pergamon Press.

Huse, E. F. 1980. *Organization Development and Change,* rev. ed. St. Paul: West.

——. 1975. *Organization Development and Change.* St. Paul: West.

Huse, E. F., and Beer, M. 1971. "Eclectic Approach to Organizational Development." *Harvard Business Review* 49(5): 103–12.

Jaques, E., and Brown, W. 1965. *The Glacier Papers.* London: Heinemann.

Jayaram, G. K. 1976. "Open Systems Planning." In *The Planning of Change,* 3rd ed. W. G. Bennis, K. D. Benne, R. Chin, and K. Corey, pp. 275–83. New York: Holt, Rinehart, and Winston.

Jones, J. E. 1980. "Quality Control of OD Practitioners and Practice." In *Trends and Issues in OD: Current Theory and Practice,* ed. W. W. Burke and L. D. Goodstein, pp. 333–45. San Diego: University Associates.

Jongeward, D., and contributors. 1973. *Everybody Wins: Transactional Analysis Applied to Organizations.* Reading, Mass.: Addison-Wesley.

Kahn, R. L. 1974. "Organizational Development: Some Problems and Proposals." *Journal of Applied Behavioral Science* 10: 485–502.

Kahn, R. L.; Wolfe, D. M.; Quinn, R. P.; Snoek, J. D.; and Rosenthal, R. A. 1964. *Organizational Stress: Studies in Role Conflict and Ambiguity.* New York: Wiley.

Kanter, R. M. 1977. *Men and Women of the Corporation.* New York: Basic Books.

Kast, F. E., and Rosenzweig, J. E. 1976. *Experiential Exercises and Cases in Management.* New York: McGraw-Hill.

Katz, D., and Kahn, R. L. 1978. *The Social Psychology of Organizations,* 2nd ed. New York: Wiley.

——. 1966. *The Social Psychology of Organizations.* New York: Wiley.

Kepner, C. H., and Tregoe, B. B. 1965. *The Rational Manager.* New York: McGraw-Hill.

Kerr, S. 1975. "On the Folly of Rewarding A, While Hoping for B." *Academy of Management Journal* 18(4): 769–83.

Kimberly, J. R., and Nielsen, W. R. 1975. "Organization Development and Change in Organizational Performance." *Administrative Science Quarterly* 20: 191–206.

King, A. 1974. "Expectation Effects in Organizational Change." *Administrative Science Quarterly* 19: 221–30.

King, D. C. 1972. "Selecting Personnel for a System 4 Organization." In *Contemporary Organization Development: Conceptual Orientations and Interventions,* ed. W. W. Burke, pp. 201–11. Washington, D.C.: NTL Institute.

King, D. C.; Sherwood, J. J.; and Manning, M. R. 1978. "OD's Research Base: How to Expand and Utilize It." In *The Cutting Edge: Current Theory and Practice in Organization Development,* ed. W. W. Burke, pp. 133–48. La Jolla, Calif.: University Associates.

Kipnis, D. 1976. *The Powerholders.* Chicago: University of Chicago Press.

Kobayashi, M. K., and Burke, W. W. 1976. "Organization Development in Japan." *Columbia Journal of World Business* 11(2): 113–23.

Kolb, D., and Frohman, A. 1970. "An Organization Development Approach to Consulting." *Sloan Management Review* 12(1): 51–65.

Kotter, J. P.; Faux, V. A.; and McArthur, C. C. 1978. *Self-Assessment and Career Development.* Englewood Cliffs, N.J.: Prentice-Hall.

Landen, D. L. 1977. *Evolution of QWL as a Movement Within Society, Government and General Motors.* Detroit: General Motors Corporation.

Lawler, E. E., III. 1977. "Reward Systems." In *Improving Life at Work,* ed. J. R. Hackman and J. L. Suttle, pp. 163–226. Santa Monica: Goodyear.

———. 1973. *Motivation in Work Organizations.* Monterey, Calif.: Brooks/Cole.

———. 1972. "Secrecy and the Need to Know." In *Managerial Motivation and Compensation,* ed. H. L. Tosi, R. J. House, and M. D. Dunnette, pp. 455–76. East Lansing: Michigan State University Press.

———. 1966. "Managers' Attitudes Toward How Their Pay Is and Should Be Determined." *Journal of Applied Psychology* 50: 273–79.

Lawler, E. E., III; Nadler, D. A.; and Cammann, C. 1980. *Organizational Assessment: Perspectives on the Measurement of Organizational Behavior and the Quality of Work Life.* New York: Wiley-Interscience.

Lawrence, P. R., and Lorsch, J. W. 1969. *Developing Organizations: Diagnosis and Action.* Reading, Mass.: Addison-Wesley.

———. 1967. *Organization and Environment: Managing Differentiation and Integration.* Boston: Division of Research, Harvard Business School.

Lazer, R. I., and Wikstrom, W. S. 1977. *Appraising Managerial Performance: Current Practices and Future Directions.* New York: The Conference Board.

Lehner, G. F. J. 1972. "From Job Loss to Career Innovation." In *New Technologies in Organization Development: 1,* ed. W. W. Burke, pp. 213–23. La Jolla, Calif.: University Associates.

Lesieur, F. G., ed. 1958. *The Scanlon Plan.* Cambridge, Mass.: Technology Press of M.I.T.; New York: Wiley.

Lesieur, F. G., and Puckett, E. 1969. "The Scanlon Plan Has Proved Itself." *Harvard Business Review* (September-October), pp. 109–18.

Levinson, H. 1975. *Executive Stress.* New York: Harper.

———. 1972a. *Organizational Diagnosis.* Cambridge, Mass.: Harvard University Press.

———. 1972b. "The Clinical Psychologist as Organizational Diagnostician." *Professional Psychology* 3: 34–40.

Levinson, D. J.; Darrow, C. N.; Klein, E. B.; Levinson, M. H.; and McKee, B. 1978. *The Seasons of a Man's Life.* New York: Knopf.

Lewicki, R. J., and Alderfer, C. P. 1973. "The Tensions Between Research and Intervention in Intergroup Conflict." *Journal of Applied Behavioral Science* 9(4): 423–68.

Lewin, K. 1958. "Group Decision and Social Change." In *Readings in Social Psychology,* ed. E. E. Maccoby, T. M. Newcomb, and E. L. Hartley, pp. 197–211. New York: Holt, Rinehart and Winston.

———. 1951. *Field Theory in Social Science.* New York: Harper.

———. 1948. *Resolving Social Conflicts.* New York: Harper.

383

————. 1946. "Action Research and Minority Problems." *Journal of Social Issues* 2: 34–46.

Lieberman, M. A.; Yalom, I. D.; and Miles, M. B. 1973. *Encounter Groups: First Facts.* New York: Basic Books.

Likert, R. 1967. *The Human Organization.* New York: McGraw-Hill.

————. 1961. *New Patterns of Management.* New York: McGraw-Hill.

Lippitt, R., and Lippitt, G. 1975. "Consulting Process in Action." *Training and Development Journal* 29(5): 48–54; 29(6): 38–44.

Lippitt, R.; Watson, J.; and Westley, B. 1958. *Dynamics of Planned Change.* New York: Harcourt, Brace.

Lodahl, T. M., and Williams, L. K. 1978. "An Opportunity for OD: The Office Revolution." *OD Practitioner* 10(4): 9–11.

Lodge, G. C. 1974. "Business and the Changing Society." *Harvard Business Review* 52(2): 59–72.

Lundberg, C. C., and Raia, A. P. 1976. "Issues in the Practice of Organizational Development Consultancy." *Proceedings of the Annual Meeting of the Academy of Management,* pp. 190–95.

McCall, M. W., and Lombardo, M. M. eds. 1978. *Leadership: Where Else Can We Go?* Durham, N.C.: Duke University Press.

McClelland, D. C. 1975. *Power: The Inner Experience.* New York: Irvington.

————. 1965. "N Achievement and Enterpreneurship: A Longitudinal Study." *Journal of Personality and Social Psychology* 1: 389–92.

McClelland, D. C., and Burnham, D. H. 1976. "Power Is the Great Motivator." *Harvard Business Review* 54(2): 100–110.

Maccoby, M. 1976. *The Gamesman: The New Corporate Leaders.* New York: Irvington.

McGregor, D. 1967. *The Professional Manager.* New York: McGraw-Hill.

————. 1960. *The Human Side of Enterprise.* New York: McGraw-Hill.

Mancuso, J. R. 1978. "How to Name and Not to Name a Business." *Harvard Business Review* 56(6): 20–26.

Mann, F. C. 1957. "Studying and Creating Change: A Means to Understanding Social Organization." In *Research in Industrial Human Relations.* Industrial Relations Research Association, Publication No. 17.

Margulies, N. 1978. "Perspectives on the Marginality of the Consultant's Role. In *The Cutting Edge: Current Theory and Practice in Organization Development,* ed. W. W. Burke, pp. 60–69. La Jolla, Calif.: University Associates.

Margulies, N., and Raia, A. P. 1978. *Conceptual Foundations of Organizational Development.* New York: McGraw-Hill.

Marris, P. 1975. *Loss and Change.* New York: Anchor.

Marrow, A. J. 1969. *The Practical Theorist.* New York: Basic Books.

Marrow, A. J.; Bowers, D. G.; and Seashore, S. E. 1967. *Management by Participation.* New York: Harper & Row.

Maslow, A. H. 1954. *Motivation and Personality.* New York: Harper & Brothers.

May, R. 1972. *Power and Innocence.* New York: Norton and Company.

Mayo, E. 1933. *The Human Problems of an Industrial Civilization.* Boston: Harvard University Graduate School of Business.

Merton, R. K. 1948. "The Self-Fulfilling Prophecy." *Antioch Review* 8: 193–210.

Michael, S. R.; Luthans, F.; Odiorne, G. S.; Burke, W. W.; and Hayden, S. 1981. *Techniques of Organizational Change.* New York: McGraw-Hill.

Miles, M. B.; Hornstein, H. A.; Callahan, D. M.; Calder, P. H.; and Schiavo, R. W. 1969. "The Consequences of Survey Feedback: Theory and Evaluation." In *The Planning of Change,* 2nd ed., ed. W. G. Bennis, K. D. Benne, and R. Chin. New York: Holt, Rinehart and Winston.

Miller, E. C. 1978. "The Parallel Organization Structure at General Motors: An Interview with Howard C. Carlson. *Personnel* 55(4): 64–69.

Moore, B., and Goodman, P. 1973. *Factors Affecting the Impact of a Company-Wide Incentive Program on Productivity.* Report submitted to the National Commission on Productivity, January.

Morrison, P. 1978. "Evaluation in OD: A Review and an Assessment." *Groups and Organization Studies* 3: 42–70.

Nadler, D. A. 1977. *Feedback and Organization Development: Using Data-Based Methods.* Reading, Mass.: Addison-Wesley.

Nadler, D. A.; Hackman, J. R.; and Lawler, E. E., III. 1979. *Managing Organizational Behavior.* Boston: Little, Brown.

Nadler, D. A.; Mirvis, P. H.; and Cammann, C. 1976. "The Ongoing Feedback System: Experimenting with a New Managerial Tool." *Organizational Dynamics* 4(4): 63–80.

Nadler, D. A., and Tushman, M. L. 1977. "A Diagnostic Model for Organization Behavior." In *Perspectives on Behavior in Organizations,* ed. J. R. Hackman, E. E. Lawler, and L. W. Porter, pp. 85–100. New York: McGraw-Hill.

Nadler, D. A.; Tushman, M. L.; and Hatvany, N. G., eds. Forthcoming. *Concepts and Cases for Managing Organizational Behavior.* Boston: Little, Brown.

Nord, W. R. 1978. "Dreams of Humanization and the Realities of Power." *Academy of Management Review* 3(3): 674–79.

Ouchi, W. G., and Jaeger, A. M. 1978. "Type Z Organization: Stability in the Midst of Mobility." *Academy of Management Review* 3: 305–14.

Ouchi, W. G., and Price, R. L. 1978. "Hierarchies, Clans, and Theory Z: A New Perspective on Organization Development." *Organizational Dynamics* 7(2): 25–44.

Pasmore, W. A., and Sherwood, J. J., eds. 1978. *Sociotechnical Systems: A Sourcebook.* La Jolla, Calif.: University Associates.

Pate, L. E.; Nielsen, W. R. and Bacon, P. C. 1977. "Advances in Research on Organization Development: Toward a Beginning." *Group and Organization Studies* 2: 449–60.

Perls, F. S. 1969. *Gestalt Therapy Verbatim.* Lafayette, Calif.: Real People Press.

Perls, F. S.; Hefferline, R. F.; and Goodman, P. 1951. *Gestalt Therapy.* New York: Dell.

Perrow, C. 1977. "The Bureaucratic Paradox: The Efficient Organization Centralizes in Order to Decentralize." *Organizational Dynamics* 5(4): 3–14.

Pfeiffer, J. W., and Jones, J. E. 1978. "OD Readiness." In *The Cutting Edge: Current Theory and Practice in Organization Development,* ed. W. W. Burke, pp. 179–85. La Jolla, Calif.: University Associates.

Plovnick, M. S.; Fry, R. E.; and Rubin, I. M. 1975. "New Developments in OD Technology: Programmed Team Development." *Training and Development Journal* 29(4): 19–27.

Polster, E., and Polster, M. 1973. *Gestalt Therapy Integrated: Contours of Theory and Practice.* New York: Brunner/Mazel.

Porras, J. I. 1979. "The Comparative Impact of Different OD Techniques and Intervention Intensities." *Journal of Applied Behavioral Science* 15: 156–78.

———. 1978. "The Impact of Organization Development: Research Findings." *Academy of Management Review* 3(2): 249–66.

Porras, J. I., and Berg, P. O. 1978. "Evaluation Methodology in Organization Development: An Analysis and Critique." *Journal of Applied Behavioral Science* 14: 151–73.

Porras, J. I., and Patterson, K. 1979. "Assessing Planned Change." *Group and Organization Studies* 4: 39–58.

Porras, J. I., and Wilkens, A. 1980. "Organization Development in a Large System: An Empirical Assessment." *Journal of Applied Behavioral Science* 16: 506–34.

Porter, L. W.; Lawler, E. E., III; and Hackman, J. R. 1975. *Behavior in Organizations.* New York: McGraw-Hill.

Quinn, R. P., and Shepard, L. 1974. *The 1972-1973 Quality of Employment Survey.* Ann Arbor: Survey Research Center, University of Michigan.

Quinn, R. P., and Staines, G. L. 1978. *The 1977 Quality of Employment Survey.* Ann Arbor: Survey Research Center, University of Michigan.

Rice, A. K. 1965. *Learning for Leadership.* London: Tavistock.

——. 1958. *Productivity and Social Organization: The Ahmedabad Experiment.* London: Tavistock.

Rioch, M. J. 1975. "Group Relations: Rationale and Technique." In *Group Relations Reader,* ed. A. D. Colman and W. H. Bexton. Washington, D.C.: A. K. Rice Institute.

——. 1970. "The Work of Wilfred Bion on Groups." *Psychiatry* 33: 56–66.

Roethlisberger, F. J., and Dickson, W. J. 1939. *Management and the Worker: An Account of a Research Program Conducted by the Western Electric Company.* Cambridge, Mass.: Harvard University Press.

Rogers, C. R. 1968. "Interpersonal Relationships: U.S.A. 2000." *Journal of Applied Behavioral Science* 4: 265–80.

——. 1951. *Client Centered Therapy.* Boston: Houghton Mifflin.

Rokeach, M. 1973. *The Nature of Human Values.* New York: Free Press.

Rosenthal, R. 1976. *Experimenter Effects in Behavioral Research,* enlarged ed. New York: Halsted Press.

Rosow, J. M. 1979. "Organizational Issues in the 80's: Shifts in the Work Force, Changing Values, New Patterns of Work." *OD Practitioner* 11(2): 1–7, 14.

Ross, R. 1971. "OD for Whom?" *Journal of Applied Behavioral Science* 7: 580–85.

Rubin, I. 1967. "Increasing Self-Acceptance: A Means of Reducing Prejudice." *Journal of Personality and Social Psychology* 5: 233–38.

Rush, H., and McGrath, P. 1973. "Transactional Analysis Moves into Corporate Training." *The Conference Board Record* 10(7): 38–44.

Schein, E. H. 1980. *Organizational Psychology,* 3rd ed. Englewood Cliffs, N.J.: Prentice-Hall.

——. 1978. *Career Dynamics: Matching Individual and Organizational Needs.* Reading, Mass.: Addison-Wesley.

——. 1972. *Organizational Psychology,* 2nd ed. Englewood Cliffs, N.J.: Prentice-Hall.

——. 1969. *Process Consultation.* Reading, Mass.: Addison-Wesley.

Schein, E. H., and Bennis, W. G. 1965. *Personal and Organizational Change Through Group Methods: The Laboratory Approach.* New York: Wiley.

Schein, V. E. 1977. "Political Strategies for Implementing Organizational Change." *Group and Organizational Studies* 2(1): 42–48.

Schein, V. E., and Greiner, L. E. 1977. "Can Organization Development Be Fine Tuned to Bureaucracies?" *Organizational Dynamics* 5(3): 48–61.

Schmuck, R. A., and Miles, M. B., eds. 1971. *Organization Development in Schools.* Palo Alto: National Press.

Schneider, B. 1980. "The Service Organization: Climate Is Crucial." *Organizational Dynamics* 9(2): 52–65.

——. 1976. *Staffing Organizations.* Pacific Palisades, Calif.: Goodyear.

Schroder, M. 1974. "The Shadow Consultant." *Journal of Applied Behavioral Science* 10: 579–94.

Schutz, W. C. 1967. *The FIRO Scales: Manual.* Palo Alto: Consulting Psychologists Press.

——. 1958. *FIRO: A Three Dimensional Theory of Interpersonal Behavior.* New York: Holt, Rinehart and Winston.

Scott, W. G., and Hart, D. K. 1979. *Organizational America.* Boston: Houghton Mifflin.

Seashore, S. E., and Bowers, D. G. 1970. "Durability of Organizational Change." *American Psychologist* 25 (March): 227-33.

Selznick, P. 1957. *Leadership in Administration.* New York: Harper and Row.

Shepard, H. A. 1960. "Three Management Programs and the Theory Behind Them." In *An Action Research Program for Organization Improvement.* Ann Arbor: Foundation for Research on Human Behavior.

Sherif, M. 1958. "Superordinate Goals in the Reduction of Intergroup Conflict." *American Journal of Sociology* 43: 349-56.

Sherif, M.; Harvey, O. J.; White, B. J.; Hood, W. R.; and Sherif, C. W. 1961. *Intergroup Conflict and Cooperation: The Robbers Cave Experiment.* Norman, Okla.: Institution of Group Relations, University of Oklahoma Book Exchange.

Sherif, M., and Sherif, C. W. 1953. *Groups in Harmony and Tension.* New York: Harper & Row.

Sirota, D., and Wolfson, A. 1972. "Job Enrichment: What Are the Obstacles?" *Personnel* 49(3): 8-17.

Skinner, B. F. 1971. *Beyond Freedom and Dignity.* New York: Knopf.

——. 1953. *Science and Human Behavior.* New York: Macmillan.

——. 1948. *Walden Two.* New York: Macmillan.

Slater, P., and Bennis, W. G. 1964. "Democracy Is Inevitable." *Harvard Business Review,* 42: 51-59.

Spence, J. T., and Helmreich, R. L. 1978. *Masculinity and Feminity: Their Psychological Dimensions, Correlates, and Antecedents.* Austin: University of Texas Press.

Spier, M. S.; Sashkin, M.; Jones, J. E.; and Goodstein, L. D. 1980. "Predictions and Projections for the Decade: Trends and Issues in Organization Development." In *Trends and Issues in OD: Current Theory and Practice,* ed. W. W. Burke and L. D. Goodstein, pp. 12-37. San Diego: University Associates.

Steele, F. I. 1973. *Physical Settings and Organization Development.* Reading, Mass.: Addison-Wesley.

Stein, B. A., and Kanter, R. M. 1980. "Building the Parallel Organization: Creating Mechanisms for Permanent Quality of Work Life." *Journal of Applied Behavioral Science* 16: 371-88.

Steiner, I. D. 1972. *Group Process and Productivity.* New York: Academic Press.

Stogdill, R. M. 1974. *Handbook of Leadership: A Survey of Theory and Research.* New York: Free Press.

Tannenbaum, A. S., and Kahn, R. L. 1958. *Participation in Union Locals.* Evanston, Ill.: Row Peterson.

——. 1957. "Organizational Control Structure: A General Descriptive Technique as Applied to Four Local Unions." *Human Relations* 10: 127-40.

Tannenbaum, R., and Davis, S. A. 1969. "Values, Man, and Organizations." *Industrial Management Review* 10(2): 67-83.

Taylor, F. W. 1911. *Scientific Management.* New York: Harper and Row.

Taylor, J., and Bowers, D. G. 1972. *The Survey of Organizations: A Machine Scored Standardized Questionnaire Instrument.* Ann Arbor: Institute for Social Research.

Tichy, N. M. 1978. "Demise, Absorption or Renewal for the Future of Organization Development." In *The Cutting Edge: Current Theory and Practice in Organization Development,* ed. W. W. Burke, pp. 70-88. La Jolla, Calif.: University Associates.

——. 1974. "Agents of Planned Social Change: Congruence of Values, Cognitions, and Actions." *Administrative Science Quarterly* 19: 164-82.

Tichy, N. M.; Hornstein, H. A.; and Nisberg, J. N. 1977. "Organization Diagnosis and Intervention Strategies: Developing Emergent Pragmatic Theories of Change." In *Current Issues and Strategies in Organization Development,* ed. W. W. Burke, pp. 361-83. New York: Human Sciences Press.

Tichy, N. M., and Nisberg, J. N. 1976. "When Does Work Restructuring Work? Organizational Innovations at Volvo and GM." *Organizational Dynamics* 5(1): 63-80.

Trist, E. 1978. "Adapting to a Changing World." In *A New Role for Labour: Industrial Democracy Today,* ed. G. Sanderson. Toronto: McGraw-Hill Ryerson.

———. 1960. *Socio-technical Systems.* London: Tavistock Institute of Human Relations.

Trist, E. L., and Sofer, C. 1959. *Explorations in Group Relations.* Leicester: Leicester University Press.

Tushman, M. L., and Nadler, D. A. 1978. "Information Processing as an Integrative Concept in Organizational Design." *Academy of Management Review* 3: 613-24.

Vaill, P. B. 1978. "Toward a Behavioral Description of High-Performing Systems." In *Leadership: Where Else Can We Go?* ed. M. W. McCall, Jr., and M. M. Lombardo, pp. 103-25. Durham, N.C.: Duke University Press.

———. 1971. "OD: A Grammatical Footnote." *Journal of Applied Behavioral Science* 7(2): 264.

Vaillant, G. E. 1977. *Adaptation to Life.* Boston: Little, Brown.

Van de Ven, A. H., and Ferry, D. L. 1980. *Measuring and Assessing Organizations.* New York: Wiley-Interscience.

Van Zelst, R. H. 1952. "Sociometrically Selected Work Teams Increase Production." *Personnel Psychology* 5: 175-85.

von Bertalanffy, L. 1956. "General System Theory." In *General Systems,* Yearbook of the Society for the Advancement of General System Theory, vol. 1, pp. 1-10.

Votaw, D. 1966. "What Do We Believe About Power?" *California Management Review* (Summer) pp. 71-88.

Vroom, V. 1964. *Work and Motivation.* New York: Wiley.

Vroom, V. H., and Yetton, P. W. 1973. *Leadership and Decision Making.* Pittsburgh: University of Pittsburgh Press.

Walker, J. W. 1980. *Human Resource Planning.* New York: McGraw-Hill.

Walters, R. W., and Associates. 1975. *Job Enrichment for Results.* Reading, Mass.: Addison-Wesley.

Walton, R. E. 1975. "The Diffusion of New Work Structures: Explaining Why Success Didn't Take." *Organizational Dynamics* 3(3): 2-22.

———. 1973. "Quality of Working Life: What Is it?" *Sloan Management* Review 15(1): 11-22.

———. 1969. *Interpersonal Peacemaking: Confrontations and Third Party Consultation.* Reading, Mass.: Addison-Wesley.

Walton, R. E., and Warwick, D. P. 1973. "The Ethics of Organization Development." *Journal of Applied Behavioral Science* 9: 681-98.

Weisbord, M. R. 1978. *Organizational Diagnosis: A Workbook of Theory and Practice.* Reading, Mass.: Addison-Wesley.

———. 1977. "How Do You Know It Works If You Don't Know What It Is?" *OD Practitioner* 9(3): 1-8.

———. 1976. "Organizational Diagnosis: Six Places to Look for Trouble With or Without a Theory. *Group and Organization Studies* 1: 430-47.

———. 1973. "The Organization Development Contract." *OD Practitioner* 5(2): 1-4.

Weiss, C. H. 1972. *Evaluation Research: Methods of Assessing Program Effectiveness.* Englewood Cliffs, N.J.: Prentice-Hall.

White, S., and Mitchell, T. 1976. "Organization Development: A Review of Research Content and Research Design." *Academy of Management Review* 1: 57–73.

Whyte, W. F. 1955. *Money and Motivation.* New York: Harper and Row.

Winter, D. G. 1973. *The Power Motive.* New York: Free Press.

Wolfe, T. 1979. *The Right Stuff.* New York: Farrar, Straus and Giroux.

Yager, E. 1979. "Examining the Quality Control Circle." *Personnel Journal* (October), pp. 682–84, 708.

Yankelovich, D. 1978. "The New Psychological Contracts at Work." *Psychology Today* 11(12): 46–50.

Yukl, G., and Latham, G. 1975. "Consequences of Reinforcement Schedules and Incentive Magnitudes for Employee Performance: Problems Encountered in an Industrial Setting." *Journal of Applied Psychology* 60: 294–98.

Zaleznik, A. 1977. "Managers and Leaders: Are They Different?" *Harvard Business Review* 55(3): 67–78.

Zand, D. E. 1974. "Collateral Organization: A New Change Strategy." *Journal of Applied Behavioral Science* 10: 63–89.

NAME INDEX

391

SUBJECT INDEX

397